Palgrave Studies in Economic History

Series Editor
Kent Deng, London School of Economics, London, UK

Palgrave Studies in Economic History is designed to illuminate and enrich our understanding of economies and economic phenomena of the past. The series covers a vast range of topics including financial history, labour history, development economics, commercialisation, urbanisation, industrialisation, modernisation, globalisation, and changes in world economic orders.

More information about this series at
https://link.springer.com/bookseries/14632

Mabel Winter

Banking, Projecting and Politicking in Early Modern England

The Rise and Fall of Thompson and Company
1671–1678

Mabel Winter
University of Sheffield
Sheffield, UK

ISSN 2662-6497   ISSN 2662-6500   (electronic)
Palgrave Studies in Economic History
ISBN 978-3-030-90569-9   ISBN 978-3-030-90570-5   (eBook)
https://doi.org/10.1007/978-3-030-90570-5

© The Editor(s) (if applicable) and The Author(s), under exclusive license to Springer
Nature Switzerland AG 2022
This work is subject to copyright. All rights are solely and exclusively licensed by the
Publisher, whether the whole or part of the material is concerned, specifically the rights
of translation, reprinting, reuse of illustrations, recitation, broadcasting, reproduction on
microfilms or in any other physical way, and transmission or information storage and
retrieval, electronic adaptation, computer software, or by similar or dissimilar methodology
now known or hereafter developed.
The use of general descriptive names, registered names, trademarks, service marks, etc.
in this publication does not imply, even in the absence of a specific statement, that such
names are exempt from the relevant protective laws and regulations and therefore free for
general use.
The publisher, the authors and the editors are safe to assume that the advice and information in this book are believed to be true and accurate at the date of publication. Neither
the publisher nor the authors or the editors give a warranty, expressed or implied, with
respect to the material contained herein or for any errors or omissions that may have been
made. The publisher remains neutral with regard to jurisdictional claims in published maps
and institutional affiliations.

Cover illustration: Harnett/Hanzon

This Palgrave Macmillan imprint is published by the registered company Springer Nature
Switzerland AG
The registered company address is: Gewerbestrasse 11, 6330 Cham, Switzerland

For Dad

ACKNOWLEDGEMENTS

First and foremost, thank you to the team at Palgrave Macmillan for their assistance and advice in the production of this book. Three reviewers provided constructive advice that helped to shape the structure of the book and prompted me to think about the material in ways I had not done previously.

Special thanks go to my Ph.D. supervisor Professor Phil Withington for all his help, guidance, and support over the many years that I have studied with him at the University of Sheffield, where this work was first conceived and developed. I would also like to thank my secondary Ph.D. supervisor, Dr. Tom Leng, for discussions, archival sources from his own research at the Hamburg State Archives and for an early look at his latest book, *Fellowship and Freedom*. My Ph.D. viva examiners, Professor Mike Braddick and Dr. Perry Gauci, also offered some constructive criticism on the topic and discussion with them has influenced the content of this book.

The majority of the research for this book was undertaken during my Ph.D. which was funded by the Arts and Humanities Research Council through the White Rose College of Arts and Humanities, and I thank them for the opportunities the grant provided. Many archives were visited over the course of this research, and I would like to thank the archivists and staff at the British Library, Borthwick Institute for Archives, Guildhall Archive, Hull History Centre, London Metropolitan Archives, and the National Archives. Special thanks also go to the partners of Hoare's bank

vii

and archivist Pamela Hunter for granting me access to look at their private archive.

There are also people I would like to thank on a personal level. Many thanks go to my mum, brother, and grandparents, who have supported me on both a personal and professional level and without whom my academic career and this book would not have been possible. Finally, to Jamie, thank you for your love, support, and incredibly insightful comments on my work.

CONTENTS

1	Introduction	1
2	Thompson and Company	27
3	Early Modern Banking	57
4	An Early Modern 'Project'	83
5	Family Network	103
6	Credit Networks	131
7	Bankruptcy	157
8	Why Did Thompson and Company Collapse?	181
9	Aftermath	207
10	Conclusion	229
	Appendix	241
	Bibliography	257
	Index	295

Abbreviations

BL	The British Library
Case of Richard Thompson and Company	*The Case of Richard Thompson and Company. With relation to their creditors.* London, 1677
CSP Venice	British History Online. *Calendar of State Papers Relating to English Affairs in the Archives of Venice, Volume 38, 1673–1675.* https://www.british-history.ac.uk/cal-state-papers/venice/vol38. Accessed 20 May 2020
HHC	Hull History Centre
HoP	The History of Parliament: British Political, Social & Local History. http://www.historyofparliamentonline.org/
Letters Addressed to Sir Joseph Williamson	Christie, W. D. 1874. *Letters Addressed from London to Sir Joseph Williamson while Plenipotentiary at the Congress of Cologne in the Years 1673 and 1674*, 2 vols. London: Camden New Series 8–9
LMA	London Metropolitan Archives
LoC, MD	Library of Congress, Manuscript Department, Washington, DC
ODNB	Oxford Dictionary of National Biography. https://www-oxforddnb-com.sheffield.idm.oclc.org/

xii ABBREVIATIONS

Reasons most humbly offered to the consideration of Parliament — *Reasons most humbly offered to the consideration of Parliament, why a bill now depending before them, against Richard Thompson and partners should not be passed.* London, 1677/8

Reasons offered by several of the creditors of Richard Thompson and partners — *Reasons offered by several of the creditors of Richard Thompson and partners, for stopping all proceedings upon the statute, and for the speedy acceptance of their proposal of 6s. 8d. per pound.* London, 1677/8

RoLLCo — Institute of Historical Research. *Records of London's Livery Companies Online: Apprentices and Freemen 1400–1900* https://www.londonroll.org

SPO — State Papers Online

TNA — The National Archives

LIST OF FIGURES

Fig. 5.1   Family tree showing the relationship between Edward Nelthorpe, Richard Thompson, and the Thompson brothers of York   108

Fig. 5.2   Family tree showing the relationship between the wider Nelthorpe and Thompson families   110

Fig. 5.3   Family tree showing the relationship between the Thompson, Nelthorpe, and Popple families   113

Fig. 5.4   The Thompson family's involvement with the market and the state   124

Graph 2.1   Creditors by place of residence   47

Graph 2.2   Percentage of creditors by occupation/status   49

Graph 2.3   Lifecycle of Thompson and Company based on amounts claimed to be on their books   50

Image 2.1   Map of London (*Source* British Library Board 06/07/2021, Maps.Crace II.61, John Ogilby and William Morgan, LARGE AND ACCURATE MAP OF THE CITY OF LONDON. Ichnographically describing all the Streets, Lanes, Alleys, Courts, Yards, Churches, Halls and Houses, &c [London, 1677])   39

Image 2.2   Map of Woolchurch Market (*Source* British Library Board 06/07/2021, Maps.Crace II.61, Detail)   40

LIST OF TABLES

Table 4.1	Factors of Thompson and Company	92
Table 6.1	Creditors who were common councillors	141
Table 6.2	Creditors who were MPs	142

CHAPTER 1

Introduction

Thompson and Company was founded in January 1671 when Richard Thompson and Edward Nelthorpe made the acquaintance of John Farrington and Edmund Page. All four men were merchants residing in London, who had been trading in pairs prior to 1671 and had accumulated significant estates. The aim of the venture was to pool their resources to create an institution that was primarily a bank but with an added mercantile element that allowed the partners to continue their trading exploits. Thus, the partners maintained their mercantile occupations and identities alongside their new roles as city bankers. Additionally, partners Thompson and Nelthorpe were religious nonconformists or dissenters who were involved in civic politics, sitting on London's Common Council in the 1670s. Therefore, the partners had networks and roles in the fields of finance, commerce, and politics. Thompson and Company went bankrupt in 1678 when three separate statutes of bankruptcy were issued against the partners. By the end of that year, only two of the partners, Richard Thompson and John Farrington, were still alive. From 1678 onwards, a series of Chancery court cases surrounding the bankruptcy and the partners' attempts to draw in their debts began. These legal and other sources reveal that during their seven active years the partners of Thompson and Company built up significant commercial and social networks and attracted business from over 200 male and female

© The Author(s), under exclusive license to Springer Nature
Switzerland AG 2022
M. Winter, *Banking, Projecting and Politicking in Early
Modern England*, Palgrave Studies in Economic History,
https://doi.org/10.1007/978-3-030-90570-5_1

1

2   M. WINTER

customers. This study accordingly uses the bank of Thompson and Company as a case study or microhistory to identify and illuminate wider financial practices, social and commercial networks, and the relationship between finance, commerce, religion, and politics in the later seventeenth century.

The venture known as Thompson and Company is rarely commented on in the historiography of seventeenth-century commerce or finance. One practical reason for this is that Thompson and Company's ledgers, papers, and account books were lost or destroyed following their bankruptcy. Therefore, there are no direct sources relating to the bank or its business transactions. Other reasons for the lack of attention paid to Thompson and Company include its unique business model that does not fit neatly into an institutional categorisation, and the partners' inclusion in works of literary history that focus on the social and economic relationships of their relative Andrew Marvell. Of these reasons, lack of source material provides the most significant barrier to studying Thompson and Company. The main surviving sources concerning the bank are a pamphlet written by the partners and published in 1677 and legal cases heard in the court of Chancery, which were taken out by or against the partners both prior to and following their bankruptcy. Other material such as printed pamphlets, personal and state correspondence, institutional records, genealogical sources, government papers, and newsletters can also provide some further insight. Whilst this material can in no way provide the complete story, it offers an opportunity to reconstruct the institution of Thompson and Company, the identities, activities and networks of its partners, the identity of its creditors, and the events and circumstances that led to its collapse.

The intense focus of this study and methodological approach makes it a microhistory, defined as a practice 'based on the reduction of the scale of observation, on a microscopic analysis and an intensive study of the documentary material'.[1] The use of Chancery records demands this kind of in-depth analysis. Sara Butler argues that when using Chancery records, 'historians are inevitably required to assume the role of detective, ferreting out any niggling, gnawing glimpses of fabrication and providing

---

[1] Giovanni Levi. 2001. On Microhistory. In *New Perspectives on Historical Writing*, 2nd edn, ed Peter Burke, 97–119. Cambridge: Polity Press. 99.

1 INTRODUCTION 3

the best explanation possible given the evidence'.[2] The metaphor used by Butler, of the historian as a detective, is one frequently used to describe the microhistorian, who uses any trace of surviving material to reconstruct their subject matter. Court records are just one example of indirect sources used to reconstruct an individual or group's life or a particular event and have been famously used by microhistorian Carlo Ginzburg in *The Cheese and the Worms*. Studies such as Ginzburg's aim to recover something that would be otherwise unknown, an exceptional case but one that reveals more about the typical beliefs or values of a wider social group or age.[3] This book has a similar aim, as each chapter reconstructs an aspect of the bank as an institution, the networks it built on and facilitated, or the social and political lives of the partners and their families. It is important to reconstruct all aspects of the bank and the lives of its four partners because, as David Hancock has emphasised, business histories do not 'take place in a vacuum'.[4] We need to examine the wider social life of a business in order to understand success and failure. This is particularly the case for Thompson and Company, whose partners conducted a diverse range of business and political activities. Through an economic microhistory, this book reveals what the case of Thompson and Company can tell us about the broader social, political, and economic atmosphere in which it existed.

---

[2] Sara M. Butler. 2004. The Law as a Weapon in Marital Disputes: Evidence from the Late Medieval Court of Chancery, 1424–1529. *Journal of British Studies* 43: 296.

[3] Carlo Ginzburg. 1980. *The Cheese and the Worms: The Cosmos of a Sixteenth-Century Miller*, trans. John and Anne Tedeschi. Maryland: The John Hopkins University Press. xx; John Brewer. 2010. Microhistory and the Histories of Everyday Life. *Social and Cultural History* 7: 99, 103; Matti Peltonen. 2001. Clues, Margins, and Monads: The Micro–Macro Link in Historical Research. *History and Theory* 40: 356; Sigurdur Gylfi Magnússon and István M. Szijártó. 2013. *What is Microhistory? Theory and Practice*. Oxford: Routledge. 5, 19; Levi. On Microhistory: 101; Keith Wrightson. 2011. *Ralph Tailor's Summer: A Scrivener, His City and the Plague*. New Haven: Yale University Press. xii.

[4] David Hancock. 1995. *Citizens of the World: London Merchants and the Integration of the British Atlantic Community, 1735–1785*. Cambridge: Cambridge University Press. 5.

I

No dedicated study of Thompson and Company exists. The institution is absent from economic historiography, featuring as neither a case study nor part of larger surveys of trade and banking in the seventeenth century. Ironically, the majority of existing scholarship regarding Thompson and Company and its partners have been conducted by literary historians looking to contextualise the works of the poet and politician Andrew Marvell, who was a friend and distant relative of partners Thompson and Nelthorpe. The reason behind this focus comes from a 1684 Chancery case first examined by Fred Tupper in 1938, which concerned Marvell's estate after his death in 1678. Tupper's article investigated the identity of 'Mary Marvell', whose name features in the preface to the 1681 edition of Marvell's works and who was a defendant in the 1684 Chancery case against complainant and bank partner, John Farrington.[5] The case reveals that Mary Marvell—or Palmer—had claimed to be the wife of Andrew Marvell, although others believed her to be his housekeeper, and that, in 1677, she had taken out a lease of a house in Great Russell Street, London, for the purpose of hiding a bankrupt friend, kinsman, and business associate of his, Edward Nelthorpe. The case primarily concerned a bond of £500 deposited with goldsmith Charles Wallis by Nelthorpe but recorded under the name of Andrew Marvell. Nelthorpe died just one month after Marvell and John Farrington, who had obtained letters of administration regarding Nelthorpe's estate, was arguing that the £500 was the rightful property of Nelthorpe. Mary Marvell, or Palmer, was arguing the reverse: that the £500 was Marvell's proper money and part of his estate, over which she had obtained letters of administration. Tupper painstakingly reconstructed the proceedings and revealed for the first time the bankruptcy of Thompson and Company and the identity of its four partners. Despite unearthing Thompson and Company from the records, Tupper's study did not spark further investigation of the institution itself or any attempts to situate it within seventeenth-century finance and culture.

Therefore, the little that is known about the bank and its partners is primarily due to Marvell studies, despite the fact that Marvell scholars are

---

[5] Fred S. Tupper. 1938. Mary Palmer, Alias Mrs. Andrew Marvell. *Modern Language Association* 53: 367–392; Andrew Marvell. 1681. *Miscellaneous Poems by Andrew Marvell Esq.* London. 'To the Reader'.

not interested in the bank itself. For example, Marvell biographer Nigel Smith labelled the formation of the bank a 'smaller-scale event' that was only important for the 'profound impact' it had in Marvell's later life.[6] In the 1950s L. N. Wall conducted a short study into the 'earlier history of the firm of Thompson, Nelthorpe & Co.', which included political disputes in the Corporation of London, as well as a brief mention of a conflict between partners Thompson and Nelthorpe and the East India Company. However, Wall's primary focus was still the 'interesting speculations about Marvell's own connection with the events described' and his analysis of Thompson and Company did not extend beyond the surface level.[7] Pauline Burdon unearthed important familial connections between Marvell and the Popple, Thompson, and Nelthorpe families, and situated Marvell's 'generous practical friendship' with Thompson and Nelthorpe within the political and religious controversies that Marvell was 'so deeply committed to'. Burdon was also the first to examine some of Nelthorpe's additional business activities, but did not relate these activities to the bank or attempt to explain the bank venture.[8] Martin Dzelzainis uncovered Nelthorpe's financial involvement in William Penn's Quaker undertaking to found a colony in West New Jersey.[9] Caroline Robbins focus was on Marvell's 'beloved' nephew William Popple, who along with his business partner Robert Stewart acted as 'agents' of Thompson and Company in 'Spain, Portugal, France, Ireland, and Scotland', illuminating the wider business network of the bank partners.[10] In his study of urban political culture, Phil Withington further examined the complicated identity of 'Mary Marvell', and highlighted the 'urban' and 'corporate' identities of the bank partners as well as the importance of 'political companionship'

---

[6] Nigel Smith. 2012. *Andrew Marvell: The Chameleon.* Hampshire: Yale University Press. 240.

[7] L. N. Wall. 1959. Marvell's Friends in the City. *Notes and Queries* 6: 204–207.

[8] Pauline Burdon. 1985. Marvell and his Kindred: The Family Network in the Later Years—II Nelthorpes, Thompsons, and Popples. *Notes and Queries.* 172–180.

[9] Martin Dzelzainis. 2013. Andrew Marvell, Edward Nelthorpe, and the Province of West New Jersey. *Andrew Marvell Newsletter* 5: 20–25.

[10] Caroline Robbins. 1967. Absolute Liberty: The Life and Thought of William Popple, 1638–1708. *The William and Mary Quarterly* 24: 198.

6   M. WINTER

in Marvell's life.[11] These studies are therefore limited in what they can reveal about Thompson and Company, the four partners, and the collapse of the bank. Instead, they have raised further questions about both the larger significance of the bank as an institution and its intersection with different aspects of Restoration society and culture. This book seeks to answer those questions.

In the history of finance in England, Thompson and Company fits between the era of goldsmith-banking and the onset of what is often called the 'Financial Revolution'.[12] Goldsmith-banks emerged in the early seventeenth century and their business expanded during the mid-century and Civil War, becoming England's dominant form of domestic bank to both the crown and the public. However, many prominent goldsmith-banks failed following the 1672 Stop on the Exchequer, when the crown stopped payment of its debts. Whilst this did not affect all goldsmith-banks, as some did not loan to the crown, the largest banks did slowly break down and collapse as a consequence of the Stop.[13] The Stop therefore caused a depletion of credit facilitators and financial institutions that was not rectified until the 1690s and the height of what is referred to as England's 'Financial Revolution'. In the 1690s, England's financial outlets increased in both number and variety and new investment opportunities opened to the public, such as joint-stock companies, private and

---

[11] Phil Withington. 2005. *The Politics of Commonwealth: Citizens and Freemen in Early Modern England*. Cambridge: Cambridge University Press. 125, 126, 224–227; Phil Withington. 2011. Andrew Marvell's Citizenship. In *The Cambridge Companion to Andrew Marvell*, eds Derek Hirst and Steven N. Zwicker, 102–121. Cambridge: Cambridge University Press. 117–118.

[12] P. G. M. Dickson. 1967. *The Financial Revolution in England: A Study in the Development of Public Credit 1688–1756*. London: Routledge; Henry Roseveare. 1991. *The Financial Revolution 1660–1760*. London: Longman; Peter Temin and Hans Joachim Voth. 2008. Private Borrowing During the Financial Revolution: Hoare's Bank and Its Customers 1702–24. *Economic History Review* 61: 541–564; Carl Wennerlind. 2011. *Casualties of Credit: The English Financial Revolution, 1620–1720*. Cambridge: Cambridge University Press; Anne L. Murphy. 2013. Demanding "Credible Commitment": Public Reactions to the Failures of the Early Financial Revolution. *The Economic History Review* 66: 178–197; A. M. Carlos, E. Fletcher and L. Neal. 2015. Share Portfolios in the Early Years of Financial Capitalism: London, 1690–1730. *Economic History Review* 68: 574–599; Anne L. Murphy. 2009. *The Origins of English Financial Markets: Investment and Speculation Before the South Sea Bubble*. Cambridge: Cambridge University Press.

[13] J. Keith Horsefield. 1982. The "Stop of the Exchequer" Revisited. *The Economic History Review* 35: 523–525.

1 INTRODUCTION 7

state lotteries, and government annuities.[14] This ushered in the beginning of public finance, the national debt, and the founding of the Bank of England in 1694. Thompson and Company therefore existed between these two eras of English finance. As an institution, it carried forward some of the older practices of the goldsmith-bankers of the first half of the seventeenth century but also experimented with new business models and practices that predate the expansion of financial practices in the last decade of the seventeenth century.

The earliest concise history of banking in England was conducted by R. D. Richards in 1929 and has been cited frequently ever since. Thompson and Company occupy just one footnote in Richards' study and do not appear in any subsequent historical works concerning the development of banking in England. The focus of Richards' work was the goldsmith-bankers of London, namely Edward Backwell, one of the only goldsmith-bankers whose records survive in significant numbers. Richards argued that the goldsmith-bankers of London were the precursors to the Bank of England, particularly in their development of a rudimentary mode of paper money in the form of goldsmiths' promissory notes.[15] Whilst historians of banking recognise that other forms of financial agent came before and existed alongside the goldsmiths, it is the goldsmith-bankers that dominate the narrative of financial development in England.[16] Consequentially, the 1672 Stop on the Exchequer, which caused the collapse of a great number of goldsmith-bankers, is

---

[14] Dickson. *Financial Revolution.* 6; C. D. Chandaman. 1975. *The English Public Revenue, 1660–1688.* Oxford: Oxford University Press. 2; K. G. Davies. 1952. Joint-Stock Investment in the Later Seventeenth Century. *The Economic History Review* 3: 292; Anne L. Murphy. 2009. Trading Options before Black–Scholes: A Study of the Market in Late Seventeenth-Century London. *The Economic History Review* 62: 9; Anne L. Murphy. 2005. Lotteries in the 1690s: Investment or Gamble? *Financial History Review* 12: 227–246.

[15] R. D. Richards. 1929. *The Early History of Banking in England.* London: Routledge. 16 n.1; R. D. Richards. 1928. A Pre-Bank of England English Banker—Edward Backwell. Reprinted from *The Economic Journal* 38, Supplement No. 3: 335–355.

[16] Frank T. Melton. 1986. *Sir Robert Clayton and the Origins of English Deposit Banking, 1658–1685.* Cambridge: Cambridge University Press. 14; Jongchul Kim. 2011. How Modern Banking Originated: The London Goldsmith-Bankers' Institutionalisation of Trust. *Business History* 53: 939–959; Stephen Quinn. 1997. Goldsmith-Banking: Mutual Acceptance and Interbanker Clearing in Restoration London. *Explorations in Economic History* 34: 411–432; Dorothy Clark. 1971. A Restoration Goldsmith-Banking House: The Vine on Lombard Street. In *Essays in Modern English History: In Honour of Wilbur*

8   M. WINTER

seen as marking the end of an era of English finance. Other banks that were not destroyed by the Stop tend to be studied separately and are not integrated into the longer trajectory of banking in England.[17] Gary De Krey's incorrect identification of Thompson and Company's partners as members of the Goldsmiths' Company further exemplifies the dominance of goldsmith-bankers in the historiography.[18] Whilst 'the merchant, the broker, the scrivener and the goldsmith' all emerged as 'pioneers' of new credit techniques and financial institutions in the seventeenth century, it was under the 'aegis of the goldsmith' that such techniques developed and were subsequently written about by historians.[19] The case of Thompson and Company suggests that other financial institutions should be included in this discussion and that these institutions can reveal more about the financial practices of a broader range of society.

In order to understand the implications of an institution in the wider social and economic world, it is important first to understand the institution itself and how it operated. Avner Greif has argued that microhistorical studies are incredibly useful in this regard, as 'the relevance of a particular institution' can only be understood through a 'micro-level, detailed examination of the evidence'.[20] This book undertakes this kind of institutional microhistory with Thompson and Company as its focal point. As such, it agrees with historians and economists who have stressed that 'institutions matter'.[21] In contrast, however, to those economists

---

Cortez Abbott, 3–47. London: Harvard University Press; Eric Kerridge. 1988. *Trade and Banking in Early Modern England*. Manchester: Manchester University Press. 81.

[17] Peter Temin and Hans Joachim Voth. 2013. *Prometheus Shackled: Goldsmith Banks and England's Financial Revolution after 1700*. Oxford: Oxford University Press; Peter Temin and Hans Joachim Voth. 2006. Banking as an Emerging Technology: Hoare's Bank, 1702–1742. *Financial History Review* 13: 149–178; Peter Temin and Hans Joachim Voth. 2005. Credit Rationing and Crowding Out During the Industrial Revolution: Evidence from Hoare's Bank, 1702–1862. *Explorations in Economic History* 42: 325–348; Melton. *Sir Robert Clayton*.

[18] Gary S. De Krey. 2005. *London and the Restoration 1659–1683*. Cambridge: Cambridge University Press. 413.

[19] Richards. *Early History of Banking*. 22.

[20] Avner Greif. 1998. Historical and Comparative Institutional Analysis. *The American Economic Review* 88: 81.

[21] Bruce G. Carruthers. 2007. Rules, Institutions, and North's Institutionalism: State and Market in Early Modern England. *European Management Review* 4: 40. For more on the importance of institutions, see Thomas Leng. 2020. *Fellowship and Freedom: The*

1 INTRODUCTION 9

and historians who see the importance of institutions only in their key role in 'economic growth' and the 'development of markets', the case of Thompson and Company demonstrates the importance of institutions in periods of economic change and even stagnation.[22] Thompson and Company's importance lies in its innovative and experimental institutional identity during a period when both the government and the people were suffering from a lack of credit and coin shortage.

Thompson and Company was innovative and entrepreneurial in its combination of a traditional early deposit banking with a commercial venture designed to provide interest-bearing deposits to customers and increase their own profits. As Chapter 4 demonstrates, the institution of Thompson and Company brings together two separate financial and commercial historiographies, those of experimental financial ventures and commercial projecting. The emergence of experimental financial ventures in the second half of the seventeenth century was a response to the coin shortage, lack of credit circulation, and the need to support rapidly expanding foreign trade.At the beginning of the century, money was inevitably bound up with precious metals but by the end of the century, England was operating on a system of paper currency and public debt.[23] The changing conceptualisation of money across the seventeenth century is reflected in the growing number of economic theories and schools of thought that emerged, such as political economy, mercantilism, and the balance of trade. J. Keith Horsefield, P. G. M. Dickson, Carl Wennerlind and others have identified a variety of new financial institutions aimed at increasing credit circulation and encouraging trade that ranged from a

Merchant Adventurers and the Restructuring of English Commerce, 1582–1700. Oxford: Oxford University Press; Phillip J. Stern. 2011. *The Company State: Corporate Sovereignty and the Early Modern Foundations of the British Empire in India.* Oxford: Oxford University Press; Phillip J. Stern. 2014. Companies: Monopoly, Sovereignty, and the East Indies. In *Mercantilism Reimagined: Political Economy in Early Modern Britain and Its Empire,* eds Phillip J. Stern and Carl Wennerlind, 177–195. Oxford: Oxford University Press; Sheilagh Ogilvie. 2011. *Institutions and European Trade: Merchant Guilds, 1000–1800.* Cambridge: Cambridge University Press.

[22] Carruthers. Rules, institutions, and North's institutionalism. 43; Douglass C. North and Barry R. Weingast. 1989. Constitutions and Commitments: The Evolution of Institutions Governing Public Choice in Seventeenth-Century England. *The Journal of Economic History* 49: 803.

[23] Christine Desan. 2015. *Making Money: Coin, Currency, and the Coming of Capitalism.* Oxford: Oxford University Press. 5, 9, 10, 231, 267.

10   M. WINTER

national exchange bank to small networks of regional banks, from land banks to Lumbard banks and pawnshops.[24] Historians have treated these financial proposals and ventures separately from other entrepreneurial and innovative ventures of the seventeenth century known as 'projects'. Daniel Defoe first discussed 'Projects' and 'projecting' in the 1690s in his *Essay Upon Projects*, in which he described a 'Projecting Age' that began in 'the Year 1680', although 'it had indeed something of life in the time of the late Civil War'.[25] Historians studying projecting have pushed its origins further back in time than Defoe. Joan Thirsk has argued that 'project' was a seventeenth-century 'key word' characterising a new era of 'material concerns' that were manifested in 'schemes to manufacture, or produce on the farm, goods for consumption at home'.[26] More recently, however, Koji Yamamoto has taken a much wider definition. He defines projects as business initiatives, whether implemented or just proposed, which demonstrate 'the commercial exploitation of useful knowledge and techniques'.[27] Whilst historians have demonstrated the importance of credit and new financial mechanisms to the operation of commercial projects, none have identified or studied a bank as a 'project'. As such, the historiographies of financial and commercial development remain largely separate.

However, by positing foreign trade and the advent of the transatlantic slave trade as progenitors of 'capitalism', the so-called 'new history of capitalism' does combine some aspects of financial and commercial development, albeit through a largely 'America-centric' outlook.[28] The case of Thompson and Company does not involve the Atlantic trade to a

---

[24] Dickson. *Financial Revolution*. 6–7; J. Keith Horsefield. 1960. *British Monetary Experiments 1650–1710*. Cambridge: Harvard University Press. 94, 95; Wennerlind. *Casualties of Credit*. 95–108; Paul Slack. 2015. *The Invention of Improvement: Information and Material Progress in Seventeenth-Century*. England. Oxford: Oxford University Press. 93, 109, 142.

[25] Daniel Defoe. 1697. *An Essay Upon Projects*. London. 1, 24.

[26] Joan Thirsk. 1978. *Economic Policy and Projects: The Development of a Consumer Society in Early Modern England*. Oxford: Oxford University Press. 1, 3.

[27] Koji Yamamoto. 2018. *Taming Capitalism before Its Triumph: Public Service, Distrust, and 'Projecting' in Early Modern England*. Oxford: Oxford University Press. 1, 5, 8, 68. See also: Mordechai Feingold. 2017. Projectors and Learned Projects in Early Modern England. *The Seventeenth Century* 32: 63–79.

[28] Trevor Burnard and Giorgio Riello. 2020. Slavery and the New History of Capitalism. *Journal of Global History* 15: 226.

significant degree and, as far as is known, none of the partners invested or engaged in the slave trade. Yet the methodology of the new history of capitalism does speak to this study's aims of uncovering the wider social and cultural underpinnings and implications of the institution of Thompson and Company. As Sven Beckert and Christine Desan have outlined, the new history of capitalism centres on 'lived experience' and identifies the individuals at the helm of new businesses as 'influential actors' within 'social networks'.[29] As such, this study also examines the social, political, and commercial networks of the partners and emphasises the importance of London within the history of capitalism, as a financial and political hub that facilitated the emergence of new technologies and forms of commerce across the globe.[30]

In bringing a greater social and cultural element to bear on institutional history, this book also combines the history of financial and commercial institutions with the wider, more socially embedded history of exchange, which includes foreign exchange, domestic exchange, coin, and credit. This history is more interpersonal in focus and centres around the moral, as opposed to the monetary, economy. Important for this study is what Craig Muldrew has described as an early modern 'culture of credit', which developed earlier than banks and other financial institutions in England to counteract the scarcity of coin and promote trade. Credit was based on social relationships and defined by Muldrew as 'the reputation for fair and honest dealing of a household and its members'. Individuals and households would be judged on their creditworthiness or reputation in social and economic dealings to determine whether or not they could be trusted. Muldrew argues that as the economy grew, these judgements became more important, and society increasingly came to be defined 'as the cumulative unity of the millions of interpersonal obligations which were continually being exchanged and renegotiated'. As networks expanded, however, it became more common for individuals

---

[29] Sven Beckert and Christine Desan. 2019. *American Capitalism: New Histories*. New York: Columbia University Press. 11–12.

[30] Nuala Zahedieh. 2010. *The Capital and the Colonies: London and the Atlantic Economy, 1660–1700*. Cambridge: Cambridge University Press; Nuala Zahedieh. 2013. Colonies, Copper, and the Market for Inventive Activity in England and Wales, 1680–1730. *Economic History Review* 66: 805–25; Pat Hudson. 2014. Slavery, the Slave Trade and Economic Growth: A Contribution to the Debate. In *Emancipation and the Making of the British Imperial World*, eds Catherine Hall, Nicholas Draper, and Keith McClelland, 36–59. Manchester: Manchester University Press. 45–47.

12   M. WINTER

to default on their payments and networks of credit broke down when individuals or households failed to meet their financial obligations. As a result, their social reputation would be damaged. Therefore, alongside the growth in credit networks was an increasing number of lawsuits, and the legal system became a central part of credit negotiations as an arbitrator of disputes. In the case of Thompson and Company, credit in social terms was vital for the establishment of the bank and attracting customers through the reputations of its partners. Credit also played a significant role in the collapse of the bank in 1678, further emphasising the important role of the legal system in the breakdown of credit networks and the extreme lengths individuals would go to in order to recover their estate and reputation.

However, the case of Thompson and Company also presents two points of conflict with Muldrew's argument. The first relates to the place of institutions within this model of credit. Whilst Muldrew argues that 'Informal credit, money and written instruments of credit all existed in tandem, and played specific roles in increasingly complex systems of exchange', he does not examine the role of financial institutions, which largely dealt with money and written instruments, in these systems. The primary institution Muldrew examines is the household and he only attributes changes or alterations in the credit system to the establishment of the Bank of England in 1694 and not to any of the banks or financial institutions earlier in the century.[31] Like the household, Thompson and Company relied on the 'reputation for fair and honest dealing' of the institution and its members and their shared credit was mutually dependent. They were not, however, a household, but an institution or 'company' and therefore had a corporate identity. This suggests that the development of institutions therefore needs to be included in a more dynamic culture of credit in order to assess how such corporations came to be the favoured financial institutions of the 1690s. The second point concerns the relationship between credit and reputation, and how networks of credit broke down. Thompson and Company is an extreme example of the breakdown of credit networks, one that proceeded to bankruptcy and Chancery proceedings. The extensive measures taken by creditors against Thompson and Company, such as refusing offers

---

[31] Craig Muldrew. 1998. *The Economy of Obligation: The Culture of Credit and Social Relations in Early Modern England.* Basingstoke: Palgrave Macmillan. 6, 91, 98, 115, 116, 123, 124, 148, 285, 328.

1 INTRODUCTION 13

of compositions and getting a parliamentary committee to investigate, suggest that the collapse of the bank was about more than just the partners inability to meet their financial obligations. Instead, the collapse of Thompson and Company appears to have been politically motivated, with their reputations collapsing before their ability to meet their obligations.

Reputation and status were therefore key to Thompson and Company's success and failure. To be trusted and creditworthy was extremely important in both finance and commerce, and maintaining a positive reputation took up much of the partners' time and effort. Historians have identified the ways and means by which creditworthiness could be defended through looking at behavioural ideals. For example, Wennerlind identified those behavioural ideals as 'honesty and punctuality, transparency, and severe punishment'; Keith Wrightson as 'reliability in the honouring of obligations, financial probity and honest dealing'; Muldrew as 'honesty ... followed by upright and fair dealing in market transactions'; and Laurence Fontaine as 'honouring one's commitments' and being 'honest'.[32] Alexandra Shepard has further linked these creditworthy behavioural traits to gender, associating being 'thrifty', 'courageous', 'plain-dealing' and 'self-governed' with the dominant form of masculinity in this period, 'patriarchal manhood'. All four partners of Thompson and Company met many of these ideals and therefore had a good claim to creditworthiness on this basis: all four were Englishmen between the ages of 'thirty-five and fifty', middling sort, married, and enfranchised householders.[33] However, whilst these basic values can provide a basis for defining creditworthiness, maintaining a positive reputation was far more complicated in practice and other considerations related to an individual's life and character come into play. The fate of Thompson and Company shows how religious and political beliefs could affect an individual's reputation and who would do business with them. Credit could also be affected by the number of different roles an individual took on and how widespread their credit was over those roles. In the case of Thompson and Company, the partners' multifaceted careers, acting as

---

[32] Wennerlind. *Casualties of Credit*. 97; Keith Wrightson. 2000. *Earthly Necessities: Economic Lives in Early Modern Britain*. London: Yale University Press. 127; Laurence Fontaine. 2014. *The Moral Economy: Poverty, Credit, and Trust in Early Modern Europe*. Cambridge: Cambridge University Press. 275, 276.

[33] Alexandra Shepard. 2005. From Anxious Patriarchs to Refined Gentlemen? Manhood in Britain, circa 1500–1700. *Journal of British Studies* 44: 290, 291, 293, 294.

14   M. WINTER

bankers, merchants, and politicians, placed further strain on their ability to meet a wide variety of obligations and maintain their reputations. However, this study is not just concerned with the masculine identity and credit of the four partners. It also examines women's roles in household and institutional credit by looking at the partners' wives and the female creditors of the bank. Women's roles and agency in banking, finance, and credit have only recently been incorporated into the historiography on a large scale. Much of this recent work has focussed on women's economic lives after 1690, during the height of the 'Financial Revolution'.[34] However, the large number of female creditors of Thompson and Company suggests that women were involved to a greater extent and earlier on in financial markets in seventeenth-century England. In this regard, this study builds on the work of Judith Spicksley, Misha Ewen, and Barbara Todd, who have all argued that women acted as financial investors or financial actors prior to the 1690s.[35] The fate of the partners' wives reinforces this argument and demonstrates the multifaceted ways in which women could use their social and economic agency to improve their situation and avoid, or lessen the impact of, total legal and economic subordination under coverture. Much of this was done through legal means in the court of Chancery, and this study complements other work on women's legal identities and legal visibility in the various courts of early modern England.[36] The economic roles and status

---

[34] Amy M. Froide. 2017. *Silent Partners: Women as Public Investors during Britain's Financial Revolution, 1690–1750.* Oxford: Oxford University Press. 59; Anne Laurence. 2008. The Emergence of a Private Clientele for Banks in the Early Eighteenth Century: Hoare's Bank and Some Women Customers. *The Economic History Review* 61: 565–586; Carlos, Ann M., and Larry Neal. 2004. Women Investors in Early Capital Markets, 1720–1725. *Financial History Review* 11: 197–224.

[35] Judith Spicksley. 2008. Usury Legislation, Cash, and Credit: The Development of the Female Investor in the Late Tudor and Stuart Periods. *The Economic History Review* 61: 277–301; Misha Ewen. 2019. Women Investors and the Virginia Company in the Early Seventeenth Century. *The Historical Journal* 62: 1–22; Barbara J. Todd. 2014. Fiscal Citizens: Female Investors in Public Finance before the South Sea Bubble. In *Challenging Orthodoxies: The Social and Cultural Worlds of Early Modern Women,* eds Melinda S. Zook and Sigrun Haude, 53–74. Ashgate: Routledge. 53–74.

[36] Amy Louise Erickson. 1993. *Women and Property in Early Modern England.* London: Routledge; Craig Muldrew. 2003. "A Mutual Assent of Her Mind"? Women, Debt, Litigation and Contract in Early Modern England. *History Workshop Journal* 55: 47–71; Butler. The Law as a Weapon. 291–316; Emma Hawkes. 2000. "[S]he will … protect and defend her rights boldly by law and reason …": Women's Knowledge of Common Law

1 INTRODUCTION 15

of the partners' wives and the female creditors of the bank demonstrate that economic gender ideals and prescribed gender roles were not necessarily put into practice, and that women could possess credibility and economic agency that was not the same as that of men but could be just as powerful. The main difference being that male economic credit was far more deeply entwined with masculinity itself and caused a much more significant blow to a man's social status when lost.

Aside from credit networks, this study examines a wide range of other social, commercial, and political networks. Here, networks are defined as a group of individuals with a common purpose or with common interests who aid one another socially or practically. Of primary importance for analysing Thompson and Company are commercial merchant networks of agents, factors, and goods, social networks of kin and friends, and political networks in official government bodies as well as more informal political associations. This study therefore undertakes an 'analysis of the relationships between actors', which has been described as the 'fundamental' basis of social network analysis.[37] Obviously this is done in a historicised way and the networks are reconstructed before they are analysed. Through this analysis, it is evident that a variety of formal and informal networks underpinned the formation and operation of the bank of Thompson and Company, with mercantile networks important for its formation, and social networks facilitating communication to attract customers, as well as each of its partner's individual careers and roles, which were aided by networks of kin as well as commercial associates. Additionally, networks also played a large part in the collapse of the bank in 1678 as facilitators of rumour and gossip through formal and informal channels.

Formal networks include the partners' membership of guilds and chartered companies, their own four-way partnership, their religious communities, and their political roles in civic government. The partners' informal networks include their immediate and wider kinship ties, local community relationships, friends, and associates. Both the formal

and Equity Courts in Late-Medieval England. In *Medieval Women and the Law*, ed. Noel James Menuge, 145–161. Woodbridge: Boydell Press. 145–161; Amy Louise Erickson. 1990. Common Law Versus Common Practice: The Use of Marriage Settlements in Early Modern England. *Economic History Review* 43: 21–39.

[37] Emily Erikson. 2013. Formalist and Relationalist Theory in Social Network Analysis. *Sociological Theory* 31: 219–242; Emily Erikson and Sampsa Samila. 2015. Social Networks and Port Traffic in Early Modern Overseas Trade. *Social Science History* 39: 151–173.

16   M. WINTER

and the informal networks the partners' established and participated in had social and economic functions, and they reflect the changing nature of the seventeenth-century economy, political landscape, and social and cultural environment. Wrightson has argued that relationships and networks changed to reflect the changing nature of society, which was becoming 'more urbanised and commercialised, more diverse, more inter-connected, more dynamic economically, culturally and politically, and more engaged with a larger world'. Therefore, 'new bonds of mutuality and *collective* identity' emerged in line with the growth of new institutions, corporations, and urban ways of living.[38] The case of Thompson and Company demonstrates this in practice, as the partners navigated new financial, commercial, and political environments by drawing on their established social relationships as well as forming new associations of mutuality and obligation, to both positive and negative ends.

Historians have mostly focussed on the positive outcomes of networks, particularly the positive, status-affirming attributes of merchant networks in the early modern period.[39] These were not just trading networks, however, but encompassed networks of 'family, place of origin, occupation, religion, or political convictions', meaning that an individual occupied a multitude of different networks at one time.[40] Of growing significance since the mid-sixteenth century was the overlapping of merchant and political networks. The wealth of merchants had been

[38] Keith Wrightson. 2005. Mutualities and Obligations: Changing Social Relationships in Early Modern England. *Proceedings of the British Academy* 139: 177, 186, 188.

[39] Ian Anders Gadd and Patrick Wallis. 2002. Introduction. In *Guilds, Society and Economy in London 1450–1800*, eds Ian Anders Gadd and Patrick Wallis, 1–14. London: Institute of Historical Research. 10; Perry Gauci. 2002. Informality and Influence: The Overseas Merchant and the Livery Companies, 1660–1720. In *Guilds, Society and Economy in London 1450–1800*, eds Ian Anders Gadd and Patrick Wallis, 127–139. London: Institute of Historical Research. 127, 129, 130, 133, 134; Perry Gauci. 2007. *Emporium of the World: The Merchants of London 1660–1800*. London: Hambledon Continuum. 73, 83, 84; Hancock. *Citizens of the World*. 2, 16–17; Wrightson. *Earthly Necessities*. 294; Ogilvie. *Institutions and European Trade*. 6; Regina Grafe and Oscar Gelderblom. 2010. The Rise and Fall of the Merchant Guilds: Re-thinking the Comparative Study of Commercial Institutions in Premodern Europe. *The Journal of Interdisciplinary History* 40: 487; Emily Erikson. 2014. *Between Monopoly and Free Trade: The English East India Company, 1600–1757*. Princeton: Princeton University Press. 20, 21, 181.

[40] Zahedieh. *The Capital and the Colonies*. 106; Perry Gauci. 2001. *The Politics of Trade: The Overseas Merchant in State and Society, 1660–1720*. Oxford: Oxford University Press. 9.

1 INTRODUCTION   17

increasing steadily since the 1550s as mercantile companies in England expanded, setting up new trade links across Europe and further afield to the Caribbean and Americas. Robert Brenner has argued that, as a result, there was a growing recognition of the need for cooperation between merchants, government, and the crown: merchants 'needed government intervention' to obtain privileges such as monopolies and to keep out foreign and, more importantly, domestic competitors, whilst the crown needed 'financial and political support' for foreign warfare. Therefore, merchants realised they could use 'political levers to obtain privileges which would allow them to limit risk and raise profits'.[41]

However, whilst the mutually beneficial relationship between mercantile and political power has been identified, the potential risks of this relationship have largely been neglected. Hancock argues that whilst networks were often 'solutions to problems', particularly the mercantile issue of 'doing business over oceanic distances', they also 'created their own management challenges'. Networks relied on trust and reputation, which were difficult to communicate and maintain across large distances and miscommunication 'could be costly in lost business and poor trades'. Personal disagreements were also common and social, economic, and political factors outside of an individual or firm's control affected the dynamics of networks. As such, networks 'failed as often as they succeeded'.[42] Whilst Hancock's insights are an important contrast to the overtly positive and often idealised discussion of early modern networks, he only deals with merchant networks and the problems inherent within them. In contrast, this study examines a wider range of networks and the interaction between multiple networks across the different 'fields' of finance, commerce, and politics, arguing that whilst there were many positive outcomes of networks there were also significant risks.

The use of the term 'field' throughout the book is a historicised version of social theorist Pierre Bourdieu's concept that describes a social space comprised of 'agents' and their 'objective power relations' with one

---

[41] Robert Brenner. 1993. *Merchants and Revolution: Commercial Change, Political Conflict, and London's Overseas Traders, 1550–1653*. Cambridge: Cambridge University Press. 113, 199, 210.

[42] David Hancock. 2005. The Trouble with Networks: Managing the Scots' Early-Modern Madeira Trade. *The Business History Review* 79: 473, 478.

another, which are determined by their levels of 'capital'. Capital represents a set of 'powers' which are specific to each field and can be in the 'form of material properties', in the 'embodied state', and 'legally guaranteed'. For Bourdieu, the main types of capital are 'economic', 'social', 'cultural', and 'symbolic', the amount and employment of which affect an individual's position within the field.[43] Fields are therefore places of contest and competition, as individuals aim to accumulate capital and improve their position within it. Thompson and Company's partners, as bankers, merchants, and officeholders, occupied the three principal fields of finance, commerce, and politics. Occupying multiple roles was a common occurrence, and Michael Braddick and John Walter have described this in terms of an 'early modern power grid'. Similar to Bourdieu's negotiation of capital in fields, Braddick and Walter argue that the early modern power grid was made up of a 'number of hierarchies', which were both distinct and interrelated. An individual's power was determined by how many hierarchies they had access to and the 'mutually reinforcing' nature of their 'ranking' within those hierarchies, which could vary spatially and temporally. This model allows us, according to Braddick and Walter, to analyse the 'dynamics of power *between* hierarchies', a relationship that has been previously neglected.[44] However, this grid of power does not account for individuals who purposefully challenged their own ranking or position within the grid, by assuming roles that placed them in a higher position of power than that dictated by the hierarchy or field. It also does not acknowledge the fact that numerous roles within numerous hierarchies could not only be mutually reinforcing but could undermine one another, as damage to a ranking in one hierarchy would damage placing within the others. The case of Thompson and Company demonstrates both scenarios in practice, highlighting the role of agency, strategy, and power that Bourdieu's fields model and Braddick and Walter's 'power grid' do not account for.

In the case of Thompson and Company, the partners used their agency and power in all three fields to further their own positions and status,

---

[43] Pierre Bourdieu. 1985. The Social Space and the Genesis of Groups. *Social Science Information* 24: 196, 197.

[44] Michael J. Braddick and John Walter. 2010. Introduction. Grids of Power: Order, Hierarchy and Subordination in Early Modern Society. In *Negotiating Power in Early Modern Society: Order, Hierarchy and Subordination in Britain and Ireland*, eds Michael J. Braddick and John Walter, 1–42. Cambridge: Cambridge University Press.

1 INTRODUCTION   19

but it was in the political field that their use of agency and strategy were most risky. Partners Richard Thompson and Edward Nelthorpe were civic politicians elected to London's Common Council in the late 1660s and 1670s, during which time their bank was established and collapsed. In these roles they grew to prominence as part of an opposition faction, which challenged the political power structure, or grid of power. English politics during this period was characterised by conflict and further complicated by the relationship between politics and religion. This is because, as a number of historians have argued, religious disputes underpinned political discontent throughout the Restoration.[45] Historians view the close relationship between politics and religion in the Restoration as an unresolved conflict from the Civil War. Despite Charles II's promise of toleration in the 1660 Declaration from Breda, the Restoration religious settlement was an Anglican Church settlement. Dissent from this settlement was penalised and enforced by acts such as the Uniformity and Corporation Acts of 1661 and the Conventicle Acts of 1664 and 1670, and Anglican success was further demonstrated by the rapid repeal of the 1672 Declaration of Indulgence. This meant that concerns over the reformed Church of England, which had been a significant cause of Civil War conflict, remained unsettled at the Restoration and parliamentary politics remained deeply embedded in 'the language of church politics' and issues of conformity, dissent, and popery.[46]

Whilst most historians agree that the 1670s witnessed political conflict, the precise nature of that conflict is debated. On the one hand, De Krey argues that this 'realignment of most citizens into conformist and

---

[45] De Krey. *London and the Restoration*; Douglas R. Lacey. 1969. *Dissent and Parliamentary Politics in England, 1661–1689: A Study in the Perpetuation and Tempering of Parliamentarianism*. New Brunswick: Rutgers University Press; Tim Harris. Introduction: Revising the Restoration. In *The Politics of Religion in Restoration England*, eds Tim Harris, Paul Seaward, and Mark Goldie, 1–28. Oxford: Oxford University Press; Mark Goldie. 1990. Danby, the Bishops and the Whigs. In *The Politics of Religion in Restoration England*, eds Tim Harris, Paul Seaward, and Mark Goldie, 75–105. Oxford: Oxford University Press; Jonathan Scott. 1990. England's Trouble: Exhuming the Popish Plot. In *The Politics of Religion in Restoration England*, eds Tim Harris, Paul Seaward, and Mark Goldie, 107–131. Oxford: Oxford University press; Tim Harris. 1990. "Lives, Liberties and Estates": Rhetorics of Liberty in the Reign of Charles II. In *The Politics of Religion in Restoration England*, eds Tim Harris, Paul Seaward, and Mark Goldie, 217–241. Oxford: Oxford University Press.

[46] Harris. Introduction: Revising the Restoration. 9; Goldie. Danby, the Bishops and the Whigs. 79.

20 M. WINTER

nonconformist camps also provided the groundwork for the emergence of political parties in London in the crisis of 1679–82'.[47] He argues that there was a conformist or Anglican 'court party', which can be viewed as the predecessors of the Tory party, and a nonconformist 'country party', which was the predecessor of the Whigs. In contrast, historians such as Tim Harris argue that although these two groups 'had developed a rudimentary organisational structure' they were not unified 'parties' with a common ideology and do not simply feed into the later development of Whig and Tory parties. This is because 'court' and 'country' were divided primarily over religious issues, which often 'cut across' the 'constitutional tensions between the Crown and Parliament' that underpinned the divide between Whig and Tory.[48] In 'court' and 'country' divisions, the monarch switched sides depending on who could provide much needed economic and political support.[49] As such, divisions between 'court' and 'country' factions are viewed as less aggressive and divisive than those between Whig and Tory, which fuelled the later Popish Plot and the Exclusion Crisis.

However, that does not mean that distinctions between 'court' and 'country' are not useful. On a large scale it may be impossible to distinguish two neatly divided parties, but when examining groups of politicians on a smaller scale who were deeply involved in the debates and issues surrounding dissent, parliamentary corruption, and popery, the distinct concepts of 'court' and 'country' are useful tools for discussion. In this study, Thompson and Nelthorpe, and others in their networks, can be defined as distinctly 'country' politicians as they were closely associated with one of the leading 'country' lords after 1673, the earl of Shaftesbury, were promoters of religious toleration, and, like their kinsman Andrew Marvell, were deeply suspicious of court corruption. In addition to this, the banking partners were known enemies of the 'court' faction leader, the earl of Danby. In this sense, Thompson and Nelthorpe were part of a 'country' party or faction that defined itself against, and regularly came into conflict with, an opposing 'court' faction. Thompson and Nelthorpe are not referred to as 'early' or 'proto' Whigs in this study, as De Krey's

[47] De Krey. *London and the Restoration.* 73–74.

[48] Tim Harris. 1993. *Politics under the Later Stuarts: Party Conflict in a Divided Society 1660–1715.* London: Routledge. 63–65; J. R. Jones. 1963. *The First Whigs: The Politics of the Exclusion Crisis 1678–1683.* London: Oxford University Press.

[49] Goldie. Danby, the Bishops and the Whigs. 75.

1 INTRODUCTION   21

argument suggests and as some previous scholarship has claimed, because they were forced to relinquish their political roles prior to the development of partisan politics during the constitutional crises after 1679.[50] But this study does show how some members of the partners' wider kinship networks developed from 'country' party to Whig politicians, suggesting that there was at least some continuity between these two groups. The case of Thompson and Company highlights the significance of 'court' and 'country' divisions in 1670s London, demonstrating how divisive these factions could be and examining the personal vendettas they inspired. It particularly emphasises that 'court' and 'country' factions were not only divisive politically but socially and economically, a point that historians have previously missed. The political roles of Thompson and Company's partners and their strategies within those roles had significant implications for the fate of their financial and commercial venture, as well as their wider social and credit networks.

II

Without Thompson and Company's 'books of original entry' such as 'ledgers, journals and correspondence, supplemented by waste books … petty cash accounts, sale and order books, abstracts for ready reference and memoranda', which are described by Richard Grassby as essential to analyse 'success and failure' in business, Chancery records offer the best possible opportunity to analyse Thompson and Company.[51] Indeed, analysing businesses through alternative sources is a common method because most original entry books and papers do not survive, particularly if that business failed. As such, this study uses Chancery court cases from across the period 1660–1690 as its primary source for reconstructing Thompson and Company.

Chancery was the court of the Lord Chancellor, which developed to form its own jurisdiction that was distinct from the common law. Chancery followed equity law, which was based on conscience rather than

---

[50] Nicholas von Maltzahn. 2019. Marvell, Writer and Politician, 1621–1678. In *The Oxford Handbook of Andrew Marvell*, eds Martin Dzelzainis and Edward Holberton, 3–25. Oxford: Oxford University Press. 24; Wall. Marvell's Friends in the City. 204.

[51] Richard Grassby. 1995. *The Business Community of Seventeenth-Century England*. Cambridge: Cambridge University Press. 12.

22 M. WINTER

'the strict rules of evidence' and could try cases that required examination of the wider facts and circumstances or required consideration of new and developing aspects of 'merchant law' and financial customs that were not yet recognised in the common law. As such, it was often used for cases in which 'no remedy' could be found through common law. Chancery proceedings were recorded in English by clerks of the court. The complainant would enter a bill of complaint, which the defendant then replied to in a written testament by way of a sworn answer, disclaimer, demurrer, a plea, or a cross bill. Once responses had been made, proceedings were closed, and the court moved on to collect documentary evidence surrounding the case in the form of depositions and original documents. Few cases made it through to a final hearing or decree, as proceedings were expensive, and it was easier to settle outside of court.[52]

Despite recognising that Chancery proceedings are an incredibly rich source of information for historians, its documents 'have rarely been explored'.[53] Historians that have used the proceedings have done so in two distinct ways. On the one hand, historians have used broad surveys of Chancery records to examine certain phenomena, such as property rights or marital disharmony, over a wide range of examples, often using quantitative data.[54] On the other hand, historians have used Chancery records to collate and reconstruct a specific series of proceedings relating to an

[52] John Baker. 2019. *Introduction to English Legal History*. 5th edn. Oxford: Oxford University Press. 106–111; Christopher W. Brooks. 2008. *Law, Politics and Society in Early Modern* England. Cambridge: Cambridge University Press. 11, 25, 239, 396; P. Tucker. 2000. The Early History of the Court of Chancery: A Comparative Study. *The English Historical Review* 115: 795; Henry Horwitz. 1995. *Chancery Equity Records and Proceedings 1600–1800: A Guide to Documents in the Public Record Office*. London: Stationery Office Books. 9; Henry Horwitz and Patrick Polden. 1996. Continuity or Change in the Seventeenth and Eighteenth Centuries? *Journal of British Studies* 35: 37, 42; Christine Churches. 2000. Business at Law: Retrieving Commercial Disputes from Eighteenth-Century Chancery. *The Historical Journal*, 43: 940.

[53] Erickson. *Women and Property*. 31; Butler. The Law as a Weapon. 294; Brooks. *Law, Politics and Society*. 12, 307; Churches. Business at Law. 938.

[54] Erickson. *Women and Property*; Maria L. Cioni. 1982. The Elizabethan Chancery and Women's Rights. In *Tudor Rule and Revolution: Essays for G. R. Elton from his American friends*, eds Delloyd J. Guth and John W. McKenna, 159–182. Cambridge: Cambridge University Press; Butler. The Law as a Weapon; Sean Bottomley. 2014. Patent Cases in the Court of Chancery, 1714–1758. *The Journal of Legal History* 35: 27–43; Adam Hofri-Winogradow. 2012. Parents, Children and Property in Late 18th-Century Chancery. *Oxford Journal of Legal Studies* 32: 741–769; Richards. *Early History of Banking*.

1 INTRODUCTION 23

individual or set of people to illuminate wider trends and characteristics in early modern commercial and business life, or to shed light on previously unnoticed or under-examined aspects of a single subject's life.[55] This book employs the latter method, combining and cross-referencing Chancery proceedings with other material from different sources and following various paper trails to reconstruct and analyse Thompson and Company.

Other sources of importance include the partners' own pamphlet, *The Case of Richard Thompson and Company: With Relation to their Creditors*, which was first published in 1677 and has been widely cited in the existing scholarship concerning the bank. Pamphlets are small books that deal with a specific subject matter and were relatively cheap to buy. As Alexandra Halasz and Joad Raymond have argued, pamphlets were crucial in the formation, maintenance, and deconstruction of credit, as they could 'circulate like gossip' and 'exercised social influence' as 'part of the everyday practice of politics'.[56] Demand for and wide readership of Thompson and Company's pamphlet is evident from its reprinting in 1678, and pamphlets written by bankrupts themselves appear to have been relatively common in cases of bankruptcy, with both Emily Kadens and Aaron Graham citing pamphlets in the same 'case of' formula in their respective studies of eighteenth-century bankruptcy cases.[57]

---

[55] Emily Kadens. 2010. The Pitkin Affair: A Study of Fraud in Early English Bankruptcy. *American Bankruptcy Law Journal* 84: 483–570; Churches. Business at Law; 2016. Military Contractors and the Money Markets, 1700–15. In *The British Fiscal-Military States 1660–c.1783*, eds Aaron Graham, and Patrick Walsh, 83–112. London: Routledge; Kathleen Kamerick. 2013. Tanglost of Wales: Magic and Adultery in the Court of Chancery circa 1500. *The Sixteenth Century Journal* 44: 25–45; Alison A. Chapman. 2018. The Lay Reader's Guide to *Milton v. Cope*: Trust, Debt, and Loss in Chancery. *Milton Quarterly* 52: 113–127; David Farr. 1994. Notes and Documents: Oliver Cromwell and a 1647 Case in Chancery. *Historical Research* 71: 341–346; Andrew Hadfield and Simon Healy. 2012. Edmund Spenser and Chancery in 1597. *Law and Humanities* 6: 57–64.

[56] Alexandra Halasz. 1997. *The Marketplace of Print: Pamphlets and the Public Sphere in Early Modern England*. Cambridge: Cambridge University Press. 3, 14; Joad Raymond. 2003. *Pamphlets and Pamphleteering in Early Modern Britain*. Cambridge: Cambridge University Press. 26.

[57] 1678. *The Case of Richard Thompson and Company: With Relation to their Creditors*. London; Kadens. The Pitkin Affair. 483–570; Graham. Military Contractors and the Money Markets. 83–112. See also Churches. Business at Law. 949–950.

24   M. WINTER

Alongside the partners' own pamphlet are two pamphlets written by anonymous creditors of the bank. The first pamphlet is dated as published in 1678 and implores all creditors to settle the dispute with the bank outside of court to prevent 'the injury of all' involved.[58] The second pamphlet was published in response to a parliamentary enquiry taken out against the banking partners and argued against the passing of a Bill that would enforce stricter punishment on the partners than was already enforced by the bankruptcy laws. This pamphlet is cited being as published in 1677 but must have been published later as it refers to the other pamphlet in the text, noting that most of the creditors were willing to settle with the partners outside of court and had 'publickly declared' the same 'in print before the meeting of Parliament'.[59] Previous scholarship has not used these pamphlets, and both offer new insights into the bank, its partners, and the bankruptcy. Similarly used to great effect are genealogical sources, which are used most commonly in family history but are here employed to trace Thompson and Company's partners, families, associates, and creditors. Of primary importance in this regard is Percival Boyd's Inhabitants of London, a database that collates birth, marriage, and death records with guild records and other sources to 'create individual family histories' for '59,389 family groups' from the sixteenth to the eighteenth centuries.[60] Other sources used include personal and state correspondence, corporate records, Privy Council records, newsletters, account books, notebooks, and government records from the Corporation of London and the Houses of Parliament.

III

The book reconstructs Thompson and Company, from its establishment in 1671 to its collapse and bankruptcy which extended into the 1680s, and can be roughly divided into three parts. Chapters 2–4 focus on the institution of Thompson and Company, reconstructing it and

---

[58] *Reasons offered by several of the creditors of Richard Thompson and partners.*

[59] *Reasons most humbly offered to the consideration of Parliament.*

[60] Boyd's Inhabitants of London & Family Units 1200–1946—Unpublished Index accessed via *Findmypast*, https://search.findmypast.co.uk/search-world-records/boyds-inhabitants-of-london-and-family-units-1200-1946; Peter Razzell and Christine Spence. 2007. The History of Infant, Child and Adult Mortality in London, 1550–1850. *The London Journal* 32: 273–274.

resituating it within the historiography of both financial and commercial institutions in seventeenth-century England. Chapter 2 reconstructs Thompson and Company primarily using Chancery court proceedings thereby providing a model for future studies of forgotten institutions and demonstrating the utility of Chancery proceedings for microhistorical and business case studies. Chapter 3 takes the reconstructed institution of Thompson and Company and resituates it within the historiography of early modern banking, comparing it to contemporary institutions and suggesting why individuals were using banks in the 1670s. Whilst Thompson and Company has an important place in the history of banking, Chapter 4 argues that it has an equally important place in the history of commerce and mercantile trade. Therefore, to incorporate Thompson and Company's institutional hybridity, the chapter situates the institution in the history of 'projecting' and as an early modern 'project'.

Chapters 5 and 6 turn to the social networks that underpinned Thompson and Company, and the social networks that were facilitated by Thompson and Company. Chapter 5 examines the partners' kinship networks and shows how their family backgrounds shaped the venture that was Thompson and Company, providing not only business support but a network of religious and politically likeminded individuals. Chapter 6 uses surviving evidence from Thompson and Company's creditors to investigate their relationship to the partners, suggest why they might have decided to do business with them, and examine how they described their financial activities. Chapters 7–9 deal with the collapse and bankruptcy of Thompson and Company. Chapter 7 reconstructs Thompson and Company's bankruptcy, outlines the unusually harsh procedures the partners faced, and demonstrates the wider significance of their collapse within the historiography of bankruptcy law in England. Having reconstructed the collapse, Chapter 8 analyses the commercial, financial, and political reasons behind it, weighing up the causes to establish why Thompson and Company collapsed in 1678. Finally, Chapter 9 examines the aftermath of the collapse and the ways in which Thompson and Company's bankruptcy affected their wider kinship and social networks.

CHAPTER 2

Thompson and Company

In their 1677 pamphlet Thompson and Company's partners began by describing their venture: 'That we being severally possessed of considerable Estates, did upon the second day of *January* [1671] (as is frequent with other Merchants) enter into a Society amongst ourselves, giving our joynt Bonds for security to all such Persons as offered Money to be deposited with us'. The partners explained that they offered 'the usual Interest' and 'paid every one duly, whether Principal, or Interest, as demanded'.[1] The ultimate aim of the pamphlet, however, was not to provide an exhaustive description of the operation of the partners' business but to offer an explanation to their creditors, and the wider public, of the hardships that had brought about the collapse of the bank and their subsequent actions. Historians discussing the bank, in the few other studies in which it features, have often used the pamphlet as their primary source when outlining and defining Thompson and Company's business model, without delving further into Chancery or other manuscript sources. This has led to Thompson and Company being labelled in a variety of conflicting ways. Tupper merely labelled it a 'bank' in 'quadripartite partnership', Kavanagh and Wall broadly refer to the partners as 'merchant bankers', De Krey wrongly identifies Thompson and Nelthorpe

---

[1] *Case of Richard Thompson and Company.* 3–4.

© The Author(s), under exclusive license to Springer Nature Switzerland AG 2022
M. Winter, *Banking, Projecting and Politicking in Early Modern England*, Palgrave Studies in Economic History, https://doi.org/10.1007/978-3-030-90570-5_2

28   M. WINTER

as goldsmith-bankers, Withington has referred to them as both a 'joint-stock company' and a 'partnership of citizens', and Dzelzainis simply calls it a 'joint bank'.[2] The only mention of the bank in a dedicated economic study is by Richards, who briefly referred to the bank as a partnership 'accepting deposits as a specialised business'. However, Richards mistakenly described the business as not 're-issuing the money deposited in the form of loans, but for the purpose of personally using such money in trading transactions'.[3] The inaccurate labelling of Thompson and Company reflects the fact that whilst the partners have attracted some attention as individuals, the bank as an institution has been largely overlooked, leaving no trace in the history of English finance and banking.

The lack of attention paid to Thompson and Company is largely due to three factors. Firstly, the bank does not feature in any contemporary directory of merchants or bankers, the first of which, the *Little London Directory*, was published in 1677. The directory features a list of names and addresses of active merchants as well as goldsmiths who held running cashes—which meant that they were first and foremost goldsmiths by trade but also engaged in pawn broking and moneylending activities—but not other businesses active in the capital. Whilst the directory is useful for tracing merchants and goldsmith credit facilitators, it does not record different business models and misses out Thompson and Company. Secondly, the relatively short life span of the bank restricted its impact, as it features in few surviving sources and is overlooked in broader studies. Third, after their bankruptcy the partners lost or destroyed the account books, ledgers, and other papers of the bank. However, by carrying out a microhistorical investigation of the Chancery proceedings this chapter reconstructs Thompson and Company. It outlines the identities and backgrounds of its four partners, the articles of agreement that underpinned its formation, the day-to-day operation of the bank, the geographical and occupational range of its creditors, and the economic

---

[2] Tupper Mary Palmer. 368; Art Kavanagh. 2013. Andrew Marvell "in want of money": The Evidence in John Farrington v. Mary Marvell. *The Seventeenth Century* 17: 207; Wall. Marvell's Friends in the City. 204; De Krey. *London and the Restoration*. 413; Withington. Andrew Marvell's Citizenship. 118; Withington. *Politics of Commonwealth*. 192; Dzelzainis. Andrew Marvell, Edward Nelthorpe. 20.

[3] Richards. *Early History of Banking*. 15–16.

2 THOMPSON AND COMPANY 29

instruments used by the partners to provide a variety of financial services for their customers.

I

Of the four partners of Thompson and Company, Richard Thompson and Edward Nelthorpe have received the most attention due to their relationship with Andrew Marvell. Partners John Farrington and Edmund Page tend to be treated separately or not at all, and information about all four partners largely concerns their activities during their bankruptcy or in later life. However, all four had successful careers prior to the formation of their four-way partnership in 1671. Prior to this date Farrington and Page had traded 'together in partnership', combining 'the trade of a wholesale mercer in London & abroad Merchants in divers particular wares & merchandyes in parts beyond the sea'. Nelthorpe and Thompson had also traded together in partnership as merchants in 'wines and other comodities'.[4] As well as being merchants, all four men were citizens of London meaning each partner was a member of one of London's livery companies or guilds. Guilds could be entered in three ways: through redemption, patrimony, or, most commonly, apprenticeship. Of the four partners, Edmund Page entered the Haberdashers' guild through patrimony, Edward Nelthorpe the Drapers' through apprenticeship, John Farrington the Haberdashers' through apprenticeship and Richard Thompson's entry to the Clothworkers' guild is unknown. Membership of these companies was highly significant for the partners' identities, social status, and their individual and collective credit. It demonstrated that they were economically substantial householders, that they had political privileges such as the right to vote in elections for civic government and be elected to it, and socially it provided access to important political and commercial contacts.[5]

The Chancery records identify Farrington as a citizen, haberdasher, and merchant of London. The Haberdashers' Company records confirm this identification, showing that Farrington began his apprenticeship by servitude in 1647 for a term of eight years under his Master Tobias Dixon and

---

[4] TNA: C 7/581/73. Farrington v Thompson. 7 July 1684; C 6/283/87. Thompson v Farrington. 30 May 1684.

[5] Withington. Andrew Marvell's Citizenship. 105; Gauci. Informality and Influence. 130; Gadd and Wallis. Introduction. 10.

30 M. WINTER

obtained his freedom of the Company in 1654.[6] Farrington's parentage and the value of his apprenticeship bond are unknown, but the fact that he completed an apprenticeship gives an insight into his family background as the family must have had 'the means to finance the investment in training' for their son.[7] Edmund Page's status as a citizen is harder to trace. The court cases simply refer to Page as 'late of London merchant', with no specific guild affiliation. However, other records demonstrate that, like Farrington, Page was a Haberdasher. He obtained freedom of the company in 1641 by patrimony, through the membership of his father, also named Edmund Page, meaning that Page was considerably older than Farrington and the other partners and already had an established career when Farrington joined the Haberdashers' guild later in the 1650s.[8] Page's father was also a citizen, meaning the young Edmund Page grew up in a citizen's household and probably had a grammar school education.

In the Chancery proceedings concerning the bankruptcy, Farrington and Page's early careers are only hinted at. However, other records show that Farrington and Page had been in business together since at least 1665. The books of sales of a later creditor of Thompson and Company, Sir William Turner, a London woollen draper, reveal that Farrington and Page had previously traded in partnership with another merchant, Charles Michell. The book of sales features the account of 'Mr Edmond Page Mr Charles Michell & Mr Farrington' on 9 March 1665. Turner referred to them collectively as 'Mr Edmond Page and Company' and they purchased cloth from him to the value of £1199 6s 1d.[9] The three-way partnership never appears in the accounts again, so how long it continued is therefore unknown. However, it was certainly no longer operational in

[6] Guildhall Archives: MS 15858/1. Index to registers of freemen of Haberdashers Company; CLC/L/HA/C/011. Register of apprentice bindings for the Haberdashers Company. f. 59.

[7] Tim Leunig, Chris Minns, and Patrick Wallis. 2011. Networks in the Premodern Economy: The Market for London Apprenticeships, 1600–1749. *The Journal of Economic History* 71: 418.

[8] City of London, Haberdashers, Apprentices And Freemen 1526–1933, accessed via *Findmypast*, https://www.findmypast.co.uk/articles/world-records/full-list-of-united-kin gdom-records/education-and-work-records/city-of-london-haberdashers-apprentices-and-freemen-1526-1933, 1641 entry for Edmond Page; *Boyd's Inhabitants of London*, 1648 record, 166.

[9] LMA: CLC/509/MS05105. Book of Sales, 1664–71, followed by accounts relating to his personal estate, 1671–91. ff. 9–10.

the later 1660s when Page and Farrington appear together in Chancery as complainants against Walter Jago junior, a merchant of Dartmouth, Devon. The complaint concerned a bill of exchange due to Jago from 'Lewes Froment', a merchant in Paris, who was indebted to Jago for the sum of 725 and a half crowns. In order to send the bill, Froment had William Barr, another merchant in Paris, draw a bill of exchange on Farrington and Page. Barr had clearly dealt with Farrington and Page prior to this incident, described as their 'correspondent' who also sent another bill alongside the one for Jago on other business. However, Jago's first bill of exchange was never produced and went unpaid. A second bill was sent, but Farrington and Page would not pay it without a form of security guaranteeing that the first bill would not appear, and they would be forced to pay both bills.[10] The outcome of the case is unknown, but it reveals that Farrington and Page regularly dealt in and were familiar with financial instruments during the 1660s, and had a significant network of factors, agents, and correspondents across Europe with whom they traded.

Further Chancery proceedings suggest that alongside cloth and financial bills, Farrington and Page dealt in a wide variety of commodities. A 1677 Chancery complaint made against Farrington by James Holland reveals that Farrington had business in Portugal and 'Leistland', or Estonia, part of the Baltic trade. In 1676, Farrington employed a ship and took on board some of the business of its merchant part-owners, agreeing to pay the customs and charges due in each foreign port. One port was Narva in Estonia, where the ship was due to deliver salt, and where Farrington also had 'goods & merchandizes', which his factors would 'load on board the ship'.[11] Narva was an important port, over which the Eastland Company and the Merchant Adventurers held monopolies. The major export from England to the Baltic was cloth, in return for imports of 'corn, hemp, flax, timber, and saltpetre', and Farrington's goods most likely consisted of such products.[12] Additionally, Farrington's 1683 bill of complaint against James Nelthorpe, Edward Nelthorpe's uncle, refers to factors in Aleppo and India, suggesting they were also principal trading ports for the partners and that they traded in their principal exports of

---

[10] TNA: C 5/59/43. Page v Jago. 1671.

[11] TNA: C 7/522/35. Holland v Farrington. 29 January 1677.

[12] Maud Sellers. 1917. *The Acts and Ordinances of the Eastland* Company. York. x.

32 M. WINTER

cloth, coffee, silk, and spices.[13] Farrington claimed that he and Page, 'upon there owne distinct and separate accounts', had 'acquired a very considerable estate in money & stock' and 'gained a good esteme in the world'.[14]

The Chancery records describe Richard Thompson as a citizen and member of the clothworkers' company. There is no surviving record of Richard's entrance into the guild, but there is information about his early life and education. Richard was born in 1630 to Robert and Ellen Thompson in the parish of St. Mary Woolchurch, London, and was educated at the Merchant Taylor's grammar school where he was enrolled in December 1640 at 10 years old.[15] Richard's father, Robert, was a confectioner by trade and a member of the Clothworkers' Company, which suggests Richard entered the guild through patrimony. Richard first followed in his father's footsteps as a 'comfit maker' or confectioner before becoming a merchant and forming a partnership with his cousin, Edward Nelthorpe.[16]

Edward Nelthorpe was the son of Edward Nelthorpe of Walkington, a village near Beverley in the East Riding of Yorkshire, and Catherine Stephenson. Edward's education prior to his apprenticeship is unknown but provision was made for his education and career. His father, a Yorkshire gentleman, died in 1640 and left his estate to his wife until their son turned 20 years old with the instruction that she educate their 'sonne Edwarde well'.[17] Through apprenticeship Nelthorpe became a member of the Drapers' Company and of the London Merchant

[13] TNA: C 10/484/71. Farrington v Nelthorpe. 12 April 1683; Alfred C. Wood. 1935. *A History of the Levant Company*. Oxford: Oxford University Press. 75–76, 162–163.

[14] TNA: C 7/581/73.

[15] Joseph Foster. 1874. *Pedigrees of the County Families of Yorkshire*, vol. 3, *North and East Riding*. London: W. Wilfred Head. 'Pedigree of Thompson, of Escrick and Marston'; J. M. S. Brooke. 1886. *Transcript of the Registers of the United Parishes of St Mary Woolnoth and St Mary Woolchurch Law*. London: Bowles and Sons. 232; Burdon. Marvell and his Kindred: The Family Network in the Later Years—II Nelthorpes, Thompsons, and Popples. 175; C. J. Robinson. 1882. *A Register of the Scholars Admitted into Merchant Taylor's School, from A.D. 1562 to 1874*, vol. 1. London. 148, 164.

[16] TNA: C 6/283/87; Burdon. Marvell and his Kindred: The Family Network in the Later Years—II Nelthorpes, Thompsons, and Popples. 176; C 7/581/73.

[17] Borthwick Institute for Archives: 'Will of Edward Nelthorpe of Walkington', July 1640.

Adventurers Company.[18] The Merchant Adventurers were a regulated company trading primarily in cloth to the Netherlands and Germany. The company was 'comprised of overseas merchants trading on their own accounts according to collective regulations' decided by a 'governing body' which 'negotiated monopolies and other privileges' and set up 'facilities abroad'.[19] Membership was obtained through a fee, which would allow the merchant to trade independently under the Company's name. Nelthorpe took his apprenticeship through servitude to Master Draper and Merchant Adventurer Nathaniel Lowns, who traded mainly with Hamburg where the principal base of the Merchant Adventurers was situated and where Nelthorpe spent part of his apprenticeship before earning his freedom in 1661.[20] Nelthorpe's career progression took the standard form for Merchant Adventurers, serving 'the earlier part of their careers overseas, acquiring the experience and assets necessary to assume economic independence before returning home to enjoy this status in their own households', which Nelthorpe did in 1662.[21] Although Nelthorpe already had the assets from his father's estate, the experience and skills learnt during his apprenticeship were vital in enabling him to set up his own business.

Nelthorpe's business during the 1660s as a Merchant Adventurer was varied, trading in France, Stockholm, Hamburg, and, of course, London, as well as acting as an agent for other Merchant Adventurers in London.[22] However, his trading activity shifted focus in the mid-late 1660s, away from the Merchant Adventurers and towards alternative partnerships and schemes. This shift was most likely due to the change in fortune of the Merchant Adventurers Company from the 1660s to the 1680s. The Navigation Acts and the Anglo-Dutch wars, which saw trade depressions, were

[18] *RoLLCO*, Search for 'Edward Nelthorpe', 'Drapers' Company' 1610–1680. https://www.londonroll.org [accessed 12 May 2020]; TNA: C 7/581/73.

[19] Thomas Leng. 2016. Interlopers and Disorderly Brethren at the Stade Mart: Commercial Regulations and Practices Amongst the Merchant Adventurers of England in the Late Elizabethan Period. *The Economic History Review* 69: 824; Ogilvie. *Institutions and European Trade*. 36.

[20] TNA: C 6/148/7, Archdale v Lownes, 1661; Hamburg State Archives: MS 521-1. Register book of the Church of the English Court.

[21] Leng. *Fellowship and Freedom*. 15.

[22] TNA: C 109/24. Attwood v Ware: Letters and Accounts of William Attwood, Merchant: London, Exeter, York; Hamburg, Genoa etc. 1660–1689. Twyford to Attwood, 17 November 1666, 20 February 1666/7, 13 July 1667.

34 M. WINTER

predominantly responsible for the downturn, particularly the successful petitioning of interlopers during the Second Anglo-Dutch War. The Navigation acts were a series of acts beginning in 1651 that attempted to regulate and strengthen England's import and export trade and were specifically targeted at reducing England's reliance on the Dutch, which was a blow to the Merchant Adventurers who depended on Dutch towns for the export of English cloth. During the Second Anglo-Dutch War interlopers—merchants who were not company members but wanted to trade in the areas monopolised by the Merchant Adventurers—successfully petitioned the government to revoke the company's monopoly, which undermined their privilege and threatened profits. In addition to this, in the 1660s the Company's mart-system of permanent company residences in towns in the Netherlands and Germany broke down, and with it the individual fortunes of each Company member. The Second Anglo-Dutch war had a personal effect on Nelthorpe, who lost one of his ships when the Dutch attacked a Merchant Adventurers' fleet in the river Elbe near Hamburg on 24 August 1666. The owners of the ships involved, including Nelthorpe, blamed their mart-town 'hosts', Hamburg, for their loss and sought compensation from the city, much to the incredulity of its citizens.[23] An agreement with Hamburg for compensation was not reached until 1676, when £35,000 was distributed to the affected merchants, of which Nelthorpe received £883 16s 4d in compensation for an estimated loss of £1458 5s 11d.[24] Given the steady decline of the Merchant Adventurers and his own specific losses, it is not surprising that Nelthorpe began looking for other ways to make money in 1660s London. Thus, Nelthorpe's partnership with Thompson first appears in the records in 1667 when they, along with another cousin, Edward Thompson, were involved in a £3000 bond for a prize ship.[25]

[23] Leng. *Fellowship and Freedom.* 13–15, 21, 154–155, 278–279, 291; David Ormrod. 2003. *The Rise of Commercial Empires: England and the Netherlands in the Age of Mercantilism, 1650–1770.* Cambridge: Cambridge University Press. 32, 35, 37, 41, 121, 141.

[24] TNA: CO 389/11. Entry Books of Commissions, instructions, petitions, warrants, correspondence, etc. 1673–1684. f. 19; Report of Sir Leoline Jenkins in the case of Sir John Shorter and the Hamburgher. *SPO*, SP 82/16. ff. 38–39, 31 May 1676.

[25] Wall. *Marvell's Friends in the City.* 204; Note of a bond of Edward Thompson of York, Richard Thompson of Stepney, and Edward Nelthorpe in 3000 l to Edward Smith and Edward Lee, merchants of London. *SPO*, SP 29/193. f. 8, 1 March 1667.

2 THOMPSON AND COMPANY   35

Shortly after starting up their partnership, Thompson and Nelthorpe also began pursuing political careers through civic office holding within the governing body of the Corporation of London. Being elected to civic office further exemplified their status as wealthy traders and householders and demonstrated their credit and good reputation in the city. The Corporation governed the square mile of the City of London and consisted of a Lord Mayor elected each year from the Court of Aldermen, 26 Aldermen elected for life, and a Common Council made up of 234 annually elected citizens. The Lord Mayor and Court of Alderman dominated decision making in the city, but the common council also played an important role and a position on the council demonstrated that an individual was part of a 'civic elite'.[26] Thompson was elected as common councillor for Walbrook ward in 1669, holding that position until the collapse of the bank in 1677. Nelthorpe joined Thompson later as a common councillor for Walbrook ward in 1671, again retaining the position until 1677.[27]

Nelthorpe and Thompson were also confirmed religious nonconformists or dissenters: opponents of the Anglican Church settlement that Charles II enforced in 1662. Dissenters referred to a broad range of religious identities, including Sectarians, Quakers, Baptists, Presbyterians, Independents, and many others. The partners' beliefs had important implications for their political activities and affiliations because religious disputes between dissenters and Anglicans underpinned political discontent throughout the Restoration. Nelthorpe and Thompson became 'pivotal figures' in a group of dissenting common councillors from 1667 onwards, which De Krey has labelled the 'civic opposition': a nonconformist faction opposed to the strict regulations placed on the metropolitan population in the Uniformity and Corporation acts. The 'opposition' group grew in prominence after 1673 in response to the failure of the 1672 Declaration of Indulgence and the promotion of Thomas Osborne, the earl of Danby, to the position of Lord Treasurer. However, the political influence of the 'civic opposition' was not restricted to the Corporation of London but part of a wider 'country' faction that

---

[26] Gary Stuart De Krey. 1985. *A Fractured Society: The Politics of London in the First Age of Party 1688–1715*. Oxford: Clarendon Press. 3, 10, 11; Gauci. *Politics of Trade.* 79.

[27] J. R. Woodhead. 1965. *The Rulers of London 1660–1689*. London: London & Middlesex Archaeological Society. 119, 161.

36   M. WINTER

included MPs and Lords, and members of the civic opposition were often linked to their parliamentary counterparts by ties of kinship and friendship.[28]

Whether Farrington and Page were also dissenters or nonconformists is harder to fathom. Further evidence of Nelthorpe's beliefs have been uncovered by Dzelzainis, who revealed Nelthorpe and Farrington's subscription of funds to the Quaker undertaking to West New Jersey led by William Penn. Both Nelthorpe and Farrington signed the 'constitution' for the new colony in 1677 at the moment the bank was collapsing. Dzelzainis highlights the two partners' involvement as evidence of 'Nelthorpe's religious preferences' but dismisses the idea that Farrington's involvement could also demonstrate his religious preferences. Instead, he views Farrington's involvement as 'legal action' designed 'to lay claim to a share that had been solely in Nelthorpe's name from the start'.[29] However, there is no solid basis for this interpretation. A perfectly valid alternative reading is that Farrington held a shared religious belief with his partners as a religious dissenter, or at least sympathised with their cause. Whatever Farrington and Page's beliefs were, they and their joint banking venture inevitably became caught up in the political feuds of their partners by association.

The social and economic identities of Thompson and Company's partners as wealthy, well-educated, and well-connected male citizens were crucial markers of creditworthiness in the business world of seventeenth-century London and vital for cultivating trust. At the time of the bank's formation, all four partners were wealthy citizens, enfranchised due to their guild membership, educated in a manner appropriate for a career in trade, and owners of urban, and in Nelthorpe's case rural, property. In addition, Thompson and Nelthorpe both held civic office. In Chancery proceedings the partners describe themselves and were described by others as citizens of London. In other sources, the Earl Marshall, Henry Howard, described the banking partners as 'considerable citizens' and

---

[28] De Krey. *London and the Restoration.* 71–73, 87, 93, 116–117, 129–134, 140, 148; John Spurr. 2008. Later Stuart Puritanism. In *The Cambridge Companion to Puritanism*, eds John Coffey and Paul C. H. Lim, 89–106. Cambridge: Cambridge University Press. 90; Lacey. *Dissent and Parliamentary Politics.* 123–125.

[29] Dzelzainis. Andrew Marvell, Edward Nelthorpe. 20–25; 1758. *The Grants, Concessions, and Original Constitutions of the Province of New-Jersey. The acts passed during the proprietary governments, and other material transactions before the surrender thereof to Queen Anne.* Philadelphia. 409.

the second creditors' pamphlet called them 'eminent citizens'.[30] Clearly, their urban dwelling and civic political roles shaped their identities. As such, Withington has described the partners as part of 'a new generation of "educated classes" and "capitalists" who came to social, urban, and public prominence in the later seventeenth or "long eighteenth century"' and who 'would seem to personify the "town" and the new generation of men that made it'.[31] The partners' growing estates and reputations meant that, by 1671, they were able to embark on their new joint venture.

II

In the Chancery proceedings, Farrington and Thompson both recalled the 'second day of January' 1671 as the date when their partnership began. According to Farrington, the venture was designed by Thompson and Nelthorpe, which—as Thompson's original idea—could explain the name Thompson and Company as opposed to using the names of the other partners, and he and Page agreed to join as they believed Thompson and Nelthorpe to be 'likewise owners of an estate at least equall' to their own. The main practice of the venture was 'borrowing & takeing up of money at interest from diverse persons' and the overall aim was 'to turne to the best account of profitt & conduce most to there joynt & equall advantage'. This was to be achieved through putting their own money and that of their clients into a 'Comon or Joynt Banke shared betweene all the said partners', which could then be used by them 'in a way of Merchandise & trade' as the 'greater number of them should think fitt & agree'.[32] They also gave out loans and dealt in financial instruments. To this end, the partners drew up articles of agreement detailing how the bank would function on a day-to-day basis and the rules and regulations that applied to each partner. Written articles of agreement were fairly commonplace for businesses and reflected the 'reciprocal choice of those involved' and detailed the 'mutual advantages gained and liabilities shared'.[33] The partners' pamphlet does not refer to the articles, and, as all

---

[30] Thomas Birch. 1757. *The History of the Royal Society of London for Improving of Natural Knowledge, from Its First Rise.* London. vol. 3. 130; *Reasons most humbly offered to the consideration of Parliament.*

[31] Withington. *Politics of Commonwealth.* 125.

[32] TNA: C 7/581/73.

[33] Hancock. *Citizens of the World.* 105.

38   M. WINTER

the papers of the bank were either lost or destroyed by the partners, there is no trace of the original agreement. However, a Chancery case between Farrington and Thompson provides evidence of seven discernible articles.

First, the stock was made up equally, of 'foure fourths' and used 'for carrying on such joynt trade & dealings & for haveing & bearing the profitt & loss thereof'. This first article, and the repetition of the word 'joynt' throughout all descriptions of the bank, is highly significant. It made each of the four partners equally responsible for the fortunes of the bank, binding them together as a 'company'. The second article stated that 'the said partnershipp was to continue for the space of three yeares' from 2 January 1671, but it was renewed in 1674. Third, they agreed that any other trade agreements, outside of the four-way joint-partnership, should not be 'hindred or obstructed by such new partnershipp'—the partners were permitted 'lawfully' to 'manage & profit any other manner of trade merchandizeing or dealing whatsoever'. Fourth, the partners agreed that the 'common Bank of money books of account touching the same' was to be kept at 'Thompsons then dwelling here in woollchurch markett in London', which was at the intersection of Cornhill, Threadneedle Street, and Lombard Street, the financial heart of London which was home to the Royal Exchange and, later, the Bank of England (see Images 2.1 and 2.2). For the use and upkeep of Thompson's rooms, the other partners were to give Thompson 'sixty pounds per annum', which in today's money would be a yearly rent of approximately £13,000.[34]

The fourth article therefore provides information about the physical space of the bank, which is important when considering how the business was conducted day-to-day. Thompson's dwelling was designated as 'the said office or banke whereby the whole shop was' and, like all businesses in seventeenth-century England, was identifiable by the sign hanging outside, in this case 'the Signe of the Golden Cock'.[35] The premises is described as 'fronting Woolchurch market' and the partners

---

[34] TNA: C 7/581/73; Inflation Calculator. *Bank of England.* https://www.bankof england.co.uk/monetary-policy/inflation/inflation-calculator?number.Sections%5B0%5D. Fields%5B0%5D.Value=60&start-year=5.10459405001771&end-year=1110.8 [accessed 6 March 2019]; Stern. *The Company State.* 7, 9.

[35] H. M. Margoliouth, Pierre Legouis, and E. E. Duncan-Jones. 1971. *The Poems and Letters of Andrew Marvell*, vol. 2. 3rd edn. Oxford: Clarendon Press. 329; TNA: C 7/581/73.

2 THOMPSON AND COMPANY 39

Image 2.1 Map of London (*Source* British Library Board 06/07/2021, Maps.Crace II.61, John Ogilby and William Morgan, LARGE AND ACCURATE MAP OF THE CITY OF LONDON. Ichnographically describing all the Streets, Lanes, Alleys, Courts, Yards, Churches, Halls and Houses, &c [London, 1677])

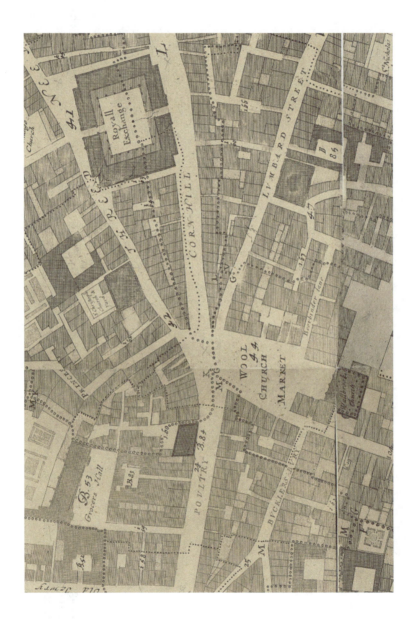

Image 2.2 Map of Woolchurch Market (*Source* British Library Board 06/07/2021, Maps.Crace II.61, Detail)

had use of 'the ground roome & part of the cellar', which had previously been used by Thompson and his father for their confectionary trade.[36] This suggests that the bank occupied what had previously been a trade shop, with a typical layout consisting of a shop entered from the street with a separate section, the cellar, used for storage or preparation.[37] The term 'shop' was commonly used to describe a bank's premises in the seventeenth century, probably due to the association of banking with the goldsmith and scrivener trades who combined their trade shops with a bank service.[38] Rather than confectionary or gold plate, however, Thompson and Company were *selling* themselves as reputable and creditworthy persons with whom individuals could entrust their money and receive interest on it, as well as *selling* instruments of credit such as loans, bills of exchange, or bonds.

To have a physically demarcated space for the business served both a symbolic and a practical purpose. This is evident first from the bank's location. Lombard Street was particularly renowned as the historic centre of banking in England since the thirteenth century and was the home of many goldsmith-bankers in the seventeenth century, including the famous shops of Edward Backwell and Sir Robert Vyner. Likewise, the nearby Royal Exchange was a hub for shopping, trading, and for obtaining information, such as commercial and shipping news or political gossip. The location of the bank was therefore situated within both the historic banking centre and the commercial hub of the city, where many merchants, city traders, and politicians would come to conduct their business and socialise. This enviable location no doubt provided Thompson and Company with a certain symbolic status, as well as the practical benefit of passing trade. The bank's premisses also played an important symbolic role in what Anne Murphy describes as the 'performance' of credit. Murphy argues that the public credit of the Bank of England was embodied within architecture, structure, and 'the very visible

---

[36] TNA: C 10/484/71; C 7/581/73.

[37] Frank E. Brown. 1986. Continuity and Change in the Urban House: Developments in Domestic Space Organisation in Seventeenth-Century London. *Comparative Studies in Society and History* 28: 578, 582; Jon Stobart, Andrew Haan, and Victoria Morgan. 2007. *Spaces of Consumption: Leisure and Shopping in the English Town, c. 1680–1830.* Oxford: Routledge. 117–119; 1932. *Hoare's Bank, A Record.* London. 8.

[38] 1676. *The Mystery of the New Fashioned Goldsmiths or Bankers.* London. 6, 7; Melton. *Sir Robert Clayton.* 46, 49, 67; Quinn. Goldsmith-Banking. 416, 425, 426.

42 M. WINTER

actions of its clerks and the technologies they used to record ownership and transfer of the national debt'.[39] More broadly, retail historians have emphasised the integral role of 'shops' in building business identity, representing not only the goods for sale but the social status and credit of the proprietor(s) and Claire Walsh has particularly emphasised the shop's importance for goldsmiths, whose outward show of expense was necessary to convince customers not only of their craft abilities but also their ability 'to manage long-term credit'.[40] Thompson and Company's shop would therefore have played an important role in cultivating trust.

Practically, the shop was the everyday place of business where customers would go to deposit money, receive interest payments, take out a loan or financial instrument, and discuss business with the partners. That customers physically went to the bank to conduct business is evident from the minutes of one of their creditors, the Corporation of Trinity House of Deptford Strond, London—the guild for the 'Masters, Rulers and Mariners of the King's Navy'. On 21 August 1677, the minutes record that the partners' sent an invitation to members of the corporation to 'meet them in the afternoone at their Office at Woolchurch Markett to receive Proposalls'. Earlier in 1676, the Corporation's secretary reported that he had discoursed with someone who had examined the accounts of Thompson and Company, most likely in the bank's premisses.[41] The shop or office is also where individuals would have gone to receive interest payments on their deposits. For example, in September 1676, Trinity House ordered their wardens to go to the bank and 'receive the Eight part of our Mony' that they had been promised by the partners.[42] The bank's shop also hosted general meetings for creditors, such as the one detailed in their pamphlet that was held at 'Mr Thompson's'.[43] In addition to

[39] Anne L. Murphy. 2019. Performing Public Credit at the Eighteenth-Century Bank of England. *Journal of British Studies* 58: 58–78.

[40] Stobart, Haan and Morgan. *Spaces of Consumption.* 112; Claire Walsh. 1995. Shop Design and the Display of Goods in Eighteenth-Century London. *Journal of Design History* 8: 163, 171; Patrick Wallis. 2008. Consumption, Retailing, and Medicine in Early-Modern London. *The Economic History Review* 61: 47–48.

[41] LMA: CLC/526/MS30307. List of masters, deputy masters, elder brethren and secretaries. 1660–1950. 5; CLC/526/MS30004/005. *Corporation of Trinity House.* Court Minutes 1676–1681. 56; CLC/526/MS30004/004. *Corporation of Trinity House.* Court Minutes 1670–1676. 229.

[42] LMA: CLC/526/MS30004/005. 12.

[43] *Case of Richard Thompson and Company.* 18.

business, shops also acted as places of sociability and Thompson and Company was no different. In February 1676 the Secretary of State, Sir Joseph Williamson, recorded in his intelligence notes that Lord O'Brien had been to Thompson's and found him, Nelthorpe and their friend Sir Thomas Player 'full' of news.[44] Given the location of Thompson and Company's bank and the political and commercial interests of its partners, sociability and discussing news was probably a prominent part of daily activity in the shop.

The fifth article stated that the partners could only withdraw money for their own business interests at 'the consent of the most' and were required to repay 'the principall ... with interest'. This fifth article is the most unusual as it essentially stipulates that the partners were allowed to be customers of their own bank, taking out loans for mercantile trade and paying it back with interest. The sixth article stated that 'any debts contracted by any' of the partners 'in their owne particuler & distinct dealings ... should remaine & be as before the said partnershipp', which meant that if one of their individual trade deals went wrong the bank and joint stock would not be responsible for the debt. Finally, it was agreed that the partners were 'onely answerable & accountable each to other' for what was 'gained or lost in the management or disposall of the money advanced or taken into the said banke Joyntly' and that a 'cashier & book-keeper' should be 'mutually chosen' and 'imployed' to keep accounts.[45] Evidence that this article was carried out comes from the witness deposition of Edmond Portmans in the 1682 case of the £500 bond, in which Portmans identified himself as 'cacheere & booke keeper' to the partners from 1672 to 1677. The depositions also reveal the identities of two further employees of the partners. Gersham Proud, a 29-year-old 'citizen and haberdasher' of London, stated that he had been a 'servant to him the said Edward Nelthorpe & partners' and was able to relay information about the bank and its 'bookes'. Proud was therefore a servant or clerk of the bank business as a whole. Another employee was Thomas Speede, a 38-year-old 'London cittizen and draper' who identified himself as 'servant to the sayd Edward Nelthorpe' and recalled information concerning

---

[44] Note by Williamson. *SPO*, SP 29/379. f. 73.

[45] TNA: C 7/581/73.

'Mr Nelthorpes bookes' only.[46] Both men could have lived in the partners' households, Proud at Thompson's where the shop was located and Speed at Nelthorpe's managing his personal business.

Although the original articles of agreement are lost, the information in the proceedings provides enough evidence to reconstruct some of the key regulations outlined in them. Additionally, the phrasing of this information reflects the terms and language used in standard articles of agreement for a four-way partnership exemplified in a contemporary manual by attorney Nicholas Covert, *The scrivener's guide*. Covert states that 'Copartners and Joint-traders together' should work 'for their most benefit, advantage and profit' upon a 'Joint-stock' that 'shall be occupied and imploied together ... both in profit and loss'. The articles should specify who was to have 'sole' control over the physical keeping of money and goods, who would be responsible for 'true keeping and custody of the Books', the timeframe or 'term' of the partnership, and he advises that each member should 'take the advice and direction of the rest' when doing business concerning 'the said Joint-trade'.[47]

The reconstructed articles of agreement reveal that the partners were operating a form of early deposit bank, taking in deposits at interest from some customers and using that money to lend to others and themselves. This type of banking relied on the premise of fractional reserve, whereby the bank would loan out more money in paper bonds and bills than it actually possessed in specie, holding only enough specie to be able to pay a certain percentage of its creditors if they requested a repayment of their deposited funds.[48] A fractional reserve bank therefore depended on its creditors not all wanting to withdraw their money at the same time, a phenomenon known as a run on the bank. The partners' pamphlet confirms their use of this system. The pamphlet states that as individuals 'chose to imploy their Money in our hands, that the debt must necessarily exceed our Estate', maintaining only a proportion of the total

---

[46] TNA: C 24/1069. Interrogatories. 'Edmond Portmans', 1 July 1682, 'Gersham Proud', 4 July 1682 and 'Thomas Speede', 24 July 1682.

[47] Nicholas Covert. 1700. *The Scrivener's Guide Being Choice and Approved Forms of Presidents of All Sorts of Business Now in Use and Practice, in a Much Better Method Than Any yet Printed, Being Useful for All Gentlemen, but Chiefly for Those Who Practice the Law.* London. 293–296.

[48] Hal W. Snarr. 2014. *Learning Macroeconomic Principles Using MAPLE.* New York: Business Expert Press. 100–101.

deposited funds. The partners argued that their creditors understood the system, as they 'could not at the same time be ignorant, yet were not distrustful', instead 'intrusting us with several summs to a great value' of which 'they found so little cause to repent of or suspect'. The partners further described their actions as constituting a 'tacit contract', whereby the creditor places their money with the debtor, in the bank, who can then 'imploy the money' to earn profit and pay the creditor 'interest'. In return the creditor, implicitly, agrees not to 'joyn' with other creditors and demand their money back all at once, which would 'make it impossible to discharge the principal'. The partners stated that this 'contract' was 'unwritten, and unattested, yet ... firm as humanity to the Debtor, Equity to fellow creditors, Truth to a Man's proper Concern, and Security can make it'.[49] This 'contract', however, would only be effective if the partners could maintain a sufficient reserve of cash to meet the demand of withdrawals and, more importantly, the trust of their customers.

III

The loss of Thompson and Company's books, ledgers, and papers has made a full study of their business transactions and the transactions of their customers impossible to carry out. However, it is possible to partially reconstruct the identities of Thompson and Company's creditors and how much money they collectively put in the bank through a previously unused 1679 Chancery case entered by 211 creditors of the bank. The Chancery complaint accuses the four partners of fraud and concealing their estates, and states that through such actions the partners 'became indebted' to the creditors to the sum of £103,000 and had subsequently become bankrupts and fled.[50] The full extent of the complaint will be examined in Chapter 7, but what is of interest for this chapter is the 211 names provided at the beginning of the bill of complaint. The list begins with titled individuals such as viscounts, lords, and sirs, before listing the rest in alphabetical order. This is not a complete list. The complaint states that it represents the 211 named plus 'other the Creditors', whose number and names are unknown. Some of these 'other' creditors likely

---

[49] *Case of Richard Thompson and Company.* 3, 5; Robert Ashton. 1960. *The Crown and the Money Market 1603–1640.* Oxford: Clarendon Press. 13.

[50] TNA: C 8/328/50. Lord Grandison v Thompson. 12 February 1679.

46   M. WINTER

already received their money prior to the statute of bankruptcy, as the partners recorded that they paid out £60,000 prior to March 1676 and a further £50,000 by the beginning of the year 1677, which could explain their absence.[51] However, as the account books, ledgers, and papers of the bank were destroyed or lost, and as the legal practice of keeping 'Docket Books' in cases of bankruptcy—which recorded 'the name, occupation and address' of petitioning creditors—was not a common practice until 1710, the 211 names represent the best possible means by which to investigate the creditors of Thompson and Company.[52] Four other creditors, not on the list, have been identified by chance mentions in other source material: namely, the Post Office Record Office letter books, a churchwarden's inventory from St. Mary Woolchurch, and Edward Nelthorpe's Irish business correspondence. All in all, this means it is possible to discuss 215 creditors.

To further identify these 215 creditors, various searches were carried out in a multitude of databases and archives. Whilst the names are of great value, searching for individuals in this way throws up three key obstacles to making a robust and likely identification. The first obstacle is the lack of standardised spelling, which means each search must be carried out with multiple versions of the same name and wildcards. Secondly, the number of results for any search can vary wildly, with some producing hundreds and others only a few. Finally, there are untraceable individuals. For example, the proverbial 'John Smith' is impossible to identify outright, foreign names often do not produce any results in English search engines, and there are some creditors who have simply left little trace in the surviving archival material, resulting in only a rudimentary identification. Despite these setbacks, it is possible to identify the majority of the 211 creditors at a basic level and outline two important sets of data about the creditors of Thompson and Company.

The first is the geographical spread of the creditors by place of residence. In January 1678, Edward Nelthorpe wrote a letter to Sir Joseph Williamson, in which he asked that a meeting with Thompson and Company's creditors be advertised in the *London Gazette* to inform all creditors, including those 'liveing out off towne in their places of

---

[51] *Case of Richard Thompson and Company. 7*, 28.

[52] Julian Hoppit. 1987. *Risk and Failure in English Business 1700–1800*. Cambridge: Cambridge University Press. 43.

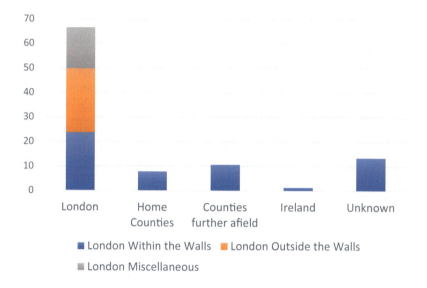

Graph 2.1 Creditors by place of residence

habbitationes unknown'.[53] Whilst unknown to Nelthorpe, it is possible to discover the places of habitation for many of the creditors. These figures are not perfect but present the best possible representation of the geographical spread of creditors. Graph 2.1 demonstrates that geographically the 215 creditors were predominantly from London with 144 (66.98%) found to reside in the capital and the other 71 (33.02%) outside of London. Of these, 17 (7.91%) creditors lived in the Home Counties, here classified as Berkshire, Buckinghamshire, Essex, Hertfordshire, Kent, Sussex and Surrey, 22 (10.23%) lived in counties further afield (Cornwall, Devon, Gloucestershire, Hull, Oxford, Plymouth, and Yorkshire) and 3 (1.4%) are believed to have resided in Ireland. Only 29 (13.49%) are untraceable and their place of residence unknown. Where wealthy creditors had more than one residence, their primary residence has been counted. For example, Sir John Churchman, a gentleman of the Inner Temple London, owned a large estate in Norfolk alongside his London

---

[53] Edward Nelthorp to Williamson. *SPO*, SP 29/400. f. 181, 25 January 1678.

48   M. WINTER

residence.[54] As he mainly resided in the capital, where he did business and where his will was entered, he is included amongst the London-based creditors in the graph.

The second is the occupational range of the creditors. Graph 2.1 represents the 211 customers of Thompson and Company sorted by occupation or status. This has been done using the following seven categories: merchants, mariners, and captains; citizens; widows, wives, and spinsters; professionals; gentlemen; yeomen; and institutions. The categories widows, wives and spinsters, and institutions are self-explanatory, but the others require a definition. Merchants are defined as those who traded overseas, a definition that is used in historiography and was recognised by contemporaries.[55] Citizens are defined as those who were freemen: members of a London guild who made their living through domestic trade. The professionals are slightly harder to define. Brooks includes 'doctors, lawyers and clergymen' in his definition. He claims that professionals are a distinct social category and not 'mere adjuncts of the elite', particularly given that the majority of the professions required training via apprenticeship and lived in urban centres rather than on country estates.[56] Earle includes teachers and public servants alongside doctors, lawyers, and clergymen in his classification of the professions, and characterises them as city dwellers, most notably residing in London.[57] However, these definitions present difficulties when placing individuals such as John Buller, a younger brother in a gentry family who trained in the law but spent the majority of his career in public service and as an MP.[58] In this study, individuals like John Buller have been categorised as professionals as they did work for a living and were not solely dependent

---

[54] TNA: PROB 11/395/360. Will of Sir John Churchman of Inner Temple, Middlesex. 13 June 1689.

[55] Susan E. Whyman. 1997. Land and Trade Revisited: The Case of John Verney, London Merchant and Baronet, 1660–1720. *The London Journal* 22: 18; Peter Earle. 1991. *The Making of the English Middle Class: Business, Society and Family Life in London, 1660–1730*. London: University of California Press. 34; Gauci. *Emporium of the World*. 1–2.

[56] Christopher W. Brooks. 1998. *Lawyers, Litigation and English Society Since 1450*. London: Hambledon Press. 231–2.

[57] Earle. *Making of the English Middle Class*. 17, 65–69, 73.

[58] M. W. Helms and Paula Watson. Buller, John (c.1632–1716), of the Middle Temple and Morval, nr. East Looe, Cornw. *HoP* http://www.historyofparliamentonline.org/vol ume/1660-1690/member/buller-john-1632-1716 [accessed 12 February 2018].

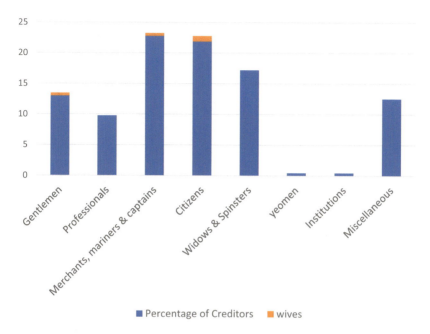

Graph 2.2 Percentage of creditors by occupation/status

on land. Only one creditor is defined as a yeoman, Daniel Barnard 'of Essex'. This category follows Wrightson's definition of an individual who possessed freehold land of a yearly rent of 40 shillings or more, and therefore had 'relative dependence' over his land and the right to vote.[59] An eighth, miscellaneous category represents those creditors that are untraceable by occupation, of which there are 27 (12.56%) named individuals (Graph 2.2).

The 211 named creditors claimed to have collectively deposited approximately £103,000.[60] This would mean each creditor would have an average credit of approximately £488, although certain creditors would have held far greater amounts in the Bank, and others much smaller

---

[59] TNA: PROB 4/8496. Barnard, Daniel, of Walthamstow, Essex, yeoman. 13 September 1686; Keith Wrightson. 2004. *English Society 1580–1680*. London: Routledge. 39.

[60] TNA: C 8/328/50.

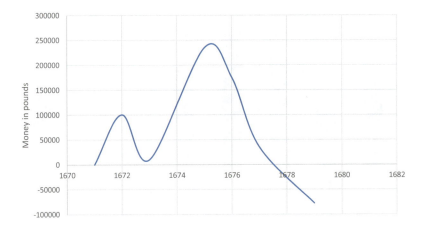

Graph 2.3 Lifecycle of Thompson and Company based on amounts claimed to be on their books

amounts. However, the partners' pamphlet suggests that prior to the statute of bankruptcy the overall amount of money the bankers had recorded in their books was considerably more than that which remained indebted to the creditors, and provides a broad outline of the lifecycle of the bank. It states that prior to 9 March 1676, the bankers had already paid out £60,000 to creditors who took part in the first run on the bank in 1675. Then, 'when the Books were first visited by the Creditors' in 1676, they showed a total of about £175,000, of which £50,000 had then also been paid out to creditors and £90,000 represented a 'Catalogue of our Losses'.[61] Prior to the first run on the bank, then, the partners claimed to be in control of approximately £235,000. The reliability of this figure is questionable as we have only the bankers' word, but it does suggest that the bank was successful in attracting a wide range of clients and trusted with significant sums of money (Graph 2.3).

However, whilst evidence is available for creditors and money deposited, that of debtors and the amount of money loaned is less forthcoming. A newsletter written by London merchant John Verney to his father, the MP Ralph Verney, informing him of the latest London gossip

---

[61] *Case of Richard Thompson and Company.* 7, 28.

2 THOMPSON AND COMPANY 51

claimed that following Thompson and Company's bankruptcy the partners 'enter'd 150 actions against such as owed them money'.[62] The exact
nature of these loans, whether personal or business, is unknown, as is
the identity of the debtors. Debtors are less likely to appear in Chancery
proceedings unless the partners took out a complaint against them.
Indeed, there is only qualitative evidence available for two debtors of
the bank through Chancery court proceedings, a London brewer named
Edward Billing and the partners' friend and relative Andrew Marvell, who
will be discussed in more detail in Chapter 6. Although the identity of
the majority of the debtors and other customers of the bank is unknown,
there is evidence of the instruments and means through which Thompson
and Company lent money and provided financial services.

IV

For the purposes of taking and lending money and carrying out other
financial services, the partners predominantly used three financial instruments: the 'bill obligatory', the 'bond', and the 'bill of exchange', all three
of which were very common by the seventeenth century. The bill obligatory was essentially a 'promissory note' that stipulated the repayment of
the principal amount along with interest.[63] An example of Thompson and
Company using the bill obligatory can be found in the account book of
creditor Sir William Turner, who acted as a London banker or agent for
his friend and fellow creditor Thomas Belasyse, Viscount Fauconberg. In
Fauconberg's account dated 1675, Turner recorded that he had received
£100 'by Bill upon Mr Ed. Nelthorpe dated 25 Aug'. The bill would be
paid by Nelthorpe on '26 September' with interest.[64] The bill obligatory
differed from the bill of exchange, which settled payments abroad, in that
this instrument had a specified place for repayment within England. Turner's accounts also record the use of inland bills of exchange, which were
similar to bills obligatory in that they were for local use to pay for goods
and services within England but brought in a third party to the credit
transaction. An individual who owed money to Fauconberg would draw

[62] BL: Microfilm 636/29. *Verney Papers from Claydon House*. 'John Verney to Sir Ralph
Verney' 16 March 1676.

[63] Wennerlind. *Casualties of Credit*. 29.

[64] LMA: CLC/509/MS05107/002. Miscellaneous accounts, chiefly clients', but also
some private accounts, 1673–1692. 'June the 24th 1675'.

a bill on Thompson and Company, which would be payable at a specified date in the future. For example, in 1674 Turner records that Fauconberg had received £300 'of Mr Thompson' by way of a 'Bill drawn by Mr Hore', which was dated 10 March 1674 and was payable just over a year later on 11 April 1675.[65] The inland bill was therefore both an instrument of debt and an order to pay.[66]

The bond was more formal and precise. Bonds specified a repayment date, which if not met would incur a penalty clause, agreed upon when the bond was signed.[67] The court cases offer a good example of the partners' use of the bond. In the Cowper family case of 1683–4 Farrington stated that in 1674 'Thompson & Nelthorpe or one of them did lend & pay two thousand pounds or thereabouts or some other great sume part of the said moneys … to Nicholas Cowper late of Blakehall in the county of Essex'. For security, this bond came with a penalty fee of £4000. Although it was Nelthorpe and Thompson who dealt directly with Cowper, the bond was made out by the bank and so Farrington 'became bound together with the said Thompson Nelthorpe & Page', giving them equal responsibility for the debt or credit in each situation as a collective company.[68] This meant that if the debt went unpaid the security, the penalty of £4000, would be due to the bank and the profit shared between the four partners.

The final type of financial instrument used by the bankers and described in the Chancery proceedings is the bill of exchange, a foreign financial instrument used most by merchants when trading abroad. The purpose of the bill of exchange, as Jongchul Kim explains, was for the bill to move further away from the 'original debtor', allowing for long distance trade to take place as the bill was cleared and passed on through various intermediaries along the way before reaching its final destination.[69] The bill was assigned to the intended drawer of the bill, ordering them to pay the bearer, not a specific person, by a specified date and settle the debt. The partners use of bills of exchange is referenced in the Chancery cases between Farrington and Page and Walter Jago, and in

---

[65] LMA: CLC/509/MS05107/002. Miscellaneous accounts. 'My Ld Viscount Fauconberg his account 23 May 1674'.

[66] Kerridge. *Trade and Banking*. 45–46.

[67] Ashton. *The Crown and the Money Market*. 3.

[68] TNA: C 6/249/35. Farrington v Foach. 22 April 1684.

[69] Kim. How modern banking originated. 942.

the case between Farrington and Thompson and Company's Bordeaux agents William Popple and Robert Stewart.[70] Another example can be found in Turner's account book. In 1674, Turner records that, on behalf of Fauconberg, he had received 'a bill of exchange dated' 17 July 'drawen by Mr Mascall' of £200, which was 'payable by Mr Nelthorpe' on 1 September.[71]

Another financial instrument mentioned in the court cases is the mortgage. John Farrington suggested that Thompson and Company used a mortgage to loan money in the court case over the Cowper family estate. Farrington argued that, as well as the £4000 penalty mentioned above, for 'further security for repayment ... Nicholas Cowper did mortgage severall of his messuages & Lands in the county'. He argued that prior to granting this particular financial instrument, Thompson ensured that the said Nicholas Cowper had 'a good title & was able to secure the said two thousand pounds or other such sume as aforesaid by his Lands'. This was supposedly after they 'did advise with councell' and 'were thereupon informed they might safely proceed'. However, it appears that Farrington was misinformed. In his answer, Richard Thompson agreed that the bank did give a loan to Nicholas Cowper in 1674 but that 'they did not take any mortgage or other security for the two thousand pounds then the statute and Defeazance' of £4000. This 'statute' was a 'statute staple', in which the borrower had to 'guarantee the loan with some form of real security'. In this case the lender, Nicholas Cowper, would secure his loan by providing or assigning a bond, which he had given out to one of his debtors for the same value. This meant that the debts owed to Nicholas Cowper by his creditor would be reassigned to pay off his debt to the bank. The defeasance meant that the agreement would become null and void when full payment was made via the statute. If the bond went unpaid, then the £4000 penalty would be due. Cowper's death, however, meant that there was an outstanding loan of £2000 with interest, which

[70] TNA: C 5/59/43; C 6/526/178. Farrington v Unknown (Popple and Stewart). 31 March 1684.

[71] LMA: CLC/509/MS05107/002. Miscellaneous accounts. 'My Ld Viscount Fauconberg his account 23 May 1674'.

54   M. WINTER

would be extracted from his estate in the usual course of paying off debts as instructed in his will.[72]

The confusion over the mortgage had arisen as Thompson and an associate by the name of John Hall, described as a 'citizen and merchant Taylor of London', were involved in a separate business arrangement with Cowper. In 1671, Cowper assigned his lands, tenements, and other property to Richard Thompson and John Hall 'for life' in a deed. The terms of this deed were as follows: upon Cowper's death Thompson and Hall 'should out of the Rents and proffitts ... or by sale thereof' raise and pay debts owed by Nicholas and any legacies he bequeathed; they should 'raise two thousand two hundred pounds' as portions for each of his daughters; and they 'should pay deliver and convey the Remainder' to his son John Cowper'. As the final decree makes clear, this deed was separate to the loan made out in 1674.[73] Whilst the partners did not use mortgages, this case shows they were aware of them and used other economic practices such as the statute staple and defeasance.

V

Through an economic microhistory, this chapter provides the first in-depth account of Thompson and Company as a financial institution and demonstrates the possibilities offered by Chancery proceedings for recovering lost or forgotten institutions and business practices. The survival rate of seventeenth-century English business papers is so low and, as a result, scholarship has tended to focus on large institutions such as the Bank of England or the East India Company, missing out on a great deal of entrepreneurship and enterprise on a smaller scale. This chapter has demonstrated that through microhistory and historical reconstruction it is possible to reconstruct these smaller and less formal commercial and financial enterprises and reintroduce them into the historiographical narrative. It therefore brings into question how many more

---

[72] TNA: C 6/249/35; TNA: PROB 11/347/293. Will of Nicholas Cowper, Gentleman of Bobbingworth, Essex. 10 March 1675; Melton. *Sir Robert Clayton.* 134–137, 142.

[73] TNA: C 10/212/10. Cowper & Thompson v Foach, Farrington and Nelthorpe. 14 July 1683; PROB 11/347/293. Will of Nicholas Cowper; Chancery Final Decree C 78 1133 no. 3. Accessed via *The Anglo-American Legal Tradition.* http://www.uh. edu/waalt/index.php/C78_1684. Robert Cowper, John Cowper, Richard Thompson, and John Hall v. John Foach, John Farrington, and Mary Nelthorp. 9 May 1684.

business ventures have been lost from the historical record and offers a methodological model for their reconstruction.

Reconstructing Thompson and Company has also highlighted the utility of Chancery proceedings, which have not been widely used by historians. The low usage of Chancery records is largely due to the difficulty of searching in the proceedings, which are not grouped by individual cases but by document type. Each case must be pieced together, a task that is both time-consuming and often to no avail as many Chancery cases have not survived in full. However, as this chapter has demonstrated, there are many benefits to Chancery records. The proceedings are easily accessible because the bills are in English and use less formulaic legal language than other courts of the period. Chancery also attracted a wide range of clientele, including a significant number of women.[74] Most significant for this chapter, Chancery proceedings also provide in-depth descriptions of the wider context surrounding a conflict rather than just the conflict itself. Christine Churches argues that the court's insistence upon 'a much more expansive story-telling to relate how the complainant had become embroiled in the particular dilemma' meant that 'suing in Chancery could be made to serve a purpose well beyond that of determining a dispute'.[75] As such, Chancery proceedings also offer the historian a wealth of additional information and means that this chapter has been able to outline the formation, operation, customer base, and extent of Thompson and Company and showed it to be a more significant venture than has previously been suggested by historians. The following chapters will use this reconstruction as a foundation from which to further explore the financial, commercial, political, and social life of the bank of Thompson and Company and its four partners.

[74] Erickson. *Women and Property*. 114; Henry Horwitz. 1997. Record-keepers in the Court of Chancery and their "Record" of Accomplishment in the Seventeenth and Eighteenth Centuries. *Historical Research* 70: 47, 48; Horwitz. *Chancery Equity Records*. 23, 29; Horwitz and Polden. Continuity or Change. 29–30; Chapman. The Lay Reader's Guide to *Milton v. Cope*. 118; Butler. The Law as a Weapon. 296; Erickson. *Women and Property*. 31; Brooks. *Law, Politics and Society*. 309.

[75] Churches. Business at Law. 944.

CHAPTER 3

Early Modern Banking

In a 1684 Chancery case John Farrington neatly summed up the venture known as Thompson and Company: 'a bank' engaged 'in takeing & disposeing money at Interest & other things'. Throughout the Chancery proceedings Thompson and Company is referred to by its partners and other litigants as a 'bank'. For example, Mary Marvell stated that Thompson, Nelthorpe, Farrington and Page were 'partners in a Banke trade', John Hall that they were each 'Copartner ... in A Banke', John Greene that they 'tride as Bankers', and Mary Nelthorpe that her husband and the other three were partners in a 'banke'. Outside of legal records, the Corporation of Trinity House referred to the partners as 'the Bankers', in wider London gossip Lieutenant of the Tower Sir John Robinson referred to the 'Bankers in partnershippe' in his letter to the Secretary of State, and London merchant John Verney similarly labelled them as 'the Bankers'.[1] Despite their interest in what Farrington loosely described as 'other things', a reference to their prior and concurrent

---

[1] TNA: C 6/249/35; C 7/589/82. Wallis v Farrington. 11 January 1682; C 6/411/29. Farrington v Hall. 18 July 1684; C 6/275/120. Wallis v Marvell. 16 November 1681; C 10/216/74. Thompson v Nelthorpe. 8 November 1684; CLC/526/MS30004/004. 223, 229; Sir John Robinson to Williamson. *SPO*, SP 29/379. f. 265, 10 March 1676; BL: Microfilm 636/29. *Verney Papers*. 'John Verney to Sir Ralph Verney', 16 March 1675/6.

© The Author(s), under exclusive license to Springer Nature Switzerland AG 2022
M. Winter, *Banking, Projecting and Politicking in Early Modern England*, Palgrave Studies in Economic History,
https://doi.org/10.1007/978-3-030-90570-5_3

58   M. WINTER

mercantile careers, the partners were clearly known as bankers. Thompson and Company's identification as a bank and as bankers is important because each partner did have a previous guild and mercantile identity, which although referred to in their identification as citizens of London and as merchants were clearly subsumed by their collective identity in the joint bank. This chapter situates the reconstructed Thompson and Company within the wider historiography of banking in England and Europe. It outlines the similarities and differences between Thompson and Company and other English and European banks, and makes comparison between Thompson and Company, in terms of size, clientele, and services offered, to its immediate seventeenth-century English contemporaries.

I

Banking was not a seventeenth-century innovation and nor was it of English origin. Before the seventeenth century, English banking consisted mostly of royal moneylending or foreign exchange. The term banker referred to an exchange specialist, whose profits were dictated by the fluctuations of exchange rates across Europe, and they did not engage in domestic banking practices such as cash keeping or dealing in domestic bonds and bills. Before the seventeenth century, England largely relied on the banking services of Europe to conduct its financial affairs. For example, the Elizabethan financier Sir Thomas Gresham was primarily a royal factor in Antwerp, a political and economic role that involved diplomacy and negotiation in order to raise loans, cancel debts, and maintain lines of communication.[2] Agents like Gresham dealt with the great banking houses of Europe such as the mediaeval Italian firms of Peruzzi or Medici, the fifteenth- and sixteenth-century Fuggers of Augsburg, and the early Venetian deposit banks. These businesses were based on family ties and consisted of partnerships, rather than individual-led businesses. They made their money not only through banking but through significant mercantile and commercial activities, becoming important political figures as well as merchants and financiers. To conduct their mercantile and commercial activities the bankers used not only their own funds, but

---

[2] Raymond de Roover. 1949. *Gresham on Foreign Exchange: An Essay on Early English Mercantilism with the Text of Sir Thomas Gresham's Memorandum for the Understanding of the Exchange.* London: Harvard University Press. 4, 20–21, 26–27, 101–103, 170–171.

the funds of their depositors in order to provide interest payments and make a profit for themselves. The financing power of these companies and their profit-seeking goals also led them to become leading monetary lenders to monarchs, emperors, and other political and religious rulers. However, this was a risky practice as monarchs could easily repudiate their debts at any time. Indeed, the failure of monarchs and other rulers to pay their debts contributed to the downfall of many of the banking houses of mediaeval and early modern Europe.[3]

In response to high levels of risk and the devaluing of coin through financial agents, European countries set up exchange banks such as the Rialto bank of Venice (1589) and the Amsterdam Exchange bank (1609). Exchange banks did not loan money but operated purely as deposit banks that could carry out exchange between accounts, holding a 100% ratio between the deposited specie and paper bills of exchange. Therefore, by simply storing and moving credit between accounts, these banks significantly reduced the risks involved in foreign banking and commercial exchange.[4] England's economic writers drew upon these European archetypes when proposing their own banks. For example, in *England's Treasure by Forraigne Trade*, Thomas Mun recognised that other European nations 'have Banks both publick and private, wherein they do assign their credits from one to another daily for very great sums with ease and satisfaction by writings only'. Mun framed his discourse in terms of the 'balance of trade' and emphasised the need for England to match its foreign counterparts and claim their proportion of international trade,

---

[3] Raymond de Roover. 1948. *The Medici Bank: Its Organization, Management, Operations, and Decline*. New York: New York University Press; Edwin S. Hunt. 1994. *The Medieval Super Companies: A Study of the Peruzzi Company of Florence*. Cambridge: Cambridge University Press; Mark Häberlein. 2012. *The Fuggers of Augsburg: Pursuing Wealth and Honour in Renaissance Germany*. Virginia: Virginia University Press; Frederic C. Lane. 1937. Venetian Bankers, 1496–1533: A Study in the Early Stages of Deposit Bankiing. *Journal of Political Economy* 45: 187–206; Kerridge. *Trade and Banking*. 3.

[4] Desan. *Making Money*. 304; Larry Neal and Stephen Quinn. 2001. Networks of Information, Markets, and Institutions in the Rise of London as a Financial Centre, 1660–1720. *Financial History Review* 8: 9; Stephen Quinn and William Roberds. 2007. The Bank of Amsterdam and the Leap to Central Bank Money. *American Economic Review* 97: 262–265.

60   M. WINTER

whilst preserving their own specie at home.[5] Samuel Lambe particularly praised the Exchange Bank of Amsterdam as the prime example of modern banking, claiming that the 'profitable use of Bankes' by the Dutch had raised them 'from Poor, Distressed, to High and mighty states'.[6] Andrew Yarranton similarly lauded the Dutch model, stating that 'if we write by their Copies, we shall do the great things they now do, and I dare say out-do them too'.[7] However, the exchange banks of Europe did not only reduce risk but restricted the amount of money in circulation by preventing the extension or creation of credit. Rather than copying foreign institutions, then, a 'peculiarly English system of private, and later public, banking' developed instead.[8]

Historians have long argued that the expansion of trade at the turn of the seventeenth century created demand for a more sophisticated and prolific banking system to sustain it and to further enrich the nation—a need recognised not only by the merchant community, but also increasingly by the monarch and the state.[9] More recently, Desan has argued that seventeenth-century England underwent a 'monetary revolution', which reimagined money itself in response to a growing need for credit and ushered in 'the political economy of modern capitalism'.[10] All of these studies highlight the second half of the seventeenth century as an important period of development, which witnessed significant economic change that would inspire many ideas for new credit systems to counteract the scarcity of physical coin. In contrast to European banks which focussed on foreign exchange, English banking developed first and foremost in the

[5] Thomas Mun. 1664. *England's Treasure by Forraigne Trade. Or The Ballance of Our Forraign Trade Is the Rule of Our Treasure.* London. 15–33, 42.

[6] Samuel Lambe. 1657. *Seasonable Observations Humbly Offered to His Highness the Lord Protector.* London. 9.

[7] Andrew Yarranton. 1677. *England's Improvement by Sea and Land.* London. 7–8.

[8] Kerridge. *Trade and Banking.* 68; Roseveare. *Financial Revolution.* 27; Wennerlind. *Casualties of Credit.* 8.

[9] Richards. *Early History of Banking.* 2; Horsefield. *British Monetary Experiments.* 93; Dickson. *Financial Revolution.* 4–6; Muldrew. *The Economy of Obligation.* 6, 114, 115; Roseveare. *Financial Revolution.* 13, 16–17; Wennerlind. *Casualties of Credit.* 2, 5, 17–19; Brenner. *Merchants and Revolution.* 46; Ashton. *The Crown and the Money Market.* 186.

[10] Desan. *Making Money.* 12, 15.

3 EARLY MODERN BANKING 61

private, domestic sphere and culminated with the Bank of England in 1694.

English domestic 'bankers' emerged in the seventeenth century and began their trade as simple moneylenders, lending their own money at interest. These individuals were associated with specific trades, notably 'the merchant, the broker, the scrivener, and the goldsmith', all of whom had gained knowledge of financial instruments and processes in the course of their career.[11] Eric Kerridge argues that goldsmiths first took on banking activities from 1622 onwards, when they began 'discounting and selling inland bills of exchange, as well as some outland ones and bills obligatory'.[12] The next significant milestone was the outbreak of the Civil War, when the goldsmiths expanded their financial services and began offering services to the public rather than just the crown and state. According to one contemporary pamphlet, when merchants' servants left their positions to go into the army, they left 'their Masters in the lurch' over who to entrust their money with. Instead of merchants trusting their money to an apprentice, whom they 'knew not how to confide in', they turned to the goldsmiths, who over time became 'the Merchants cash-keepers'.[13] Although this narrative has been critiqued, throughout the seventeenth-century goldsmiths evolved from simple moneychangers to bankers who provided loans to others using funds deposited by clients at interest—the beginnings of fractional reserve banking.[14]

The narrative of the rise of goldsmith-bankers has dominated historiography surrounding seventeenth-century English finance. The goldsmiths' biggest contribution to English banking was one particular instrument: the goldsmith's promissory note. Kim argues that the promissory note represents modern 'transferable paper money'. They were inland bills intended for local use and included the clause 'payable to X or bearer', meaning that the goldsmith-banker who issued the note was always the debtor but the creditor could be continually reassigned as the note passed

[11] Richards. *Early History of Banking*. 2.

[12] Kerridge. *Trade and Banking*. 67.

[13] 1676. *The Mystery of the New Fashioned Goldsmiths or Bankers*. London. 3.

[14] Roseveare. *Financial Revolution*. 1–11; Kim. How Modern Banking Originated. 942; David Mitchell. 1995. Innovation and the Transfer of Skill in the Goldsmiths' Trade in Restoration London. In *Goldsmiths, Silversmiths and Bankers: Innovation and the Transfer of Skill, 1550 to 1750*, ed. David Mitchell, 5–22. London: Sutton Publishing. 5.

62 M. WINTER

from hand to hand.[15] The development of such notes was significant, but the point at which the goldsmith-bankers began to dominate England's market for financial services was when certain goldsmiths agreed to accept the notes of their rival bankers. None of the bankers would charge interest in these transactions and accounts were settled on a regular basis: accepted notes were added up and cancelled against one another, leaving a difference which would result in a negative balance for one banker (in debit) and a positive balance for the other (in credit).[16]

Despite the establishment of a working system of transferable credit, the goldsmith-bankers did experience a major setback in the 1670s: the 'Stop on the Exchequer'. The Stop was the result of government overspending and the use of unstable financial instruments known as Treasury orders, which were government-issued interest-bearing promissory notes. Treasury orders had been common since the mid-1660s to encourage lending to the crown and facilitate wartime borrowing. The security behind these orders-to-pay was a specific tax revenue, so as taxes were collected those with orders were paid. However, between 1667 and 1671 the number of these orders grew and were no longer secured against specific tax revenues but the ordinary revenue, which was not guaranteed and, therefore, not secure. Most order holders sought to exchange the orders for cash through the goldsmith-bankers who, as a result, became the most significant holders of Treasury orders by 1671. When the Stop was enacted, the creditors or depositors of the goldsmiths immediately began a run on the banks, demanding their money from the bankers whose credit networks and trustworthy reputations had been destroyed by the public declaration of the Stop. Despite promises made by the crown and government guaranteeing repayment, a significant proportion of the debts owed to the goldsmith-bankers were still outstanding at the beginning of the eighteenth century. The failure of Treasury orders was therefore the latest problem experienced in the development of the public debt after the outbreak of the Civil War.[17]

---

[15] Kim. How Modern Banking Originated. 939, 942.

[16] Quinn. Goldsmith-Banking. 411–432.

[17] Desan. *Making Money*. 10, 244–248, 254, 262, 280–289; Horsefield. The "Stop of the Exchequer" Revisited. 511; Kerridge. *Trade and Banking*. 79.

3   EARLY MODERN BANKING   63

Although the Stop of the Exchequer, along with the financial impact of the Third Anglo-Dutch War, caused a 'financial debacle' and trade depression, it did not affect all bankers.[18] This is because two distinct types of goldsmith-bankers had evolved since the 1650s. The first type included Sir Robert Vyner's *The Vine* and Edward Backwell's *The Unicorn*, both on Lombard Street, which were the largest banks of the seventeenth century. Vyner and Backwell dealt not only with private individuals but with the government, crown, and large institutions such as the East India Company. The second type were smaller goldsmith-banks, whose clientele was restricted to private individuals. The smaller goldsmith-bankers, who were not crown lenders, escaped the ruin and bankruptcy that befell the likes of Backwell and Vyner, who as the two primary crown lenders held the majority of the defunct Treasury orders.[19]

Additionally, goldsmiths were not the only bankers in existence and, arguably, were not the first to engage in the techniques of modern banking. The goldsmith was preceded by the scrivener-banker. Scriveners were legal notaries, whose extensive knowledge of the financial transactions and contracts they drew up, led to them acting as agents for other services such as property conveyancing, rent collecting, and banking. The most famous scrivener-bank, and arguably one of the most successful English banks of the seventeenth century, was Clayton and Morris. The institution had been operating since 1635, when it was under the proprietorship of Robert Clayton's uncle, Richard Abbott. Clayton and John Morris took over the business in 1658, but both had worked for Abbott since the 1640s. Like the smaller goldsmith-banks, Clayton and Morris never lent to the crown and did not trade in foreign bills of exchange. The scriveners were also responsible for the development of a financial instrument: the mortgage. Mortgages were primarily used for 'large-scale and long-term debts' and required 'professional land assessment' alongside the usual financial paperwork. The land was assessed and formed the security for the loan, so as rent payments were made the loan was paid off. Thus, the borrower had longer to repay the debt and the lender, who would be receiving regular repayments over time, offered a greater

---

[18] Horsefield. The "Stop of the Exchequer" Revisited. 524; Roseveare. *Financial Revolution.* 22–26; J. R. Jones. 1996. *The Anglo-Dutch Wars of the Seventeenth Century.* Essex: Routledge. 192, 212.

[19] Mitchell. Innovation and the Transfer of Skill. 9–10; Clark. A Restoration Goldsmith-Banking House. 3–47; Richards. A Pre-Bank of England English Banker. 335–355.

loan than he would otherwise be able to under the terms of a bond. Whilst mortgages were common amongst scrivener-bankers throughout the second half of the seventeenth century, other banks would not use it regularly until the 1680s and 1690s. Despite their innovation, scriveners such as Clayton and Morris remain obscured by the vast historiography preoccupied by goldsmith-banks in England. The scriveners' company declined in the later seventeenth century, as the legal and banking professions became increasingly specialised and distinct, which has further obscured their place in the historical record.[20]

Aside from the goldsmiths and scrivener, the seventeenth century also witnessed a marked increase in experimentation in the world of finance. The scarcity of coin, demand for credit, domestic and foreign warfare, and the 1672 Stop caused a dearth of credit facilitators and therefore prompted proposals for new financial institutions. Many of the new proposals took a very different form to the guild-based, fractional reserve banks that the goldsmiths and scriveners represented. Instead of using a fractional reserve of specie, these proposals envisioned banks using 'commodities or land' or 'the public revenue' as the bases for their lending. Despite the myriad of proposals, however, few were realised and those that were, such as land banks, had limited success.[21] As neither goldsmiths nor scriveners, Thompson and Company were an unusual and experimental banking institution, but still retained similarities to their contemporaries through their use of the fractional reserve system. In order to fully situate them within the historiography of banking it is necessary to see how they compare to the more traditional goldsmith and scrivener institutions.

II

Whilst the records of most seventeenth-century banks do not survive, or survive in a partial or reduced state, it is possible to make a rough comparison between Thompson and Company and other contemporary banks in terms of size and the social composition of their creditors.

---

[20] Melton. *Sir Robert Clayton*. 14, 24, 28, 33, 44, 53–57, 81, 96, 113, 215, 216, 226; Graham. Military Contractors and the Money Markets. 106; Richards. *Early History of Banking*.

[21] Horsefield. *British Monetary Experiments*. 94–95, 103; Ashton. *The Crown and the Money Market*. 189; Wennerlind. *Casualties of Credit*. 95, 120–121.

3 EARLY MODERN BANKING 65

Comparisons by size are made possible by using approximate calculations derived from an institution's surviving books or from calculations made upon their collapse. These figures show that contemporary banks were trading in numbers far exceeding the £103,000 for which Thompson and Company went bankrupt and the £235,000 they claimed was in their books. For example, the scrivener-bank of Clayton and Morris was dealing with clients' deposits that totalled over £1 million in some years. Similarly, the two largest goldsmith-banks, *The Vine* and *The Unicorn*, dealt with single accounts that totalled more than Thompson and Company ever held. After the 1672 Stop on the Exchequer, the government calculated a large proportion of the holdings of Backwell and Vyner to organise a scheme for repayment, offering an insight into the size and scope of these institutions. In 1675, in crown debts alone, Backwell's Unicorn was owed £229,845 4s, over double the amount Thompson and Company were recorded as going bankrupt for. The Vine boasted even greater accounts. In crown debts alone, including interest accrued over five years, the amount owed to Vyner in 1677 stood at £416,724 13s 1.5d: approximately four times the amount Thompson and Company went bankrupt for.[22] Therefore, compared to these institutions Thompson and Company was relatively small.

However, Clayton and Morris, The Unicorn, and The Vine had been in existence for much longer than Thompson and Company and had built up a clientele base over many years, which Thompson and Company did not have the opportunity to do. In terms of size, Thompson and Company more closely resembled the smaller goldsmith-banks. Hoare's bank, whose records survive in the family-owned bank today, is a good comparison. Sir Richard Hoare established the bank in 1672 at the sign of the Golden Bottle in Cheapside before moving to Fleet Street in 1690. In its earliest days, Hoare's was considerably smaller than Thompson and Company. The first customer ledger, covering the years 1673–1683, lists only 89 names, compared to Thompson and Company's incomplete list of 211 names. However, Hoare's fortunes changed in the eighteenth century when the bank expanded rapidly. Peter Temin and Hans-Joachim Voth have calculated that between 1695 and 1724 Hoare's ledgers feature 721 individual borrowers or '206 customers per quinquennium', similar

---

[22] Muldrew. *Economy of Obligation*. 115; Melton. *Sir Robert Clayton*. 228; Richards. A Pre-Bank of England English Banker. 341, 348; Horsefield. The "Stop of the Exchequer" Revisited. 516.

66   M. WINTER

to the number Thompson and Company attracted earlier in the 1670s.[23] Therefore, whilst Thompson and Company was not amongst the largest banks of its day, it appears to have been a relatively significant venture compared to others established at a similar time.

Another point of comparison can be made between the clientele of these banks. Chapter 2 revealed the varied clientele of Thompson and Company, which features a low proportion of wealthy gentry and a high concentration of City-dwelling tradespeople. This is important when considering the type of people typically believed to have been using banks in this period. Whilst historians recognise the move from large-scale government lending and in joint-stock companies to the more localised role of goldsmith and scrivener banks, they have always been assumed to have had a limited clientele, confined to wealthy professionals and merchants, until the 'Financial Revolution' in the 1690s, which opened investment opportunities to those with lesser means.[24] However, other historians have emphasised the role of the small investor prior to the 1690s. Clay has argued that it was actually those 'who could least afford to purchase the social advantages of a landed estate' who were most attracted to 'new forms of investment', particularly as urban spaces developed and fostered new status distinctions not based on rural estates.[25] The largely urban and civic nature of the creditors of Thompson and Company certainly attests to that.

Thompson and Company's clientele demonstrates some significant similarities and differences to other contemporary banks. Henry Roseveare briefly examined the clientele of Edward Backwell and Robert Vyner's banks in the 1660s and 1670s and found that their clientele was largely London based, but with 'nearly one-third' residing outside of London. This mirrors Thompson and Company's creditors, of whom nearly two thirds were London residents. This geographical commonalty is not surprising given that all three banks had their shops in London.

---

[23] 1932. *Hoare's Bank: A Record 1673–1932.* London. 6, 7; Hoare's Bank Archive. HB/5/F/1. Customer Ledger 1673–1683; Temin and Voth. Private Borrowing. 547.

[24] Muldrew. *Economy of Obligation.* 115; Roseveare. *Financial Revolution.* 19; Temin and Voth. Banking as an Emerging Technology. 150; Laurence. The Emergence of a Private Clientele for Banks. 565–567; Anne L. Murphy. 2006. Dealing with Uncertainty: Managing Personal Investment in the Early English National Debt. *History* 91: 201.

[25] Theodore K. Rabb. 1966. Investment in English Overseas Enterprise, 1575–1630. *The Economic History Review* 19: 70.

However, Vyner and Backwell's clientele was 'widely drawn from government officials and the professions, as well as from merchants, tradesmen and the landed gentry'. For Vyner the largest group were those labelled 'Esq.' or 'Gent'. and comprised 42.7 per cent of Roseveare's sample. As Backwell's accounts confirmed 'this picture', Roseveare concluded that the evidence attested 'to a well-established "banking habit" in the moneyed community'.[26] In contrast, Thompson and Company's largest group of creditors were merchants (22.79%) closely followed by citizens or tradesmen (21.86%) and widows or spinsters (17.21%). Gentlemen (13.02%) and professionals (9.77%) made up a smaller percentage of their clientele than other banks in this period, possibly reflecting the mercantile and trading backgrounds of its partners. Other bankers of the period were mostly goldsmiths or scriveners rather than merchants or traders, and so did not possess the same contacts in those fields. All of which suggests that the social composition of the creditors of Thompson and Company was significantly different to other contemporary banks.

The evidence of Thompson and Company's creditors similarly problematises Roseveare's use of the term 'moneyed community', which suggests only the wealthiest were using banks. However, Thompson and Company's creditors came from more varied financial backgrounds. The two creditors' pamphlets argued for the relief of 'poor Families' and of those 'in a very low condition'. In the 1679 case of the creditors, the complainants stated that some creditors were 'poore Tradesmen & widdows', who had become further 'impoverished' due to the commission of bankruptcy. The use of 'poor' here is clearly rhetoric to provoke sympathy and encourage action to be taken. The less wealthy creditors of Thompson and Company cannot have been destitute as they had enough spare capital to put money in the bank, but that capital could have been vital for their maintenance in later life. Less wealthy creditors are much harder to trace, and it is probable that many of the untraceable names fall into this category. However, there is some surviving evidence pertaining to a few of the less wealthy. Grissilla Thorold, for example, was a 'poore' widow of London, who's short will stated that she 'owes a greate deale of moneys'. Similarly, Mary Norman, a spinster of St Martin in the Fields, bequeathed the total sum of £35 to friends and relatives in her 1698 will and mentioned no other estate or goods of value, suggesting she had very

---

[26] Roseveare. *Financial Revolution*. 19.

68 M. WINTER

little else. The mention of 'poore Tradesmen' could refer to those creditors who were London citizens, such as tailor Richard Seymour. In his 1685 will Seymour left his remaining estate of 'five shillings a piece' to his three sons William, Richard and Edward, his daughter Mary, his wife's sister Mary Coxen, and his nephew William Abbott.[27] Whilst Seymour clearly was not a wealthy citizen, he could have deposited just a small amount at the bank to earn more at interest from the little he had.

In contrast, the largest category of creditors consisted of merchants and mariners who were a significantly wealthier group of individuals. For example, merchant Edward Watts was a Levant Company member, used multiple London banks, and owned a large property in the parish of All Hallows Staining, London.[28] Most banks had a large mercantile clientele, for whom banking was a business necessity rather than a choice. Additionally, many merchants accumulated significant wealth and looked to further it through investment or make a profit by utilising interest-bearing deposits. The number of merchants also reflects the partners' own mercantile backgrounds, and the number of citizens— who represent the second largest category of creditors—is consistent with the partners' civic backgrounds and membership of London guilds. The citizen creditors of Thompson and Company represent a range of occupations, from goldsmiths and grocers to upholders and joiners, and are significant because they comprise much smaller numbers of bank clientele in other studies. Like merchants, citizens and tradesmen dealt in credit in their day-to-day business and often took up political roles alongside their commercial occupations, but often had less spare capital due to their larger overhead costs.[29] However, certain citizens were wealthier

---

[27] *Reasons Most Humbly Offered to the Consideration of Parliament*; *Reasons Offered by Several of the Creditors of Richard Thompson and Partners*; TNA: C 8/328/50; PROB 11/380/471. Will of Grissilla Thorold. 23 July 1685; PROB 11/447/76. Will of Mary Norman, Spinster of Saint Martin in the Fields, Middlesex. 4 August 1698; LMA: DL/AM/PW/1685/067. Will of Richard Seymour. 1685.

[28] *Records of London's Livery Companies Online*, Livery Companies—home (london roll.org), Search for 'Edward Watts', master to apprentices in 1664 and 1666; *The Little London Directory*; Search for Edward Watts in the *London Hearth Tax: City of London and Middlesex, 1666*, https://www.british-history.ac.uk/london-hearth-tax/london-mddx/1666/all-hallows-staining, accessed via *British History Online* [accessed 2 March 2020].

[29] Muldrew. *Economy of Obligation*. 185; Gadd and Wallis. Introduction. 4; Earle. *Making of the English Middle Class*. 137, 140.

3 EARLY MODERN BANKING 69

than others. For example, creditor William Piggot was a member of the Grocers' Company, a druggist by profession, and a churchwarden of St Mary Woolchurch. Churchwardens were governors of the parish alongside the overseers of the poor and the constable and expected to be of sufficient wealth and status within the parish. The role of churchwarden would therefore act as a further mark of their respectability and social standing.[30] Piggot's position suggests he might have had more spare capital to put in the bank than others.

Thompson and Company's creditors also featured a significant number of women. The role of women in early modern finance has been much explored in recent years. This scholarship has largely focussed on women's financial activity from the 1690s onward, showing that more financial options became open to women and that they were not passive investors but active participants in a changing financial climate.[31] However, as Ewen argues, 'there has been very little study of women's roles as investors' before the 1690s and little recognition of the importance of 'women from various backgrounds'.[32] The evidence of Thompson and Company's creditors suggests that, prior to the 1690s, women were taking advantage of bank services and putting out their money at interest to further their capital wealth. Additionally, that the names of so many female creditors appear in the court case suggests that women understood the legal system and were keen to engage with it when necessary to support their financial activities.

---

[30] *Boyd's Inhabitants of London*, 1647 record, 3830; Mark Goldie. 2001. The Unacknowledged Republic: Officeholding in Early Modern England. In *The Politics of the Excluded, c.1500–1850*, ed. Tim Harris, 153–194. Basingstoke: The MacMillan Press. 160, 164, 166; Peter Earle. 1994. The Middling Sort in London. In *The Middling Sort of People: Culture, Society and Politics in England, 1550–1800*, eds Jonathan Barry and Christopher Brooks, 141–158. Basingstoke: The MacMillan Press. 157.

[31] B. A. Holderness. 1984. Widows in Pre-Industrial Society: An Essay Upon Their Economic Functions. In *Land, Kinship and Life-Cycle*, ed. R. M. Smith. Cambridge: Cambridge University Press. 423–442; Froide. *Silent Partners*; Eleanor Hubbard. 2012. *City Women: Money, Sex, and the Social Order in Early Modern London*. Oxford: Oxford University Press; Alexandra Shepard. 2015. Minding Their Own Business: Married Women and Credit in Early Eighteenth-Century London. *Transactions of the Royal Historical Society* 25: 53–74; Todd. Fiscal Citizens. 53–74; Spicksley. Usury Legislation, Cash, and Credit. 277–301; Laurence. The Emergence of a Private Clientele for Banks. 565–586; Carlos and Neal. Women Investors. 197–224; Erickson. *Women and Property*.

[32] Ewen. Women Investors. 4.

70   M. WINTER

The female creditors of Thompson and Company were predominantly widows and spinsters (17.21%), who exercised greater financial agency than married women. The importance of widows and spinsters to early modern English finance has largely focussed on informal and rural credit markets.[33] However, most widows interacting with Thompson and Company were Londoners and active in urban financial markets. For example, creditor Elizabeth Farrer was a London resident and the widow of a London common councillor and brewer, who clearly gained control over funds after her husband's death.[34] Whilst widows are easier to trace than spinsters, as they can be found in family documents, there are instances, such as for Jane Coles, Anne Radford, and Mary Russell, whereby the records are too limited to ascertain whether the creditor was a widow or a spinster.

Spinsters are much harder to trace than widows, with only two wills of spinsters found in this study, but they were equally as important in credit networks. Spicksley argues that spinsters were important moneylenders in informal and formal credit networks, 'engaging in loans that were secured by recognized credit instruments' and were 'interest-bearing'. The motivation behind such activity was to extend the portion received in their inheritance or upon adulthood, lending to friends, family, acquaintances, and, later, investing in local businesses and corporations. Both widows and spinsters have not been included in studies of urban finance or as customers of banks prior to the 1690s, with Laurence only identifying female customers of Hoare's Bank after 1690.[35] Evidence of Thompson and Company's creditors shows that widows and spinsters were engaging with urban financial institutions in the 1670s, even if they had little money to spare. This suggests that female financial practices were well established by the later seventeenth century as banks like Thompson and Company offered new mechanisms for women to participate in financial markets, bridging the gap between household and corporate credit.

---

[33] Holderness. Women in Pre-Industrial Society. 435, 436.

[34] *Boyd's Inhabitants of London*, 1663 record, 20431; Woodhead. *Rulers of London*. 68.

[35] TNA: PROB 11/375/341. Will of Elizabeth Irby of Saint Margaret Westminster, Middlesex. 8 March 1684; PROB 11/447/76. Will of Mary Norman; Judith Spicksley. 2007. "Fly with a duck in thy mouth": Single Women as Sources of Credit in Seventeenth-Century England. *Social History* 32: 188–191, 197–199, 205; Laurence. The Emergence of a Private Clientele for Banks. 565–586.

The small number of wives, however, attests to the dominance of the common law concept of coverture in women's financial lives, which dictated that a married couple 'were one person' in the eyes of the law and a woman was unable to 'contract', 'sue', or 'be sued independently of her husband'.[36] Whilst wives may have been financially active in their household, they remained legally subsumed under their husband's financial identity, and only became financially independent in widowhood. Of the female creditors of Thompson and Company, only 4 (1.86%) can be identified as wives. Mary Chetwind, wife of merchant Phillip Chetwind, inherited her husband's estate in his will of 1683.[37] Hester Churchman was the wife of gentleman Sir John Churchman of Norfolk, who was also a creditor.[38] Anne Berry was from a wealthy family, the daughter of Sir Robert Wolesley who was clerk to the patents office, and could have retained some control over a portion of her finances.[39] Finally, Elizabeth Dixon was either the wife of fellow creditor and felt maker John Dixon, or the wife of goldsmith Charles Dixon.[40] Elizabeth appears to have been of a lower, more middling, status than the other three, possibly using the bank for financial transactions for the household business.

III

The evidence of Thompson and Company's creditors, and those of other banks, demonstrates an appetite for financial opportunities amongst a wide range of the population in seventeenth-century England. Historiographical discussion surrounding increased financial activity in this period has largely focussed on the final decades and the 'Financial Revolution' of the 1690s, attributing increased activity to the separation of the crown from English finance in 1688 and the greater security perceived in the

---

[36] Erickson. *Women and Property.* 19, 114.

[37] *Boyd's Inhabitants of London*, 1636 record, 43084; TNA: PROB 11//372/258. Will of Phillip Chetwind, Clothworker of London. 19 February 1683.

[38] John P. Ferris. GORE, Sir John (1621–97), of Sacombe, Herts. *HoP*, http://www.historyofparliamentonline.org/volume/1660-1690/member/gore-sir-john-1621-97 [accessed 27 June 2018]; *Francis Blomefield. 1739. An Essay Towards a Topographical History of the County of Norfolk*, vol. 1. London: W. Miller. 304.

[39] Woodhead. *Rulers of London.* 29. *Boyd's Inhabitants of London*, 1674 record, 11543.

[40] TNA: C 8/328/50; *Boyd's Inhabitants of London*, 1651 record, 24947, or 1672 record, 4239.

national debt.[41] The reasons behind the earlier development of banks and financial engagement with institutions has received less attention. The growth of banks in the seventeenth century has been attributed to the necessities of state finance and warfare, but these studies have not fully addressed why people increasingly turned to banks for their own personal finances.[42] Therefore, the following section aims to provide some wider reasons why individuals increasingly turned to financial institutions before the 1690s and how this might have affected the appeal of Thompson and Company.

Historians have shown that there was a general growth in national wealth across the seventeenth century, which translated into prosperity and higher real wages across all levels of the social strata.[43] Slack argues that this economic change was part of a wider seventeenth-century cultural development that altered the way England viewed its own progress. This was the introduction of the idea of 'improvement', or at least its acceptance into contemporary political and economic thought. Improvement is reflected in the doubling of 'Agricultural and industrial output', a 'fivefold' rise in the value of foreign trade, and significant 'urbanisation' which was largely centred on London. Slack demonstrates contemporary recognition of 'improvement' through the rising number of literary publications on the topic, and through the development of the discipline of political economy. By the 1670s, Slack argues, 'improvement had become part of the collective mentality of the cultural and political elite'.[44] However, increase in national wealth and the culture of 'improvement' are macroeconomic changes and the extent to which they would have affected the mindset of individuals is difficult to gauge. More pertinent reasons behind the motivation of the non-elite to use financial institutions are specific life events or experiences, such as those hinted at by the partners of Thompson and Company who stated that they had been successful despite the 'difficulties' experienced in recent years.[45]

---

[41] North and Weingast. Constitutions and Commitment. 803–4; Murphy. *Origins of English Financial Markets.* 1, 13–15, 37; Temin and Voth. Private Borrowing. 541–564.

[42] Richards. *Early History of Banking.* 38; Roseveare. *Financial Revolution.* 4.

[43] Wennerlind. *Casualties of Credit.* 92–94; Murphy. *Origins of English Financial Markets.* 13; Susan E. Whyman. 1999. *Sociability and Power in Late-Stuart England: The Cultural Worlds of the Verneys 1660–1720.* Oxford: Oxford University Press. 17.

[44] Slack. *The Invention of Improvement.* 12, 115, 116, 123.

[45] *Case of Richard Thompson and Company.* 4.

Two of these difficulties, which encouraged rapid financial development and affected the ways in which people thought about their property and finances, were the Civil War and the Great Fire of London. Whilst both events are recognised as significant for the development of England's trade and manufacturing sectors, they are given less prominence when explaining the reasons behind the growth of financial activity. For example, Ben Coates argues that the pamphlet *The Mystery of the New Fashioned Goldsmiths*, which argued for the importance of the Civil War for goldsmith-banking, 'was a government inspired attempt to justify the 1672 stop on the Exchequer', that the 'origins of English banking were probably much less dramatic' than the pamphlet suggests, and that the Civil War 'did not result in a major change in the London money market, at least as far as public finance was concerned'.[46] However, if instead of looking to the Civil War for the origins of public finance, we look at its impact on the expansion of private banking services then its significant impact on the money market, particularly in London, becomes evident. In 1640 Charles I requisitioned £200,000 worth of London merchants' coin and bullion kept in the Mint for the war effort, an act which Richards and Kerridge argue shattered the Mint's reputation. As a result, merchants looked for places to safely deposit surplus funds and paved 'the way towards a system of private banking'.[47] The Civil War did not only impact upon merchants. Through an examination of witness depositions in ecclesiastical courts, Shepard found a 'growing reluctance of witnesses to divulge their net worth in goods' across the seventeenth century. This was, she argues, 'in all likelihood one of the many consequences of the disruption of civil war' which witnessed the 'extraction of goods and the destruction of property' that 'jeopardised trust in goods as security for credit'.[48]

Although less commented on, the Great Fire of 1666 also represents a decisive moment for English finance, and, as such a large proportion of Thompson and Company's creditors were London-based, could have

---

[46] *The Mystery of the New Fashioned Goldsmiths or Bankers.* 3; Ben Coates. 2004. *The Impact of the English Civil War on the Economy of London, 1642–50.* Ashgate: Routledge. 85, 89.

[47] Richards. *Early History of Banking.* 35–36; Kerridge. *Trade and Banking.* 69.

[48] Alexandra Shepard. 2015. *Accounting for Oneself: Worth, Status, and the Social Order in Early Modern England.* Oxford: Oxford University Press. 288–289; Desan. *Making Money.* 244.

been a significant factor in creditors' decision to put money in Thompson and Company. The fire inflated fears surrounding the security of cash kept in houses and money in property, evident from the instigation of fire insurance in the later seventeenth century.[49] Both the fire and the Civil War made land a less attractive investment, due to rising debts, disruption and requisitioning, and the land tax introduced to fund the war. However, as the appeal of land decreased a range of other financial institutions appeared. In 1677 Yarranton claimed that the security on land was 'so uncertain and bad' that it forced the 'monied men ... into *Lombard-street*' and the goldsmith-banks that resided there. Aside from the 'monied men', this change could also apply to the middling sorts trying to improve themselves. Builder and fire insurance entrepreneur Nicholas Barbon claimed it was the high interest rate in England that was causing 'the Fall of Rents' and attracting more individuals to rent rather than buy. For example, individuals such as Samuel Pepys rented throughout their lifetime, demonstrating a tendency to avoid land as a form of personal wealth.[50]

The same high interest rates that deterred land investment could have attracted more customers to bank services. Interest only became a recognised concept in 1571 when it replaced the term usury, which referred to the illegal practice of making a profit out of moneylending by charging the debtor for the time it took to repay the loan. The first act regarding usury in 1545 allowed lenders to charge 10 per cent interest but was repealed in 1552. It was reinstated in 1571, under the name interest, and the legal maximum that could be charged dropped to 6 per cent in 1651. Richards has argued that the change in public opinion regarding usury, or interest,

---

[49] Harold E. Raynes. 1948. *A History of British Insurance.* London: Sir Isaac Pitman & Sons. 78; H. A. L. Cockerell and Edwin Green. 1976. *The British Insurance Business 1547–1970: An Introduction and Guide to Historical Records in the United Kingdom.* London: Heinemann Educational. 18.

[50] Jacob F. Field. 2018. *London, Londoners and the Great Fire of 1666: Disaster and Recovery.* Oxford: Routledge. 101; Muldrew. *Economy of Obligation.* 153; Wennerlind. *Casualties of Credit.* 94; Whyman. *Sociability and Power.* 15, 77; Whyman. Land and Trade Revisited. 26; C. G. A. Clay. 1984. *Economic Expansion and Social Change: England 1500–1700, vol. 1, People, Land and Towns.* Cambridge: Cambridge University Press. 163; Yarranton. *England's Improvement.* 17–18; Nicholas Barbon. 1690. *A Discourse of Trade.* London. 84; Muldrew. *Economy of Obligation.* 171.

reflected in the statutes led to the 'release of more capital seeking investment' and growing demand for banks and other financial institutions.[51] The interest offered by bankers on deposits varied, but any amount could act as a 'magnet compelling clients to place their deposits with bankers'.[52] As the previous chapter outlined, Thompson and Company offered the legal maximum of six per cent interest on their client's deposits, which would certainly have compelled individuals to part with their funds.

Other financial institutions include commercial trading companies, such as the East India and Royal African companies, who sold their bonds and stocks to the public. Like banks, these companies relied on their reputation or credit, along with the potential for significant profits, to attract customers. Although different companies had different minimum investment criteria—some more affordable than others—the majority of investors were gentry, who had the financial means to invest, and merchants, who had both financial means and direct experience of mercantile ventures. However, other people did invest in companies, and it was not just a male practice as Ewen has demonstrated that women were amongst company investors in the early seventeenth century. Whilst merchant companies could offer significant profits, investments in companies could not provide clients with a guaranteed return: they relied largely on speculation and were subject to fluctuations in trading markets and accidents at sea.[53] Although Thompson and Company was certainly not risk free, like other banks they did promise clients a guaranteed return on their deposit and the ability to demand the return of their money whenever they pleased, something trading companies did not do.

Similar to financial involvement with companies, ship shares and shipping also attracted capital in this period. Ships were sometimes under sole ownership but were more often divided into shares and sold off as easily transferable capital investments. Ship shares offered the possibility

---

[51] Richards. *Early History of Banking*. 19, 20, 22; Muldrew. *Economy of Obligation*. 114.

[52] Roseveare. *Financial Revolution*. 20; Melton. *Sir Robert Clayton*. 39, 49, 213–214, 216.

[53] Edmond Smith. 2018. The Global Interests of London's Commercial Community, 1599–1625: Investment in the East India Company. *The Economic History Review* 71: 1121–1124, 1135–1136; Ewen. Women Investors. 1–22. See also: Brenner. *Merchants and Revolution*. 5, 10, 12, 13, 16, 33, 35, 109; Rabb. Investment in English Overseas Enterprise. 72–4, 80; K. G. Davies. 1952. Joint-Stock Investment in the Later Seventeenth Century. *The Economic History Review* 3: 295, 298–299.

76   M. WINTER

of significant profits as they usually operated on a profit-share basis and were relatively easy to manage as money could be withdrawn or shares could be sold if an individual needed funds. Owning ship shares therefore appealed to a wide range of people. However, it was not without its risks. Ships were subject to bad weather conditions, good could be damaged or destroyed, and there was also the risks of privateering and piracy.[54] Owning ship shares therefore held some similarities to using early deposit banks, a flexible form of investment that did not have the same wealth margins as companies, but still did not offer a promised return by way of interest like Thompson and Company and other early modern banks did.

However, it is not necessarily the case that people only used one type of financial institution at the same time. There is evidence to suggest that some individuals, usually the wealthier gentry and merchants, created diverse financial portfolios by spreading their spare capital amongst various institutions with the hope of increasing profit and minimising risk. Scholarship concerned with diversification of financial portfolios has mostly focussed on the 1690s onwards, but this practice has also been evidenced earlier.[55] For example, Edmond Smith has shown that early seventeenth century members of the East India Company had divers investment portfolios, spreading funds across different trading companies, privateering, and colonial ventures.[56] In his examination of the middling sort in London from 1660–1730, Earle found occupational and age determinants associated with an individual's propensity to invest. 'Rentiers and money-lenders' as well as wealthy merchants were important in financial circles, the likelihood of investing increased with age as individual's were less active in employment, and retailers were less likely to invest as their assets were largely 'tied up in stock in trade and trade credit'. Whilst Earle identifies an 'increasing spread of investors' in the 1690s, he does recognise that such investment practices were prevalent earlier in the century.[57] Evidence from Thompson and Company's creditors corroborates this.

Two such creditors who recorded economically diverse portfolios were Thomas Belasyse, viscount and later earl Fauconberg, and Sir

---

[54] G. V. Scammell. 1972. Shipowning in the Economy and Politics of Early Modern England. *The Historical Journal* 15: 397–405.

[55] Carlos, Fletcher, and Neal. Share Portfolios. 575; Murphy. Dealing with Uncertainty. 201, 202.

[56] Smith. The global interests of London's Commercial Community. 1119, 1123–1124.

[57] Earle. *Making of the English Middle Class.* 143, 144, 149.

3 EARLY MODERN BANKING 77

William Turner. Fauconberg's financial notebook, and a range of account books, books of sale and letter books of Turners have survived in the archives.[58] These two creditors are particularly interesting because alongside their involvement with Thompson and Company they also had a close personal and financial relationship. Both men hailed from Yorkshire gentry, Belasyse was the eldest son of a nobleman and succeeded to the Fauconberg titles, and Turner was a younger son of a gentleman who took up trade, becoming a wealthy London woollen draper. How the two men knew each other is not revealed in either of their records but by 1674 Turner was acting as a London agent for Fauconberg, disbursing and collecting money on his behalf in the capital.[59] Turner therefore managed not only his own portfolio but part of Fauconberg's as well, and the accounts are therefore very similar in their contents.

Turner's portfolio consisted of loans to individuals, money invested in small companies of merchants (signified by 'X and company') and large chartered trading companies such as the East India and African Companies, ship shares, and property. He also recorded the plate and gold he held, along with what he had in cash that physically contributed to his personal wealth.[60] Interestingly, although Turner was a customer of goldsmith-banker Edward Backwell in the 1660s, he appears never to have used the services of another London bank alongside or after his business with Thompson and Company.[61] Fauconberg was similarly a customer of Backwell's and supplied personal loans and mortgages to friends, held stock in the Royal African Company and East India Company from the 1670s to the 1690s, and was of course a creditor of Thompson and Company. The key difference between the two is that Turner's accounts are professional accounts formulated by a woollen draper who was used to extending credit as part of his business, whereas Fauconberg's are personal accounts concerned with his estate. As such,

---

[58] BL: Add MS 41255. Note-Book of Thomas Belasyse; LMA: CLC/50. Sir William Turner.

[59] LMA: CLC/509/MS05107/002. Miscellaneous Accounts. 'My Ld Viscount Fauconberg his account 23 May 1674'.

[60] LMA: CLC/509/MS05105. Book of Sales, 1664–71, followed by accounts relating to his personal estate, 1671–91.

[61] Customer Account Ledgers of Edward Backwell, 1663–72. *Royal Bank of Scotland Heritage Hub.* https://www.rbs.com/heritage/people/edward-backwell.html [accessed 28 March 2019]. 243.

Fauconberg had a greater amount of land in his portfolio than Turner did, owning his own estate as well as acting as a rentier, and did not invest in ships as Turner did.

Fauconberg's accounts also change slightly in the 1690s, whilst Turner's remain the same. In 1696 Fauconberg purchased '100 lottery tickets', a growing form of investment that Turner does not seem to have taken up. Private lotteries had existed in England since the mid-sixteenth century, and their growing popularity meant that by the end of the seventeenth century 'the English government hit on the idea of turning the fad for lotteries into a way to raise money to fund its wars', such as the funding of the Nine Years' War in the 1690s. Fauconberg could have invested in one of the state lotteries, like the 'Million Adventure' in 1694, or in one of the many private lotteries that were carried out throughout the 1690s. Further demonstrating the widespread involvement in lotteries, and Fauconberg's use of lottery tickets in financial transactions, is his loan to Lady Russell 'upon Malt Ticketts', which were tickets from the 'Malt Lottery' of 1697. In addition to these new investments, Fauconberg also had dealings with another bank, Hoare's Bank, from 1692 until his death.[62]

Fauconberg and Turner's varied and diverse portfolios demonstrate that, alongside more traditional financial activities such as lending money and owning land, individuals also put their money into companies and took advantage of new opportunities in commerce and state finance. Both men lost substantial sums over the course of their portfolios. Turner lost £1200 to Thompson and Company, often recorded arrears of debts, and from 1689 onwards began recording 'doubtful' debts in his bi-annual accounts. Fauconberg had to accept compositions on two of his investments in the late 1670s and early 1680s: the deposit he made with Thompson and Company and repayment of capital put into Royal African Company stock. In both cases Fauconberg had £875 remaining with the companies and received a final pay-out of just £131 5s. However, both men also minimised risk by not investing all their capital in one venture. So, although they both lost significant sums, this did not result in financial ruin.

---

[62] BL: Add MS 41255. Note-Book of Thomas Belasyse; Customer Account Ledgers of Edward Backwell. 22; Richards. *Early History of Banking*. 58–59; Froide. *Silent Partners*. 30, 31; Murphy. Lotteries in the 1690s. 228, 230, 234.

Unfortunately, none of the other creditors left such detailed records as Fauconberg or Turner but surviving evidence does suggest that others also developed diverse investment portfolios in the 1670s. Most of these individuals were either merchants or gentry, suggesting this kind of financial activity was restricted to wealthier individuals before the 1690s, and no evidence has been found to suggest that female creditors undertook this type of financial activity. Merchant John Crisp was an investor in both the East India and Royal African Company, with £500 worth of shares in each, demonstrating his significant wealth.[63] Ferdinando Gorges, inherited the province of Maine from his father, the military officer and coloniser Sir Ferdinando Gorges who had colonised it in 1629, and sold the province in 1676 to the King for £11,000. Gorges was also a director of and owned stock in the Royal African Company as well as depositing funds in Thompson and Company.[64]

Alongside his business with Thompson and Company, the merchant John Dubois was an East India Company personal account holder and had shares in and became a director of the Royal African Company.[65] Merchant Sir Jonathan Keate had an account at Hoare's Bank from 1675 onwards and owned East India Company stock from 1671 to 1675 at the same time as he put funds into Thompson and Company.[66] Indeed, many of the creditors of Thompson and Company had business with the East India Company. The majority were merchants, with 21 of the merchant-creditors either having a personal trading account, stocks and shares, or correspondence with the Company. Other creditors who held bonds with the East India Company in the 1670s include the gentleman Israell Mayo and the lawyer Thomas Medlicott. Additionally, 9 other merchant-creditors held stock in the Royal African Company (Appendix).

[63] De Krey. *London and the Restoration*. 415.

[64] Charles E. Clark. 2004. Gorges, Sir Ferdinando (1568–1647). *Oxford Dictionary of National Biography*. https://doi-org.sheffield.idm.oclc.org/10.1093/ref:odnb/11098 [accessed 11 August 2018]; BL: Add MS 28089. *Papers Relating to the English Colonies in America*. 24 February 1676, f.1; William Pettigrew. 2013. *Freedom's Debt: The Royal African Company and the Politics of the Atlantic Slave Trade, 1672–1752*. Chapel Hill: University of North Carolina Press. 238.

[65] Pettigrew. *Freedom's Debt*. 237.

[66] Hoare's Bank Archive: HB/5/F/1. Customer Ledger A. f. 31, 89.

80   M. WINTER

Aside from the merchants and gentlemen who evidently had varied financial portfolios, there is one citizen who also shows evidence of financial experimentation and diversity alongside his involvement with the bank. 'Button seller' Francis Savile was involved in a mercantile partnership from 1671 to approximately 1676, when the partnership broke down and the case was taken to the Chancery court. Savile's partner was goldsmith William Cordary, who in 1671 began a new 'trade into fflanders in the way of merchandizing'. According to Cordary, Savile 'very much sollicited' to partner with him in the trade and offered 'severall sumes of money'. Eventually a partnership was agreed, and Savile put up £200 'as his share for a stake to bee adventured upon the said trade'. The partners drew up an 'Agreement', similar to Thompson and Company's, whereby they would 'beare an equall share of all expenses Customes Losses' and receive a fair portion of the 'profits gaines and Advantages ariseing'. However, their merchandising was unsuccessful, and the partnership broke down as the two partners tried to recover their funds.[67] Despite their lack of success, the case suggests that Savile had sufficient funds to be a creditor of the bank as well as experiment in a mercantile partnership in the 1670s, and that he was prepared to put money in different places for different purposes and intended outcomes.

The above factors all have important ramifications for Thompson and Company, and for banking in England in the later seventeenth century. By the 1670s banks were well-established institutions and legal and social developments made certain financial practices more widespread and acceptable. However, there was one significant setback in the 1670s that could have discouraged the use of banks—the 1672 Stop on the Exchequer. Rather than hinder Thompson and Company, though, the Stop seems to have worked in their favour. As outlined earlier, Thompson and Company were similar to the goldsmith-bankers in many of their financial practices but were significantly different enough that potential customers could have seen them as a viable alternative once the major goldsmith-banks had collapsed. Indeed, Clay argued that despite suffering in the 'financial crisis of 1672', the opportunities offered by banks were still 'perceived by investors as sufficiently safe to divert a growing proportion

[67] TNA: C 8/327/60 Cordary v Savile. 19 May 1676.

3 EARLY MODERN BANKING 81

of the surplus capital generated in economic activities other than agriculture away from the purchase of land'.[68] This is reflected in Nicholas Barbon's claim that despite the Stop, the 'Dispatch and Ease in Trade is so great by such Notes, that the Credit is still in some Measure kept up'.[69] The appeal of banks lay in their flexibility—the ability to put in and withdraw money on demand. For example, the *Mystery of the New Fashioned Goldsmiths or Bankers* argued that banks gave 'hopes to everybody to make Profit of their money until the hour they spent it' and the 'conveniency ... to command their money when they please, which they could not do when lent at interest upon personal or reall Security'.[70] Additionally, banks were useful for individuals who were unfamiliar with financial practices. For example, Thomas Mun argued that 'The Bankers are always ready to receive such sums of mony as are put into their hands by men of all degrees, who have no skill or good means themselves to manage the same upon the exchange to profit'.[71] Clearly, the benefits outweighed the risks.

The willingness of individuals to use banks despite the 1672 Stop was also recognised by Thompson and Company's partners who stated that creditors 'found so little cause to repent or suspect' the bank 'notwithstanding the Calamity which about a year after [their establishment] fell upon Bankers, and consequently upon so many hundreds of Persons concerned with them in the Exchequer'.[72] Indeed, many of Thompson and Company's creditors previously did business with the goldsmithbanks of Backwell and Vyner. Of the 215 known creditors, 47 names (21.86%) match those found in Backwell's customer list and seven names (3.26%) match those found in the Exchequer books of receipt for Vyner's bank (Appendix). These are not necessarily definite matches and common names could lead to over-counting, but it suggests that a significant number of people were keen to retain the service of a bank. This is not necessarily the case for merchants, who often held accounts at several different institutions, each intended for a different purpose or place.[73]

---

[68] Clay. *Economic Expansion*. vol. 1. 163.

[69] Barbon. *A Discourse of Trade*. 28–29.

[70] *The Mystery of the New Fashioned Goldsmiths or Bankers*. 4–5.

[71] Mun. *England's Treasure by Forraigne Trade*. 124.

[72] *Case of Richard Thompson and Company*. 3.

[73] Neal and Quinn. Networks of Information. 13.

82   M. WINTER

Additionally, a few of the creditors clearly used multiple banks, featuring in the records of both Backwell and Vyner.

IV

Thompson and Company were part of a wider transformation of England's money markets in the seventeenth century. One that saw the emergence of private banking and an increased appetite amongst the population for a place in which they could not only store but increase their capital wealth. They were from neither goldsmith nor scrivener backgrounds but did have many similarities to them; a private fractional reserve bank that extended credit through the provision of transferable financial instruments and interest-bearing deposits. In their clientele, Thompson and Company had a more diverse group of creditors, demonstrating that it was not only the wealthiest who used banks and that a significant number of women used banks. The composition of Thompson and Company's creditors therefore challenges the arguments made about pre-1690s financial involvement in London and beyond. It suggests that financial practices may be more widespread but the lack of evidence surrounding creditors of smaller, more informal, institutions make such practices harder to identify and uncover.

However, Thompson and Company was not only an early deposit bank, but, as their articles of agreement state, they used bank funds to continue their commercial activities. Thompson and Company therefore have similarities with the earlier mediaeval banking houses, such as the Peruzzi, Medici, and Fuggers, as a partnership of merchants who maintained commercial interests alongside their banking venture, although on a much smaller scale than those European banking houses. Additionally, two of Thompson and Company's partners pursued political careers alongside their mercantile and financial endeavours. The following chapter explores the mercantile and commercial aspect of Thompson and Company more closely. It argues that as well as situating Thompson and Company in the history of banking, it also needs to be situated in the history of commercial ventures. As such it is a hybrid institution that benefits from inclusion in the wider historiography of early modern 'projecting'.

CHAPTER 4

An Early Modern 'Project'

In his 1684 complaint to the Chancery court, Farrington stated that Nelthorpe was 'an adventerous young man' and that he was 'wholly influencing' Thompson 'who was altogether unskillfall'. He claimed both men were 'ambitious', with a design to 'engage in divers chargeable & Hazardous under takeings' in the hope of becoming 'suddainly rich'. As such, they embarked upon 'expencefull & fruitlesse projects'. In order to fund these projects, Farrington claimed that Thompson and Nelthorpe 'drew out the cash in bank', which was permitted by their articles of agreement.[1] The partners' pamphlet also hints at projecting activities, stating that they embarked on 'various Business and Adventures' and on 'several advantagious or probable Trades ... omitting nothing within the compass of our ingenuity'.[2] Thompson and Company has never before been included in the historiography of projects and projecting nor have the partners been described as projectors. Thompson has, however, been described as 'entrepreneurial' and Nelthorpe as 'a man of many parts', 'a

---

[1] TNA: C 7/581/73.

[2] *Case of Richard Thompson and Company.* 4.

© The Author(s), under exclusive license to Springer Nature Switzerland AG 2022
M. Winter, *Banking, Projecting and Politicking in Early Modern England*, Palgrave Studies in Economic History, https://doi.org/10.1007/978-3-030-90570-5_4

83

man of energy and initiative', and as 'prone to highly speculative commercial projects'.[3] These descriptions highlight a divide in the quadripartite partnership, between the adventurous and risky Thompson and Nelthorpe and the unfortunate Farrington and Page who, according to Farrington's account, were unwittingly caught up in their schemes. Although Farrington's Chancery statements are clearly partisan, none of the projects connected to the bank in the 1670s can be directly linked to Farrington or Page. However, both Farrington and Page were partners in the most significant project of them all, the bank itself. This chapter argues that Thompson and Company represents a hybrid of early modern institutions and business models, that whilst outwardly acting as a bank can be better situated and explained as an early modern 'project'.

The previous chapter outlined the extent to which banking evolved in seventeenth-century England, demonstrating the lack of tradition and longevity of financial institutions that indicate an experimental and entrepreneurial culture in English finance, which served as an important context for the establishment of Thompson and Company. The historiography describing new banks and financial ventures often refers to them as 'proposals' or 'schemes' but given their experimental nature they could also fit under the category of 'projects' and, I argue, should be included within a wider historiography of 'projecting' in England.[4] The financial 'schemes' and the bank of Thompson and Company fit well within Yamamoto's wide definition of 'projects', as business initiatives, whether implemented or just proposed, which demonstrate 'the commercial exploitation of useful knowledge and techniques' that were intended both for public benefit and private profit. Although not specifically analysing any banks or banking proposals in his study, Yamamoto does include 'banking proposals', 'banks', and schemes concerned with 'public credit' as examples of projects and argues that the 1660s and 1670s witnessed a large number of 'projects for economic improvement and innovations' due to 'the return of Charles II, the Great Fire, the establishment of the Royal Society, the Anglo-Dutch Wars, and increasing

[3] Withington. *Politics of Commonwealth.* 125; Dzelzainis. Andrew Marvell, Edward Nelthorpe. 20; Burdon. Marvell and His Kindred: The Family Network in the Later Years—II Nelthorpes, Thompsons, and Popples. 176; Smith. *Andrew Marvell.* 240.

[4] Dickson. *Financial Revolution.* 6–7; Horsefield. *British Monetary Experiments.* 94, 95; Wennerlind. *Casualties of Credit.* 95–108; Defoe. *An Essay Upon Projects*; Thirsk. *Economic Policy and Projects.* 1, 9, 11.

colonial trade and real wages amid a stabilising population'. Additionally, according to Yamamoto, the 'culture of projecting changed its institutional outlook' throughout the seventeenth century, 'from predatory monopolies and fiscal experiments under the early Stuarts to business partnerships under the later Stuarts and joint-stock companies in Defoe's projecting Age'.[5] Drawing together the history of financial development and commercial projecting, this chapter argues that Thompson and Company was a project that fits perfectly within this time frame and description as one of the 'business partnerships' that emerged in the Restoration era.

I

Described as 'innovative in theory and entrepreneurial in practice', Thompson and Company were not the first to use fractional reserve banking or written financial instruments and they acted as bankers in the ordinary sense, receiving money as deposits and acting as loan-brokers who lent out their client's money to others at interest.[6] Projecting is often associated with novelty and innovation, but, as Yamamoto and Grassby have argued, innovation and entrepreneurship rarely constitute something wholly new but refer to the use of existing knowledge or practices in different ways.[7] Whilst Thompson and Company did do what banks were designated to do, 'borrow from some in order to lend to others', they added a further speculative aspect to their venture and demonstrate the kind of 'institutional experimentation', which, Ann Carlos and Stephen Nicholas argue, was a growing trend in 'seventeenth-century English overseas trade'.[8] Thompson and Company's innovation and entrepreneurship is therefore evident in the way they combined banking and mercantile trade, acting as intermediaries who took their clients deposits and funnelled them into riskier ventures with the promise

[5] Yamamoto. *Taming Capitalism.* 1, 5, 15, 21, 60, 225.

[6] Withington. *Politics of Commonwealth.* 191. Withington does use the word 'project' here but not in the sense of 'projecting' or in reference to the historiography surrounding it, rather as a synonym for 'business' or 'venture'.

[7] Yamamoto. *Taming Capitalism.* 3; Grassby. *Business Community.* 172.

[8] Melton. *Sir Robert Clayton.* 10; Ann M. Carlos and Stephen Nicholas. 1996. Theory and History: Seventeenth-Century Joint-Stock Chartered Trading Companies. *The Journal of Economic History* 56: 917.

86   M. WINTER

of a steady six per cent return. They did this before the widespread acceptance and rise of 'public subscription' as a way of raising funds for new initiatives and are, therefore, a perfect example of what Yamamoto describes as the 'little-known interface between the culture of projecting and the world of everyday financial credit'.[9]

Whilst the venture was known as a bank and the partners as bankers, the name they used to portray themselves in their pamphlet was Thompson and *Company*. The pamphlet describes the four partners entering 'into a *society* among our selves' and described each partner as 'One of our *company*'.[10] Whilst others most often described Thompson and Company as a bank and the partners as bankers, there are instances when they too used the name Thompson and *Company*. For example, Robert Yard referred to them as 'Thompson and the rest of his company', the churchwardens' inventory of St. Mary Woolchurch referred to a bond from 'Mr Richard Thompson and Company', Fauconberg referred to them as 'Mr Thompson and Company' in his accounts and Turner switched between 'Mr Thompson and Company' and 'Mr Thompson and partners'.[11] There are also a number of instances where the institution was referred to as 'Mr Nelthrope & Company' and 'Mr Nelthorpe & his partners in company'.[12] The use of the word *Company* is significant. As Withington has argued, the term *company*, along with *society*, had a different and more specific meaning in early modern England than in the modern day. Both terms were used as synonyms to describe the same sorts of 'voluntary and purposeful association' and reflected 'a culture of early modern corporatism' that facilitated a 'collective good' or 'collective agency' which was unattainable for the individual and highly beneficial in sharing costs and accessing greater market power.[13] The

---

[9] Yamamoto. *Taming Capitalism*. 134, 170, 229.

[10] *Case of Richard Thompson and Company*. 3, 12.

[11] *Letters Addressed to Sir Joseph Williamson*. vol. 2. No. 148—From Robert Yard. 81–83; LMA: P69/MRY15/B/013/MS01009. Churchwardens' vouchers; BL: Add MS 41255. Note-Book of Thomas Belasyse. f. 15; LMA: CLC/509/MS05105. Book of sales. ff. 16–32.

[12] POST 94/19. *Letter book, Ireland*. 57; POST 94/17. *Letter book, England*. 47; BL: IOR/B/32. Court Minutes. 22 April 1672–10 April 1674. f. 153.

[13] Phil Withington. 2010. *Society in Early Modern England: The Vernacular Origins of Some Powerful Ideas*. Cambridge: Polity Press. 104–105, 116; Regina Grafe and Oscar Gelderblom. 2010. The Rise and Fall of the Merchant Guilds: Re-thinking the

term *company*, however, was usually associated with chartered mercantile 'trading companies', 'Urban corporations and common councils', and 'theatrical' companies.[14] Further linking company to commerce, Ian Anders Gadd and Patrick Wallis defined 'companies' as 'places to develop the loose networks of sociability and association which allowed the mercantile economy to function'.[15] The use of the word *company* intimated commercial rather than simply financial activities, and whilst there were plenty of mercantile trading companies, none of the banks or financial institutions prior or contemporary to Thompson and Company—such as the famous goldsmith-banks of Backwell, Vyner, and Hoare or the scrivener-bank of Clayton and Morris—used the word 'company' or engaged in mercantile trade. Therefore, even the name links Thompson and Company to a broader mercantile or commercial culture, which is viewed as separate to the financial culture of the period.

The *company* aspect of the venture is evident from the articles of agreement, which state that alongside the bank the partners were permitted to carry out additional mercantile ventures using the bank stock which in turn would enable the partners to pay interest on their creditors' deposits. As they described it, once creditors had chosen to 'imploy their money in our hands' the partners would then embark on 'several advantagious or probable Trades', which would allow them to meet their 'Obligations to so many worthy Persons'.[16] The articles of agreement outline exactly how this trade worked, with each partner permitted to withdraw sums of money for their own business interests outside of the bank, provided they return the original amount plus interest.[17] Therefore, the bankers were essentially loaning to themselves—acting as both creditor and debtor in the same transaction. This differs from previous descriptions of the bank, such as Richards' description that 'The deposits were invested in various

---

Comparative Study of Commercial Institutions in Premodern Europe. *The Journal of Interdisciplinary History* 40: 488.

[14] Phil Withington. 2007. Company and Sociability in Early Modern England. *Social History* 32: 298.

[15] Gadd and Wallis. Introduction. 10.

[16] *Case of Richard Thompson and Company.* 3–4.

[17] TNA: C 7/581/73.

88   M. WINTER

trading enterprises, and the depositors received joint bonds as securities'.[18] Instead, the partners were operating outwardly as a bank, not only taking in deposits but giving out loans to debtors and dealing in instruments of foreign and domestic exchange. Their outward role as a bank is also evident from the fact that the partners offered interest payments on deposits rather than a share of the profits, the latter being the normal procedure for subscribed to mercantile ventures of the kind described by Richards. The partners' own business ventures were funded by loans to themselves that carried the same rules, regulations, and interest rates as the loans they extended to customers. The interest they paid back to the bank on their own loans, along with the interest paid on customers' loans, would then provide a fund from which they could pay interest on deposits. Their own separate trade was therefore an addition to the bank, a distinct yet financially intertwined merchant partnership that saw them dealing across 'Spaine Italy Portugall & ffrance' in 'Wine, that of Silk, that to Russia, parts of East-India Shipping, the private Trade to East-India, Lead-Mines, the Irish Manufactures' as well as foreign 'Exchange'.[19]

Thompson and Company was therefore a hybrid of various seventeenth-century business models, which complicates its place within the history of English finance. The confusion over Thompson and Company's institutional identity is evident in the Chancery material, which regularly refers to the 'joynt banke', 'joynt partners', and 'common bank'. Given the varying and vague descriptions used, it is no surprise that the bank has been labelled in various conflicting ways in previous scholarship. The constant reference to 'joint', for example, suggests that Thompson and Company was similar to a joint-stock company, which sold shares to create a joint stock that was used to fund ventures by company merchants. The profit from these ventures would then be shared out amongst shareholders. The Chancery proceedings also refer to each partners' individual and 'distinct' trading account, which was funded by the bank stock but the profit derived was for their own individual benefit. Operating in this way suggests a similarity to a regulated company, which was 'comprised of overseas merchants trading on their own accounts according to collective regulations' set up by a 'governing

---

[18] Richards. *Early History of Banking.* 16 n.1.

[19] TNA: C 6/526/178; C 10/484/71; *Case of Richard Thompson and Company.* 4.

body'.[20] However, Thompson and Company was neither a joint stock nor a regulated company. Most significantly, Thompson and Company did not possess a charter, did not have membership qualifications, and were too small in number to be counted amongst such institutions. Instead, the mercantile aspect of the venture resembles a merchant partnership. Richards recognised Thompson and Company as a 'partnership of merchants' in the 1920s and, more recently, Smith identified them as a 'partnership of several merchants' and Withington as 'a partnership of citizens'.[21] Despite this recognition, however, what exactly a merchant partnership was or how Thompson and Company operated as one have not been explored.

Private merchant partnerships are a common, yet little discussed form of business association in early modern England.[22] Private merchant partnerships were typically small firms that were not in possession of a charter granted by the monarch but operated under a set of articles of agreement, which they drew up themselves. Partnerships were formed to maximise profits, exploit new commodities and territories, expand each individual partner's geographical reach and commercial network, and mitigate risks. Individuals chose partners according to their 'proven talents or obvious assets', which would allow them to 'compete more effectively on a national and international basis'.[23] Whilst in general partnership all partners contributed to the management and organisation of the business, partnerships were 'usually dominated by one individual' and the 'ordering of names' was important as it signified who the chief figure within the firm was.[24] In the case of Thompson and Company, then, Thompson was clearly the chief, and the institution fits more widely with the common tropes of a merchant partnership. In his complaint to Chancery in 1684,

---

[20] TNA: C 7/581/73; C 6/283/87; Ogilvie. *Institutions and European Trade*. 36; Leng. Interlopers and disorderly brethren. 824.

[21] Richards. *Early History of Banking*. 16 n.1; Smith. *Andrew Marvell*. 240; Withington. *The Politics of Commonwealth*. 192.

[22] Grassby. *Business Community*. 401; Pierre Gervais. 2017. In Union There Was Strength: The Legal Protection of Eighteenth-Century Merchant Partnerships in England and France. In *Market Ethics and Practices, c. 1300–1850*, eds Simon Middleton and James E. Shaw, 166–183. Oxford: Routledge.

[23] Hancock. *Citizens of the World*. 105, 106, 107; Gauci. *Emporium of the World*. 84.

[24] Bram Von Hoftstraeten. 2016. The Organization of Mercantile Capitalism in the Low Countries: Private Partnerships in Early Modern Antwerp (1480–1620). *TSEG* 13: 11; Grassby. *Business Community*. 401; Gauci. *Emporium of the World*. 103.

90 M. WINTER

John Farrington described how each partner and prior two-way partnerships had their own talents and contacts. Farrington stated that he and Page dealt in 'divers particular wares & merchandyes in parts beyond the sea', and that Thompson and Nelthorpe did 'deale together in partnershipp in wines and other comodities'. He further emphasised that each partner was believed to have 'money', 'stock', and 'a good esteme in the world'. Collectively their aim was 'drawing in the world' of 'whatever would unquestionably turne to a great amount of profitt'.[25] This statement highlights the fact that each partner was recruited to 'draw' in a different aspect of world trade through his own resources and assets for their collective benefit.

As well as having the possibility to turn a great profit through collectivisation, however, partnerships were also notoriously risky.[26] Unlike joint-stock and regulated companies, partnerships had little protection at law. They were private contracts between a specific group of individuals who were personally liable for their collective debts and whose creditors could seize company and personal assets if they failed.[27] There was also an unreliable human element to partnerships, as partners could attempt to defraud one another, and relationships could break down. In the case of Thompson and Company, their collective identity broke down under the pressure of insolvency and the partners began to blame each other for their collective predicament.

The merchant partnership of Thompson and Company was further complicated by the fact that it was not a closed partnership. Their four-way partnership was an open partnership, in which Thompson, Nelthorpe, Farrington, and Page were all permitted to trade outside of the banking venture and develop other partnerships and associations, which were more casual and only operated for a singular venture or contract. They did this using 'factors': professionals working on commission who, unlike formal partnerships, had an informal and flexible relationship with the commissioning merchant and worked for them on an ad hoc basis.[28] A factor would communicate trade news from abroad and regularly act as 'a

[25] TNA: C 7/581/73.

[26] Earle. *Making of the English Middle Class.* 111; Grassby. *Business Community.* 402.

[27] Giuseppe Dari-Mattiacci, Oscar Gelderblom, Joost Jonker, and Enrico C. Perotti. 2017. The Emergence of the Corporate Form. *The Journal of Law, Economics, and Organization* 33: 195, 201.

[28] Leng. *Fellowship and Freedom.* 46, 69, 74.

4 AN EARLY MODERN 'PROJECT' 91

bank for his clients', with the commissioning merchant and their clients drawing on them for money, meaning cash did not need to travel overseas.[29] Farrington gave several examples of factors used by the partners in Chancery and even explained their utility (see Table 4.1). In the 1683 case between Farrington and James Nelthorpe, Farrington stated that he drew on factors 'beyond the seas' to repay a debt to James Nelthorpe in 1676, when the bank was experiencing difficulties and could not simply remit the money at the shop.[30] In the 1684 case of the Bordeaux agents, William Popple and Robert Stewart, Farrington stated that he and Nelthorpe 'desired' the 'assistance' of Popple and Stewart in transmitting some goods and money away from their 'most remote' places of trading 'to drive a trade in France Ireland & other parts adjacent'. They requested Popple and Stewart's assistance because they believed them to have 'better correspondencyes in diverse of those Countrys' and so 'could more easily & speedily gett the said effects transmitted'.[31] Popple's wife, Mary, also referred to a variety of associates of the bank partners in a letter she wrote to Edward Nelthorpe in 1677. However, she only referred to these individuals and partnerships by their initials. Mary stated that 'G & G hath accepted your first bill', that she had 'writ to DC ... but have yet noe answer', that 'S & B will not remit any more money nor suffer me to draw upon them', that she 'will be mindfull of AR's commission of Christall tartar', and that 'In JF busynesse there is nothing new'.[32] Without further details, these individuals and partnerships are unidentifiable. However, the named factors, detailed in the Table 4.1, give a better idea of the breadth and depth of the partners' trading networks in the 1670s. This is not an exhaustive list of Thompson and Company's other partners and factors, but it goes some way to showing how prevalent these additional short-term agreements were.

The wider prevalence of merchant partnerships is well attested in Gerard Malynes *Law Merchant*, in which he identified two forms of 'Associations' through which trade was conducted. The first was formed 'by publicke authoritie of Princes or States, upon Graunts made by Letters

---

[29] Hancock. *Citizens of the World.* 128.

[30] TNA: C 10/484/71; C 7/581/73.

[31] TNA: C 6/526/178.

[32] Hertfordshire Archives and Local Studies: DE/P/F81/77. Letter from Mary Popple to Edward Nelthorpe. 26 June 1677.

92   M. WINTER

Table 4.1   Factors of Thompson and Company

Name	Location	Year drawn on	Money	Goods	Transmitted to
John Ivatt	Aleppo, Syria	1676	Bill of Exchange for 800 dollars or £192 16s 8d		James Nelthorpe senior
Thomas Johnson	Fort St. George, India	1676	Bill of Exchange for 1000 dollars or £256		James Nelthorpe senior
Thomas Patten	Port St. Maria, Spain	1677	1000 Crownes (c.£250)	Plus, goods worth £2000	Popple and Stewart
Robert Ball & Francis Gosfright	Leghorn (Livorno), Italy	1677	Bill of 1500 Crownes (c.£375) and another for 2000 dollars (c.£500)		Popple and Stewart
George Davies	Naples, Italy	1677	Bill of 400 dollars (c.£100)		Popple and Stewart
Robert Welch & George Stiles	Genoa, Italy	1677		Goods amounting to £800	Popple and Stewart
Alexander Southerland	Wales	1677		Goods and services amounting to £500	Popple and Stewart
Barnard Mervin & Thomas Monsch	Lisbon, Portugal	1677		Goods and services amounting to £400	Popple and Stewart
Blackwood & Blare	Scotland	1677	Bills amounting to £184		Popple and Stewart

Source TNA: Chancery C 10/484/71, Farrington v Nelthorpe, 12 April 1683 and TNA: Chancery C 6/526/178, Farrington v Popple and Stewart, 31 March 1684. Exchange rates: 1 Crown = 5 shillings. Dollars done on the rough calculation from John Farrington's calculations in the 1683 court case: 4 dollars = £1

Patents' and 'properly called Societies', such as the chartered Merchant Adventurers, the East India, Levant, Virginia, and Bermuda companies. The second association was formed 'by and between Merchants of their owne authoritie, ioyning themselues together for to deale and trade either for yeares or voyages' and 'properly called Partnership'.[33] As a form of business association, therefore, partnerships were second only to the large companies that traded with Europe and the East. Aside from the Virginia Company, trade and colonialism in the West was largely expanded on the basis of partnerships, particularly merchant–planter partnerships.[34] As a more corporate form of business association, and playing an important part in empire building, historians have identified partnerships as playing a key role in the transition to modern capitalism.[35]

The broader significance of partnerships makes the lack of discussion surrounding them even more surprising. Lack of scholarly attention appears to arise from the poor survival rate of written agreements, the often-short existence of such ventures, and the fact that many partnerships were formed through oral agreements only. However, many partnerships, like Thompson and Company, ended in disputes and disorder, and many entered formal legal proceedings. The reconstruction of Thompson and Company using Chancery proceedings reveals some of the formal, not extant, agreements that underpinned their partnership, how it worked in practice, and why it ultimately failed. Another partnership was also revealed in the previous chapter, that of creditor Francis Savile, and many more such legal cases can be found in the Chancery proceedings. This chapter, along with the reconstruction of Thompson and Company in Chapter 2, highlights the potential of such methodology to reconstruct other partnerships from this period and uncover the wider culture surrounding this important form of association.

---

[33] Gerard Malynes. 1622. *Consuetudo, vel lex mercatoria, or the ancient law-merchant.* London. 210–211.

[34] Earle. *Making of the English Middle Class.* 111; Brenner. *Merchants and Revolution.* 95, 104.

[35] Dari-Mattiacci, Gelderblom, Jonker, and Perotti. The Emergence of the Corporate Form. 225; Francesca Trivellato. 2020. Renaissance Florence and the Origins of Capitalism: A Business History of Perspective. *Business History Review* 94: 239.

94 M. WINTER

II

Operating as an open partnership meant that whilst the bank itself was a project, it could also act as a base from which Thompson and Nelthorpe could develop and fund a network of other joint and singular projects. This was useful because, as Yamamoto argues, seventeenth-century projects struggled to secure investment, partly due to coin shortage but also because 'backers were careful not to waste money on "projects" that might turn out to be unsuccessful or even deceitful'.[36] The 'bank' of Thompson and Company gave the partners a way around this. It provided an opportunity to access the capital of others without having to persuade them of the potential benefits or profits arising from each of their 'projects'. All the partners' commercial projects were funded by a publicly subscribed-to stock—their creditor's deposits. How far creditors were aware of this is unclear. By using the established label and financial instruments of a 'bank', which pointed to the traditional gold-smith and scrivener institutions, the partnership provided creditors with a written promise that they could demand the return of their money whenever they wished and engendered trust in their project through association with familiar practices and institutions.

One of the most significant projects undertaken jointly between Nelthorpe and Thompson was their negotiation of a Prize goods contract from the King in 1673, which consisted of the contents of four Dutch East India ships captured during the Third Anglo-Dutch War and were the subject of a Chancery case in 1676.[37] The Prize goods contract will be discussed further in Chapter 8. Although Thompson and Nelthorpe may have embarked on other projects, evidence suggests that Nelthorpe was the most active 'projector' in the 1660s and 1670s. Alongside his new bank partnership, Nelthorpe maintained his previous trading connections and embarked on a variety of his 'owne distinct' trading activities in the 1670s.[38] In 1672 Nelthorpe and fellow Merchant Adventurer, and future director of the Royal African Company, Francis Townely were trading in wine and Brandy between France, Stockholm, and London.[39]

---

[36] Yamamoto. *Taming Capitalism.* 140, 157.

[37] Jones. *Anglo-Dutch Wars.* 212; TNA: C 8/296/106.

[38] TNA: C 7/581/73.

[39] William A. Shaw. 1909. *Calendar of Treasury Books Preserved in the Public Record Office,* vol. 4, *1672–1675.* London: His Majesty's Stationery Office. 37, 38; TNA: T

4 AN EARLY MODERN 'PROJECT'   95

This trade must have brought him into contact with Alexander Waddell, a Scottish merchant in Stockholm who fell into difficulties in 1672 after acting as an agent for another London partnership, Marescoe-Joye, who extended him more credit than they had the means to support. Not being able to retrieve his money, Waddell was declared a 'Fugitive Bankrupt of Sweden' and 'given no choice but transfer his London stocks to another agent, Edward Nelthorp'.[40] As well as trade with Sweden, Nelthorpe also secured a contract to provide the Navy with 30 tons of 'good sound merchentable' French wine vinegar in 1672.[41] Therefore, as allowed by the partners' articles of agreement, Nelthorpe frequently acted and traded on his own account when opportunities arose. Of the four partners, he appears to have had the most available capital to put into alternative ventures, the widest variety of trading connections, and the entrepreneurial ideas needed to put his economic and social capital to use. Therefore, Farrington's claim that the bank was the brainchild of Nelthorpe, and to a lesser extent Thompson, seems accurate, as does his claim that Nelthorpe was an 'adventurous' man who took on a variety of 'hazardous' and risky ventures.

However, as well as taking risks Nelthorpe also obtained some key markers of credit and reputation in London's trade and manufacturing circles. Yamamoto has identified inventions and obtaining letters patent for inventions as one of the key outputs and identifying markers of a projector, and one that gave them greater credibility in their proposals and schemes.[42] In the post-Restoration era, the increase in inventions and projecting activities was supported by the instigation of the Royal Society of London, which Nelthorpe became a member of in 1666.[43]

70/601. Company of Royal Adventurers Trading with Africa. Home Ledger 3, 1678–1680. f. 30.

[40] Henry Roseveare. 1987. *Markets and Merchants of the Late Seventeenth Century: The Marescoe-David Letters, 1668–1680.* Oxford: Oxford University Press. 126, 128; Order in Council on the petition of William Strangh, citizen and merchant of London. *SPO* SP 29/370 f. 284, 19 May 1675.

[41] Contract by Edward Nelthorp with the Navy Commissioners, for delivering 30 tuns of vinegar, made of French wines, at 14*l*. 10*s*. per tun. *SPO*, SP 29/325 f. 135, 25 May 1672.

[42] Defoe. *Essay Upon Projects.* 6, 14, 33, 35; Yamamoto. *Taming Capitalism.* 15, 29, 35–37, 237.

[43] Yamamoto. *Taming Capitalism.* 180, 183; Birch, *The History of the Royal Society of London for Improving of Natural Knowledge.* 97, 99, 243, 302.

96 M. WINTER

The reason behind Nelthorpe's membership of the Society is evident from an invention of his patented in 1677 for 14 years of 'a certaine engine or mill for the hulling of black pepper and barley'.[44] As the patent was entered as the bank was failing, and to avoid it being affected by the commission of bankruptcy, it was submitted under the name of Nelthorpe's business associate Charles Milson. Nelthorpe most likely developed the mill in a factory of his in Caversham, Oxford, which produced 'Pearle Barley or French Barley'.[45] Aside from Caversham, Farrington stated that Nelthorpe had many other factories in 'remote' places, such as a 'woollen & silke' factory in Ireland, a factory in 'Mosco', and another in 'Narva', Estonia.[46] The factories at Moscow and Narva are untraceable, but significant evidence of the factory project in Clonmel, Ireland, survives in the correspondence of James Butler, duke of Ormond, who acted as a patron to the project. In October 1674 Nelthorpe wrote to Ormond, explaining that he had been 'encouraged by some intelligent clothiers to set up a considerable manufactory in Ireland' to further the woollen industry. Nelthorpe was putting up a stock of between £30 and £40, part funded by the bank, and it was claimed that the manufacture would be of both private and public benefit. It would be a 'great service' to Ormond personally and, as the factory would provide 'employment for a great many idle poor people', it would also be 'an advantage to the whole country'. In return for Nelthorpe's stock and manufacture, Ormond was to provide 'convenient work-houses and dwelling-houses in Clonmel ... without paying any rent for twenty-one years' and allowing English workers employed by Nelthorpe 'their freedoms and liberties in Clonmel ... without charge'.[47]

The factory in Ireland perfectly demonstrates how Nelthorpe's projecting activities interacted with the bank and the risks associated with indirectly funding projects using creditors' deposits. Evidence for this is found in a series of letters between Edward Nelthorpe and Ormond's half-brother, Captain George Matthews. In May 1676, two months after the bank fell into difficulties and two years after the factory project began,

[44] 1876. *Patents for Inventions. Abridgments of Specifications Relating to Grinding Grain and Dressing Flour and Meal, A.D. 1623–1886.* London. 3.

[45] TNA: C 7/510/27. Poyntz v Nelthorpe. December 1673.

[46] TNA: C 7/581/73.

[47] Royal Commission on Historical Manuscripts. 1912. *Calendar of the manuscripts of the Marquess of Ormond, K. P. Preserved at Kilkenny Castle,* vol. 3. London. 352–354.

Nelthorpe informed Matthews that he was concerned his assets in Ireland might be 'seized' as they were 'threatened withal'. Of particular concern to Nelthorpe were the actions of Sir John Temple, who was attempting 'to secure his moneys' through seizure of the factory in Clonmel. This suggests that Temple was a creditor of Thompson and Company, who was aware of the partners' additional projecting activities. Fearing the loss of his money in the London bank, Temple decided to reclaim his money through one of the projects Nelthorpe had embarked on using bank funds. Given the fact that limited liability did not apply to partnerships at this time, Temple possibly viewed himself as a sort of stockholder in the factory. According to Nelthorpe, 'Should [Temple] attempt and succeed in his design others will be encouraged to use the same course, and I dread the fatal consequences'. These fatal consequences involved his business in London at the bank. Nelthorpe informed Matthews that 'Most of our creditors have signed', by which he meant that Thompson and Company's creditors had signed an agreement to settle their debt informally outside of court. He wrote that 'if such a misfortune should happen to me in Ireland as the seizure of my effects, besides the ruin it menaces that affair withal, it would also have a malign influence against it', referring to the bank in London and the composition that had been offered. Although the factory was Nelthorpe's project, it was bank-financed and therefore at risk from creditors who knew about its existence, such as Sir John Temple. To placate Temple, Nelthorpe enlisted Mr. John Morphy, a merchant of Waterford, who owed 'considerably more' to Nelthorpe than Nelthorpe did to Temple, as a third party 'of known ability and reputation' to act as security for him. Despite Nelthorpe's attempts to save the factory, however, in March 1677 he sold it to 'Mr Nic. White'.[48] The partners, explaining their decision to sell the factory in their pamphlet, stated that one of them had 'published a journey for Ireland' to 'gather in Debts and dispose of that Manufacture, because it was most ready at hand' and 'of the greatest improvement'.[49] Despite the sale of the

---

[48] Toby Barnard. 2008. Butler, James, first duke of Ormond (1610–1688). *ODNB* https://doi-org.sheffield.idm.oclc.org/10.1093/ref:odnb/4191. Accessed 10 January 2020; Royal Commission on Historical Manuscripts. 1912. *Calendar of the Manuscripts of the Marquess of Ormond, K. P. Preserved at Kilkenny Castle*, vol. 4. London. 11–12, 20–21.

[49] *Case of Richard Thompson and Company*. 12.

98 M. WINTER

factory, however, the bank collapsed and was issued with a commission of bankruptcy.

III

The above discussion has highlighted that certain creditors, like Sir John Temple, were clearly aware of the projecting activities of the bank of Thompson and Company and used it against them once they ran into difficulties. This brings into question how the wider body of creditors viewed the bank, what financial activity they thought they were getting involved in, and the extent of their knowledge of the workings of the institution. The 1679 Chancery case entered by creditors of Thompson and Company, the two creditors' pamphlets, and other surviving source material written by creditors or contemporaries can provide some insight. However, it is difficult to establish creditors' level of understanding of the financial practices they engaged in. This is because surviving sources written by creditors or contemporaries were often written retrospectively at the time of economic troubles or collapse, which influences how they portray themselves and the level of their involvement in or portrayed knowledge of the situation. As Todd argues, in some contexts creditors could deliberately represent themselves as naïve to suggest they had been taken advantage of, whereas in other contexts they could assert their knowledge in order to prosecute or convict the debtor of fraud or negligence.[50] As the writer or writers of the two creditors' pamphlets are unknown, and the Chancery case was probably led by a small group of those 211 named who merely recruited the rest to join in their endeavours, the exact motivation behind these sources is unclear. Additionally, both the pamphlets were published, and the Chancery case entered into, after the partners' published their own pamphlet detailing some of their activities. Thus, it is possible that knowledge of the partners business activities only emerged to the majority of creditors in 1677. These sources are not therefore representative of the entire body of creditors and can offer no individual responses or opinions. However, the pamphlet and the Chancery case are evidence that at least some people were aware of the business operation of Thompson and Company, and that this information subsequently became public knowledge through these means.

[50] Todd. Fiscal Citizens. 57.

Both the pamphlets written by anonymous creditors and the 1679 Chancery case suggest that at least some of the creditors knew how the business worked. The second creditors' pamphlet states that the partners were engaged 'in taking up and giving Security for great summs of Moneys', like a bank, and that the partners 'did as all other Merchants imploy their Moneys in Foreign parts in the most probable trades', like a merchant partnership. It argues that the 'Security' offered by the partners, the fractional reserve, 'was made good by them for above five years' and that 'no man all that time was refused either Principle or Interest when demanded'. The partners engaged in additional mercantile trade, according to the pamphlet, in order 'to enable them to pay interest' on creditors' deposits. The pamphlet writer, or writers, even acknowledged that upon their insolvency, the partners began to draw in their 'Effects at home or abroad', probably referring to assets like Nelthorpe's factory, to pay their petitioning creditors.[51]

The first creditors' pamphlet is less concerned with justifying the procedures of the bank and the actions of its partners than the second pamphlet. Instead, it focusses on the commission of bankruptcy and persuading other creditors to put an end to it for the benefit of them all. However, the pamphlet does recognise certain aspects of Thompson and Company's business. For example, the writer, or writers, state that the partners extended their 'estate', or stock, through their trade as 'Merchants that trade beyond the seas'. It also reveals that creditors received a good deal of information at the meetings the partners set up to discuss compositions. The creditors had view of the partners' books and the partners gave them an 'Account of losses' of the bank, which detailed what the losses were and that they amounted to about £90,000.[52] The complainants in the 1679 case of the creditors similarly recognised that Thompson and Company were 'acteing & tradeing in Company togeather & upon theire joynt stocke', suggesting that they were 'acteing' as a bank and 'tradeing' as merchants.[53] Both creditors' pamphlets and the 1679 case suggest that at least some of the creditors' could have been aware of the hybrid nature of Thompson and Company

---

[51] *Reasons most humbly offered to the consideration of Parliament.*

[52] *Reasons offered by several of the creditors of Richard Thompson and partners.*

[53] TNA: C 8/328/50.

and knew, to some extent, the kind of organisation into which they were putting their money, or certainly did from 1677 onwards.

The response of the creditors to the collapse of the bank in the pamphlets and court cases also reveal that the partners' additional projects had become a point of conflict since their collapse. In order to put their projects into action, projectors had to show that their endeavours were for public benefit as well as private gain. The term projector accrued negative connotations because some projects were set up purely for private gain and gained notoriety for 'draining money from investors', which is exemplified in the case of Thompson and Company by Farrington's negative testimony about Thompson's schemes to become 'suddainly rich'.[54] Defoe's *Essay Upon Projects* demonstrates the delicate balance between positive and negative depictions of the projector, distinguishing between the honest and dishonest projector. The 'Honest' projector was one whose projects were based on 'Ingenuity and Improvement' for public benefit, whereas the 'Dishonest' projector thrived on 'pretences', seeking only personal profit.[55] The problem for projectors and entrepreneurs was that if their venture failed, for any reason, petitioning creditors could draw on the negative discourse of projecting and private interest. Thompson and Company's creditors did exactly that upon the collapse of the bank. The second creditors' pamphlet states that the partners were accused by certain creditors of putting money into 'several Factories beyond the seas' so that it would be 'beyond the reach and power of any Commission of Bankrupt'. Interestingly, this pamphlet refers to the bank throughout as 'Richard Thompson and partners' rather than using the partners' own term 'company'.[56] This could be simply the personal preference of the writer, or it could be a specific recognition of the merchant partnership aspect of the venture, which had created additional animosity between the partners and their creditors since the collapse of the bank. The petitioning creditors in the 1679 Chancery case made the same accusation. The creditors argued that the partners had 'placed the Bulk of theire Estates in

---

[54] Slack. *Invention of Improvement*. 53, 104; Yamamoto. *Taming Capitalism*. 2, 3, 130, 140; TNA: C 7/581/73.

[55] Defoe. *Essay Upon Projects*. 10–13.

[56] *Reasons most humbly offered to the consideration of Parliament*.

4 AN EARLY MODERN 'PROJECT'   101

fforeaigne partes & out of the reach & power of the Laws of this Kingdome of England', further demonstrating that the partners' additional
projects had become a rallying point for criticism and legal action.[57]

IV

This chapter has revealed the hybrid nature of Thompson and Company,
which combined an early fractional reserve bank with a merchant partnership in what can best be described as a seventeenth-century 'project'.
The hybridity of Thompson and Company, providing services concurrent with contemporary banking institutions but also using the term
company and carrying out various trading exploits under the model of a
merchant partnership, clearly point to a different kind of institution that
combined different aspects of seventeenth-century business models. That
the institution was known as a 'bank' but operated as a multifaceted partnership or project suggests a lack of distinction between different kinds
of credit facilitating institutions in seventeenth century England and a
willingness amongst the population to explore different financial options
and entrepreneurial enterprises. However, like many other contemporary
projects, Thompson and Company struggled to maintain the delicate
balance between public good and private profit, and eventually their
projecting schemes were used against them in public discourse and in
the law courts. The case of Thompson and Company demonstrates that
financial schemes did get put into practice by entrepreneurial individuals,
and that these schemes were not only directed at public finance but at
private finance as well. The institution was aimed at aiding the problems
of everyday credit whilst also allowing its partners to make a profit. It
therefore suggests that the historiography of commercial projecting and
financial schemes should not be treated separately by historians but should
be treated as complementary, often overlapping phenomena.

Additionally, through acting as a collective, or *company*, Thompson
and Company represent a shift towards institutional as opposed to
interpersonal credit. Across the seventeenth century, both finance and
commerce witnessed a move towards more corporate, collective models.
In finance, the shift took place from the more interpersonal goldsmith
banks, which were in most cases run by one individual, towards the

---

[57] TNA: C 8/328/50.

102   M. WINTER

more corporate nature of the financial institutions of the 1690s.[58] The same is true for commerce and mercantile ventures, which also witnessed the emergence of more frequent and 'greater associations' across the seventeenth century alongside the already dominant chartered trading companies.[59] Thompson and Company combined these financial and commercial developments in one institution, demonstrating the importance of experiment and the lack of defined institutional identity in pre-1690s England.

The first three chapters have reconstructed, resituated, and re-evaluated the institution that was Thompson and Company, revealing it to have been a multifaceted project that reflects greater trends in the commercial and financial development of early modern England, but was entrepreneurial in its combination of banking and mercantile trade. The following chapters turn to focus more on the social and political aspects of Thompson and Company, revealing the wider family networks that fostered the skills necessary to embark on such a venture, the social composition of the bank's customers, and how and why the institution collapsed in 1678.

[58] Muldrew. *Economy of Obligation.* 115, 116; Wennerlind. *Casualties of Credit.* 95–96; Michael J. Braddick. 2000. *State Formation in Early Modern England c.1550–1700.* Cambridge: Cambridge University Press. 259–260.

[59] Gauci. *Politics of Trade.* 107.

CHAPTER 5

Family Network

In March 1656 Henry Thompson, York wine merchant and aldermen, wrote to his brother Stephen, who was conducting the family business as a factor in Bordeaux, to inform him of some recent business developments. Henry states that he has 'sent Ned to Yarmouth about' their business as he has 'a letter of credit to a friend theire to assist him in the businesse' and expects to hear from him 'next weeke'. Towards the end of the same letter, Henry writes of Stephen securing some business in London, in which he hopes 'my cozen Thompson may serve yow'.[1] This letter, along with the others in Henry Thompson's letter book from the years 1652–1657, provide evidence of a large family network that was both socially and economically intertwined. 'Ned' was the name used by members of the Thompson family to refer to their cousin Edward Nelthorpe and 'cozen Thompson' was Lieutenant Colonel Robert Thompson, a confectioner of London and father of Richard Thompson. Throughout Henry Thompson's letter book many other Thompson and Nelthorpe relatives appear as recipients and subjects of his letters. The previous chapter argued that Thompson and Company was an early modern project that combined the provision of everyday credit with a profit-seeking, high-risk

[1] HHC: U DDFA/37/5. Journal of Henry Thompson at Bordeaux. Letter to Stephen 8 March 1656.

© The Author(s), under exclusive license to Springer Nature Switzerland AG 2022
M. Winter, *Banking, Projecting and Politicking in Early Modern England*, Palgrave Studies in Economic History, https://doi.org/10.1007/978-3-030-90570-5_5

103

104   M. WINTER

mercantile partnership, and facilitated the funding and operation of many other projects. This chapter demonstrates that, in addition to being a multifaceted project, Thompson and Company was part of an even wider web of mercantile businesses that connected London to York, Hull, and Scarborough, as well as abroad to Bordeaux and Amsterdam. Whilst these businesses were distinct, each with their own capital and goods, they relied on each other for news, services, and support, and all stemmed from the same core family group.

The Thompson family of York has been described as one of the city's 'most important merchant dynasties', who dominated both trade and politics in the seventeenth century. The merchants of the family traded primarily in wine and cloth, and were councillors, aldermen, mayors, and MPs of their respective cities. They intermarried with other successful trading and political families in their local area and built up their estates over time by purchasing rural residences but retained city addresses for trade and political purposes. The Thompson family can therefore be viewed as a 'dynastic family', a concept which has been defined by Alan Everitt as 'the core of dominant families' in provincial society 'who for one reason or another came to form the focus of influence within it' dominating and shaping politics, trade, and local society. Similar concepts have been identified by Anne Mitson, who focussed on the parish and local officeholding, and Lewis Namier, whose focus was on the county and national political roles as MPs. The concept of 'dynastic' families has also been attributed to trading families by Grassby in his concept of the 'business family' or 'family firm', which acted as a 'holding company' distributing and transferring wealth and property across the generations to fund various discontinuous businesses linked by their common kinship connection. Whilst politics features in Grassby's model as a way for an individual to enhance their family's status, political roles are also viewed as a potentially damaging pursuit that could undermine the business family, as it privileged personal over family values.[2] This chapter highlights the

---

[2] Gauci. *Politics of Trade*. 147; Alan Everitt. 1985. *Landscape and Community in England*. London: A&C Black. 312; Anne Mitson. 1993. The Significance of Kinship Networks in the Seventeenth Century: South-West Nottinghamshire. In *Societies, Cultures and Kinship 1580–1850*, ed. C. Phythian-Adams. Leicester: Leicester University Press; Sir Lewis Namier. 1960. *The Structure of Politics at the Accession of George III*. 2nd edn. London: Macmillan; Richard Grassby. 2001. *Kinship and Capitalism: Marriage, Family, and Business in the English-Speaking World, 1580–1740*. Cambridge: Cambridge University Press. 3, 262, 269, 358, 382, 402.

Thompson family's successful combination of all these traits of 'dynastic' families, providing a commercial, political, and economic backdrop for the careers of Edward Nelthorpe and Richard Thompson, and for the establishment of Thompson and Company as a hybrid financial and mercantile institution.

Existing scholarship on Thompson and Company has predominantly focused on the partners' kinship connection to Andrew Marvell, at the expense of other important familial networks that influenced the partners' financial, commercial, and political lives through the provision of capital, skills, and contacts. It is important to note that early modern notions of family are not the same as modern concepts and did not necessarily rely on ties of 'blood and marriage' but were flexible and could refer to blood-relatives, relatives by marriage, and those who were not relatives in the modern meaning of family at all.[3] In terms of politics and business, the genealogical proximity between kin was less important than the services they could provide, and distant kin could take a much more prominent role in an individual's life than immediate kin due to their mutual interests. As little can be discovered about the wider kinship networks of Farrington and Page, this chapter focusses primarily on the Thompson and Nelthorpe family networks. It demonstrates the importance of examining the wider socio-economic background of a business venture and how the four partners' backgrounds shaped the venture known as Thompson and Company.

I

In order to understand how Thompson and Company's partners acquired the necessary skills and capital to embark on such a risky venture it is crucial to examine their wider kinship network. Kin were fundamental in organising early education, facilitating apprenticeships, providing commercial connections, and offering economic and social support. The importance of kinship networks for 'merchant success' has been particularly emphasised, as 'family reputation and credit' could provide vital contacts and security for new entrants in the trade and 'bonds of family

---

[3] Naomi Tadmor. 2001. *Family and Friends in Eighteenth-Century England: Household, Kinship, and Patronage*. Cambridge: Cambridge University Press. 106, 123, 125, 150.

obligation and solidarity could be brought to bear to reinforce commercial relationships'.[4] Such networks could also facilitate the transmission of credit through established contacts and the positive reputation associated with a name. Therefore, the reputation and credit of an individual's wider kinship network affected their own status.

The most significant kinship connection in the partners' networks was Richard Thompson and Edward Nelthorpe's link to the Thompsons of York, whose wealth and credit derived from the 'wine trade and through small lending' in the seventeenth century.[5] Most important in this family network for the banking partners were the brothers Sir Henry and Edward Thompson, whose mercantile and political connections were a useful source of prestige and assistance throughout Richard Thompson and Edward Nelthorpe's careers. Henry and Edward were both wine merchants and members of York's mercantile companies, of which there were three, the York Merchant Adventurers, the residency of the Merchant Adventurers of England, and the residency of the Eastland Company. Such companies offered significant 'political connection' both locally and in London, and this may have aided the brothers' later political careers.[6] Henry Thompson became free of the York branch of the Eastland Company in 1649, and, from 1667 to 1672, also served as governor of the Merchant Adventurers of York. Henry also purchased a rural estate, Escrick, in 1668 but retained his city address for trade and political purposes. His brother Edward was also a wine merchant and member of the Eastland Company, obtaining his freedom in 1672.[7] Edward also built up a landed estate, buying the estate of Sheriff Hutton Park in 1676.[8]

---

[4] Whyman. *Sociability and Power*. 48; Wrightson. *Earthly Necessities*. 294.

[5] Smith. *Andrew Marvell*. 235–236.

[6] Gauci. *Politics of Trade*. 144, 146.

[7] Anna B. Bisset. 1996. *The Eastland Company York Residence: Register of Admissions to the Freedom 1649–1696*. York: Borthwick Institute Publications. 12, 25; G. C. F. Forster. 1969. Hull in the 16th and 17th Centuries. In *A History of the County of York East Riding*, vol. 1, *The City of Kingston Upon Hull*, ed. K. J. Allison, 90–173. London. Victoria County History. 142; Eveline Cruickshanks. THOMPSON, Sir Henry (c.1625–83), of York and Marston, Yorks. *HoP*, http://www.historyofparliamentonline.org/volume/1660-1690/member/thompson-sir-henry-1625-83. Accessed 13 June 2019.

[8] Foster. *Pedigrees*, 'Pedigree of Thompson, of Kirby Hall, Sheriff Hutton'; Sheriff Hutton Park. *Historic England*, https://historicengland.org.uk/listing/the-list/list-entry/1001462. Accessed 13 June 2019.

5 FAMILY NETWORK   107

Henry and Edward's membership of the Eastland Company is significant. The Eastland Company traded in the Baltic, and Thompson and Nelthorpe may have obtained contacts and agents for their own trade in this region through their cousins.[9] Both brothers were also close friends of Andrew Marvell, exchanging frequent correspondence between York and London throughout the 1660s and 1670s.

Previous scholarship has identified Richard Thompson varyingly as either the brother or cousin of Henry and Edward.[10] Further study of the family pedigrees and personal family documents confirms that the banking partner Richard Thompson was the cousin of the York wine merchants. The fourth Thompson brother of York was indeed named Richard Thompson, but was a landowner 'of Kilham', a village in the East Riding of Yorkshire. The Richard Thompson of the banking partnership, however, was related to Sir Henry, Edward, and Stephen through their grandfather William Thompson, thus making him their second cousin (see Fig. 5.1).[11] Through Robert and Richard the London branch of the family was established, providing vital kinship links between York and the capital.

Edward Nelthorpe was also a cousin of the wine merchants of York, related through the mother of Sir Henry and Edward, Anne Nelthorpe, who had married Richard Thompson of Humbleton and had five sons together.[12] Both Richard Thompson and Edward Nelthorpe could have benefitted from these mercantile-landed connections, bolstering their economic and social reputations, and offering them established connections in mercantile trade. That the cousins formed an epistolary network as well as a kinship network is evident from Henry Thompson's letter book and the correspondence of Marvell. In December 1670 Marvell apologised to Edward Thompson for not 'answering yours of the former

[9] Maud Sellers. 1917. *The Acts and Ordinances of the Eastland Company.* York. xi.

[10] Identified as a brother in: H. M. Margoliouth. 1967. *The Poems and Letters of Andrew Marvell,* vol. 2. 2nd edn. London. 372; Withington. Andrew Marvell's Citizenship. 118; Wall. Marvell's Friends in the City. 204; Nicholas Von Maltzhan. 2005. *An Andrew Marvell Chronology.* Basingstoke: Palgrave Macmillan. 122. Identified as a cousin in: Burdon. Marvell and His Kindred: The Family Network in the Later Years—II Nelthorpes, Thompsons, and Popples. 173; Tupper. Mary Palmer. 368.

[11] Foster. *Pedigrees.* 'Pedigree of Thompson, of Kirby Hall, Sheriff Hutton' and 'Pedigree of Thompson, of Escrick and Marston'.

[12] Foster. *Pedigrees.* 'Pedigree of Thompson, of Humbleton and Kilham'.

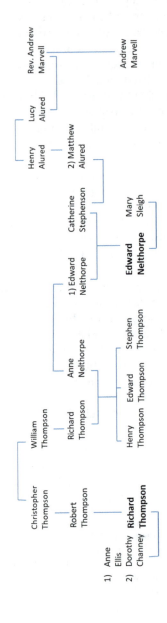

Fig. 5.1 Family tree showing the relationship between Edward Nelthorpe, Richard Thompson, and the Thompson brothers of York

5 FAMILY NETWORK 109

post', stating that he had instead 'transferd that debt upon a more responsible man your Cosin Ned'.[13] Aided by their mercantile cousins, both Edward Nelthorpe and Richard Thompson established themselves in the wine trade.

However, this family business extended beyond these sets of cousins. The Thompson brothers of York conducted a vast family business that incorporated various members of the wider kinship network. This is evident in the 1650s from Sir Henry Thompson's letter book and in the 1660s from Edward Thompson's account book. In the 1640s Henry had been in Bordeaux conducting his trade in person, but by the 1650s was back in York and had sent his younger brother Stephen to Bordeaux to manage 'our interest in the sayle of the goods & the exchange & the buying of the goods'. As well as employing his younger brother, Henry also relied on other family members to operate his business across England and Europe. This included his 'cozen William Thompson' in Hull, his 'uncles' John and James Nelthorpe, 'cozen Robert Thompson', and his cousin 'Richard Thompson' (see Fig. 5.2).[14] Henry's business with William Thompson and John and James Nelthorpe was mainly commercial, organising shipment of goods and the exchange and payment of bills. Henry's business with Robert and Richard Thompson, however, was primarily financial. Robert and Richard appear to have acted as London brokers, exchange specialists, or bankers for Henry throughout the 1650s and may have done so later, although the book does not cover the later years.

Henry Thompson's letter book suggests that he aided his cousin Richard, the banking partner of Thompson and Company in London, in his mercantile and banking career. Henry regularly sent bills and bonds to Robert Thompson via 'carrier' to be paid to various agents and associates in London, and Robert also found business for Henry, evident from Henry's thanks to Robert in 1654 for the 'commission yow got me'. Henry's gratitude for his cousin's service can further be seen in his statement that 'iff ever I be able yow shall fynde me willing to answer it by service'. Robert Thompson also acted as a financial go-between

---

[13] *The Poems and Letters of Andrew Marvell*, vol. 2. 319.

[14] HHC: U DDFA/37/5. Journal of Henry Thompson. Letter to Stephen, 16 May 1654; Letters dated: 5 June 1655, 16 February 1656, 19 June 1655, 27 May 1656, 17 June 1656, 1 July 1656, 4 July 1656, 21 October 1656, 5 June 1653, 3 April 1654, 15 September 1654, 13 March 1655, 19 June 1655, 11 September 1655, 22 October 1656.

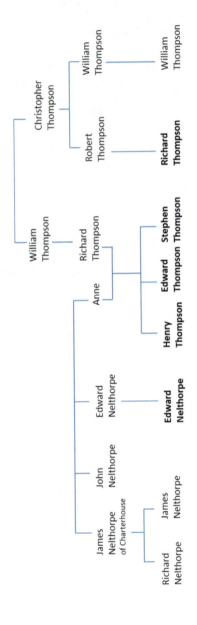

Fig. 5.2 Family tree showing the relationship between the wider Nelthorpe and Thompson families

5 FAMILY NETWORK 111

for the Thompsons and Nelthorpes. Henry wrote to his uncle James Nelthorpe that he had sent 'cosen R. Thompson a bill of Exchange for him' of £59, which evidences interaction between the London Thompsons and the Nelthorpe family before Edward Nelthorpe came to London in the 1660s. By 1655, Richard too was involved in Henry's business dealings. In September of that year, Henry wrote to Richard to ask for his help in 'findeing out a good honest wyne Cooper' to get '10 or 12 Bottles of good sound Sherryes' and 'the like number of green low priced Canaryes'. In a July 1656 letter to Robert Thompson, Henry stated that he was 'thankefull' to Richard 'yor son' and 'sorry' that he experienced 'trouble', presumably on Henry's behalf.[15] The business activities Richard conducted on behalf of Henry would have provided him with good experience and reputation in London with other merchants and traders, and meant that Thompson and his dwelling house, where the bank's shop was later located, would already have a good reputation in London's mercantile and trading circles.

Edward Thompson's account book similarly shows evidence of a wider family business. The book covers the years 1662–1665, when Edward was in Bordeaux. Unfortunately, the book is badly water damaged and ripped along the edges, which obscures a great deal of content. However, the remaining accounts show that Edward was also conducting business with their cousin William Thompson, uncles John and James Nelthorpe, and Richard Thompson in London—this time without his father Robert, who had died in 1662. Richard received money and bonds for Edward and provided other services, such as that on 2 May 1664 when Richard received one shilling and four pence 'for breaking up a writ'.[16] Both Edward and Henry's merchant books demonstrate the familial nature of their business, transferring goods and bills between kin and providing vital services in various parts of the country. The Thompson and Nelthorpe families had been aiding each other's businesses since at least the 1650s and would have been keen to introduce their younger kin to continue the mutual benefits arising from a family-based mercantile network. This therefore helps to explain how and why Richard Thompson and Edward

[15] HHC: U DDFA/37/5. Journal of Henry Thompson. 15 September 1654, 11 September 1655, 30 June 1655, 4 July 1656.

[16] HHC: U DDFA/37/6. Wine merchant's account book (Edward Thompson). ff. 62, 63, 71, 95, 118, 125, 135, 142, 143, 198; Brooke. *Transcript of the Registers*. 406.

Nelthorpe became business partners, and how they gained the necessary mercantile and banking experience.

The mercantile connections of the Thompson family also included the more distantly related Marvell and Popple families (see Fig. 5.3). The connection between the Nelthorpe and Marvell families derives from Edward Nelthorpe's mother, Catherine. Edward Nelthorpe senior died in 1640, and Catherine was remarried two years later to Matthew Alured of Hull. The Alured family were related to the Marvell family through marriage. Andrew Marvell's mother died in 1638 and his father, the Reverend Andrew Marvell, remarried that same year to Lucy Harries, née Alured. Matthew Alured was Lucy's nephew and Edward Nelthorpe's stepfather, making Edward a distant cousin of Andrew Marvell. The Alured-Marvell connection was further solidified when Andrew Marvell's nephew, William Popple, married Matthew Alured's daughter, Mary, in 1663. Popple left London in 1670 to set up in Bordeaux as a wine merchant, and his particularly close friendship with Marvell is evident from the many letters Marvell wrote to his nephew in Bordeaux, whom he was 'always thinking of'. Marvell had a significant role in the progress of William Popple's career, using his connection with Sir Henry and Edward Thompson to aid his nephew's entrance in the wine trade in Bordeaux. Popple also became involved in Thompson and Company's business, working as an agent for them in Bordeaux and was later accused in Chancery of concealing money from Farrington and Thompson. However, this was not just a commercial relationship, and Popple established friendships with his distant relations. Edward Nelthorpe carried letters from London to Popple in Bordeaux on Marvell's behalf and turned to William and his wife Mary when the bank collapsed for advice on where to put his money and information on the current state of bills that Nelthorpe was negotiating abroad. The Thompsons were also part of this friendship network, evident from correspondence between Dorothy

5 FAMILY NETWORK 113

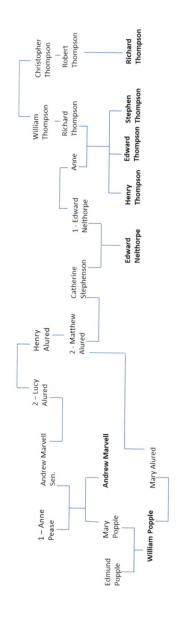

Fig. 5.3 Family tree showing the relationship between the Thompson, Nelthorpe, and Popple families

Thompson and Mary Popple.[17] These mutual acts of passing information and helping out relatives and friends were crucial for furthering the careers of young kinsmen, enhancing the reputation and credit of the entire family.

As well as introductions to commercial life, the family network also provided practical assistance for the banking partners. The wider family's concern for the welfare of the bank and its partners is evident from correspondence between Andrew Marvell and Sir Henry Thompson. In December 1675 Marvell informed Sir Henry of the struggles recently met by the 'Goldsmith Banquiers in Lombard Street' who had been 'laid at by their Creditors and so much money drawn from them that I believe it will never more find the same Chanell'. Marvell believed that their 'intention' was 'Wholy to breake all credit of that nature' and he further informed Henry that although the conflict had 'skirted upon our friends in Woollchurch market ... they proceed Cock-sure'.[18] Clearly, Marvell was a useful source of information for Sir Henry, passing on news that concerned their family business in London.

The family also provided financial assistance. Another surviving instance of the kinship network providing practical support occurred in 1675 and was recounted in the 1683 Chancery case between John Farrington and James Nelthorpe. Farrington stated that the banking partners 'borrowed' money from James Nelthorpe on 21 June 1675, taking a bond from him for £1000 at the penalty of £2000, but that James Nelthorpe had tried to trick the partners to repay more money than he was due. Farrington went on to argue that James Nelthorpe had carried out a fraudulent tobacco deal with him, from which Farrington saw none

---

[17] David Scott. 2015. Alured, Matthew (*bap.*1615, *d.*1694). *ODNB*, https://doi-org.sheffield.idm.oclc.org/10.1093/ref:odnb/66498. Accessed 13 June 2019; Pauline Burdon. 1982. The Second Mrs Marvell. *Notes and Queries*. 33; Burdon. Marvell and His Kindred: The Family Network in the Later Years—II Nelthorpes, Thompsons, and Popples. 172, 175; HHC: U DDBA/8/35. Lease at peppercorn rent: Edward Nelthorpe, citizen merchant of London and his wife Mary to Matthew Alured of Beverly, esq. 6 March 1665; Robbins. Absolute Liberty. 191, 196; Borthwick Institute for Archives: Will of Matthew Alured of Harthill. September 1694; *The Poems and Letters of Andrew Marvell*, vol. 2. 317, 313–318, 321–323, 327–328, 341–343, 346–348, 357; TNA: C 6/526/178; C 6/283/87; Hertfordshire Archives and Local Studies: DE/P/F81/77. Letter from Mary Popple to Edward Nelthorpe. 26 June 1677; Reference to correspondence with 'sister Pople' in Madam D. Thompson to Madam Braman. *SPO*, SP 29/402 f. 223, 30 March 1678.

[18] *The Poems and Letters of Andrew Marvell*, vol. 2. 343.

5 FAMILY NETWORK 115

of the profits. However, the more important aspect for this case is the lending and borrowing of money between the partners and the 'neer relacion of ... Edward Nelthorpes'. James Nelthorpe was not a normal creditor of the bank, but provided a personal loan to the partners, and Farrington distinguished him from the 'other creditors' of the bank.[19] James *lent* the £1000 to the partners prior to the first run on the bank in September 1675, which suggests that they were low on funds earlier that year. Although the money was intended to help the partners, it could also have fuelled rumours that the bank was struggling, and possibly being bailed out by family, thereby causing a loss of confidence.

Whether Farrington and Page's families provided mercantile or commercial aid to the partners is harder to establish. This is because these two partners are much harder to trace. The Chancery material describes John Farrington as 'of London'.[20] However, Tupper pointed to Farrington's origins in Chichester where there was a prominent family of the same name. Unfortunately, the pedigree of the Chichester Farrington family does not include a John Farrington who lived in London during the 1660s and 1670s, was a merchant, or a member of the London Haberdashers guild. The only John Farrington of the correct age in the Chichester pedigree was an MP for Chichester educated at Oxford and Gray's Inn, not the Haberdasher and citizen of the bank partnership.[21] Additional confusion arises from another John Farrington who was a common councillor for Cheapside in the 1670s. Once again, this is not the John Farrington of the banking partnership. The common councillor John Farrington was a member of the Cordwainers' Company, an administrator in the Court of Delegates and married in 1661 and again in 1677.[22] Therefore, he does not fit with the information provided in the court cases of the banking partner, whose exact London origins remain unknown. Edmund Page's origins are also obscure. In the Chancery cases, Page is identified only as 'late of London merchant' and of his family little

---

[19] TNA: C 10/484/71.

[20] TNA: C 7/581/73; C 10/484/71.

[21] M. W. Helms and B. M. Crook. FARRINGTON, John (c.1609–80), of Chichester, Suss. *HoP*, http://www.historyofparliamentonline.org/volume/1660-1690/member/farrington-john-1609-80. Accessed 26 June 2019.

[22] Woodhead. *Rulers of London*. 67.

is known other than that his father, Edmund Page senior, also lived in the London parish of St. Mary Woolchurch.[23]

Although little is known regarding Page's background, it is possible that he also had a connection to the Thompson family prior to the establishment of the bank in 1671. A 1673 Chancery case suggests that, despite Farrington's claim that he and Page first made Thompson and Nelthorpe's 'acquaintance' in 1671, Page knew of the Thompson family prior to the formation of the bank partnership. The 1673 Chancery Court case was taken out by complainants Sir Henry Thompson and James Nelthorpe and concerned the last will and testament of Sir Francis Bickley. Prior to his death in 1670, Sir Francis Bickley had handed over management of a family trust to none other than Edmund Page, along with Sir Jonathan Keate and Bickley's grandson, also called Sir Francis Bickley. Sir Henry Thompson and James Nelthorpe were involved because they were buying some of the Bickley family's land, the proceeds of which would go towards paying the legacies left by the deceased Sir Francis. Henry Thompson and James Nelthorpe accused Keate, Page and the younger Sir Francis Bickley of breaching the terms of the trust and refusing 'to make any conveyances of the said mannors and premisses'. The case ended with Keate agreeing to the terms of the trust and continuing his managerial role, and Page refusing to have any further part in it. Page stated that Sir Francis left a clause to 'revoke determine & make void' any of the directions, which 'did thereby acquitt & discharge [Page] of or from all such monies as should be soo received'.[24] It could be that Page's duties as a banker in his new partnership held precedent over other ventures or commitments at this time. Whatever his reason, the case demonstrates that Page could have had contact with the Thompson family prior to his agreement to go into partnership with one of their family members.

II

Once the partners had all received their training and set up in business, the next step was marriage and forming their own household families. Making a good marriage was of primary importance for dynastic and business families. Marriages could provide much-needed capital, reinforce

[23] TNA: C 7/581/73; *Boyd's Inhabitants of London*, 1648 record, 166.

[24] TNA: C 8/178/138. Thompson v Bickley. 1673.

5 FAMILY NETWORK 117

alliances, or create new networks of influence. For the partners, marriage was a crucial aid to creditworthiness in the capital and, as such, marriage partnerships were just as contested and subject to debate as business partnerships. Marriage was also the first step towards setting up a household, the basic economic and social unit on which early modern life rested and a crucial aspect of citizenship and public life.[25] The household was made up not just of the nuclear family but of a variety of individuals including servants and apprentices, and Chancery and other records show that the partners' households also included these contractual members.[26] Servant was a term used broadly to describe 'dependents who lived in the household of another' whether for domesticity or business, and as live-in members of the household they also contributed to the wider household credit and were important witnesses to both the public and private life of their employer.[27] Indeed, the servants and employees of Thompson and Company comprised 60% of the deponents called to give evidence in the £500 bond case in Chancery in 1682. Apprentices could also be described as servants, but their role in the household differed significantly as they paid to be included in the household and learn their master's trade for a specified number of years. Like servants, apprentices also contributed to the wider credit of the household, extending it even further as they 'consolidated and managed' the business networks of their master.[28]

Little information survives regarding the marriages and households of John Farrington and Edmund Page. Farrington's conjugal relationship is only evident through his wife's will and parish records. Farrington married Margaret Bearblock in London in 1662 and they had three sons and two daughters. Margaret's will reveals that the couple had a marriage settlement, whereby Margaret retained control over a portion of her own

[25] Muldrew. "A Mutual Assent of Her Mind"?. 52; Muldrew. *Economy of Obligation.* 9, 148, 202, 274; Jan de Vries. 2008. *The Industrious Revolution: Consumer Behaviour and the Household Economy, 1650 to the Present.* Cambridge: Cambridge University Press. 7–10, 36; Gauci. *Politics of Trade.* 75–76.

[26] Tadmor. *Family and Friends.* 27–28.

[27] Amanda Flather. 2011. Gender, Space, and Place. *Home Cultures* 8: 172; Muldrew. *Economy of Obligation.* 158.

[28] Leng. *Fellowship and Freedom.* 34.

118   M. WINTER

estate, and that Farrington outlived his wife.[29] Other than the information in Margaret's will, there is little evidence available of this couple's partnership or life together. Edmund Page's conjugal partnership is even more difficult to uncover. Page married Mary Stevens in 1639 and they had five children between 1640 and 1656, three of whom survived into adulthood.[30] Neither Edmund nor Mary left an extant will and, despite being a partner, Page features rarely in the Chancery proceedings. Both Farrington and Page lived in St. Mary Woolchurch with their families. Farrington's household also included at least one servant and two apprentices: Jerome Rawstone who was bound to Farrington for seven years in June 1661 and Francis Michell who was bound for nine years in 1672.[31] There are no records of Page as a master to apprentices or any information about his wider household.

Richard Thompson married twice. First to Anne Ellis in 1653, with whom he had four sons and one daughter, with only their daughter Anne and son Robert surviving to adulthood. Richard's wife Anne died in 1667 and he was remarried the following year to Dorothy Channey, with whom he had five children, only two of which survived to adulthood. Richard's household in the 1670s was therefore made up of both his children from his first marriage and those he had with Dorothy. The household also could have included a servant or employee of the bank, such as Gersham Proud, and likely included an apprentice or apprentices. There are four possible apprentice records for Richard Thompson: Veneables Bowman in 1661, Benjamin Macy in 1669, Matthew Hungerford in 1669, and Richard Saunders in 1674.[32] Unfortunately, these records do not provide enough detail to ascertain for definite that it is the correct Richard Thompson.

---

[29] *Boyd's Inhabitants of London*, 1670 record, 1903; Brooke. *Transcript of the Registers*. 61, 65; TNA: PROB 11/421/381. Will of Margarett Farrington, Wife of London. 1 October 1694.

[30] *Boyd's Inhabitants of London*, 1648 record, 166 and 1447; Brooke. *Transcript of the Registers*. 243.

[31] TNA: C 6/283/87; City of London, Haberdashers, Apprentices and Freemen 1526–1933. Accessed via *Findmypast*, https://www.findmypast.co.uk, 1661 and 1672 records for John Farrington.

[32] *Boyd's Inhabitants of London*, 1653 record, 1701; RoLLCo, Search for Richard Thompson in the Clothworkers' Company, records from 29 April 1661, 2 January 1668, 2 November 1669, and 4 August 1674. Accessed 23 January 2020.

5 FAMILY NETWORK   119

The details of Richard's first marriage or any economic benefits that may have arisen from either his first or second marriage are unknown, but his marriage to Dorothy forged useful connections to other prominent political families, primarily the Braman family of Chichester. Dorothy's sister Elizabeth was married to Major John Braman, a parliamentarian in the New Model Army, an exclusionist MP from 1679 to 1685, and a nonconformist plotter in the Restoration who was involved in the Rye House Plot and the Monmouth Rebellion. The kinship link is evident from surviving letters between the sisters in the late 1670s, and a letter from Dorothy to Major Braman in which she addresses him as 'Deare Brother'. Richard Thompson's letters to Major Braman similarly start with the familiar and affectionate 'Dear Bro' and speak of their shared interest in politics as Richard sent news and gossip from London. Richard also discussed his business problems with his brother-in-law. In June 1678, Richard wrote to Braman about 'The Bill' which 'moves slowly and the statute mongers seem to be of the quickest in their intended proceedings, for so they threaten, but I abandon the subject that begins to molest me, before it transport me'.[33] The Braman family connection not only provided family support and political and religious alliance but practical assistance, hiding Thompson in their own house when the bank collapsed and the partners fled into hiding.

Tupper suggested that the Thompson-Braman kinship link also included bank partner John Farrington. Major Braman's stepdaughter is referred to as 'Elizabeth Farringdon' in two petitions to the King requesting access to visit Braman in prison in the 1680s. Tupper believed 'Farringdon' could have been a misspelling of Farrington thereby suggesting that the Bramans and John Farrington were kin, although he did not examine this network further. Evidence supporting his claim can

---

[33] Zaller, 2006. Breman [Braman], John (*bap.* 1627, d.1703). *Oxford Dictionary of National Biography*, https://doi-org.sheffield.idm.oclc.org/10.1093/ref:odnb/67420. Accessed 13 May 2020; Braman, John (1627–1703), of Chichester, Suss. *The History of Parliament: British Political, Social & Local History*, http://www.historyofparliamenton line.org/volume/1660-1690/member/braman-john-1627-1703. Accessed 14 June 2019; Madam D. Thompson to Madam Braman. *SPO*, SP 29/402 f. 223, 30 March 1678; E B[raman] to Madame [Thompson]. *SPO*, SP 29/402 f. 305, 6 April 1678; Dorothy Thompson to her brother-in-law, Major Braman. *SPO*, SP 29/401 f. 330, 7 January 1678; Richard Thompson to Major Braman. *SPO*, SP 29/404 f. 275, 27 June 1678; Richard Thompson to Major Braman, his brother[-in-law]. *SPO*, SP 29/404 f. 257, 25 June 1678.

120   M. WINTER

be found in a letter from Dorothy Thompson to Major Braman, in which she wrote an endnote that expressed her 'hartey servis' not only to her sister and brother-in-law, but to 'mr and madam Farington'. However, the Elizabeth 'Farringdon' or Farrington of the petitions and letter was the wife of Richard Farrington of Chichester, and no relation to the bank partner John Farrington of London.[34]

Of all four partners, Edward Nelthorpe appears to have made the most advantageous marriage. Nelthorpe married in 1662, a year after gaining his freedom from the Drapers' Company and Merchant Adventurers. His bride was the 16-year-old orphan Mary Sleigh, daughter of Edmond Sleigh, a wealthy Alderman from a prominent Derbyshire family, who died in 1657. Sleigh's wealth is evident from his will, in which he left a third of his considerable estate to be divided between his four children, plus additional legacies to each of them when they reached the age of 21 or got married. Edmund Sleigh left Mary a legacy of £1200, which along with money raised from his estate, brought her marriage portion to just under £5000. This was a significant portion for the mid-seventeenth century, at the upper-end of typical 'gentry portions', which ranged 'from £1000 to £5000'. At the time of marriage, Mary's portion was under the control of the Court of Aldermen, who, according to her Chancery statement in 1684, required that Edward make her a 'jointure' of £300 a year. A jointure essentially signified 'the number of years a woman had to survive her husband in order to get full value out of her portion', in Mary's case it would take 17 years.[35] Although the money was not within her immediate control, the jointure gave Mary financial security in

---

[34] Elizabeth Farringdon to the King. *SPO*, SP 29/429 f. 400, July 1683; Elizabeth Farringdon to the King. *SPO*, SP 29/429 f. 401, 1683; Tupper. Mary Palmer. 371; Dorothy Thompson to her Brother-in-law Major Braman. *SPO*, SP 29 401 f. 330, 7 January 1678; B. M. Crook. FARRINGTON (FARINGTON), Richard (c.1644–1719), of South Street, Chichester, Suss. *HoP*, http://www.historyofparliamentonline.org/vol ume/1660-1690/member/farrington-%28farington%29-richard-1644-1719. Accessed 16 July 2019.

[35] Burdon. Marvell and His Kindred: The Family Network in the Later Years—II Nelthorpes, Thompsons, and Popples. 172; A. P. Beaven. 1908. *The Aldermen of the City of London, temp. Henry III.-1908: With Notes on the Parliamentary Representation of the City, the Aldermen and the Livery Companies, the Aldermanic Veto, Aldermanic Baronets and Knights*, etc. vol. 2. London: Corporation of the City of London. 81; TNA: PROB 11/262/31. Will of Edmund Sleigh, Alderman of London. 3 February 1657; HHC: U DDBA/8/15. Account of monies due to Mary Sleigh, a daughter of Edmund Sleigh, esq. citizen and Alderman and mercer, under will of her father. 1657–1662; Erickson.

5 FAMILY NETWORK 121

widowhood and a recourse to the law should she not receive her money. Nelthorpe's marriage to Mary therefore brought with it economic wealth and social status.

Alongside wealth and status, Nelthorpe's marriage also brought with it further connections to networks of politico-religious dissent. After the death of Mary's father her mother, Elizabeth, remarried the following year to John Ireton. The Iretons were a puritan family from Derbyshire, and John and his brother Henry were both active in the Civil War on the Parliamentarian side. Whilst Henry took a more active role in the army before his death at the siege of Limerick in 1651, John benefitted from sequestration and rose in the political ranks, aided by his brother's marriage to one of Cromwell's daughters in 1646. John Ireton was imprisoned three times after the Restoration and his commitment to the nonconformist cause in the following years is further evident from his contribution of £200 to the 1670 'dissenting loan' to Charles II—an attempt by 155 Londoners to 'influence Charles's religious policy'.[36] A kinship connection to such a prominent puritan and dissenting family certainly would have affected the reputation of the banking partners.

In the 1660s and 1670s Nelthorpe set up his household in the parish of St. Michael Bassishaw in London and he and Mary had three children: Edward, Mary, and James. At least one 'servant' of the Nelthorpe family can be identified in the Chancery records, Thomas Speed, and he likely lived with the family. Nelthorpe also took on apprentices. In 1664 he became master to 'John Chaplin' under an 8-year bond of £1000, and in 1665 an identical bond was made for 'Sanckeleare Umfreavil'. However, another apprentice does not feature in the Drapers' Company records. Boyd's Inhabitants of London records that in 1662 James Nelthorpe, son of James Nelthorpe of Charterhouse London and Edward Nelthorpe's

---

Women and Property. 86; TNA: C 10/216/74; Erickson. Common law versus common practice. 31.

[36] Gary S. De Krey. 2008. Ireton, John [created Sir John Ireton under the protectorate]. *ODNB*, https://doi.org/10.1093/ref:odnb/14453. Accessed 31 May 2019; Ian J. Gentles. 2004. Ireton, Henry (*bap.* 1611, *d.* 1651). *ODNB*, https://doi-org.sheffield.idm.oclc.org/10.1093/ref:odnb/14452. Accessed 14 June 2019; De Krey. *London and the Restoration.* 125, 407.

122   M. WINTER

cousin, was set up in an apprenticeship with Edward.[37] This apprenticeship was likely less formal and less costly than Chaplin and Umfreavil's due to the kinship ties between master and apprentice. The households that the partners formed allowed them to further their mercantile and political careers, building up their economic and social credit within the community and establishing useful commercial and political connections.

III

As suggested above with the connections to the Ireton and Braman families, the kinship network of the Thompson and Nelthorpe families was not just a commercial network but a religious and political network. Kinship ties provided ready-made connections for political alliances. In the case of the Thompson and Nelthorpe families it provided links between the civic politics that Edward Nelthorpe and Richard Thompson were engaged in and the court politics of their MP cousins, creating an 'intersecting and endogamous dissenting social milieu'.[38] Burdon has argued that 'the deepest kinship among these families [the Thompsons, Nelthorpes, Alureds, and Popples] centred in their shared Puritanism'.[39] This shared puritanism matched onto their political identities and activism, with many members of the family affiliated with a Parliamentarian, a nonconformist, and then a 'Whig' political outlook. This is significant because, as Harris has argued, the 'struggles which emerged in the 1670s and 1680s' were in many ways 'continuities' of struggles that began in the first half of the seventeenth century, and the individuals 'who led or shaped the opposition to the restored monarchy in the 1670s and 1680s' were those who 'had gained their formative experience during the struggles of the 1640s and 1650s'. These individuals of the 'old' struggle were joined by 'new' individuals of the 'younger generation', united in their shared beliefs.[40] The political networks of the bank partners show that one significant way in which 'old' and 'new' were united was through kinship

[37] TNA: C 10/216/74; RoLLCo, Search for Edward Nelthorpe as a master in the Drapers' Company between 1654 and 1678; *Boyd's Inhabitants of London*, 1662 record, 38,185.

[38] De Krey. *London and the Restoration.* 130.

[39] Burdon. Marvell and His Kindred: The Family Network in the Later Years—II Nelthorpes, Thompsons, and Popples. 178.

[40] Harris. Introduction: Revising the Restoration. 6–8.

ties, sharing experience and inspiring beliefs in the younger generation to create lineages of like-minded individuals taking up the same cause. This therefore demonstrates the importance of studying the wider kinship networks of an individual, in order to understand why they believed what they did and how this shaped the roles they took up and their actions within those roles (Fig. 5.4).

The most politically prominent member of the family network was Andrew Marvell, who sat as MP for Hull from 1659 to his death in 1678.[41] Marvell acted as a 'political liaison' between dissenters in the City, such as Richard Thompson and Edward Nelthorpe, and those in the House of Commons, as well as connecting North and South through his regular correspondence with his friends and kin in York, Sir Henry and Edward Thompson, and with the Corporation of Hull.[42] However, both the Thompson and Nelthorpe families had a long history of participation in civic politics in York and Beverley and in national politics throughout the seventeenth century. Richard's father Robert Thompson was a Parliamentarian army officer who rose to the position of Lieutenant Colonel, and his political allegiance was shared by many other members of the Thompson family.[43] York was a parliamentarian strong hold in the Civil War, with the governing body extending their civic authority and ridding the city of royalists in 1644 and 1649. Although their authority was reduced at the Restoration, the civic and godly ideals of York's civic community re-emerged in the Restoration as puritanism and nonconformity grew in the city. This is reflected in the election of York MPs in the 1670s, when the city turned decisively against the 'Court' interest and elected individuals such as Sir Henry and Edward Thompson.[44]

[41] M. W. Helms and John P. Ferris. MARVELL, Andrew (1621–78), of Highgate Hill, Mdx. and Maiden Lane, Covent Garden, Westminster. *HoP*, http://www.historyofparliamentonline.org/volume/1660-1690/member/marvell-andrew-1621-78. Accessed 13 June 2019.

[42] De Krey. *London and the Restoration.* 137; von Maltzahn. Marvell, Writer and Politician. 5.

[43] Burdon. Marvell and His Kindred: The Family Network in the Later Years—II Nelthorpes, Thompsons, and Popples. 175.

[44] Phil Withington. 2001. Views from the Bridge: Revolution and Restoration in Seventeenth-Century York. *Past & Present* 170: 133, 144, 151; G. C. F. Forster. 1961. York in the 17th Century. In *A History of Yorkshire: The City of York*, ed. P. M. Tillott, 160–206. London. Victoria County History. 193, 200, 205.

124　M. WINTER

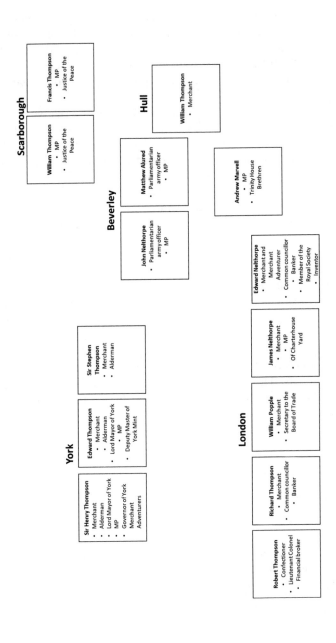

Fig. 5.4 The Thompson family's involvement with the market and the state

5 FAMILY NETWORK 125

Sir Henry Thompson's political career began with a position on York's 'County Committee of the 1640s' when he was involved in 'sequestrating royalist property in York City on behalf of Parliament'.[45] Following this, he was Alderman of York from 1652 until his death in 1683, Lord Mayor of the city in 1663–1664, and knighted in 1665, making him one of only ten York Aldermen knighted in the seventeenth century and distinguishing him as a 'merchant leader'.[46] Henry's brother Edward was also an Alderman of the city from 1681 to 1685 and from 1688 until his death in 1701, and was Lord Mayor in 1683–1684.[47] That both brothers were politically active in York is unsurprising given the dominance of merchants both economically and socially in the city and its governing body.[48] However, their influence also extended to national politics, with both brothers sitting as MPs for York in the 1670s and 1680s. They were both associated with 'country' party politics and were 'leading progenitors of what can be legitimately described as nascent Whiggism within the City'.[49] With their political and mercantile notability, Henry and Edward were important allies to the banking partners in London.

The Nelthorpe family provided links to Beverley, a town that was also characterised by parliamentarianism and puritanism. In the early 1640s Beverley was used as a base during the siege of Hull by Royalist forces, but in 1644 Royalist MPs and civic leaders were purged from Beverley and the new MPs elected in their place were John and James Nelthorpe—Edward Nelthorpe's uncles—who were 'leading townsmen' and had both 'served in the parliamentarian armies'. James Nelthorpe was an Alderman of Beverley, mayor for the year 1641–1642, and was a lieutenant colonel in the army, and John Nelthorpe was an officer in the New Model Army. John Nelthorpe served as MP until 1648 and James until 1654. In 1659 James Nelthorpe moved to Charterhouse, London, establishing

---

[45] Barbara English. 1990. *The Great Landowners of East Yorkshire 1530–1910*. Hertfordshire: Harvester Wheatsheaf. 29.

[46] Cruickshanks. THOMPSON, Sir Henry. *HoP*; Forster. York in the 17th Century. 180; Gauci. *Politics of Trade*. 90.

[47] Eveline Cruickshanks. THOMPSON, Edward (c.1639–1701), of York. *HoP*, http://www.historyofparliamentonline.org/volume/1660-1690/member/thompson-edward-1639-1701. Accessed 31 May 2019.

[48] Forster. York in the 17th Century. 179; Withington. Views from the Bridge. 127–128, 131.

[49] Withington. Andrew Marvell's Citizenship. 118.

126   M. WINTER

another important London branch of the family.[50] Another member of Nelthorpe's wider family involved in the Civil War was his stepfather Matthew Alured, who served as a Parliamentarian army officer with John Nelthorpe. Matthew Alured was also an MP for Hedon in 1659, and his 'strongly nonconformist family' had campaigned for the reformed religion since the 1580s, providing yet another source of religious and political alliance for Edward.[51]

Other members of the kinship network involved in national politics include Thompson and Nelthorpe's other cousins Francis and William Thompson, who were both MPs for Scarborough in the 1680s.[52] The Popples of Hull were also important in this network. Marvell's brother-in-law Edmund Popple was Sheriff of the City in 1658 and Marvell's nephew William, although he never held a position as an MP or civic governor, held strong religious and political views, expressed in his publications, and an administrative position on the board of Trade in the 1690s, which made him an important node in this support network.[53] Indeed, the extended family did not just represent a kinship network but a 'civic and mercantile' network of 'politically like-minded citizens'.[54]

[50] G. C. F. Forster. 1989. Beverley in the 17th Century. In *A History of the County of York East Riding*, vol. 6, *The Borough and Liberties of Beverley*, ed. K. J. Allison, 89–111. London. Victoria County History. 90–94; K. J. Allison. 1989. Lists of Officers. In *A History of the County of York East Riding*, vol. 6, *The Borough and Liberties of Beverley*, ed. K. J. Allison, 198–206. London: Victoria County History. 203; TNA: PROB 11/459/28. Will of James Nelthorpe of Charterhouse Yard, Middlesex. 8 January 1701.

[51] Scott. Alured, Matthew. *ODNB*; Burdon. Marvell and His Kindred: The Family Network in the Later Years—II Nelthorpes, Thompsons, and Popples. 172; Forster. Beverley in the 17th Century. 97.

[52] P. A. Bolton and Paula Watson, 'THOMPSON, Francis (c.1655–93), of Humbleton, Yorks', *HoP*, http://www.historyofparliamentonline.org/volume/1660-1690/member/thompson-francis-1655-93. Accessed 13 May 2020; P. A. Bolton and Paula Watson. THOMPSON, William (1629–92), of Scarborough, Yorks. *HoP*, http://www.historyof parliamentonline.org/volume/1660-1690/member/thompson-william-1629-92. Accessed 13 May 2020.

[53] Thomas Seccombe, revised by C. S. Rogers. 2013. Popple, William (1638–1708). *ODNB*, https://doi-org.sheffield.idm.oclc.org/10.1093/ref:odnb/22545. Accessed 11 July 2019; Robbins. Absolute Liberty. 191.

[54] Withington. *Politics of Commonwealth*. 193; Withington. Andrew Marvell's Citizenship. 117.

5 FAMILY NETWORK 127

Beyond official national and civic politics, the banking partners also had kinship and friendship connections to known rebels and conspirators. Whilst the partners' views were not as radical as their associates', these networks would have further bolstered their dissenting identities. Important in this regard is Richard Nelthorpe, the Rye House Plotter and conspirator executed in 1685 for high treason. Richard was Edward Nelthorpe's cousin, son of James Nelthorpe of Charterhouse, London (see Fig. 5.2). On 22 February 1679 Richard became a member of the Green Ribbon Club, a political club formed in 1674 that met at the King's Head tavern, and in 1682 became 'involved in the Rye House cabal'. The Rye House Plot, in which conspirators intended to assassinate Charles II and his brother James, was discovered in June 1683 and Nelthorpe was forced to flee the country. He managed to escape via Scarborough using his kinship connection to the Thompson family. In 1683 Stephen Thompson, merchant of Scarborough and cousin of Sir Henry, Edward and Stephen, deposed that on 24 June 'Richard Nelthrop came to his house' along with another man named 'Layne'. Stephen stated that the two men 'pretended that they were forced to flee for debt', which Stephen believed as he was unaware 'of any declaracion from his majesty for the takeing of the said Nelthrop or any other' as the 'declaracion was not knowne in Scarborough all that time'. Therefore, Stephen helped Richard and his accomplice flee in a 'vessell that was bound for Holland'. Stephen's deposition against his cousin, which informed the examiners of Richard's actions and location, appears less harsh when viewed alongside a letter from Edward Thompson to Secretary Jenkins concerning Richard Nelthorpe. Edward had been 'ordered to apprehend' Richard in 1683 but did not manage to find his cousin. In a letter to the Secretary, he wrote 'the relacion I have to Mr Nelthorpe could not lessin my duty in securing him had it been in my power'. Finally apprehended after taking part in the Monmouth Rebellion, an attempt to overthrow the newly crowned James II, Richard was 'hanged, drawn, and quartered' on 30 October 1685.[55]

---

[55] J. R. Jones. 1956. The Green Ribbon Club. *Durham University Journal* 49: 17–20; Samuel Pepys Library: MS 2875. Journal of the Green Ribband Club at the King's Head Tavern over against the Temple in Fleet Street, 14 November 1678 to 29 June 1681; copied from the original lent to S. P. by the King. 469; Robert L. Greaves. 2009. Nelthorpe, Richard (*d.*1685). *ODNB*, https://doi.org/10.1093/ref:odnb/19891. Accessed 31 May 2019; The examination and further deposition on oath of Stephen

128   M. WINTER

Another conspirator and associate of the banking partners was Sir William Cowper, who was also an associate of Shaftesbury, a Green Ribbon Club member, and an MP from 1679.[56] When faced with bankruptcy in 1677, Nelthorpe was contemplating leaving some money with Cowper, presumably for safekeeping and to avoid the funds being subsumed by the commission of bankruptcy. Knowledge of this comes from a letter written by Mary Popple in Bordeaux to her 'Deare Brother & Sister', Edward and Mary Nelthorpe.[57] The letter reveals that Mary Popple had consulted the '*abbé* in Bordeaux' for advice on Nelthorpe's situation. The '*abbé*', Maniban, was the subject of Marvell's poem '*Illustrissimo Viro Domino Lanceloto Josepho de Maniban Grammatomantis*', which, Nicholas von Maltzahn and Rory Tanner argue, reveals Marvell's concern of the influence Maniban had over the Popples.[58] In this case, the *abbé* claimed that 'if it were money lent him [Cowper] it would not be very easey to get it all again', but was unsure 'whether it weare to be money lent or onely a trust reposed upon'.[59] The letter reveals the link between Nelthorpe and Cowper, and provides further evidence of Nelthorpe looking for places to conceal his remaining money out of the reach of the commission of bankruptcy.

IV

The wider family backgrounds of Thompson and Company's partners reveal that they were part of a wealthy commercial kinship network, which provided the necessary social and economic capital as well as vital contacts needed to succeed in business. The Thompson and Nelthorpe families were also significant for their political and religious beliefs, which

Thompson. *SPO*, SP 29/428 f. 298, 13 July 1683; Cruickshanks. THOMPSON, Edward. *HoP*; Edward Thompson to Secretary Jenkins. *SPO*, SP 29/428 f. 282, 13 July 1683.

56 E. R. Edwards. COWPER, Sir William, 2nd Bt. (1639–1706), of The Castle, Hertford. *HoP*. http://www.historyofparliamentonline.org/volume/1660-1690/member/cowper-sir-william-1639-1706. Accessed 31 May 2019; Samuel Pepys Library: MS 2875. Journal of the Green Ribband Club. 469.

57 Hertfordshire Archives and Local Studies: Letter from Mary Popple to Edward Nelthorpe. 26 June 1677.

58 Nicholas von Maltzahn and Rory Tanner. 2012. Marvell's "Maniban" in Manuscript. *The Review of English Studies* 63: 764–765.

59 Hertfordshire Archives and Local Studies: Letter from Mary Popple to Edward Nelthorpe. 26 June 1677.

informed and reinforced the partners' own beliefs, and provided a support network of political allies and a wealth of experience that stretched back to and beyond the Civil War. Alongside this, however, the family networks also embroiled the partners within a religiously and politically dissenting network, including both high status MPs and dangerous rebels and conspirators. On the one hand, the partners' wider kinship networks had the power to enhance the partners' own status and business success socially, commercially, and economically, but, on the other hand, they further entrenched the partners within a network of opposition and dissent that increased the risk in their political roles. Therefore, in terms of their networks, finance and commerce were inseparable from politics and religion for Thompson and Nelthorpe, and the wider dynastic Thompson and Nelthorpe families. This is less so for Page and Farrington, whose family backgrounds are largely untraceable and who did not take on political roles alongside their banking and mercantile roles. Despite their lack of political engagement, Farrington and Page became entrenched in the networks and associations of their partners.

The partners kinship backgrounds had a significant influence over their later careers and, as this chapter has shown, had a positive role to play in supporting the establishment of Thompson and Company and aiding the partners during its struggles and collapse. As the following chapter demonstrates, the commercial and familial networks were also a useful tool for attracting customers to the new bank. However, whilst commercially these families were very successful, in their political and religious outlook they were involved in opposition groups that became targets in wider parliamentary disputes and contests. Kinship networks therefore not only contributed to the early success of Thompson and Company, but to its later struggles as well.

CHAPTER 6

Credit Networks

Viscount Fauconberg recorded in his notebook that on 27 September 1675 he 'put One Thousand Pounds into the hands of Mr Thompson & Company'. Underneath, he noted the interest payments he received in the year following and the proportion of his principal debt he received in November 1676. Fauconberg's financial activity with Thompson and Company appears to have combined the functions of a deposit and an investment, storing the principal amount for safe keeping but also accruing interest whilst it lay there. On the same page Fauconberg recorded a transaction with the Royal African Company, 'I put into the African Company' £1000, and listed the interest received underneath.[1] In both these accounts Fauconberg used the same language and did not distinguish between what we would now recognise as *depositing* money in a bank and *investing* in stocks or shares.

Previous chapters have emphasised the hybrid nature of Thompson and Company—a project that combined a bank and a merchant partnership—and outlined the commercial and political kinship networks that the bank relied on. In contrast, this chapter examines the outward facing credit networks facilitated by Thompson and Company: the 215 known creditors and two known debtors. It turns first to the evidence of the few

---

[1] BL: Add MS 41255. Note-Book of Thomas Belasyse. f. 15.

© The Author(s), under exclusive license to Springer Nature Switzerland AG 2022
M. Winter, *Banking, Projecting and Politicking in Early Modern England*, Palgrave Studies in Economic History, https://doi.org/10.1007/978-3-030-90570-5_6

creditors of Thompson and Company for whom surviving source material can be found in which they recorded their business with the bank, such as the accounts of Fauconberg. This kind of analysis is important for understanding how hybrid institutions, like Thompson and Company, were viewed and discussed by contemporaries in comparison to other contemporary banks and financial institutions, and to better understand how financial interaction that we now characterise as investments and deposits were discussed and conceptualised by contemporaries. It is argued that whilst historians neatly distinguish between *investments* and *deposits* in their analysis of seventeenth-century English finance,[2] such distinctions would not have been recognised by contemporaries. Instead, the language used to describe financial interaction and exchange in the 1670s was vague and ambiguous and reflects the highly interpersonal nature of credit networks that relied on reputation and recommendation, and the pervasiveness of risk in early modern society.

As few creditors have left such detailed material, however, analysis of each creditor's business with Thompson and Company or the reasons why they decided to entrust their money to the bank is not possible. Instead, the second part of this chapter expands upon the prosopographical analysis of the creditors discussed in Chapters 2 and 3 to identify and broadly categorise the interpersonal connections between groups of creditors and Thompson and Company's partners. As Laurence has argued for Hoare's Bank, private banking relied on 'personal networks' of 'kinship, religion, and politics', to do business and expand these networks through recommendation to others who moved within those same circles, and Thompson and Company were no different.[3] From the evidence of the 215 creditors, there appear to be five factors informing why individuals put their money into the bank of Thompson and Company: kinship links, political affiliation or connection, locality, recommendation, and trading association. This chapter outlines and further explores these connections, demonstrating that credit and reputation were not only central to personal financial networks but were also central to the networks underpinning larger financial institutions.

---

[2] Davies. Joint-Stock Investment. 283–301; Rabb. Investment in English Overseas Enterprise. 70–81; Murphy. Dealing with Uncertainty. 200–217; Laurence. The Emergence of a Private Clientele for Banks. 565–586; Froide. *Silent Partners*; Todd. Fiscal Citizens. 53–74.

[3] Laurence. The Emergence of a Private Clientele for Banks. 582, 585.

I

In a study of early modern lotteries, Anne Murphy argues that 'Risk was ever-present in the early modern period and methods of utilising and controlling it were varied and often involved actions that would today be classified as gambling'. Indeed, she states that historians have often viewed such practices as standing 'in direct contradiction to the progress that was being made in other areas of public and private finance in England in the late seventeenth and eighteenth centuries'. In contrast, through analysis of newspaper advertisements, published discourses, and the diary of Samuel Jeake, Murphy claims that the speculative practice of buying lottery tickets was not an act of frivolity but a 'solid form of investment' that demonstrates a lack of distinction 'between gambling and investment' in 1690s England.[4] Murphy's study emphasises the need for further historicist investigation of contemporary financial language and concepts, rather than employing modern terms and distinctions. The following section employs this methodology through an examination of the evidence left by some of the creditors of Thompson and Company. It suggests that due to the 6% interest offered on deposits and the risky, unstable nature of pre-Bank of England banks, there was a lack of distinction between what we would now recognise as a *deposit* and an *investment* in seventeenth-century England.

Creditors of early deposit banks, the Goldsmith banks as well as Thompson and Company, were depositing their money into a bank which they could retrieve on demand, but which also accrued interest and was given out in the form of loans. The Goldsmith-bankers were using these deposits to loan to others, particularly to the monarch in the 1660s and 1670s. Thompson and Company were using their creditors' deposits to loan to others and to themselves. Early deposit banks also worked on the premise of fractional reserve, only holding a percentage of their funds in physical coin at any one time and, as the Stop on the Exchequer demonstrated, the bankers' promise that funds could be withdrawn at any time on demand was no real guarantee. There was, therefore, a significant amount of risk attached to these businesses. It was not until the 1690s that English banks started offering purely safe keeping services, like the continental Exchange banks, and distinguished between demand

---

[4] Murphy. Lotteries in the 1690s. 227–246.

and time deposits.[5] Demand deposits could be recalled at any time, much like a modern current account, but offered no interest. In contrast, time deposits stipulated a fixed period in which the money could not be withdrawn and during which it accrued interest. The interest offered by banks like Thompson and Company, and the highly publicised risk attached to banking in this period, suggests that in the seventeenth century financial interaction was not distinguished through the concepts of *investment* and *deposit*.

Fauconberg's notebook documents the changes in the services offered by banks over time and the changing ways in which individuals would use their services. In 1692 Fauconberg recorded that he had opened an 'Account' with Hoare's bank. The descriptor of an 'account' marks Fauconberg's involvement with Hoare's Bank as different to that of his earlier dealing with the bank of Thompson and Company and reflects the development of banks more generally in the final decades of the seventeenth century, when Thompson and Company were no longer active. From 1690 onward Hoare's Bank, and many others, no longer offered interest on deposits. Hoare acted as an agent for individuals who wanted to increase their capital through the stock market or other speculative investments, but no longer offered interest on deposits that could be recalled on demand.[6] For Fauconberg, then, Hoare's services were more useful for money management: Hoare received merchants' bills for Fauconberg, bills due from individuals, 'bills to be received of Tradesmen', and even dealt with Fauconberg's estate after his death in 1700.[7] The changing purpose of banks and the services they offered from the 1690s onwards could explain some shift in the language used in the eighteenth century, but prior to this all financial activities with institutions involved some underlying risk and as an incentive offered the reward of annual or bi-annual interest payments. Instead of using *invest* or *deposit* then, Fauconberg described his financial activity by using the terms 'put' and in 'the hands of'. Such language can be seen in the records of other creditors of Thompson and Company.

---

[5] Richards. *Early History of Banking*. 229; Roseveare. *The Financial Revolution*. 20; Melton. *Sir Robert Clayton*. 49, 213–214, 216.

[6] Laurence. The Emergence of a Private Clientele for Banks. 567, 570.

[7] BL: Add MS 41255. Note-Book of Thomas Belasyse. ff. 82, 83, 85, 86, 89, 90, 92, 93.

6 CREDIT NETWORKS   135

Sir William Turner's account books are less discursive than Fauconberg's, but the same ambiguous language and lack of distinction between activities we would now describe as either a *deposit* or an *investment* is evident. Every six months Turner wrote up a personal account of money 'owing' or 'due' to him on various 'bonds' and 'other securities', which consists of a list of names, the principal debt, and any interest due. In the accounts Turner does not specify whether each entry is a bond, a bill, company shares, or money laid out in ships. For example, Turner was part owner of a ship, the Golden Fleece, which is simply listed as 'ship Golden Fleece' and occasionally provided small returns that were most likely profit shares. He also regularly includes the 'East India' and 'Affrica' companies in his lists but only once writes 'East India Company in stock', with the rest of the entries in the 1670s left ambiguous as to their precise nature. It is only in the 1680s that Turner begins to specify his financial engagements as 'upon bond', 'upon mortgage', or 'in stock'.[8] Additionally when Turner and Fauconberg reckoned their accounts, to calculate who was in debit and who in credit, the overall figure was always stated as the amount that remained due to Fauconberg 'in the hands of Sir William Turner'.[9]

Other examples of this language can be seen in creditor Robert Draper's 1681 will, in which he used the phrase 'in their hands' to refer to his money that 'remained' in the bank of Thompson and Company.[10] The minutes of the Corporation of Trinity House similarly use the term 'in the Bankers hands' to describe the £500 they had in the bank.[11] The minutes of the Royal Society record the recommendation of Henry Howard, Duke of Norfolk, who described Thompson and Company 'as very good men to put' their money with at interest.[12] The merchant John Verney described Thompson and Company's partners as having money 'in their hands'.[13] Roger Whitley, deputy postmaster of London, wrote to a correspondent

---

[8] LMA: CLC/509/MS05105. Book of sales, 1664–1671, followed by accounts relating to his personal estate, 1671–1691.

[9] LMA: CLC/509/MS05107/002. Miscellaneous accounts.

[10] TNA: PROB 11/366/377. Will of Robert Draper, Gentleman of Windsor, Berkshire. 31 May 1681.

[11] LMA: CLC/526/MS30004/004. 223.

[12] Birch. *History of the Royal Society of London*, vol. 3. 129.

[13] BL: Microfilm 636/29. *Verney Papers*. 'John Verney to Sir Ralph Verney', 16 March 1676.

of his hopes of securing money that he had 'in Mr Nelthorpe & partners hands'.[14] In the 1679 Chancery case the creditors of Thompson and Company argued that through fraud and intrigue the money and estates of the partners had been 'drawne out of their hands' and into the 'hands' of their confederates to prevent the creditors receiving a share of their remaining debt. They also lamented the fact that they had 'expended & laid out' over £500 in legal fees, which had been 'swallowed upp or put to the Account' of the commission of bankruptcy.[15] Additionally, the first creditors pamphlet, when imploring other creditors to allow Thompson and Company to distribute their remaining estate, stated that their money was in 'great danger of loss, in whose hands soever it is lodged' due to the pressures of the commission of bankruptcy.[16]

Surviving probate documents of the creditors demonstrates that this language was not just confined to their discussions of Thompson and Company. In her study of female public investors, Froide implies that the term *invest* emerged in the final decade of the seventeenth century. Froide states that 'When women made wills they often established financial trusts for legal minors or married female kin', and that they defined this action through the terminology to 'lay out or invest'.[17] However, an examination of some of the creditors' wills used in this study suggests that they used different language in the 1680s. For example, Robert Draper and James Nelthorpe junior both used the term 'put out': Draper requested that £350 be 'put out at interest' for his niece's children and James Nelthorpe junior requested that legacies left to his sister and his nieces and nephews be 'put out or disposed at interest'.[18] Elizabeth Bond also did not use either *invest* or *lay out*. Instead, Bond asked for the £200 bequeathed to her grandchildren to be 'paid into the Chamber of the Citty of London' to be given to them at their ages of 21. The 'interest of which money' accrued in the meantime was directed to 'be paid to their

---

[14] PORO: POST 94/19, f. 58.

[15] TNA: C 8/328/50.

[16] *Reasons offered by several of the creditors of Richard Thompson and partners.*

[17] Froide. *Silent Partners.* 125.

[18] TNA: PROB 11/366/377. Will of Robert Draper; PROB 11/381/180. Will of James Nelthorpe, Merchant of London. 2 October 1685.

father and to goe towards the increase of their portions'.[19] The language Froide found could be a result of the expansion of financial institutions in the 1690s. However, in the early 1700s, James Nelthorpe senior also did not use the term *invest* in his will but directed £500 to be 'placed or put out ... at interest' for his granddaughters.[20]

More widely, in some of the most popular contemporary pamphlets concerning finance and banking there is similarly no use of the terms *invest* and *deposit*, but a significant use of 'hands' terminology to describe financial interaction. For example, In *England's Treasure by Foreign Trade* Thomas Mun discusses money being 'in the hands of' the Dutch, of bankers and exchangers taking 'credit into their hands' and of bankers having money 'put into their hands'.[21] Gerard Malynes similarly refers to the 'Bankers hands' throughout his work 'Of Bankes and Bankers', as does Andrew Yarranton in his 1677 text.[22] In his 1662 *A treastise of taxes* William Petty made some observations of financial practices 'in several places of Europe', noting that 'in some places the State is common Cashier for all or most moneys, as where Banks are, thereby gaining the interest of as much money as is deposited in their hands'.[23] Here Petty used the concept of 'hands' to refer more broadly to the abstract state. Similar usage can be found in the diary of Samuel Pepys, who described his intentions in June 1666 to 'get as much money' as possible out of 'public hands' and into his own 'hands' in anticipation of 'a turn' he feared was imminent in the national fortunes. Earlier that year, he cleared a bond and received a 'note' from the banker Sir Robert Vyner, 'in whose hands' the money was 'lodged'.[24] Pepys did not differentiate between interpersonal, institutional, and state finances, but used the same physical, embodied language of 'hands' to describe all three.

---

[19] TNA: PROB 11/365/74. Will of Elizabeth Bond, Widow of the City of London. 17 January 1681.

[20] TNA: PROB 11/459/28. Will of James Nelthorpe, of Charterhouse.

[21] Mun. *England's Treasure*. 101, 113, 124–125.

[22] Malynes. *Consuetudo, vel lex mercatoria*. 96, 102, 108, 112, 131–134; Yarranton. *England's Improvement*. 20.

[23] William Petty. 1662. *A Treatise of Taxes & Contributions*. London. 63.

[24] Robert Latham and William Matthews. 1971. *The Diary of Samuel Peyps*, vol. 7. London: Harper Collins. 32, 188.

The use of physical and embodied language, 'hands' and 'putting', reflects the importance of interpersonal credit relations based on reputation, widespread comparisons between the circulation of money in the body politic and that of blood in the body, and the intimate relationship between handwriting, trust, and financial instruments.[25] The language used by creditors also suggests that the hybrid nature of Thompson and Company, acting as a bank and a merchant partnership, may not have been as unusual as it seems to a modern audience. If there was no hard and fast distinction between financial institutions, then combining different elements into one institutional project would not have a great effect on how it was viewed by its customers. It is possible that the increasingly diverse range of financial institutions in the 1690s changed this outlook, encouraging specialisation or professionalisation in specific fields. However, further investigation of this is outside the realms of this chapter. Important for this chapter is what the use of embodied and physical language can tell us about why and how people came to use Thompson and Company as a credit facilitator. As the following section demonstrates, the interpersonal nature of the language of 'hands' and 'putting' reflects the personal networks and recommendations through which people chose Thompson and Company to look after their money.

II

Thompson and Company's pamphlet stated that individuals 'offered Money' to be deposited with the bank and entrusted the partners with 'several summs to a great value'.[26] Whilst it has been shown that at least 215 individuals chose to entrust their money to the bank, their reasons for choosing Thompson and Company over other banks or institutions remain unknown. Without the diaries, letters, or recorded testimonies of these individuals their individual motivations behind choosing Thompson and Company cannot be recovered. However, by further investigating

---

[25] Muldrew. *Economy of Obligation*; Natasha Glaisyer. 2005. "A due Circulation in the Veins of the Publick": Imagining Credit in Late Seventeenth- and Early Eighteenth-Century England. *The Eighteenth Century* 46: 277–297; Christine Desan. 2008. From Blood to Profit: Making Money in the Practice and Imagery of Early America. *The Journal of Policy History* 20: 26–46; Randall McGowen. 1998. Knowing the Hand: Forgery and the Proof of Writing in Eighteenth-Century England. *Historical Reflections* 24: 385–414.

[26] *Case of Thompson and Company.* 3.

6 CREDIT NETWORKS   139

their individual and collective biographies, it is possible to identify five interpersonal networks that underpinned the credit network of the bank: kinship links, political affiliation or connection, locality, recommendation, and trading association. The following section outlines these connections and the individuals behind them.

As the previous chapter demonstrated, kinship links were an important connection in the business world of the seventeenth century. However, the kin of Thompson and Company's partners do not appear in the list of 215 creditors of the bank. Whilst kin such as James Nelthorpe were clearly involved financially in the bank, they were not considered 'creditors' as their contribution was intended to aid the partners, not to make profit. As well as lending the partners £1000, James Nelthorpe also made a separate agreement with John Farrington in which they would trade 159 hogsheads of tobacco, using the profits to repay the remaining debt.[27] His business with the bank was not, therefore, like that of other creditors and he does not appear on the list of names entered in Chancery. Instead, kin were vital in communicating the news and reputation of the bank to potential customers. For example, Stephen Humphrey, a gentleman from Sussex, most likely knew of the bank through Richard Thompson's brother-in-law, John Braman who acted as a witness to a lease Humphrey took out in 1682 and may have recommended the bank to him.[28] Family connections were also responsible for a known debtor of the bank, Andrew Marvell. Evidence that Marvell was a debtor arises from the proceedings and depositions taken during the £500 bond Chancery court case between John Farrington, Mary Palmer, and Charles Wallis in 1682. In the depositions, Nelthorpe's servants Gersham Proud and Thomas Speede, and the bankers' cashier and bookkeeper Edmond Portmans, all stated that Marvell was in debt to the bank in the sum of approximately £100 to £200.[29] Additionally, Farrington stated in his 1682 Chancery statement that Marvell was not worth £30 at his death and that Nelthorpe 'kept & maintained him'.[30] It is possible that other kin, particularly Henry and Edward Thompson, used the services of their

---

[27] TNA: C 10/484/71.

[28] East Sussex Record Office: SAS/DD 510. Release by way of Mortgage (following lease for a year). 2 May 1682.

[29] Kavanagh. Andrew Marvell "in want of money". 206–212; TNA: C 24/1069. Interrogatories. 1–24 July 1682.

[30] TNA: C 8/252/9. Farrington v Palmer. February 1682.

cousins' bank but because of their familial ties never entered into any of the legal cases against them.

Proximity to the bank also affected who would become a creditor, which is evident from the fact that almost two-thirds of the creditors resided in London. However, people who resided in the immediate local area of St. Mary Woolchurch, where three of the four partners lived and where the bank's shop was located, would have been the first to encounter the bank and could have personally known the partners and been encouraged to use its services. For example, two widows were residents of St. Mary Woolchurch. Mary Robinson was the widow of the local minister Ralph Robinson, and Anne Sankey was the widow of goldsmith and St. Mary Woolchurch churchwarden William Sankey. Another creditor and citizen of London, William Piggot, was also a churchwarden of St. Mary Woolchurch in 1676 and painter-stainer John Vear also lived in the parish. Whilst there are many possibilities for the identity of creditor John Hudson, the most compatible identity is the goldsmith from St. Mary Woolchurch, showing yet another local creditor with money to deposit for either business or investment. Additionally, a doctor, Charles Mason, also resided in St. Mary Woolchurch. Mason could have acted as a family doctor to the partners and their families, or simply have been aware of the bank through local networks. Proximity also accounts for a known creditor of the bank not included in the 1679 case, John Beaman, a resident of St. Mary Woolchurch and possible sideman of the churchwardens who died in 1695. Beaman's identity as a creditor of the bank is evident from a 1683 inventory or account of the belongings of the parish church, in which is listed a 'Bond of 100^{Li} for payment of 50^{Li} from Mr Richard Thompson and Company at six pounds percent per annum'. The record states that this was in Beaman's possession and that he 'doth acknowledge to have Recived' it.[31]

Political connection accounts for a good deal of the creditors of Thompson and Company. This is unsurprising given the political roles of Thompson and Nelthorpe in the 1670s, both sitting on London's Common Council, and the political connections of their wider kinship

---

[31] Brooke. *Transcript of the Registers.* lx, 48, 144, 152, 212, 274, 338, 366; *Boyd's Inhabitants of London*, 1647 record, 3830, and 1651 record, 42878; TNA: PROB 11/484/164. Will of John Hudson, Goldsmith of London. 13 September 1705; LMA: P69/MRY15/B/013/MS01009. Inventory, 27 September 1683; TNA: PROB 4/7721. Beaman alias Ballmon, John, of St. Mary Woolchurch, London. 20 February 1695.

6 CREDIT NETWORKS 141

network. Whilst the two partners' opposition affiliation and dissenting beliefs could affect who chose to become a creditor, or whom they accepted business from, this does not appear to be the case. Their politically active clientele included dissenters, Anglicans, and independents, suggesting that financial activity was not dictated by political affiliation (see Tables 6.1 and 6.2). Of the 215 known creditors, 15 sat on London's Common Council and 11 were MPs. To be an officeholder in civic and national government required status and wealth, so those who were

Table 6.1 Creditors who were common councillors

Name	Status	Ward	Years active	Persuasion
William Allen	Merchant	Bread Street	1660, 1686	Whig
John Baker	Merchant	Cordwainer	1683, 1688–1692	
Daniel Berry	Merchant	Dowgate	1669, 1672–1677, 1681	Whig
Samuel Beake	Merchant	Billingsgate	1674–1676	
Phillip Chetwind	Merchant		1648	
John Crisp	Merchant	Bread Street	1669–1683, 1689–1693	Whig
John Dubois	Merchant	Cripplegate Within	1674–1682	Whig
John Jekyll	Citizen & Haberdasher	Cheapside	1661–1662, 1668–1670	Whig
John Jeenes	Citizen & Upholder	Castle Baynard	1672	
Henry Lewis	Citizen & Scrivener	Aldgate	1683, 1690–1692	Tory
John Morice	Merchant	Bread Street	1675–1683, 1688–1692	Whig
Robert Stephenson/Stevenson	Merchant	Bishopsgate Within	1671–1674, 1681, 1683	
Richard Tilden	Merchant	Tower	1662, 1677, 1680, 1690–1696	
William Wilkinson	Citizen & Skinner	Cordwainer	1671, 1675–1683	Tory
Henry Williamson	Citizen & Upholder	Tower	1664, 1669–1680	

Sources Woodhead, *Rulers of London*, except Chetwind, for whom information derives from Brenner, *Merchants and Revolution*, 486

142   M. WINTER

Table 6.2 Creditors who were MPs

Name	Status	MP for	Years active	Persuasion
Francis Buller	Politician	Cornwall & Saltash	1659, 1660, 1661	Whig
John Buller	Lawyer	East & West Loe, Saltash, Liskeard, Grampound	Irregular intervals 1656–1692	Independent
Sir Robert Cotton	Politician	Chester/Cambridgeshire	Irregular intervals 1679–1701/2	Whig/ Tory
Sir Gilbert Gerard	Politician	Northallerton	1661, 1679, 1681	Whig
Randalph Grahme	Woollen Draper	Leominster	1661	Whig
Sir John Hoskins	Lawyer	Hertfordshire	1685	Tory
Sir Anthony Irby	Politician	Boston, Lincolnshire	Irregular intervals 1628–1681	Whig
Sir Jonathan Keate	Merchant	Hertfordshire	1679	Whig
Sir John Kempthorne	Captain	Portsmouth	1679	Independent
William Ramsden	Merchant	Kingston-Upon-Hull	1678, 1679	Whig
Sir William Turner	Woollen Draper & Silk Merchant	London	1690–1693	Tory

Sources: *The History of Parliament*, http://www.historyofparliamentonline.org/

aware of the bank through political circles would certainly have possessed enough capital to warrant the services of a financial institution.

The majority of the 15 creditors who were common councillors sat on the Common Council at the same time or for periods during the time that Thompson and Nelthorpe did between 1669 and 1676 (see Table 6.1). Only four of the common councillors, William Allen, John Baker, Phillip Chetwind, and Henry Lewis, did not sit on the council during those seven years. Additionally, two-thirds of the councillors were merchants by trade, so, if not through the Common Council, it is likely they were aware of the bank through the mercantile social circles of London. For example, William Allen and John Baker were both merchants, and so

6 CREDIT NETWORKS   143

likely knew of the bank through mercantile circles. Allen was also a dissenter, contributing £50 to the 1670 Dissenting loan to the crown, giving him a religious connection to the banking partners.[32] Henry Lewis was a scrivener and bankers commonly used scriveners to draw up financial and legal documents. Thompson and Company's partners certainly used scriveners, such as John Foach who was a defendant alongside Farrington in the Cowper family case in Chancery in 1683.[33] There is, then, a possibility that Lewis may have encountered the bankers professionally, obtaining knowledge of the bank through his trade. Merchant and former common councillor Phillip Chetwind is harder to place in direct connection to the bankers. He was on the Common Council of London in the 1640s, a member of the Clothworkers' Company like Richard Thompson, a Presbyterian, and active amongst an earlier powerful mercantile faction in metropolitan government. That Chetwind was still around in the later seventeenth century, when the bank was active, is evident from his will of 1683 and the Exchequer Books of Receipt for the compositions of the accounts of Robert Vyner, which record that Chetwind was a customer.[34] It is possible that following the 1672 Stop on the Exchequer, Chetwind decided to deposit his remaining funds elsewhere and chose Thompson and Company due to their reputation amongst political circles in London, in which Chetwind may still have been active.

Of the other 11 common councillors, some have further links to the bankers that could offer an insight into why they chose Thompson and Company. John Morice was a member of the Mercers Company, a merchant, and director of the Royal African Company and the Levant Company. Morice was later to become a deputy leader of the Whigs under William Love, suggesting deeper involvement in opposition politics and a potential friendship with the bankers through their dissenting common councillor identities.[35] John Dubois was a French Huguenot merchant born in Canterbury and raised in the French church there. On his freedom from the Weavers' Company in 1653, Dubois became a silk

[32] De Krey. *London and the Restoration*. 403.

[33] Woodhead. *Rulers of London*. 108; TNA: C 6/392/39, Cooper v Foach, 1683.

[34] Brenner. *Merchants and Revolution*. 486; *Boyd's Inhabitants of London*, 1636 record, 40384; TNA: PROB 11/372/258, Will of Phillip Chetwind, Clothworker of London. 19 February 1683; TNA: E 406/16. Goldsmiths' assignment book, Second series. 1676–1680. f. 410.

[35] De Krey. *London and the Restoration*. 418; Woodhead. *Rulers of London*. 117.

144   M. WINTER

merchant trading predominantly with France. It was through mercantile trading that Dubois first began an active political career, participating in the 1674 'scheme of trade' and identified as one of the 'small but powerful group of London merchants who were especially important in anti-French propaganda after 1670'. As a common councillor, Dubois was appointed to at least four committees alongside Thompson and Nelthorpe and prominent within the same 'civic opposition' faction in the Corporation of London, later becoming a leader of the Whigs. Dubois was a wealthy merchant whose personal property in 1686, two years after his death, was recorded at £35,205, so he could have been quite a large depositor at the bank.[36]

Similar to Dubois, John Crisp would also go on to become a leading figure in the Whig party. Crisp was a merchant and a member of the Salters' Company, becoming a master in 1683. He sat on London's Common Council for Bread Street from 1669–1683 and 1689–1693 and was appointed to a Common Council committee with Richard Thompson in 1674. Crisp was certainly in possession of spare capital and had £500 worth of shares in both the East India Company and Royal African Company, demonstrating his wealth.[37] John Jekyll, as well as being a Common Councillor, had a further link to the bankers through their cousin and friend Andrew Marvell who supported Jekyll and James Hayes when they caused the arrest and trial of London Mayor Samuel Starling in 1670. Jekyll was a Presbyterian, an exclusionist, and an unlicensed printer who was involved in the Rye House Plot and the Monmouth Rebellion.[38] His religious and political outlook, along with his association with Marvell and the Common Council, could explain why Jekyll chose to deposit his funds at the bank.

[36] Margaret Priestley. 1956. London Merchants and Opposition Politics in Charles II's Reign. *The Bulletin of the Institute of Historical Research* 29: 205, 209; Gary S. De Krey. 2008. Dubois, John (*bap.* 1622, *d.* 1684). *ODNB*, https://doi.org/10.1093/ref:odnb/67399. Accessed 12 February 2018; Woodhead. *Rulers of London*. 62; LMA: COL/AD/01/49, 'YY Letter Book 1673–76', ff. 20, 50, 71, 137; De Krey. *London and the Restoration*. 140, 225–226, 235, 315, 322.

[37] De Krey. *London and the Restoration*. 415; Woodhead. *Rulers of London*. 54; LMA: COL/AD/01/49, 'YY Letter Book 1673–76', f. 16.

[38] Elizabeth R. Clarke. 2008. Jekyll, John (1611–1690), *ODNB*, https://doi.org/10.1093/ref:odnb/67136. Accessed 16 February 2018.

6 CREDIT NETWORKS 145

In addition to these 15 members of the Corporation of London, the list of creditors features 11 MPs who similarly could have links to the bank through political circles (see Table 6.2), although three of those 11, Sir John Hoskins, Sir John Kempthorne, and Ranald Grahme, have alternate reasons for choosing the bank, which are discussed elsewhere. One of the 11 MPs, Sir Robert Cotton, is difficult to identify. For Sir Robert Cotton there are two possible options for his identity, one being Sir Robert Cotton of Cambridge, and the other Sir Robert Cotton of Combermere, Cheshire. Both Cottons became significantly active in the Exclusion crisis, Cotton of Cambridge for the Tories and Cotton of Cheshire for the Whigs and held their positions from 1679 to 1701/2. Both, however, had launched their political careers earlier after inheriting family estates, Cotton of Cambridge inheriting Hatley estate in 1662 and Cotton of Cheshire inheriting his estate in 1649.[39] Either could have been the creditor of Thompson and Company.

It is possible that some of these creditors came to know of the bank through MP, and friend and relative of the bankers, Andrew Marvell. Many of the creditors who were MPs were in the House of Commons in the same period as Marvell, who was MP for Hull from 1659 to 1678. For example, John Buller and Sir Anthony Irby were in the House of Commons at similar times to Marvell and both were friends of Lord Wharton, who was also a friend and patron of Marvell.[40] Additionally, Irby and Buller, along with Marvell and creditor and MP Sir Gilbert Gerrard, sat on the parliamentary committee for 'A Bill for the better Discovery of the Estates of *Richard Thompson, Edward Nelthrop*, and others, Bankrupts', which attempted to discover the whereabouts of the

---

[39] Eveline Cruickshanks and Richard Harrison. COTTON, Sir Robert (1644–1717), of Hatley St. George, Cambs. *HoP*, http://www.historyofparliamentonline.org/vol ume/1690-1715/member/cotton-sir-robert-1644-1717. Accessed 18 May 2020; Eveline Cruickshanks and Richard Harrison. COTTON, Sir Robert, 1st Bt. (c.1635–1712), of Combermere, Cheshire. *HoP*, http://www.historyofparliamentonline.org/volume/1690-1715/member/cotton-sir-robert-1635-1712. Accessed 18 May 2020.

[40] Helms and Watson. BULLER, John (c.1632–1716), of the Middle Temple and Morval, nr. East Looe, Cornw. *HoP*, http://www.historyofparliamentonline.org/volume/1660-1690/member/buller-john-1632-1716. Accessed 12 February 2018; M. W. Helms and Paula Watson. IRBY, Sir Anthony (1605–1682), of Whaplode, Lincs. and Westminster. *HoP*, http://www.historyofparliamentonline.org/volume/1660-1690/member/irby-sir-anthony-1605-82. Accessed 12 February 2018; Nicholas von Maltzahn. 2003. Andrew Marvell and the Lord Wharton. *The Seventeenth Century* 18: 252–265.

bankrupt partners and enforce legal action in 1678.[41] It is possible that Gerrard, Irby, and Buller's appointment to the committee was due to their familiarity with the bank as creditors.

For MPs William Ramsden and Sir Jonathan Keate their knowledge of Thompson and Company more likely arose through mercantile networks or from associations in York with the wider Thompson family, particularly Sir Henry and Edward Thompson. Ramsden was a prominent political figure in Hull and Mayor of the City from 1659 to 1660, but there is no mention of Ramsden in Marvell's correspondence, and Ramsden only became MP for Hull following Marvell's death. Instead, Ramsden's connection to the bankers could have been through the Thompsons of York and Hull. Ramsden was a York Merchant Adventurer, as were the bankers' relatives Sir Henry and Stephen Thompson, and through them he could have learnt of the bank.[42] Merchant Sir Jonathan Keate similarly sat as an MP after Marvell's death in 1679, but he did have a previous connection with the Thompson brothers of York and with banking partner Edmund Page as outlined in the previous chapter.[43] Why Keate decided to deposit funds at the bank probably arose from his acquaintance with Page and his own mercantile connections.

Another creditor with political connections was James Hickes, the senior clerk of the inland letter office of the Post Office in the 1660s and 1670s. In this role Hickes was in direct contact with the secretary of state from 1674, Sir Joseph Williamson, who was a particularly vehement enemy of the banking partners. Williamson's administrative roles led him to become 'the *de facto* head of the Restoration government's intelligence system', intercepting mail at the post office and gathering information on the plots and conspiracies of post-Restoration England, a task which

[41] *Journal of the House of Commons*, vol. 9, 1667–1687, accessed via *British History Online*, https://www.british-history.ac.uk/commons-jrnl/vol9. Accessed 15 August 2018. '2 March 1677', '12 February 1677', and '16 February 1677'.

[42] P. A. Bolton and Basil Duke Henning. RAMSDEN, William (c.1618–80), of Hull, Yorks. *HoP*, http://www.historyofparliamentonline.org/volume/1660-1690/member/ramsden-william-1618-80. Accessed 12 February 2018; Maud Sellers. 1918. *The York Mercers and Merchant Adventurers, 1356–1917*. London: Surtees Society. 293, 298, 302.

[43] E. R. Edwards and Geoffrey Jaggar. KEATE, Sir Jonathan, 1st Bt. (1633–1700), of The Hoo, Kimpton, Herts. *HoP*, http://www.historyofparliamentonline.org/volume/1660-1690/member/keate-sir-jonathan-1633-1700. Accessed 12 February 2018.

6 CREDIT NETWORKS **147**

he carried out using 'various intermediaries most of whom were drawn from the staff'. One such intermediary recruited to Williamson's 'cabinet noir' was Hickes.[44] The intelligence network and relationship between Williamson and Hickes is evident in the 244 surviving letters Hickes sent to Williamson in his years in office from 1661 to 1678, detailing plots, gossip, and foreign affairs.[45] That Hickes was one of Williamson's 'spies and informers' is of particular interest given Williamson's later surveillance of the banking partners as potential political conspirators.[46] Hickes most likely knew of the bank through political circles and knowledge of London's social and business life attained through his position at the Post office.

Many creditors of Thompson and Company likely became clients of the bank through recommendation by friends, family, or associates. This highlights the importance of credit and reputation for institutional as well as interpersonal financial networks. In their own pamphlet the partners recognised that reputation and recommendation would provide them with more clients, stating that as current creditors maintained their 'Confidence' in them 'many others chose to imploy their Money in our hands' too.[47] Recommendations demonstrate creditors' confidence in the bank's service and reputation, and highlight the role of intermediaries in expanding credit networks beyond immediate acquaintances. For example, creditor and widow Elizabeth Bond appears to have become a customer of the bank through the partners' friend and political ally Sir Thomas Player. Elizabeth was Thomas Player's mother-in-law: her daughter Joyce from her first marriage to William Kendall had married Player in 1641. In her will of 1681 Elizabeth Bond, as she had then become, left to her 'daughter Dame Joyce Player wife of Sir Thomas Player Knight five hundred pounds', and made her 'loveing sonne in

---

[44] James Hickes, senior clerk in the inland Letter Office, to the Duke of York. *SPO*, SP 29/442 f. 178, 1678; Alan Marshall. 1994. *Intelligence and Espionage in the Reign of Charles II, 1660–1685*. Cambridge: Cambridge University Press. 33, 78–95; Alan Marshall. 1996. Sir Joseph Williamson and the conduct of administration in Restoration England. *Historical Research* 69: 18–41.

[45] State Papers Online: advanced search for Author/writer: James Hickes and Recipient: Williamson.

[46] Notes by Williamson. *SPO*, SP 29/379 f. 73, 17 February 1676; Notes by Williamson. *SPO*, SP 29/379 f. 80, 18 February 1676.

[47] *Case of Richard Thompson and Company*. 3.

148   M. WINTER

law Sr Thomas Player' one of the 'overseers of this my will'.[48] Elizabeth clearly had plenty of affection for and trust in her son-in-law, making it likely that she would ask him for advice on where to place her money and Player, as a close friend and ally of the bankers, could have suggested Thompson and Company as such an institution. Similarly, creditor Elizabeth Irby was the sister of fellow creditor and MP Sir Anthony Irby. She was a spinster of Westminster who died in 1684, leaving quite significant amounts of money to friends and relatives, including 'One hundred pounds' a piece to each of her nieces and nephews, £50 to a friend, and £20 to her servant.[49] Her brother, who, as mentioned above, moved in the same political circles as the banking partners could also have recommended Thompson and Company.

Why Theophilus Birkenhead became a customer of the bank is unclear. Birkenhead was a gentleman of the parish of Saint Clement Danes, London, which also housed 'Heycock's Ordinary', a regular haunt of 'Parliament men and gallants', and the 'Palgrave's Head', which similarly hosted meetings of 'Talkers'. It is possible, therefore, that Birkenhead could have heard of the Bank's reputation through political circles gathered in those establishments. Whether this was how he knew of it or not, Birkenhead himself appears to have helped expand the bank's network or been a recipient of recommendation himself. In his 1693 will he left 'land at Islington' and 'all my houses and other my real estate' to his sister, Susan Salisbury, a widow who was also named in the 1679 Chancery case as a creditor.[50] Another sibling connection is evident in creditors Tregonwell and William Frampton, brothers from Dorset. Tregonwell Frampton was a racehorse trainer who began his career in the 1670s and acquired a sizeable estate in Newmarket. Tregonwell was the fifth son of William Frampton of Moreton, Dorset, and William was his elder

---

[48] *Boyd's Inhabitants of London*, 1641 record, 35759; Gary S. De Krey. 2008. Player, Sir Thomas (*d.* 1686). *ODNB*, http://www.oxforddnb.com/view/article/22364. Accessed 2 July 2018; TNA: PROB 11/365/74. Will of Elizabeth Bond.

[49] TNA: PROB 11/375/341. Will of Elizabeth Irby of Saint Margaret Westminster, Middlesex. 8 March 1684.

[50] LMA: ACC/0413/A/04/001. Will of Theophilus Birkenhead. 15 September 1693; John Diprose. 1868. *Some account of the parish of Saint Clement Danes*. London: Diprose and Bateman. 186; Notes by Williamson. *SPO*, SP 29/379 f. 80, 18 February 1676.

6 CREDIT NETWORKS 149

brother who inherited the estate from their father.[51] That both brothers were creditors suggests that one recommended the bank to the other. The same is true of London citizens and creditors Richard Seymour and his nephew William Abbot, both of whom were creditors of the bank.[52]

Creditors Sir John Churchman, his wife Hester, the Gore family, Ranald Grahme, and Sir William Turner could also have formed a network of recommendation. Sir John Churchman's will reveals that he was 'of the Inner Temple', held lands in London, and owned the majority of the town of Illington in Norfolk, which he left to his son William. Additional sources show that, through his wife Hester, the Churchman family were related to the Gore family.[53] Churchman's home in St. Giles in the Fields, London, was large, possessed of 10 hearths according to the 1666 hearth tax for Middlesex, further demonstrating their vast wealth.[54] Churchman's connection to Ranald Grahme is evident from Grahme's will, in which he bequeathed Churchman 'twenty pounds to buy him mourning'.[55] Grahme became a member of the Merchant Taylors' Guild through apprenticeship and worked in London as a successful Woollen Draper, evident from his purchase of the estate of Nunnington in Yorkshire in 1655 and his election as MP for Leominster in 1661.[56] Creditor Gerard Gore was originally believed to be a merchant and Alderman of London from 1656 to 1657. However, Alderman Gore died in 1660.[57]

---

[51] John Pinfold. 2007. Frampton, Tregonwell [*called* the Father of the Turf] (*bap.* 1641, *d.* 1728). *ODNB*, https://doi.org/10.1093/ref:odnb/10062. Accessed 18 July 2018; TNA: PROB 11/399/141. Will of William Frampton of Moreton, Dorset. 10 April 1690.

[52] LMA: DL/AM/PW/1685/067. Will of Richard Seymour. 1685; *Boyd's Inhabitants of London*, 1676 record, 54516.

[53] TNA: PROB 11/395/360. Will of Sir John Churchman; Blomefield. *An Essay Towards a Topographical History of the County of Norfolk*, vol. 1. 304.

[54] Search for Sir John Churchman in London Hearth Tax: City of London and Middlesex, 1666, British History Online, https://www.british-history.ac.uk/london-hearth-tax/london-mddx/1666/st-giles-in-the-fields-holborn-north. Accessed 19 May 2020.

[55] TNA: PROB 11/381/495. Will of Ranald Grahme of Nunnington, Yorkshire. 2 December 1685.

[56] Edward Rowlands. GRAHME, Ranald (c.1605–85), of Petty France, Westminster and Nunnington, Wath, Yorks. *HoP*, http://www.historyofparliamentonline.org/volume/1660-1690/member/grahme-ranald-1605-85. Accessed 26 July 2018.

[57] *Boyd's Inhabitants of London*, 1656 record, 10249; Beaven, *Aldermen of the City of London*, p. 85.

150   M. WINTER

Instead, the gentleman Gerrard Gore from Sussex, relative of the Churchman's, was the creditor of Thompson and Company. In his will, Gore refers to a lease and release for one of his properties which was made between himself, William Bleverchasset, and fellow creditor Sir William Turner.[58] Gore's acquaintance with Turner, or recommendation from his kin the Churchman family, could explain how Gore heard of the bank and why he deposited money there.

Despite the detailed accounts between William Turner and Fauconberg, there is no evidence concerning which of them first decided to do business with Thompson and Company. It is possible that the connection arose through Andrew Marvell. Fauconberg was related to Lord Fairfax, who employed Marvell as a tutor for his daughter, Mary Fairfax, from 1650 to 1652. Upon Fauconberg's marriage to Mary Cromwell in 1657, just after Marvell had ceased tutoring Oliver Cromwell's ward William Dutton, Marvell wrote 'Two Songs at the Marriage of the Lord Fauconberg', no doubt commissioned by Fauconberg's new father-in-law.[59] As well as using the bank himself, Fauconberg could then have recommended his friend or agent, William Turner, to their services, thus extending the credit network of Thompson and Company. That Fauconberg did recommend the bank is suggested by the fact that Fauconberg's aunt Frances Ingram was also a creditor of the bank. Frances was the widow of Sir Thomas Ingram, MP for Thirsk in Yorkshire, and Frances left her 'coach-horses' to her nephew, 'Thomas lord Viscount Fauconberg', in her will.[60] The relationship between Fauconberg and Ingram could explain how Ingram came to be a creditor.

Although no concrete evidence exists, the Corporation of Trinity House London also appear to have become a creditor of the bank through the recommendation of Marvell, who was an elder brother of the institution, having been elected and sworn in to the Corporation

---

[58] TNA: PROB 11/373/120. Will of Gerrard Gore of Shillinglee Park, Sussex. 21 May 1683.

[59] Smith. *Andrew Marvell*. 141–142.

[60] P. A. Bolton and Paula Watson. INGRAM, Sir Thomas (1614–1672), of Sheriff Hutton, Yorks. and Isleworth, Mdx. *HoP*, http://www.historyofparliamentonline.org/volume/1660-1690/member/ingram-sir-thomas-1614-72. Accessed 20 July 2018; TNA PROB 11/362/434. Will of Dame Frances Ingram, Widow. 1 April 1680.

6 CREDIT NETWORKS 151

on 8 May 1674. No record exists that details the Corporation's decision to deposit with the bankers, but on 9 December 1675 the minutes record that Trinity House was requesting the return of £500 they had put in Thompson and Company. In addition to their own business, Trinity House also provided a connection for another two creditors. One was captain John Kempthorne, one of the Elder Brethren of Trinity House who was made a master of the corporation in 1674. The second was John Thompson, which although is an incredibly common name could refer to a John Thompson who was elected as a younger brother of the Corporation on 7 February 1672.[61]

Whilst the Corporation of Trinity House London is the only institution named on the list of creditors, there was another institution that nearly became a creditor of the bank and would have done so through recommendation of the bank's services—the Royal Society, of which Nelthorpe was a member. In 1674 the prospect was raised of the Society itself becoming a creditor by putting a £400 legacy left by 'the late Dr Wilkins to the society' in the Bank. The minutes record that on 27 February the Earl Marshal, Henry Howard, duke of Norfolk, 'named upon occasion Mr Thomson and Mr Nelthrop as very good men to put the four hundred pounds legacy to upon use at 6 percent'. In the following meeting, the reason behind Norfolk's recommendation was revealed. The minutes record that Norfolk sent a letter to Henry Oldenburg in which he 'proposed a method of well disposing the four hundred pounds legacy to some considerable citizens', Thompson and Nelthorpe, 'with whom his friends had lodged some considerable sums of money'. This suggests that Norfolk was not a creditor himself but was aware of Thompson and Company's reputation through unnamed 'friends' who may have been creditors themselves. Despite his recommendation, the Society decided that the £400 legacy 'should be paid out to Sir John Bankes' and used to purchase 'three fee-farm rents'.[62] Although not acted on, Norfolk's

---

[61] LMA: CLC/526/MS30307, List of masters. 12, 54, 56; LMA: CLC/526/MS30004/004. 66, 227.

[62] Birch. *History of the Royal Society of London*, vol. 3. 70, 93, 129, 130, 176, 178; John Henry. 2009. Wilkins, John (1614–1672). *ODNB*, https://doi-org.sheffield. idm.oclc.org/10.1093/ref:odnb/29421. Accessed 13 February 2018; John Miller. 2004. Howard, Henry, sixth duke of Norfolk (1628–1684). *ODNB*, https://doi.org/10.1093/ ref:odnb/13907. Accessed 6 February 2018.

152   M. WINTER

recommendation and the society's consideration of his proposal, demonstrates that the bank had a good reputation in London. Like Trinity House, some members of the Royal Society were also creditors of the bank of Thompson and Company. These were Robert Boyle and Sir John Hoskins.[63] Robert Boyle was one of the founding members of the Society and a philanthropist. Boyle was familiar with finance and trade through his role as Governor of the New England Company and as a shareholder in the East India Company.[64] He was also an associate of Thompson and Nelthorpe's distant cousin William Popple, who is another possible source of recommendation for Boyle.[65] Creditor Sir John Hoskins, a master in the Court of Chancery from 1676 to 1703, was also a member of the Royal Society and briefly acted as President in 1682.[66]

Further signifying the partners' good reputation in London is the number of citizens who were creditors, suggesting that guild membership could account for how the partners' reputation circulated amongst these trading communities. Of the group of citizens listed as creditors, 18 were members of the guilds that the bankers themselves were members of; there were nine Clothworkers, five Drapers, and four Haberdashers. However, membership of any guild could explain how some of these citizens became creditors. As Gadd and Wallis argue, guilds and companies served as 'talking-shops, clearing houses for gossip and information, and places to develop the loose networks of sociability and association which allowed the mercantile economy to function'.[67] Therefore, the reputation of the bank could have spread through these kinds of urban trading associations.

More specifically, in terms of trading connections, merchant-creditors identified as Merchant Adventurers had a potential connection to bank

[63] TNA: C 8/328/50; Gail Ewald Scala. 1974. An Index of Proper Names in Thomas Birch, "The History of the Royal Society" (London, 1756–1757). *Notes and Records of the Royal Society of London* 28: 270, 293–294.

[64] Michael Hunter. 2015. Boyle, Robert (1627–1691). *ODNB*, https://doi-org.sheffield.idm.oclc.org/10.1093/ref:odnb/3137. Accessed 13 February 2018; BL: IOR/L/AG/1/1/5. Ledger D. May 1671–July 1673, f. 262(1), IOR/L/AG/1/1/6. Ledger E. August 1673–December 1675, f. 356(1).

[65] Robbins. Absolute Liberty. 206, 220.

[66] G. S. McIntyre. 2004. Hoskins [Hoskyns], Sir John, second baronet (1634–1705). *ODNB*, https://doi-org.sheffield.idm.oclc.org/10.1093/ref:odnb/13840. Accessed 15 August 2018; Birch. *History of the Royal society of London*, vol. 1. 53.

[67] Gadd and Wallis. Introduction. 10.

6 CREDIT NETWORKS 153

partner and fellow Adventurer Edward Nelthorpe. Godfrey Lawson was a Merchant Adventurer from Leeds, who became a new communicant at the Hamburg Church in 1654, six years prior to Nelthorpe's own introduction there in 1660. Mart towns such as Hamburg were places where the young apprentice or merchant could expand his social contacts and make his reputation known. It is possible, therefore, that the two merchants knew each other through the Hamburg trade in the 1660s, and that this connection led Lawson to utilise the banking services later in the 1670s. The same could be argued for creditors Samuel Beak, Robert Fenn, William Palmer, and John Smythe. William Palmer has a further link to Nelthorpe alongside being a Merchant Adventurer. Palmer's master was William Attwood, for whom Nelthorpe acted as agent in the early 1660s, and, if they did not meet as apprentices, the two men could have first made each other's acquaintance through their mutual employment by Attwood.[68]

Abraham Dixon also had a trading connection to Edward Nelthorpe, evident from a Chancery court case dispute with him in 1676. Dixon lived and worked in Somerset, part of the 'West Country clothing district', and he and Nelthorpe were defendants to a complaint entered by clothier Richard Scadding, who had accused his employee William Corbee of being indebted to him. The majority of the court case concerns the dealings of Scadding and Corbee, offering little insight for this study apart from explaining how and why Dixon was a creditor of the bank. Corbee had previously been lent money by Dixon, who had 'considerable dealing' with Nelthorpe 'in selling of wooles for him in the Country', for which purpose Nelthorpe and Dixon often assigned bills to one another to cover the costs or pay the profits.[69] This demonstrates that Nelthorpe had contacts in Somerset, and other areas of the cloth-producing district, who could have become clients of the bank for either deposits or loans. This could therefore explain how Devonshire tailor Thomas Parkman became a creditor, as Devon was also part of the cloth-producing district.

[68] Sheffield City Archive: BFM/1293. Matthew Ashton's (later Frank's) account book; Woodhead. *Rulers of London*. 27; *The Little London Directory*; Brenner. *Merchants and Revolution*. 183, 185; Hamburg State Archives: Register book of the Church of the English Court, MS 521-1; Leng. *Fellowship and Freedom*. 12, 15.

[69] TNA: C 5/551/85. Scadding v Corbee. 1676; C. G. A. Clay. 1984. *Economic Expansion and Social Change: England 1500–1700, vol. 2, Industry, Trade and Government*. Cambridge: Cambridge University Press. 13.

154 M. WINTER

Additionally, Nelthorpe's trade in Ireland could explain how George Villiers, fourth Viscount Grandison of Limerick, became a creditor. Part of the Villiers family, Grandison was the uncle of Barbara Villiers, duchess of Cleveland and mistress of Charles II, and as her trustee received her 'pension' and gifts of land from the King. Nelthorpe was active in Ireland in the 1670s due to his factory project in Clonmel under the patronage of James Butler, duke of Ormond, and Grandison's connections to Ireland and the Irish peerage could have brought Nelthorpe and the bank to his attention. Grandison certainly had available funds from the profits made on his lands in Ireland, and the substantial marriage portion of £2000 he received in 1674 when he married Dame Mary Sternell or Starling, widow of the alderman Sir Samuel Starling.[70]

Less speculatively, Nelthorpe's varied trading exploits also account for one known debtor to the bank, Edward Billing, a brewer of London. Billing was involved in a Chancery court case entered by Robert Squibb, who owned the brewhouse that Billing occupied. Edward Nelthorpe was another defendant in Squibb's case and had come into conflict with Squibb over the sale of vessels and other equipment in the brewhouse intended to satisfy each of their debts. Only Nelthorpe's answer to the case survives, but in that answer he revealed that Billing was a possible bankrupt, although Nelthorpe 'knoweth not' for certain, and that Billing was indebted to Nelthorpe' & his partners in the summe of six hundred fifty and nine pounds' along with the interest that had accumulated.[71] If Billing was a bankrupt, then the bankers may never have received the full amount owed to them, particularly given the subsequent conflict between Nelthorpe and Squibb.

---

[70] S. M. Wynne. 2008. Palmer [née Villiers], Barbara, countess of Castlemaine and suo jure duchess of Cleveland (*bap.* 1640, *d.* 1709), royal mistress. *ODNB*, https://doi.org/10.1093/ref:odnb/28285. Accessed 15 February 2018; BL: Stowe MS 201. Essex Papers vol. II. f. 410; Stowe MS 204. Essex Papers vol. V. f. 341; Stowe MS 205. Essex Papers vol. VI. f. 461; Stowe MS 207. Essex Papers vol. VIII. f. 448; Stowe MS 210. Essex Papers vol. XI. f. 442; Egerton MS 3351. vol. XXVIII. f. 90; Add MS 38849. Hodgkin Papers vol. IV. f. 112; LMA: CLC/521/MS18242. Agreement whereby Dame Mary Sternell, alias Starling (nee Garford), widow of Samuel Sternell, gives George, Viscount Grandison, her intended husband, £2000 on condition that her remaining real and personal estate will not be under his control. 18 November 1674.

[71] TNA: C 8/268/47. Squibb v Nelthorpe. 1674.

III

Through a study of language and the five categories of connection between creditors and the partners of Thompson and Company, this chapter has demonstrated the centrality of trust, credit, and reputation to a financial institution. The partners drew customers to the bank through their existing social networks and through the recommendations of existing customers, friends, and family. These interpersonal connections have been highlighted as important for informal or neighbourly credit networks, but not nearly as important for institutions. Historians such as Muldrew and Wennerlind have argued that the institutions that emerged after the 1672 Stop on the Exchequer, and particularly in the 1690s, represented a break from the interpersonal financial culture that had existed previously and was centred more explicitly on the state and public finance.[72] However, the importance of interpersonal credit remained. Many of the creditors knew one or two members of Thompson and Company on a personal basis, whilst those that did not usually had connections to another creditor, which demonstrates the importance of the practice of recommendation in extending credit networks.

The use of physical and embodied language to describe financial interaction further demonstrates the enduring importance of reputation, personal networks, and interpersonal trust, whether that be in the proprietors of institutions themselves or their existing customers. That the importance of credit and interpersonal reputation continued is evident from studies of later financial phenomenon. For example, Graham has emphasised the importance of credibility for the 1690s Exchequer bills, which relied on the example set by 'key figures in the money market' to encourage others to trade in and accept the bills, and Murphy argued that the Bank of England relied on the performance of credit through its architecture and its clerks, which 'allowed public creditors to interact with each other and to interrogate the financial stability and reputation of the state in the same ways that they could interrogate the integrity of any potential private borrower'.[73] Thompson and Company's credit networks and the language used by their creditors further reinforce the enduring

---

[72] Muldrew. *Economy of Obligation*. 115–116; Wennerlind. *Casualties of Credit*. 1–5.

[73] Aaron Graham. 2019. Credit, confidence, and the circulation of Exchequer bills in the early financial revolution. *Financial History Review* 26: 63–80; Murphy. Performing Public Credit. 61.

importance of reputation, and interpersonal credit, to institutions and corporations.

This chapter has highlighted the importance of the partners' social, commercial, and political networks for providing capital and customers for the bank venture. It therefore emphasises the positive implications of networks in building reputation and credit. However, these networks could not only spread positive reputation and forge new connections, but could also spread negative information concerning the bank, whether it be true or false, to disastrous ends. The following chapters turn to examine the collapse of the bank, demonstrating that these same roles and networks contributed to Thompson and Company's failure just as much as they did to their success.

CHAPTER 7

Bankruptcy

In 1684, Farrington stated that whilst 'in a short time the said Joint Banke & dealing got into very great creditt & esteeme', the banking venture did not proceed entirely as planned. The original articles of agreement stipulated that the venture was to last three years, so in 1674 the articles of agreement were renewed to continue the partnership. However, according to Farrington, this renewal was not a result of success but done out of necessity to avoid scandal. He argued that the bank was 'reduced soo low' that he and Page 'could not then disengage themselves from the said Nelthorpe & Thompson without present ruine to themselves'. The reason behind this 'low' was a contract for Prize goods—enemy ships captured during warfare—that were seized during the Third Anglo-Dutch war, which Thompson and Nelthorpe obtained and lost in the space of one month in 1673. In order to obtain the contract, Thompson and Nelthorpe were required to gather a vast sum of money, some of which likely came out of the bank. The circumstances surrounding the contract are discussed in the following chapter, but it is worth noting here that this was the reason behind the partners' 'low' funds. The renewed articles of agreement included one 'new or further agreement' that had not been in the original articles. This article specified that, as before, 'each of the said parties might by the consent of the rest & not otherwise contend to drawe out from the said bank any such convenient sumes as might be

© The Author(s), under exclusive license to Springer Nature Switzerland AG 2022
M. Winter, *Banking, Projecting and Politicking in Early Modern England*, Palgrave Studies in Economic History, https://doi.org/10.1007/978-3-030-90570-5_7

157

spared without inury to the creditt of the said bank' but included the caveat that each partner could 'not to exceed each other in proporcion or quantity of money soo taken'. Farrington claimed that this article was designed to prevent Thompson and Nelthorpe extracting more money than him and Page, as it was 'Thompson who kept the said Bank cash' and he and Nelthorpe had 'drawne out a farr greater sume from the said Joynt stock & cash ... for other there owne private & sinister ends'.[1] Thompson, in turn, accused Nelthorpe and Farrington of withdrawing excessive amounts of money out of the bank. Thompson claimed that it was actually Farrington and Nelthorpe who were the principal managers of the 'money that came into and belonged to the said Bank' and that it was they who drew 'out all the moneyes as they came into the Bank and disposed of the same ... to their particular uses'.[2] Regardless of who the intended target of the new article was, Thompson and Farrington would later use it in court to lay the blame on their respective former partners rather than themselves in an effort to redeem their own individual reputations.

The renewal of the partners' articles of agreement in 1674 was intended to provide them with more time in which they could recoup their losses and meet their obligations. Whilst the first year of this new agreement appears to have been without issue, trouble reappeared in 1675 and continued until the collapse and bankruptcy of Thompson and Company in 1678. The Chancery proceedings and the partners' pamphlet state that in September 1675 Thompson and Company experienced their first run on the bank, a process whereby a large number of creditors all demanded their deposits back 'at one & the same time'. At this point they were able to satisfy those customers who demanded repayment, but it did 'exhaust all those summs of Money which we still reserved'. They stated that their 'general stock, which ... had hither-to been esteemed as a grand Countersecurity to every particular Creditor' instead 'turned into an Argument of Jealousie, and Discredit', a transformation that, they argue, would 'have disordered the most responsible Person, or Society, in their private Estate and Reputation'. However, the partners managed to survive until March 1676, when, having already 'paid about the summ of Sixty thousand pounds', they 'found it necessary to summon' their

[1] TNA: C 7/581/73.

[2] TNA: C 6/283/87.

creditors to a meeting.[3] In that meeting, they offered their creditors a composition, which is a private agreement between debtor and creditor to settle the repayment of debt outside of court. Offering a composition was a standard financial practice in seventeenth-century England that was used to avoid the country's 'archaic bankruptcy framework'.[4] However, far from avoiding bankruptcy, Thompson and Company were drawn into a protracted legal battle. The bank collapsed and along with it the partners mercantile careers and dependent commercial projects.

This chapter reconstructs the collapse and bankruptcy of Thompson and Company, setting out the process of bankruptcy in seventeenth-century England and how it was applied in the case of Thompson and Company. The reconstruction identifies two opposing groups of creditors that emerged after Thompson and Company collapsed, and the different courses of action they embarked upon in response to it. This includes particularly harsh and unusual processes that the partners were subjected to, such as a parliamentary enquiry which questioned the extent and nature of bankruptcy legislation itself. The issues debated by the parliamentary enquiry and the first creditors pamphlet of 1677, foreshadow changes made to bankruptcy law in the early eighteenth century demonstrating the conflicting motives and designs of different groups of creditors and how seventeenth-century bankruptcy law could be used for a multitude of different purposes. The role played by the creditors in Thompson and Company's collapse is emphasised through comparison to the collapse of a contemporary bank in order to demonstrate that proceedings against Thompson and Company went beyond the norm of bankruptcy in this period. Finally, the chapter highlights the publicity and notoriety of Thompson and Company's collapse and the extent to which news of it spread in the social circles of early modern London and beyond.

I

In order to pursue a case of bankruptcy, creditors of 'commercial men' were required to petition the Lord Chancellor who would issue a commission of bankruptcy. At the time of Thompson and Company's bankruptcy

---

[3] *Case of Richard Thompson and Company.* 6–7; TNA: C 7/581/73.

[4] Muldrew. *Economy of Obligation.* 283–284.

the Lord Chancellor was Heneage Finch. 'Commercial men' in this instance was defined vaguely as anyone who 'exercised the trade of merchandise, or sought their living through buying and selling'. The partners' varied activities, acting as both bankers and merchants, meant they easily fitted within this vague definition and were eligible to be tried for bankruptcy. In the petition to the Lord Chancellor, creditors had to demonstrate that the debtor was indebted by over £100 and had committed an act of bankruptcy, such as 'failure to pay'. The link between bankruptcy legislation and the Chancery courts derives from the role of the Lord Chancellor and the nature of Chancery court jurisdiction. Chancery courts dealt with 'commercial and industrial content' and recognised a much wider range of financial instruments than common law courts, which could be vital to bankruptcy cases. Once a petition had been accepted, the Lord Chancellor would appoint a commission to investigate the bankrupt(s), which would consist of 'men who were familiar with the debtor, his holdings, worth and trade'. This commission would attempt to discover all the assets of the bankrupt(s) in order to divide the remaining estate and satisfy the creditors' debts.[5]

Seventeenth-century English bankruptcy legislation was particularly harsh. As the second creditors' pamphlet claimed, 'the said Laws are more severe and penal in England, than in any other part of Christendom'.[6] At the time of Thompson and Company's collapse, bankruptcy legislation had last been altered in 1662 and did not reflect progress made in commerce and trade since the first Act concerning bankruptcy in 1543.[7] As such, the law took no account of misfortune, damage to goods, or shipping losses sustained during warfare.[8] The responsibility of the debtor, and concern for the out-of-pocket creditor, was at the forefront of the legislation, resulting in the treatment of bankrupts as frauds and delinquents and offering them no chance of recovery. However,

---

[5] Jones. 1979. The Foundations of English Bankruptcy: Statutes and Commissions in the Early Modern Period. *Transactions of the American Philosophical Society* 69: 8, 21–22, 25, 40–41; D. E. C. Yale. 2004. Finch, Heneage, first earl of Nottingham (1621–1682). *ODNB*, https://doi.org/10.1093/ref:odnb/9433. Accessed 5 February 2019; Brooks. *Law, Politics and Society*. 320; Grassby. *Business Community*. 216–217.

[6] *Reasons most humbly offered to the consideration of Parliament*.

[7] Michael Quilter. 2004. Daniel Defoe: Bankrupt and Bankruptcy Reformer. *The Journal of Legal History* 25: 58, 60–61.

[8] Jones. Foundations of English Bankruptcy. 8, 9; Grassby. *Business Community*. 217.

7 BANKRUPTCY 161

despite primary concern focussing on the creditors, the legislation rarely worked out in their favour as entering a commission of bankruptcy was an expensive and lengthy process.[9] Thompson and Company's creditors recognised this fact. The first creditors' pamphlet argued that 'no Man knows how long the contest between the Commissioners and Creditors will last' and complained of the vast sums 'spent in Law-Suits, and charges of the Commissioners, and how little is like to come to the Creditors'.[10] Similarly, in the 1679 case of the creditors, the complainants stated that they had collectively 'disbursed the summe of five hundred pounds & upwards out of theire owne money towards the said prosecucion' along with the 'Estates & Effects of the said Bankruptes gained in the said prosecucion to the value of' £1200. All of which 'hath beene swallowed upp' whilst the creditors had not 'nor cann obtaine any reimbursements of theire charges much lesse any dividend att all towards the satisfaccion of theire just debts'.[11]

The law would not begin to reflect contributing factors or any rights of the debtor until 1705, after the infamous Pitkin affair, in which merchants Thomas Brerewood and Thomas Pitkin staged a 'bankruptcy fraud' in order to extract money from unsuspecting creditors, and the public interventions and petitioning taken-up by Daniel Defoe. The Act of 1705 introduced the concept of 'discharge', whereby a debtor could declare themselves bankrupt and offer up their estate to the creditors. In return for his honesty, the debtor received 'Relief', whereby the debtor received a certain percentage of their estate back so that they had a chance to recover their reputation and livelihood. Although slightly undermined by a follow-up Act of 1706, which made discharge conditional upon the agreement of 'four-fifths' of the creditors, the 1705 Act offered an incentive for debtors to be honest and comply with the law.[12] This was, however, all too late for Thompson and Company. The partners' pamphlet states that at the meeting in March 1676, they offered their creditors a composition in which they would, in 'eight six months time', repay each of the creditors 'the Principal without Interest', what they

---

[9] Brooks. *Law, Politics and Society.* 309; Quilter. Daniel Defoe. 53, 59, 61; Muldrew. *Economy of Obligation.* 283–284.

[10] *Reasons offered by several of the creditors of Richard Thompson and partners.*

[11] TNA: C 8/328/50.

[12] Kadens. The Pitkin Affair. 483–570; Quilter. Daniel Defoe. 53–73.

162   M. WINTER

claimed was 'possible' from 'an Estate (not by our fault) so mangled already, and under so shatter'd a Reputation'.[13] The phrase 'eight six months' refers to a standard repayment format, whereby the debtors would repay a certain percentage or amount of debt to their creditors every 'half years or six months' for a certain term—in this case four years.[14] Additional information concerning this meeting can be found in the news letters of the Verney family. In a letter dated 16 March 1676, John told his father that Thompson and Company had 'failed'. He reported that they had 'enter' d 150 actions against such as owed them money to prevent attachments' and that 'last weeke theire Booke-keeper mett sundry of the creditors, & desir'd eight six months time' to pay back their principal debt. John added 'Tomorrow, Sr Wm Turner & some others on there behalf (for they thinke it not secure to appear themselves) give an other meeting to the Creditors'.[15] This letter reveals that the partners were unwilling to appear themselves, instead relying on their bookkeeper and some of their creditors (such as Turner) to relay their plans to the rest of the creditors.

The partners' unwillingness to appear could have been due to fear of arrest or another aspect of bankruptcy proceedings mentioned in John Verney's letter, that of 'attachments', which were used to ensure a debtor's attendance at court and to act as a security for any repayment proposals.[16] Attachments were particularly harsh and publicised proceedings that came in two forms: attachment of the person or attachment of goods. In the case of attachment of a person, the debtor would have had to 'find two sureties or pledges for his eventual appearance' in court who would 'be held liable for the debt or damages sued for if he defaulted'. If goods were attached then 'a certain amount of his belongings, or stock, to the value of what was owed would be sealed up'. If the debtor failed to appear in court, then 'the goods would be distrained and eventually sold for recovery of the debt'.[17] In order to prevent attachments, Thompson and Company called in money they were owed. The partners' pamphlet,

---

[13] *Case of Richard Thompson and Company. 7.*

[14] Covert. *The scrivener's guide.* 308, 309.

[15] BL: Microfilm 636/29. *Verney Papers.* 'John Verney to Sir Ralph Verney' 16 March 1676.

[16] Jones. Foundation of English Bankruptcy. 24.

[17] Muldrew. *Economy of Obligation.* 202, 275.

7 BANKRUPTCY 163

whilst not specifically stating an effort to avoid 'attachments', claims that the partners tried to 'hale back whatsoever lay within our reach', recalling loans, drawing bills on agents abroad, and withdrawing investments.[18]

Whatever processes the creditors were utilising, they were not united in their response to Thompson and Company's collapse. Whilst some creditors, whose exact names and identities are unknown, agreed to the proposed composition, and were clearly not pressing for attachments; others, again unknown, persisted with the legal case of bankruptcy against the partners. Following the meeting of March 1676 and the partners' offer to repay the principal debts, certain creditors requested the 'view of our Books' in which they found about £35,000 'more Credits, than Debts'. As a result, the creditors lowered the repayment time to 'six six months' over three years. Still more creditors refused to agree to the terms and were still dissatisfied 'at the beginning of the year 1677', when they petitioned the Lord Chancellor. Indeed, the partners recounted that on 'the very same day that their Money [from the bankers' composition] first grew due' the creditors 'Petitioned the Lord Chancellor ... for a Statute of Banquerupt against us which was soon granted'. This commission was requested despite the fact that the partners had organised a 'general meeting' of their creditors on 1 February 1677, in which they were to offer another composition in the hope of avoiding the statute of bankruptcy.[19]

The February composition stipulated that the partners would repay all their creditors 6s 8d per pound of their original deposit. This sum was based on the £35,000 left, or 'the Total of what doth or can remain for Satisfaction' in the bankers' reserves, a much lower sum than the £103,000 the creditors claimed to be owed. Despite the low offer, the pamphlet states that many creditors 'subscribed' to this new composition 'upon the place'. These same creditors were probably behind the second creditors' pamphlet, which implored others to drop the statute and accept the composition. According to the partners' pamphlet, some creditors put off signing the composition as they waited to 'behold a while what the effects would be of a new statute taken out by some select Creditors'. This new statute was the second commission of bankruptcy issued against

[18] *Case of Richard Thompson and Company.* 6.

[19] *Case of Richard Thompson and Company.* 8, 10, 16, 18; *The London Gazette*, 24 January 1677.

the partners, the petitioners of which had 'procured that first to be superseded'. However, appearing unhappy with the second commission, 'they quash'd that also, and had another granted'. Within one month the bank of Thompson and Company had suffered three statutes of bankruptcy.[20]

The commissions of bankruptcy taken out against Thompson and Company achieved very little. The first creditors' pamphlet stated that despite having sat for five or six months and having examined 'the Debtors Servants, and as many others as they thought fit from whom any intelligence could be hoped', they had not made any 'discoveries' that would 'defray the Charges of the Commission' or found 'any real clear Estate to divide amongst the Creditors toward satisfaction of their vast Debts'. Indeed, the only thing discovered by the commissioners thus far was the 'Land settled by way of Joynture' between some of the partners and their wives, which could not be subsumed under the commission.[21] The most significant outcome of the bankruptcy commission was that it forced the partners to flee into hiding. The partners' pamphlet states that having offered multiple compositions and following the three statutes of bankruptcy taken out against them, the partners decided to 'the best remaining husbandry to the Body of the Creditors', that their best option would be to 'Retreat', having been deprived 'at once both of Estate and Reputation'.[22] To run away from debts reinforced the idea that a bankrupt or bankrupts were attempting to conceal assets and avoid punishment.[23] However, the partners emphasised in their pamphlet that they were 'inforced' to flee, and that it was not done 'in Fraud to our Creditors, but the better to pay every one an equal proportion as far as the Estate will reach'. They added that this would only be possible 'if equitably and timely considered'.[24] Whilst one group of creditors were prepared to settle with the partners, however, another group refused and pursued a more damaging course of action.

[20] *Case of Richard Thompson and Company.* 18, 19, 28.

[21] *Reasons offered by several of the creditors of Richard Thompson and partners.*

[22] *Case of Richard Thompson and Company.* 13, 17.

[23] Muldrew. *Economy of Obligation.* 285; Jones. Foundations of English Bankruptcy. 24.

[24] *Case of Richard Thompson and Company.* 17.

II

The importance attributed to the position and demands of creditors, as well as the significance of their actions in bankruptcy proceedings, is well acknowledged for this period.[25] Bankruptcy legislation was not designed to help the debtor but 'aimed to provide a mechanism for preventing the debtor from ruining his creditors', meaning that the creditor had ultimate power.[26] However, whilst most creditors 'would wish to be spared the cost and delay of litigation', in certain cases 'reluctant creditors' could delay proceedings for alternative purposes.[27] In the case of Thompson and Company, one group of creditors were focussed on retrieving as much money as the partners' estates would allow and were content to accept a composition to achieve this, whilst a second group were intent on punishing the partners and refusing all offers of settlement, to the extent that no money would be left for anyone involved. The opposing groups were suggested by the partners in their own pamphlet when discussing their losses. The pamphlet outlines the partners shock when viewing their books, stating that '*the losses we had sustained, and must still foresee, were such as We could yet scarce our selves believe, and therefore forbore as then to mention*'. They state that they did not conceal the losses, but distributed copies of their accounts to the bankruptcy commissioners and their creditors. They also got their bookkeepers to calculate the loss, which was found to be 'no less than' £90,000. However, this loss, or the 'greatest part of which', was not accounted for solely by their own actions, but by 'the infortunate Importunity of some Creditors'. As a result the partners claimed that they were forced to 'draw what we had therein back by Exchange at great dammage'. Despite the partners' efforts and offers of compositions, a number of creditors continued 'to obstruct any good business of this kind' and 'accounted it a more desirable thing to have their Will, than to exercise their Understanding; and to execute a causless and unprofitable Revenge, than to arrive at a just Payment'.[28]

It was not just the partners who identified the split between a group of cooperating and a group of disgruntled creditors. The two pamphlets

---

[25] Jones. Foundations of English Bankruptcy. 8; Muldrew. *Economy of Obligation*. 283; Brooks. *Law, Politics and Society*. 320–321.

[26] Kadens. The Pitkin Affair. 485.

[27] Jones. Foundations of English Bankruptcy. 36.

[28] *Case of Richard Thompson and Company*. 9–10, 15, 26.

written by anonymous creditors both identified an opposing group who were pursuing the harshest punishment for the partners. The second creditors' pamphlet argues that the partners' losses were primarily caused by 'the impatient demands of their Creditors', particularly those who 'had not complied' with the partners' offers to settle the debt and were intent on making sure the partners' 'Estates and Credits' were 'ruined and destroyed'. The pamphlet claimed that those creditors, 'for their own private advantage', were deliberately trying to 'encrease clamor' against the partners.[29] The first creditors' pamphlet similarly outlined a particular group of uncooperative creditors who were preventing the 'generality' from having even a portion of their debt repaid.[30]

The 1679 Chancery complaint entered by 211 creditors similarly suggests that two groups of creditors existed. The 211 named complainants claimed that they, 'for and on the behalf of the majority in number & value of the said creditors', did 'come to some treaty toucheing an accomodacion with the said Bankruptes' to accept 6s 8d to the pound for the remaining debt. This agreement, they argued, also entailed an end to the commission of bankruptcy, which 'should bee stayed and for borne & the persons goods and Estates of the said Bankruptes there from discharged and sett ffree'.[31] The 211 named creditors in this case, then, were most likely the 'generality' who had supposedly suffered at the hands of the uncooperative creditors. Although Thompson and Company's partners suggested that they knew the identity of those uncooperative creditors, stating in their pamphlet that they were not 'ignorant whence it all proceeded', their identity is unfortunately not revealed in the pamphlets or the court cases.[32]

[29] *Reasons most humbly offered to the consideration of Parliament.*

[30] *Reasons offered by several of the creditors of Richard Thompson and partners.*

[31] TNA: C 8/328/50.

[32] *Case of Richard Thompson and Company.* 6, 19.

III

Commissions of bankruptcy in seventeenth-century England were, then, particularly rigorous. However, in the case of Thompson and Company, certain creditors argued that the law did not go far enough. According to the first anonymous creditors' pamphlet, a certain group of creditors did not only 'violently prosecute the Statute of Bankrupt' against the partners but also 'preferred' a bill entered into the Houses of Parliament that was designed to punish the partners further. The pamphlet argued that the bill would tend 'only to the further waste and imbezlement of the remaining estate' and was for the creditors 'own private advantage'.[33] The bill, titled 'the Bill for the better Discovery of the Estates of *Thompson* and *Nelthrop*, and other Bankrupts', authorised a committee to 'inspect and peruse the statutes against Bankrupts' so that they might 'provide Remedies to supply such Defects as they shall find therein'. The committee consisted of 85 named individuals and was permitted to examine 'Persons, Papers, and Records' in order to reach their decision and, whilst the committee was in session, the House of Commons extended the 'Privilege and Protection of this House' over the bankers, meaning that no other case could be taken out against them.[34]

The exact 'defects' in bankruptcy law that the committee was debating are not recorded in the House of Commons journal, but the second creditors' pamphlet provides a list of proposals that were supposedly debated by the committee. The first suggestion made in the bill was that the 'laws and statutes' of bankruptcy 'do not sufficiently reach the evil contrivances of Richard Thompson and Partners'; second, that the partners had taken up money upon security only to 'defraud all their Creditors'; third, that in order to accomplish this they had 'disposed' the money 'beyond the seas' and 'out of the reach and power of any Commission of Bankrupt'; fourth, that the partners had 'made over their private Estates, and secured the Moneys of their Creditors' and 'did refuse to pay any of them'; and fifth, that they had 'absconded themselves, and conveyed away their Books and Estates on purpose to defraud their Creditors'. The pamphlet denied

---

[33] *Reasons offered by several of the creditors of Richard Thompson and partners.*

[34] *Journal of the House of Commons*, vol. 9, 1667–1687. British History Online. https://www.british-history.ac.uk/commons-jrnl/vol9. 12 February 1678 and 16 February 1678.

168   M. WINTER

that any of the five statements in the bill were true, and further questioned whether it was 'reasonable' to punish Thompson and Company more severely 'than ever by Law hath hitherto been provided', whether 'it stands with the Honour of Parliament' to give 'rewards' to people for information, and whether it was 'reasonable' to pass a bill that was purely against Thompson and Company rather than 'against all men' in their 'condition'.[35]

The outcome of the committee was not as severe as the proposals stated in the pamphlet. In a letter to the Corporation of Hull Marvell reported that the committee had decided on a course of action but had not fully agreed on terms: 'the Statutes of Ban route' were 'deficient' in this case 'and therefore that unless by a *blanke* day they surrendred up their persons and estates' they would be 'subject unto *blanke* penaltyes'.[36] However, in March 1678 the Corporation of Trinity House, who had £500 in the bank, reported that 'the Creditors of Tompson & partners at a meeting yesterday had agreed to a subscription to the Committee of Parliament'. The terms were firstly, that 'the majority of the Creditors may be enabled to force the rest to agree or carry on the Comission'. Secondly, 'some Provisions may be made by act of Parliament to force the Debtors to produce their persons and their books by a time assigned or soon after thereon'. Finally, that 'it may be enabled to bring in all moneys paid by the Debtors since the March 15 into a common averidge'. A majority of Thompson and Company's creditors must have wanted to continue with the commission of bankruptcy because in June 1678 the Trinity House minutes record the order 'that the Corporation doe come into the Banckruptcy against Thompson & Partners'.[37]

The collapse of Thompson and Company therefore led to questions being asked about the efficiency of bankruptcy law itself. In this regard it is similar to the case of the Pitkin Affair, which Emily Kadens argues was significant in prompting the changes to bankruptcy law in 1705 and 1706. In the Pitkin case, Thomas Pitkin and Thomas Brerewood deliberately set out to defraud their creditors by establishing a business and 'excellent credit' by prompt paying of bills and then buying up merchandise that they would sell for below cost for cash. When they had stretched

---

[35] *Reasons offered by several of the creditors of Richard Thompson and partners.*
[36] *The Poems and Letters of Andrew Marvell*, vol. 2. 215.
[37] LMA: CLC/526/MS30004/005. 77, 89.

their credit as far as they could, they would flee, exploiting the loophole in bankruptcy law that offered no solution for debtors fleeing abroad to cooperate and be brought to justice. The plan was that whilst Pitkin fled, Brerewood would remain and offer to buy Pitkin's debt, providing creditors with a composition that amounted to a much smaller sum than he and Pitkin had received for the goods. Pitkin would then be able to return and receive his share of the profits. However, the creditors caught on and the whole scheme unravelled. Like the case of Thompson and Company, Pitkin's creditors petitioned parliament to intervene and force Pitkin to appear, which they did in an Act of 1705. However, the Pitkin scandal also prompted the introduction of the more general 'Act to Prevent Frauds Frequently Committed by Bankrupts', which Kadens argues 'was little more than a generalized Pitkin bill' that punished debtors who intended to defraud their creditors with life imprisonment and pillorying. However, it was not until the act introducing discharge that debtors were given an incentive to cooperate. Kadens admits that the bankruptcy and parliamentary intervention in the Pitkin case was not without precedent but argues that the economic and commercial environment of the early eighteenth century gave the case greater impact.[38]

The case against Thompson and Company can be seen as one important case that preceded the Pitkin Affair, in which further punishment was afflicted upon debtors who were perceived as intending to defraud their creditors and which provoked wider discussion of the efficiency of bankruptcy law. Like the Pitkin case, parliament passed an act against the partners to force them to appear. This was a targeted act, restricted to the case of Thompson and Company and not a blanket reform. However, whilst legislation to reform bankruptcy laws was not passed as a result of this, the case against Thompson and Company did spark parliamentary discussions of the 'Laws concerning Bankrupts' throughout 1679 and 1680. These discussions occurred prior to the bankruptcies of goldsmith-bankers Backwell and Vyner, who were not declared bankrupt until 1682 and 1684 respectively and whose bankruptcies also caused further discussions surrounding the legislation.[39] In May 1678, after the act against

---

[38] Kadens. The Pitkin Affair. 485–486, 508, 509, 511, 518.

[39] Horsefield. The "Stop on the Exchequer" revisited. 524.

170 M. WINTER

Thompson and Company, it was ordered that a committee be appointed to consider the defects in the bankruptcy laws with the aim of providing 'more effectual Means for Discovery of their Estates; and to take care that it may not be in the Power of any particular Creditor, or small Number of them, to obstruct the Composition of the Generality of the Creditors; and to bring in a Bill for that Purpose'. In May of the following year bills 'for the more easy Recovery of Debts against Bankrupts' and 'for preventing it being in the Power of any particular Creditor, or smaller Number of Creditors of a Bankrupt, to obstruct the Compositions of the greater Number' were read. Further reference to the 'Bill to supply the Laws against Bankruptcy' were read throughout 1680.[40] These bills reflect the arguments made by the creditors of Thompson and Company that a certain group of creditors were preventing the remainder from receiving relief. Therefore, although reform was not passed for another two decades, the case of Thompson and Company was significant enough to raise debates in parliament that foreshadow some of the later reforms made to the law in the early eighteenth century.

One of the primary failings of the parliamentary committee was that it did not help the creditors obtain any more of the debt owed to them. That the creditors were unsatisfied with the result of the committee is evident from the Chancery complaint entered by 211 creditors in 1679. The creditors argued that the continuance of the commission of bankruptcy, allowed by the parliamentary committee, meant that the creditors were worse off, as they missed out on the offer of a composition of 6s 8d to the pound. The complaint also laid further accusations of fraud on the partners, stating that they deliberately deceived their creditors by exploiting the commission of bankruptcy. Brooks has shown that certain bankrupts 'went so far as to enter into collusive actions against themselves so that they could transfer assets to one creditor in order to avoid having to pay another', and this is what the partners, along with four confederates, were accused of in Chancery in 1679.[41] The creditors claimed that Thompson and Company's partners had set up a 'pretended

[40] *Journal of the House of Commons*, vol. 9, 1667–1687. British History Online. https://www.british-history.ac.uk/commons-jrnl/vol9. 27 May 1678, 7 May 1679, 16 May 1679, 24 November 1680, 11 December 1680, and 15 December 1680.

[41] Brooks. *Law, Politics and Society*. 319.

prosecucion', whereby the partners enlisted friends or 'confederates' to pretend to be creditors of the bank and take out a statute of bankruptcy against them. They named the false creditors, or 'confederates', as 'the said Lord Marquise and the said Thomas Wareing Thomas Lamb & Thomas Guy'. As creditors these confederates would claim any remaining funds that were collected as part of the commission of bankruptcy. In this scheme, whilst under the strictures of the commission of bankruptcy, the partners would also be able to claim that they were 'disabled' from collecting in their own estates and debts, particularly those that were 'in fforaigne partes', and therefore that money would never be collected to satisfy their creditors debts. According to the complaining creditors, the confederates would hold onto the funds collected under the commission of bankruptcy until the partners were released, whereupon the confederates would return the partners' money to them.[42] In short, through this elaborate scheme, the partners would never pay any of their creditors but keep the reserve funds for themselves.

Whether there was any truth in this accusation is unclear. The case did not proceed to cross-complaints or witness depositions in Chancery and the complaint is not referred to in any other records. The two creditors' pamphlets specifically refute any notion of corruption or fraud, stating that the partners of Thompson and Company were 'Men of honest Reputations' and that 'there was nothing of secret contrivance on their parts, but always in a fair open method of Negotiation'. It is therefore possible that the 1679 complaint was a strategic bid by the creditors intended to get the commission of bankruptcy superseded so that their 'Agreement' with the partners, the composition of 'six shillings & eight pence in the pound', might be met. In which case it is a good example of a group of individuals using Chancery as 'business by other means'.[43] Whether true or not, the accusation further demonstrates the volatile nature of bankruptcy proceedings and the different ways in which creditors could use the law in attempts to retrieve remaining funds.

[42] TNA: C 8/328/50.

[43] *Reasons most humbly offered to the consideration of Parliament*; TNA: C 8/328/50; Churches. Business at Law. 940.

IV

So far, this chapter has focussed on the role creditors of the bank played in the collapse of Thompson and Company. However, it must be remembered that the sources behind this information are problematic. The information all derives from interested parties, either the partners themselves or their creditors, and so is liable to be exaggerated or manipulated to serve particular ends. It is therefore important to consider the wider economic and commercial context in which Thompson and Company were established and collapsed, and to compare their collapse with another contemporary bankruptcy case in order to assess the extent to which the creditors really did play an integral part in the collapse of Thompson and Company.

As outlined in Chapter 3, Thompson and Company was established and collapsed during a period of financial change and trepidation. Whilst Thompson and Company were not directly affected, they were inevitably caught up in the wider and more general spread of distrust and fear in the capital's credit markets, establishing themselves as a new provider of credit just as previous providers were experiencing extensive difficulties. For example, despite the government attempting to alleviate the fallout from the 1672 Stop on the Exchequer by making an agreement for repayment of the goldsmiths' debt in 1674, the following year disgruntled bankers and creditors presented a petition to the House of Commons asking for relief.[44] Lack of repayment and adhering to the conditions of the agreement had caused creditors to enact runs on the banks that destroyed London's remaining credit networks. In December 1675, deputy postmaster of the General Letter Office in London, Roger Whitley, informed his correspondent in Ireland of London's economic situation. He reported that the 'Bankers are run downe by the fears, or malice, of some men, all people are drawing from them, but few receive satisfaction'. Whitley himself could 'neither Borrow of them nor receive what they have of mine to make my payments' and so asked his Irish correspondent 'to supply me as considerably, and speedily as possibly you can'.[45] Although not directly affected by the Stop, Thompson and Company were still at risk from the general depression it caused and vulnerable in the period of recovery that followed.

[44] Horsefield. The "Stop on the Exchequer" revisited. 514.

[45] PORO: POST 94/19. 7 December 1675. f. 54.

However, the rigorousness of the proceedings against Thompson and Company suggest that it was far more than just a crisis of credit that caused their downfall. The impact of the creditors in the collapse of Thompson and Company can be fully understood by comparing it to another bank that went bankrupt at a similar time. In March 1676, John Verney reported to his father that at the same time as Thompson and Company experienced a run on the bank 'Hynde (& his partner) Bankers have refusd further payments'. He predicted that John Hind and his partner would be 'the next' to fall and that 'The like is said of some others'. Verney himself was not saddened by the news but 'glad of' it, as he wished 'all Bankers broke' due to their 'ruining the trade of the whole Kingdome'.[46] Hind and his partner, Thomas Kirwood or Carwood, ran a smaller goldsmith-bank 'over against the Exchange in Cornhill'.[47] Although Hind and Kirwood appear to have suffered economically at a similar time to Thompson and Company, they did not collapse as Verney predicted. Instead, a pamphlet written by Hind, or written on his behalf, in 1685 reveals that Hind and Kirwood's creditors allowed them time to repay their debts and that shortly after Hind 'withdrew his Share and gave over, and left Kirwood in the Trade singly'. Kirwood died shortly after Hind left the partnership and at the insistence of some of his creditors Hind 'undertook the Trade again'. The pamphlet records that, in 1682 or 1683, Hind 'became (unhappily) concerned in the New Buildings at *Albermarle-House, Grayes-Inn-Fields*, and other places thereabouts'. However, at the end of July 1684 Hind's creditors 'joyned together to call in their moneys out of his hands'.[48] Thus, even though Hind and Kirwood experienced financial difficulties in 1676, Hind did not go bankrupt until the mid-1680s and was not subjected to the same Chancery or parliamentary proceedings as Thompson and Company. The survival of Hind and partners further confirms the integral role of Thompson and Company's creditors in their downfall.

[46] BL: MS 636/29. *Verney Papers*. 'John Verney to Sir Ralph Verney', 16 March 1676.

[47] *The Little London Directory*.

[48] 1685. *The Case of John Hinde Goldsmith with his Creditors Justly Stated*. London. 1–2.

174   M. WINTER

V

The extended dispute concerning the collapse of Thompson and Company, which was most likely engineered and fueled by a particular group of creditors, meant that it became widespread news and common gossip in London and beyond. In Restoration London, this discourse largely took place in the coffeehouses, which were prominent venues for political discussion. Indeed, political opposition leader the earl of Shaftesbury held regular meetings at coffeehouses, with Williamson recording that he 'vents out all his thoughts and designs' at 'John's coffeehouse'.[49] Thompson too was a regular at coffeehouses and Withington notes that 'Thompson's fondness for coffee coincided with a number of proclamations attempting to close down the coffeehouses as seminaries of subversion'.[50] Thompson's fondness for coffee and the political discussion that accompanied it is evident from Farrington's Chancery complaint in 1684 in which Farrington partially blamed Thompson's political activities for the bank's collapse. He claimed Thompson 'was by day at coffee houses & other public places & that he spent his time in publick matters & in heareing & telling unto', regarding his political duty higher than 'his duty & engagement to mind the said office or banke'.[51] Whilst this was clearly intended to injure Thompson's position in Chancery by implying that he was not paying enough attention to his financial role as a banker, the comment further illuminates the intimate relationship between the political and commercial fields and how roles in different fields could impact upon one another.

The importance of coffeehouse culture for political factionalism is evident from the government's attempt to supress the coffeehouses in 1676. Indeed, this is well illustrated by the newsletters that passed between Sir Ralph and John Verney. On 30 December 1675 Sir Ralph sent news to his son that he had heard of a 'Proclamation coming out to put downe all coffee houses' as they were deemed to be 'inventers and spreaders of fales or Failed newes'. By early January the proclamation had been issued and the coffeehouse keepers were in uproar having

[49] Notes by Williamson. *SPO*, SP 29/379 f. 80, 18 February 1676.

[50] Withington. *Politics of Commonwealth*. 154.

[51] TNA: C 7/581/73.

paid 'customes & excise' for their commodities and 'taken long leases of greate houses & furnished them for that Trade'. However, Sir Ralph believed that the proclamation would be in vain for 'noo Englishman will long endure to bee forbid meeting together' and will drink 'Sage, Belondy, & Rosemary drinkes' which 'pay neither Excise nor customes', so the 'Crowne will bee the only looser'.[52] This crack down on coffee-houses occurred just two months before John Verney reported the first meeting of Thompson and Company's creditors to discuss a composition. Alongside politics, commerce and finance were also popular topics of conversation in the coffeehouse. Like political discourse, commercial and financial discussions could be dangerous because 'A casual remark in a coffee-house or a tavern might lead creditors to suspect that their debtor had no "bottom" and to close in quickly for repayment'.[53] Therefore, coffeehouses became a vital aspect of politics, finance, and commerce, with the power to both build and destroy reputations.

Thompson and Company's pamphlet suggests that such public discourse played an important role in their collapse by emphasizing the public nature of their predicament. Indeed, the pamphlet itself is evidence that they had to justify themselves to a wider, print consuming, community of readers who were aware of their situation. This was because, in addition to coffeehouses, the seventeenth century witnessed a growth in 'commercial publications', which had a profound impact on a society that also witnessed 'an expansion of the reading public'.[54] Therefore, print played an important part in making issues of 'economic activity' and 'the fortunes and reputations of private individuals ... into issues of public concern and national interest'.[55] The partners' pamphlet argues that certain creditors ruthlessly pushed the bank into returning their whole deposit, but they were still 'not satisfied to enjoy the fruits of their victory, unless they proclaimed them all abroad, and in all places published the Particulars'. This was done through people 'divulging all upon the Exchange, and through the Countries', as well as through 'Letters, and

---

[52] BL: MS 636/29. *Verney Papers*. 'Sir Ralph Verney to his son', 30 December 1675, and 'Sir Ralph Verney to his son', 3 January 1676.

[53] Earle. *Making of the English Middle Class*. 120.

[54] Natasha Glaisyer. 2006. *The Culture of Commerce in England, 1660–1720*. London: Boydell & Brewer. 5.

[55] Miles Ogborn. 2007. *Indian Ink: Script and print in the making of the English East India Company*. London: University of Chicago Press. 160.

176   M. WINTER

in their daily discourses', which 'egged them on to prosecute us', even 'instructing them moreover how to do it in the most effectual manner'. The perpetrators, the partners claimed, 'would never cease till they had infected in a manner the whole Town with a Belief of our insufficiency' to the point where the partners lost both their 'Estate and Reputation'.[56]

Further evidence that the collapse of Thompson and Company was widely reported is found in newsletters. John Verney's newsletter to his father claimed to provide him with 'a report about the Towne', which began by stating that 'The great discourse of the Towne is of Thompson & Nelthorpe the Bankers who are failed', revealing that their collapse was part of common gossip, transmitted orally around London.[57] However, news of Thompson and Company's difficulties was not just of interest in London. Thompson and Company's creditors were not all London-based, but geographically dispersed, meaning that news of the bank would be communicated to those areas of the country and amongst networks further afield. This was made possible through the Post Office, which had been re-established at the Restoration and operated centrally from London with the assistance of various provincial offices in England and corresponded with offices across Europe.[58] Evidence that news of Thompson and Company's disputes and difficulties spread through the Post Office is found in the Post Office letter books. Deputy postmaster Roger Whitley transmitted bills sent to the Post Office in London to Thompson and Company in order for them to be paid or remitted. As well as demonstrating how London business was conducted with the provinces, Whitley's actions also reveal how news about Thompson and Company could be spread further afield. On 11 March 1676, Whitley wrote to Mr. Rigden in York, stating that he had 'received yours of 8th with your Bill, which was presented, but Mr Nelthorpe (& Comp) not appearing, & having refused other Bills, I returne it for feare of Accidents'. Whitley not only communicated the specific business relating to Rigden's bill, but also communicated the news of Thompson and Company's collapse to York. Similarly, on 18 March, Whitley wrote to Mr Cranck in Birmingham warning him of 'Mr Nelthorps misfortune',

---

[56] *Case of Richard Thompson and Company.* 13, 16.

[57] BL: Microfilm 636/29. *Verney Papers.* 'John Verney to Sir Ralph Verney', 16 March 1676.

[58] Marshall. *Intelligence and Espionage.* 78, 81.

which although he 'may not be surprised to hear' Whitley felt he should warn him as Nelthorpe was Cranck's 'security'.[59] As a result, Thompson and Company's difficulties became common knowledge in Birmingham. These are just a few surviving instances of correspondence between the metropolis and the provinces and, given the geographical spread of the creditors, there were likely many more.

The Post Office records, however, extended beyond England and there is evidence that Thompson and Company's business extended to and was discussed in Ireland. Nelthorpe's Irish enterprises meant that his actions in London were of interest to a group of business associates and creditors there. On 29 March 1676, Whitley wrote to Mr Warburton, the 'Deputy Post-master of Ireland', about a bill owed to Whitley, which Warburton had drawn on Thompson and Company. Whitley informed Warburton that 'Mr Nelthropp promised to answer yor Bill, this day his servant paid mee part of it, the rest he promises in a few dayes'. In addition to this update, Whitley also asked Warburton for his 'advise' on 'whether to press for the rest' and 'what to doe', speculating 'whether A state of Bankrupt; (though I hope there will be none in the Case) may not fetch this money againe'. By 4 April, Whitley had 'yett gott noe satisfaction' but was 'loath to come in with the Croude being in hope of A better hold'.[60] Whitley's discussion of the affairs of Thompson and Company, whilst demonstrating personal concern over his own business, spread the news of their difficulties and lack of payment to Ireland. This would have the additional result of affecting Nelthorpe's business in Ireland, which came under scrutiny in May that year.[61] Letters about personal business, such as those sent by Whitley, helped to transmit news about the banking partners' credit and reputation and make such news public. Through gossip in the town, manuscript newsletters, and print, the disputes and downturns of Thompson and Company became public knowledge and with devastating consequences.

[59] PORO: POST 94/17. f. 47, 56.
[60] PORO: POST 94/19. ff. 26, 56, 57.
[61] *Calendar of the manuscripts of the Marquess of Ormond*, vol. 4. 11.

178   M. WINTER

VI

The commission of bankruptcy against Thompson and Company finally came to an end in June 1680, having exhausted a significant amount of money in fees. At this point the surviving partners were able to take back control of their remaining estates and divide what was left amongst the creditors. In 1681 Farrington claimed to be 'makeing an Agreement with his Creditors' and pursuing the company's debtors who 'refuse to pay the moneys due from them'.[62] The nature of the court cases that occurred after 1680 confirm Farrington's actions, as they do not involve the creditors and were focussed on non-payments or debts that Thompson and Farrington claimed were owed to the bank. That some of the money recovered went towards settling the creditors' debts is evident from the surviving accounts of viscount Fauconberg and Sir William Turner. Fauconberg recorded in his accounts that he received '3s per pound in full Composition', or 15%, of the £875 he had remaining with Thompson and Company in April 1682. As he originally had £1000 with the bank, he must have been paid £225 at some point between 1677 and 1682.[63] Sir William Turner, who recorded his accounts with Thompson and Company in more detail, recorded that, in December 1677, he had £2350 with Thompson and Company. By June 1678, the amount had decreased to £1750, and by January 1679 to £1350. This suggests that Fauconberg and other creditors could have similarly been paid amounts at these intervals. Turner would not be paid again until November 1681, when he received another £41 and would receive his final payment from Thompson and Company of £100 in May 1683. Turner recorded that he was still owed £1200 in 1684, which he was never repaid.[64]

The collapse and bankruptcy of Thompson and Company was a highly controversial and public affair that provoked discussion not only of how their particular case should be treated but of the efficiency of bankruptcy legislation as a whole. Reconstructing the collapse of Thompson and Company therefore demonstrates the importance of this small bank to

---

[62] TNA: C 7/589/82.

[63] BL: Add MS 41255. Note-Book of Thomas Belasyse. f. 15.

[64] LMA: CLC/509/MS05105. Book of Sales. ff. 22, 23, 24, 28, 29, 30, 31, 32.

the wider history of bankruptcy in the seventeenth and early eighteenth centuries. The existence of two separate groups of creditors, each pursuing opposing courses of action, explains why the collapse of Thompson and Company was so drawn out. Why certain creditors refused the partners' compositions and pursued them to such a disastrous end, however, is the subject of the following chapter.

CHAPTER 8

Why Did Thompson and Company Collapse?

In 1676 the alderman, city merchant and lieutenant of the Tower of London, Sir John Robinson, wrote to Sir Joseph Williamson, the Secretary of State, to inform him that 'Thompson Nelthrope Farrington Page the Bankers in partnershippe have lost their reputations', and that 'they have summoned their creditors to meet tomorrow'. The significance of this letter to the fate of the banking partners was monumental. Robinson was a noted political enemy of partners Thompson and Nelthorpe, who, along with the Lord Treasurer the Earl of Danby, and Secretary of State Joseph Williamson, had been trying to bring 'quiet' to the Corporation of London since the failed Declaration of Indulgence in 1672. The failure of the bank and the loss of the partners' reputations resulted in the expulsion of Thompson and Nelthorpe from their political offices, and Robinson's glee is further evident from his closing statement that 'wee shall now I hope bee quiett in the Common councell the Leaders faileing'.[1]

The collapse of Thompson and Company has been documented in existing scholarship, but this scholarship has only addressed the collapse itself and has not attempted to uncover the reasons behind it. For example, Wall briefly alluded to a commercial dispute between the banking partners and the East India Company and speculated that the

---

[1] Sir John Robinson to Williamson. *SPO*, SP 29/379 f. 265, 10 March 1676.

© The Author(s), under exclusive license to Springer Nature Switzerland AG 2022
M. Winter, *Banking, Projecting and Politicking in Early Modern England*, Palgrave Studies in Economic History, https://doi.org/10.1007/978-3-030-90570-5_8

181

collapse was linked to the political activities of the partners. However, he did not follow those leads through to the end, and as a result, did not sufficiently explain why the bank collapsed. De Krey has highlighted the political repercussions of the collapse of the bank, noting that Thompson and Company's bankruptcy had a profound effect on their own political positions. However, he had no conception of the political scheming behind the collapse of the bank and failed to recognise the effect of its collapse on the wider political opposition movement. Withington has argued that the partners' 'economic efficiency was in large part dependent on the social construction and performance of "credit"' and so 'It was by the sword of credit that their bank first lived and then died'.[2] He emphasises the importance of credit and rumour but does not excavate the partisan and economic conflicts in which the partners were engaged.

This chapter explores the importance of credit and reputation in the downfall of Thompson and Company. It assesses three reasons for the collapse of the bank: accidental losses, commercial conflict, and political dispute. But it does so by examining more fully the financial, commercial, and political contexts that informed the performance and meaning of credit. In so doing, it suggests that finance, commerce, and politics were intimately interwoven in this period, using the sociological concepts of role and fields to understand how these contexts intermeshed. In Bourdieu's concept of 'fields', he argues that society is 'made up of multiple fields', or social spaces, which each have their own rules and logistics but are related to each other through commonalities that allow them to interact in a broader 'field of power'. As such, individuals can inhabit more than one role in more than one field at any one time. A 'role' in this context is a 'collectively understood' and 'continually negotiated' position of authority or power within a field, which gives that individual agency to pursue certain goals and influence the field and others within it. Within each field, individuals compete for superiority using different forms of capital, or power, specific to that field or fields. The most significant form of capital for this chapter is symbolic capital, which is 'commonly called prestige, reputation, renown' but could also be called credit.[3] Credit was

---

[2] Tupper. Mary Palmer. 367–392; Wall. Marvell's Friends in the City. 204–207; De Krey. *London and the Restoration.* 150; Withington. *Politics of Commonwealth.* 129.

[3] Patricia Thompson. 2014. Field. In *Pierre Bourdieu: Key Concepts*, ed. Michael James Grenfell, 65–80. Oxford: Routledge. 68, 70; Braddick and Walter. Introduction. Grids of Power. 5, 11–12; Bourdieu. Social Space. 197.

vital to the partners in each role and field they operated in and was the central basis for their individual and collective power. The key argument here is that whilst the cultivation of roles in multiple fields could enhance the credit and agency of an individual, it could also increase the level of social and reputational risk. Viewed in these terms, the collapse of Thompson and Company was the result of risky strategies taken up by the partners in their commercial and political roles and the damage this caused to their reputations and identities.

The benefit of inhabiting multiple roles in different fields to enhance reputation, status, and business success has been emphasised by various historians.[4] What historians have not done is explore the reverse: namely the potential for officeholding and public activity to deconstruct and destabilise economic and social credit. For an individual to succeed in multiple fields, they had to maintain good credit. However, this difficult task required constant attention. Credit, as Shepard has argued, was 'neither fixed nor secure, but spread over a series of unpredictable networks' which could not always be controlled and could change within the course of just one day.[5] The spread of news, by both print and word of mouth around London, meant public figures were subject to increased levels of rumour and gossip. Credit was therefore based on more than just calculable wealth and meeting obligations, it was also a character judgement that had significant implications not only for the individual but for the wider financial and trading markets.[6] An individual's potential exposure to rumour was increased by inhabiting multiple roles in different fields, as negative reputation would spread through different fields and in different contexts, affecting them all. It is precisely such risks that the collapse of the bank of Thompson and Company reveals.

[4] Gauci. *Politics of Trade*. 78–80, 86; Ormrod. *The Rise of Commercial Empires*. 35; Zahedieh. *The Capital and the Colonies*. 56–57; Steven C. A. Pincus. 1996. *Protestantism and Patriotism: Ideologies and the Making of English Foreign Policy, 1650–1668*. Cambridge: Cambridge University Press. 449; Brenner. *Merchants and Revolution*. 79, 199, 200, 222; Bruce G. Carruthers. 1996. *City of Capital: Politics and Markets in the English Financial Revolution*. Chichester: Princeton University Press. 12, 18, 27; Murphy. *The Origins of English Financial Markets*. 7.

[5] Alexandra Shepard. 2003. *Meanings of Manhood in Early Modern England*. Oxford: Oxford University Press. 193; Shepard. From Anxious Patriarchs to Refined Gentlemen? 291.

[6] Ogborn. *Indian Ink*. 167.

184   M. WINTER

Multiple sources reference the collapse of the bank of Thompson and Company, but the events leading up to it and reasons behind it are only hinted at in the surviving source material. Like the formation and operation of the bank, the reasons behind its collapse must be reconstructed using a wide variety of sources. The partners' pamphlet and the Chancery proceedings concerning the bankruptcy, which the majority of existing scholarship has referenced, are limited in what they reveal about why the bank collapsed, but other, previously unused, Chancery material can offer further insight. Of particular importance is a 1676 Chancery case between Edward Nelthorpe and a group of Jewish merchants working in London, and another case from 1677 between John Farrington and the London merchant James Holland. Alongside the Chancery material, state and personal correspondence, Privy Council records, East India Company records, Venetian state papers, and newsletters provide crucial insight into the disputes and conflicts that resulted in the collapse of the bank of Thompson and Company.

I

In Thompson and Company's pamphlet, the partners claim that throughout the life of the bank they had experienced the 'ordinary accidental losses', which most merchants experience during their career.[7] As the partners did not trade collectively as merchants, these losses must have occurred through their individual, but bank-funded, trading exploits and 'projects'. Farrington confirmed this in 1684, claiming that the partners had 'contracted greate debts in theire owne perticuler trades not relateing to the said Bank'.[8] Such losses could include accidental damage to goods, the destruction of a ship by storm, or losses due to piracy or theft. The second creditors' pamphlet suggests that the partners' losses were partially related to shipping and 'casualties at sea'.[9] Neither the pamphlet nor the partners' Chancery statements confirm when these casualties occurred, what goods or ships were affected, or the extent to which the losses damaged the Company's finances or reputation. However, customs records and other Chancery proceedings provide evidence of

---

[7] *Case of Richard Thompson and Company.* 15.

[8] TNA: C 7/581/73.

[9] *Reasons most humbly offered to the consideration of Parliament.*

8 WHY DID THOMPSON AND COMPANY COLLAPSE?   185

some instances in which the partners experienced shipping losses. The records reveal that the partners were financially and commercially involved in a ship called the *Constant Friendship* of London, which was the subject of Chancery proceedings in 1677 and various government documentation throughout the 1670s.

On the 18 November 1675, Edward Nelthorpe paid £1000 to the Custom House in London for the *Constant Friendship*, a ship of 'burthen 300 Tons or thereabouts' and 'made oath that himselfe was full & sole owner'.[10] This is an unusual investment for a merchant on his own because whilst owning a ship was potentially lucrative, it was also highly expensive and risky. Instead, ownership was divided into shares, which were 'sold or mortgaged' as a 'useful liquid asset'.[11] The risks posed by owning a ship are well demonstrated by the fate of the *Constant Friendship* a few months after Nelthorpe registered it. In May 1676, merchants Sir Benjamin Ayloffe and William Scrimshire entered a petition in the Privy Council, which stated that last January they had employed 'the Constant Friendship of London' for a voyage between Denmark and London, 'with her Lading, consisting in Flax, Hemp, Tarr, and other Goods'. During the voyage, the ship ran upon Læsø Island off the coast of Denmark, whereupon the inhabitants 'forcibly Boarded' the ship and 'tooke away & carryed her Lading on shore together with what they could of the Ships Tackle and apparell'. Ayloffe and Scrimshire complained to the court of Denmark for damages but were unsuccessful, and so asked the Council to prepare a letter endorsed by the king 'to demand and obtaine satsifaction'.[12] Whether Ayloffe and Scrimshire hired the ship from Nelthorpe, or were part-owners is unclear from the petition, but the damage sustained may have cost Nelthorpe a significant amount of money. This event could be one of the instances of 'casualties at sea' to which the creditors' pamphlet referred.

However, the ship was not out of action for long. On 30 June 1676, Nelthorpe again made an oath regarding the *Constant Friendship* in the customs house but did not claim to be the sole owner. He stated that the ship had been on a voyage 'for the Baltick seas for the space of twelve weekes or thereabouts now last past', dating the voyage to April

[10] Original Warrants for making free the following ships. *SPO*, SP 29/364 f. 19.

[11] Earle. *Making of the English Middle Class*. 40.

[12] Order in Council. SP 29/381 f. 97, 5 May 1676.

186   M. WINTER

1676.[13] This voyage is significant, because it was the subject of Chancery proceedings between London merchant James Holland and partner John Farrington, and details another possible instance of shipping loss. In the proceedings, no mention is made of Nelthorpe, and Farrington and Holland name only one other part-owner, Richard Bankes. There is similarly no reference to the bank or bank partnership, suggesting Farrington employed the ship for his own singular purpose and trade.

In January 1677, James Holland entered a complaint against Farrington which states that he, Holland, was 'partowner' of the *Constant Friendship*. Holland argued that, in April 1676, Farrington employed the ship for a voyage 'from London to St Tooves in Portugall & from their back againe into the downes & from thence to Ravill & Narva in Leistland & from thence' to a 'Port of Ireland'. To finance the voyage Holland borrowed £250 from Farrington via bond, with a penalty of £500 if it went unpaid. Holland entered a complaint because Farrington was pressing for repayment of the bond, which Holland argued had become 'voide' as he believed the ship had been 'totally lost & destroyed by storme & Tempest' on its return voyage. However, Farrington argued that the ship was not lost or destroyed but would have 'still beene in being if [Holland] & the rest of the partowners or some of them had not caused her to be broken up & the materials of her to be sold'. Farrington claimed that the sale of the parts took place 'in or about May 1676', just two months after the partners had met with their creditors to offer a composition and Robinson's report of their bankruptcy.[14]

The only Chancery proceedings for this case are Holland's complaint and Farrington's answer, suggesting the case was taken no further. However, the story of the destruction recounted by Farrington must be incorrect as the Customs House documents show that Nelthorpe still owned the *Constant Friendship* in June 1676, along with 'others', and on 1 July that year obtained ships pass for a voyage from La Rochelle, France, to the Baltic.[15] Whether Holland or Richard Bankes were amongst the shareholders is unknown. It is possible that the sale

---

[13] Similar affidavits by the following persons concerning the following ships, the only difference being that the ship is sometimes a foreign built ship made free. *SPO*, SP 29/389, ff. 100, 101, 30 June 1676.

[14] TNA: C 7/522/35.

[15] Passes granted for the following ships during the period included in this volume. *SPO*, SP 30/D, 1 July 1676.

referred to by Farrington was the sale of shares rather than the ship itself, and that Holland had sold his share in May 1676. Evidence that the *Constant Friendship* was eventually sold is found in the Admiralty records. In October 1677, Thomas Lewsley reported to the commissioner of the Navy that he had surveyed the *Constant Friendship*, a 'flyboate lying att Wapping', for potential purchase. Lewsley reported that it was a 'fine ship and not above 3 yeares old', dating the building of the ship to 1674 shortly before it first appears in customs records under Nelthorpe's name. He further states that 'ordinary repaires' should be carried out but confirms that the ship was neither destroyed nor deconstructed.[16] The Admiralty purchased the ship, and it was making regular journeys to Tangiers by December 1677.[17] A later sale of the ship certainly fits with the information given in the partners' pamphlet, which claims that having survived until June 1677 they then 'lay gasping'. At this point, the partners decided that although they may be 'at great loss in fixing or recalling the distracted and dispersed Estate' it would be better for the creditors if the partners, rather than the bankruptcy commission, were to recall debts and sell assets.[18] The sale of the *Constant Friendship* was included in these efforts at drawing in and redistributing the partners' estates, but shipping losses were not the primary reason for Thompson and Company's collapse.

II

Around the same time as the first run on the bank in March 1675, political disputes in the Corporation of London and Parliament became increasingly vicious, which had a significant effect on the partners' political and religious networks. From 1673 onwards, Thompson and Nelthorpe's roles as common councillors became more significant and disruptive in the Corporation of London as they were involved in numerous disputes with the Court of Aldermen and Lord Mayor, who were trying to enforce Anglican conformism within the city. The Chamberlain of London, Sir Thomas Player, joined Thompson and Nelthorpe in leadership of the

---

[16] TNA: ADM 106/236/86. 31 October 1677.

[17] TNA: ADM 106/323/139. 10 December 1677; ADM 106/323/415. 12 December 1677; ADM 106/323/143. 28 December 1677.

[18] *Case of Richard Thompson and Company.* 23.

188 M. WINTER

opposition within the Corporation. Player started his civic career as a protégé of Sir John Robinson and the Anglican leadership, acting as 'one of Williamson's sources of intelligence in the City'.[19] However, Player switched allegiances in 1673 and joined a new 'grievance committee' with Thompson, which produced a petition to the king addressing issues within the City including, 'poverty', 'dearness of coales', 'merchants that are noe freemen trading within and without the City', and 'the declining estate of the City', which demonstrates that divides were not only on religious grounds but also on staple problems of urban governance.[20] Player's friendship and political alliance with Thompson and Nelthorpe most likely began when Player became a fellow common councillor, elected to Bassishaw ward in 1672. Thompson, Nelthorpe, and Player, who all lived in close proximity of one another, were reported to hold regular meetings and were described as a 'knot of people in the City', who also colluded with politicians in the Commons and Lords.[21]

The grievance committee's petition caused a rift between the Common Council and Court of Aldermen, who felt the committee had over-stretched their authority by identifying wider problems of urban governance, which were not under the council's jurisdiction, in an attempt to gain more power.[22] Indeed, the petition never reached the king as the Court of Aldermen quashed it, and Robinson reported that the Aldermen's action 'incurr'd the displeasure of Mr Thompson'.[23] In November 1674, Nelthorpe and Thompson were assigned to a committee to 'consider and informe themselves out of the records of this City of the respective priviledges of the Lord Maior and Aldermen and of the Commons in Common Councell' particularly 'in making Laws' and to 'make report'. The committee intended to promote the authority of

[19] De Krey. Player, Sir Thomas. *ODNB.*

[20] *Letters Addressed to Sir Joseph Williamson*, vol. 1. No. 57—From Sir John Robinson. 113–115.

[21] Woodhead. *Rulers of London.* 131; Burdon. Marvell and His Kindred: The Family Network in the Later Years—II Nelthorpes, Thompsons, and Popples. 175; Notes by Williamson. *SPO*, SP 29/379 f. 80, 18 February 1676; Note by Williamson. *SPO*, SP 29/379 f. 73, 17 February 1676.

[22] De Krey. *London and the Restoration.* 135.

[23] *Letters Addressed to Sir Joseph Williamson*, vol. 1. No. 57—From Sir John Robinson. 113–115.

8 WHY DID THOMPSON AND COMPANY COLLAPSE? 189

the Common Council within the Corporation, increasing their decision-making ability and involvement in elections. The intensifying of disputes between the Common Council and Court of Aldermen reflected broader trends in parliamentary politics and the emergence of a prominent 'country' faction.[24] The links between civic politicians and MPs and lords was important in this regard. Significant for the banking partners was Thompson and Nelthorpe's kinship and close friendship with Andrew Marvell, as well as with their cousin Sir Henry Thompson who was a 'Country' MP for York from 1673. Other important associates include Player's close friend Anthony Ashley Cooper, the Earl of Shaftesbury, who similarly turned to opposition politics after being dismissed as Lord Chancellor in 1673 and then dismissed from the Privy Council in May 1674.[25] Thereafter, Shaftesbury became one of the leading opposition figures in parliament and participated in regular meetings with civic opposition leaders: Thompson, Nelthorpe, and Player.

Thompson and Nelthorpe's political activity and extensive network of allies earned them powerful enemies. Their most vehement enemy was Robinson, whose job it was, over the 1660s and 1670s, to root out nonconformists and bring 'quiet' to the City.[26] Robinson's position was strengthened by his alliance with court politicians Thomas Osborne, the Earl of Danby, and Sir Joseph Williamson. Danby had been appointed as Lord Treasurer in October 1673, a month before Shaftesbury's dismissal—an appointment that Douglas Lacey claims was 'portentous to all Dissenters' as the laws restricting dissenters' activity in public life were exacerbated following his appointment.[27] In addition to his general dislike of dissenters, Danby's appointment as Lord Treasurer had brought him into conflict with the banking partners' cousin, Sir

---

[24] LMA: COL/CC/01/01/046 (Microfilm X109/083). Common Council Journal. 20 December 1673–22 October 1678, ff. 123, 129, 144; LMA: COL/AD/01/49. Letter Book YY. 1673–1676, f. 71; De Krey. *London and the Restoration*. 137–138.

[25] K. H. D. Haley. 1968. *The First Earl of Shaftesbury*. Oxford: Oxford University Press. 328, 342, 364; W. D. Christie. 1874. *Letters Addressed from London to Sir Joseph Williamson While Plenipotentiary at the Congress of Cologne in the Years 1673 and 1674*. vol. 2. London. Camden New Series, 8–9. 154, 197–198.

[26] Paul Seaward. 2008. Robinson, Sir John, first baronet (*bap.* 1615, *d.* 1680). *ODNB*, https://doi.org/10.1093/ref:odnb/37904. Accessed 10 December 2018.

[27] Lacey. *Dissent and Parliamentary Politics*. 71, 72; Brian Weiser. 2003. *Charles II and the Politics of Access*. Suffolk: Boydell Press. 73; De Krey. *London and the Restoration*. 142–143.

190   M. WINTER

Henry Thompson, over the parliamentary seat for York, which Danby had held prior to his promotion. A letter to the Corporation of York reveals that Danby had hoped to maintain 'ties' with the city by having his 14-year-old son, Peregrine, elected to the seat and was confident in his desire as he did 'so little doubt the affection of the Citty'. However, the council replied that they were 'utterly incapable of Answering yor Lordshipps expectation', as they had already chosen a replacement out of 'our owne body', Sir Henry Thompson. In response Danby stated that he 'deserved better from the Citty'.[28] Henry Thompson himself corresponded with Danby on this issue, politely and reverently expressing his ignorance of Danby's wish and desire not 'to cross' him, but acknowledging that 'the Citty hath long protested, they would chuse me from amongst them selves'.[29] Thus, much to Danby's displeasure, 'country' politician Henry Thompson took his seat. Alongside Danby was Sir Joseph Williamson, who held the post of under-secretary to the Secretary of State from 1660 and then Secretary of State from 1674. From the mid-1670s Williamson was also engaged in promoting Anglican conformity and kept extensive intelligence notes gathered by agents in the city, some of which concerned the activities of the bank partners.[30] For these political leaders Thompson and Nelthorpe, and other civic opposition leaders, were disruptive figures whose removal from the Corporation became a priority.

These 'Court' and 'opposition' divisions, however, do not account for the position of the monarch. De Krey and Brain Weiser suggest that, from 1673 onwards, the king sided more and more with the Anglican, or 'court', faction. However, Harris and Mark Goldie have argued that the king acted independently as he 'leaned towards' different sides at different times, 'playing off' each side against each other for political and economic benefits.[31] One of the king's primary concerns in the 1660s and

---

[28] BL: Add MS 28,051. Original, correspondence of the family of Osborne, Dukes of Leeds, on matters of private business; 1669–1788. ff. 23, 31–32, 34–35; Basil Morgan. 2004. Osborne, Peregrine, second duke of Leeds (*bap.* 1659, *d.* 1729). *ODNB*, https://doi-org.sheffield.idm.oclc.org/10.1093/ref:odnb/20879. Accessed 1 June 2020.

[29] HHC: U DDFA/39/8, 'Sir Henry Thompson to Thomas Osborne, Lord Treasurer', 5 July 1673.

[30] Marshall. *Intelligence and Espionage*. 3, 30, 37, 44, 63.

[31] De Krey. *London and the Restoration*. 144–145; Weiser. *Charles II*. 4, 37, 74; Harris. *Politics Under the Later Stuarts*. 67; Goldie. Danby, the Bishops and the Whigs. 75–76, 81.

8 WHY DID THOMPSON AND COMPANY COLLAPSE? 191

1670s was finance and he relied on Parliament to provide much-needed capital. When Parliament failed to grant money, the king could turn to other sources, such as the city guilds, or appeal to political or commercial groups in return for privileges. As a result, politics could be influenced through finance, and this tactic was pursued by both 'court' and 'country' factions. That the king maintained an open dialogue with opposing factions is further evident from his meetings with civic opposition leaders throughout the 1670s. In 1675 Williamson noted that Player, Thompson and Nelthorpe 'still own that they come and drink now and then with the King at Will Chiffinch's', the Page of the King's bedchamber and keeper of the Royal Closet who often acted as a 'political go-between' for the Court and City.[32] Additionally, the banking partners were described as possessing the 'particular favour' of the king.[33] Wall has suggested that this favour arose from Thompson and Nelthorpe having 'a hand in' a loan of £40,000 to the monarch, which was supplied by City nonconformists in 1670. This gesture was most likely intended to tempt Charles towards a policy of religious toleration, such as the unsuccessful Declaration of Indulgence of 1672. However, neither Thompson nor Nelthorpe's name appear in the list of subscribers. Instead, it appears that this favour originated through their friend and political ally Sir Thomas Player, who was one of the king's regular drinking partners.[34]

That is not to say, though, that the king was not looking for loans from City nonconformists. It is possible that Charles hoped to use Thompson and Nelthorpe's influential position in dissenting circles to sway the minds and pockets of the nonconformists—particularly as Parliament became increasingly less willing to provide funds for the Third Anglo-Dutch War.[35] However, the partners' relationship with the king was a balancing act. Williamson's intelligence notes record that Thompson, Player, and Nelthorpe 'of late' seemed 'not so well satisfied of their reception by the King' and decided not to 'hazard themselves further' for fear that

---

[32] Notes by Williamson. *SPO*, SP 29/379 f. 80, 18 February 1676; David Allen. 1976. The Political Function of Charles II's Chiffinch. *Huntington Library Quarterly* 39: 285.

[33] *Letters Addressed to Sir Joseph Williamson*, vol. 2. No. 124—From Henry Ball. 44–47.

[34] Wall. Marvell's Friends in the City. 205; De Krey. *London and the Restoration*. 403–411, 123; De Krey. Player, Sir Thomas. *ODNB*.

[35] Steven C. A. Pincus. 1995. From Butterboxes to Wooden Shoes: The Shift in English Popular Sentiment from Anti-Dutch to Anti-French in the 1670s. *The Historical Journal* 38: 344–345, 351; Jones. *Anglo-Dutch Wars*. 199, 209; CSP Venice. 194–204.

192 M. WINTER

they might lose favour 'elsewhere'.[36] Whilst having a relationship with the monarch was important, and potentially lucrative, an over-reliance on the king's favour at the expense of other lucrative relationships could be damaging. The partners' political activism, connections to parliamentary court politics, and relationship with the king would be highly significant for the fate of the bank.

III

The risk caused by the partners' multiple roles came to a head in 1675, when they encountered political and commercial difficulties. Commercially, the partners ran into conflict with the East India Company in 1673 and another group of merchants in 1675 over a contract for prize goods, which resulted in legal challenges. Politically, relations within the Corporation of London and in national politics had become increasingly tense. The 'civic opposition' had caused trouble within the Corporation and their 'Country Party' allies had caused similar disruption in the houses of Parliament. The coincidence of these commercial and political struggles, I argue, gave powerful individuals and opponents an opportunity to discredit the banking partners by using their commercial misfortune as an excuse to cast doubt on their financial abilities and eject them from the Common Council. The partners' pamphlet gives no specific reason for the collapse of the bank, only stating that the partners encountered 'Affronts and Unkindnesses', 'Calumny', and pursuit by 'enemies'.[37] Whilst these insinuations could be viewed as mere excuses on the partners' behalf, the fact that the collapse of the bank coincided with commercial and political discontent suggests otherwise.

Commercially, the partners first encountered trouble in 1673 over a contract for prize goods during the Third Anglo-Dutch War. The contract concerned four Dutch East India 'prizes'—goods or vessels of a belligerent captured during warfare by the opposing side—seized during the English retaking of St Helena from the Dutch in September 1673. The taking of prize was regulated by the Prize Courts, which were set up in wartime under the jurisdiction of the High Court of Admiralty and followed the civil law, rather than the common law of England. In

[36] Notes by Williamson. *SPO*, SP 29/379 f. 80, 18 February 1676.

[37] *Case of Richard Thompson and Company*. 11, 14, 15.

the court, a judge and commissioners would deem each capture legal or illegal, and once declared lawful the goods would become crown property and any appeals dealt with by the Privy Council.[38] In 1673 the four captured Dutch ships—the *Alphon*, the *Europe*, the *Arms of Camphire*, and the *Papenburg*—were considered lawful prize and it was largely anticipated that the East India Company, which already had the ships in its warehouses, would be commissioned to sell them. Newsletters record that the prizes contained 'pepper, salt peter, cloath, some silks, and severall other Rich east India comodities adjudged alreadie to be worth abote 800000Li'. These were products that the Company already had 'magazines full' of, being part of their monopoly, which 'if they got into the hands of others they would cause notable prejudice to the company by being sold at a low price'.[39] The East India Company had already risked losing the prizes on their return voyage to England to the retaliating Dutch forces and proclaimed that if they lost them they would 'never' be able to 'hold up their heads againe'.[40]

However, on 13 October 1673 East India merchant John Paige wrote to Williamson that he had 'just had notice how his Majesty has disposed of his East India prizes on private contract', taking the prizes out of the East India Company's hands. Paige remarked 'I wish it may prove to his advantage, though I doubt it'.[41] Later that month the minutes of the East India Company confirmed the sale and recipient of the contract, recording that they were 'to sell & dispose' of the prizes to 'Mr Nelthorp & his partners', the king having 'thought fit to dispose of the Goods by private contract'.[42] The phrase 'private contract' refers to how the goods were sold. The king would sell them to Thompson and Nelthorpe for a set

---

[38] Hardinge Goulburn Giffard, Viscount Tiverton. 1914. *The Principles and Practice of Prize Law*. London: Gale. 2, 7; Jones. *Anglo-Dutch Wars*. 212; Shavana Musa. 2015. Tides and Tribulations: English Prize Law and the Law of Nations in the Seventeenth Century. *Journal of the History of International Law* 17: 48, 49, 57, 74, 80; G. E. Aylmer. 2002. *The Crown's Servants: Government and Civil Service under Charles II, 1660–1685*. Oxford: Oxford University Press. 60.

[39] LoC, MD: MSS97733 *London Newsletters Collection*. Reel 2. 16 August 1673 and 23 August 1673; TNA: ADM 106/289/7. Folio 7: Jonas Shish, A. Beare, J. Uthwat and Phineas Pett. 27 October 1673.

[40] *Letters Addressed to Sir Joseph Williamson*, vol. 1. No. 94—From Henry Ball. 190–194.

[41] John Paige to Williamson. *SPO*, SP 29/337 f. 150, 13 October 1673.

[42] BL: IOR/B/32. Court Minutes. ff. 151, 155.

194   M. WINTER

price, who would then sell the goods privately through the same means—
setting a price and selling in bulk to certain individuals. In contrast, the
East India Company would sell the goods by public auction, using a
candle to signify the time in which individuals had to bid. This practice,
it was argued, would allow everyone to access the goods and maintain a steady price, as the Company would only put up for auction the
amount of goods necessary to meet demand without overstocking or
understocking the market.[43]

That Thompson and Nelthorpe managed to obtain the contract
is remarkable. Shavana Musa argues that, throughout the seventeenth
century, the monarch had a unique relationship with the East India
Company regarding prizes, using charters to gain revenue which 'in
essence transcended the authority of Parliament'. The potential financial
gains were so high that the Privy Council would order the Admiralty
Court 'to be lenient' on the East India Company and 'bypass any rigorous
application of the law' for the benefit of the monarch.[44] The mutual
benefit arising from prizes meant that the monarch needed to appease the
East India Company to enrich all their pockets. Thompson and Nelthorpe
managed to alter this established process through personal favour, and
'upon verie considerable conditiones', demonstrating their power and
influence with the monarch, the strength of their commercial reputations,
and how power or capital in the political field could influence actions in
the commercial field.[45]

However, the established and lucrative relationship between the East
India Company and the monarch also makes it less surprising that the
contract did not remain in Thompson and Nelthorpe's hands for long.
Just days after the partners obtained the contract, a rumour circulated
that 'the King will loose 90,000l' by his decision.[46] Furthermore, the
East India Company had 'given out' publicly that 'the Goods were sold
for less by 33,700^{Li} than they would have been' by them. In order to
'avoid publique clamour', the king sent the Company a proposition that if

---

[43] 1676. *An Answer to Two Letters concerning the East-India Company*. London. 5;
1691. *Plain Dealing: In a Dialogue Between Mr. Johnson and Mr. Wary His Friend, a
Stock-Jobber, and a Petitioner Against the E– I– Company, About Stock-Jobbing, and the
Said Company*. London. 11.

[44] Musa. Tides and Tribulations. 74–75.

[45] LoC, MD: MSS97733. *London Newsletters Collection*. 18 October 1673.

[46] *Letters Addressed to Sir Joseph Williamson*, vol. 2. No. 124—From Henry Ball. 44–47.

8 WHY DID THOMPSON AND COMPANY COLLAPSE? 195

they 'would buy the goods & give 33700^{Li} more than what Mr Nelthorp was to pay for them, they should have them'. The East India Company agreed to the proposition, paying £50,000 on 30 October 1673, a further £50,000 on 6 November, and the rest, which included the extra £33,700, on 13 November.[47] This therefore reveals that Thompson and Company had agreed to pay at least £100,000 for the contract. Later in November, Robert Yard reported to Williamson that 'The East India Company have sold all the prize goods for 45,000^{Li} more than was contracted for with Thompson and the rest of his company'.[48] Public knowledge is further evident from reports of the taking and arrival of the prizes to England in the London Gazette newspaper, and from newsletters concerning the 'discourse' of the 'citizens of London' who, according to Sir Thomas Player, were discussing 'how these prizes may be disposed to the best advantage'. The prizes were such a popular topic of conversation due to the controversial nature of the Third Anglo-Dutch War and the financial state of the king, who desperately needed funds but could no longer rely on parliament voting to finance another year. It was not only Parliament who were dissatisfied, but the population at large. In his letter to Williamson, Player reported that the 'Citizens of London lookt more disconsolate then when their Citie lay in ashes' and claimed that this 'could not be otherwise' as the 'state ... thinke fitt to stifle any publick narrative wherein the French might be exposed' of 'cowardice and treachery', which he claimed was 'impossible to conceale'. But news of the prizes had provided a 'diversion' in the discourse and 'humour' of the City that, according to Player, could be used to the king's 'advantage'.[49] Therefore Player's letter further explains why the contract was transferred in favour of the East India Company: to stifle discontent amongst the people. Although this may have had repercussions for the partners' commercial reputations, economically they were not entirely ruined as Charles awarded Thompson and Nelthorpe £10,000 in compensation for their troubles.

Despite this, the conflict over the prize contract did not end in 1673. It re-emerged with greater vigour in July 1675, just before the first run

---

[47] BL: IOR/B/32. Court Minutes. ff. 154, 155.

[48] *Letters Addressed to Sir Joseph Williamson*, vol. 2. No. 148—From Robert Yard. 81–83.

[49] Sir Thomas Player to Sir Joseph Williamson. *SPO*, SP 29/337 f. 38, 9 September 1673; *The London Gazette* 813, 1 September 1673; *The London Gazette* 814, 4 September 1673; Jones. *Anglo-Dutch Wars*. 209, 212.

196   M. WINTER

on the bank in September 1675. No longer directly involving the East India Company, the renewed conflict concerned four Jewish merchants working in London—Francisco Terrezy, Antonio Gomes Serra, Alphonso Rodrigues, and Jacob Aboab—who claimed they were owed a percentage of the £10,000 compensation.[50] The Jewish merchants petitioned the Privy Council in July 1675, resulting in a summons to Nelthorpe and ten witnesses to appear at a hearing at Hampton Court, which, according to the Venetian secretary in England, was 'considered remarkable'.[51] The rival petitioners argued that their right to compensation derived from an 'agreement' with Nelthorpe that they would 'advance one Moyety' for the prize contract and in return would 'bear one Moyety of the Profit or Losse'. To this end, they argued, they delivered 'ready money & Notes' to Nelthorpe and 'drew other considerable sumes from the Bank of Holland in order to pay the whole'.[52] However, the Privy Council hearing clearly did not provide the desired outcome, and the following year Terrezy and Rodrigues entered a Chancery complaint against Nelthorpe and Thompson, of which only Nelthorpe and Thompson's answer survives.

In their answer, Nelthorpe and Thompson recounted receiving the prize contract from the king and the privy seal for the same, and confirmed that, after the Hampton Court hearing, 'the Lord Arlington discharged all persons from their attendance declaring hee would doo nothing in that affaire'. Nelthorpe stated that he and Thompson first became aware of the goods through fellow merchant Thomas Hawke, who along with another merchant Michael Levy, offered to contact 'severall Jewes' to advance money to Nelthorpe in return for 'a share of the said goods'. However, Nelthorpe denied 'that the said proposalls or discourse was done by way of partnershipp' but was 'a bare discourse'. Nelthorpe described a meeting with the Jewish merchants at the 'Vulture Taverne' on 15 October 1673 in which he produced documents 'for each of them to signe' detailing the money offered and goods desired. However, they 'refused ... and then declared they would not be concerned therein directly or indirectly'. Nelthorpe argued that their

---

[50] Maurice Woolfe. 1970–1973. Foreign Trade of London Jews in the Seventeenth Century. *Transactions & Miscellanies (Jewish Historical Society of England)* 24: 38–58.

[51] CSP Venice. 438–450.

[52] Francisco Terrezy &a. against Mr. Nelthorp touching their share in the 10000^L for relinquishing their Contract for the East India Prizes to be heard 28th· SPO, Privy Council: Registers, PC 2/64 f. 465, 14 July 1675.

8 WHY DID THOMPSON AND COMPANY COLLAPSE? 197

lack of partnership or formal agreement was evident from the absence of an 'Accompt of the charges of the private contract' and 'any obligacion or writing under their hands' which Nelthorpe 'would have taken' in the normal course of business.[53] Instead, Nelthorpe and Thompson claimed that they obtained funds elsewhere, most likely drawing on their own joint bank funds and calling in investments and loans. All of which was futile, however, as the king reversed his decision.

Aside from detailing Terrezy and Rodrigues' complaint, the Chancery answer further illuminates the wider ramifications of the loss of the prize contract in 1673 and suggests how this later conflict reignited rumours surrounding the partners' commercial abilities. According to Nelthorpe, in 1673 the East India Company heard that Serra, Rodrigues, and Terrezy had been negotiating with Nelthorpe over the prizes and approached the merchants to inform them that the 'Company was much displeased with them'. This brief comment hints at a connection between the Jewish merchants and the East India Company. Along with the da Silva's and the da Costa's, the Rodrigues family were the initiators of, and primary figures in, London's diamond trade which became part of the East India Company monopoly in the 1660s. Indeed, the da Costa and Rodrigues families became the East India Company's 'largest traders' along with 'agents at Surat and Madras'.[54] Similarly, Antonio Gomes Serra was another wealthy merchant and one of 'the most prominent among the Jewish importer'.[55] The merchants' links to the East India Company help to explain why, following their discussion with the Company, Serra and Rodrigues told Nelthorpe 'they were sorry that ever they had treated with him' and that they would neither 'buye' the goods nor 'meddle any further in that matter', fearing the East India Company 'would doo them a displeasure of a greater consequence'. The Jewish merchants also 'advised [Nelthorpe] to desist from the businesse'.

[53] TNA: C 8/296/106. Terrezy v Nelthorpe. 12 May 1676; Hawke was later rewarded for his role in the sale of the contract: Warrant to the Commissioners of Prizes to pay 100l. to Thomas Hawkes, merchant, for his services about the East India prizes, and particularly in advancing their sale. *SPO*, SP 44/26 f. 170, 28 January 1674.

[54] Edgar Samuel. 2002. Diamonds and Pieces of Eight: How Stuart England Won the Rough-Diamond Trade. *Jewish Historical Studies* 38: 25, 27–28; Walter J. Fischel. 1960. The Jewish Merchant-Colony in Madras (Fort St. George) during the 17th and 18th Centuries: A Contribution to the Economic and Social History of the Jews in India. *Journal of the Economic and Social History of the Orient* 3: 82–83.

[55] Woolfe. Foreign Trade of London Jews. 51.

The East India Company not only threatened the Jewish merchants; they also took direct action against the banking partners. Nelthorpe stated that, following the reassignment of the contract, he was 'in a great straight for money'. On top of this, Nelthorpe claimed, the East India Company used 'all ways and meanes to destroy [his] Creditt', and, as a result of the Company's public 'discourses and perswasions', some creditors of the bank 'drew their Cash' from Nelthorpe and Thompson 'to their very great prejudice and damage'.[56] This led to an economic downturn, evident from John Farrington's statement to Chancery in 1684, in which he argued that the bank ran into difficulties in 1673 as Thompson and Nelthorpe had 'drawne out a farr greater sume from the said Joynt stock & cash for the carrying on the said Profitable trade betweene them'—the prize contract.[57] Therefore, it is easy to see how, through public discourse and rumour, the East India Company's commercial actions impacted upon Thompson and Company's financial business. Reigniting the dispute in the Privy Council and Chancery Court stirred up similar concerns amongst clients of the bank, leading them, once again, to withdraw their funds.

Politically, the Corporation of London witnessed large-scale disruption in 1675. On 20 March, the Venetian Secretary in England, Girolamo Alberti, wrote to the Doge and Senate describing a 'violent dispute' between 'the Lord Mayor of London and the Common Council' over who had the right to elect a judge to the Sherriff's Court, with the councillors arguing that the position had always been 'in the gift of the Common Council'.[58] In the meeting 'John Dubois, Sir Thomas Player, Edward Nelthorpe, Richard Thompson, and other common councilmen' made a stand against the decision, to which Lord Mayor Vyner responded by dissolving the meeting.[59] Vyner was, however, in a weak position. As a banker and principal lender to the crown, the 1672 Stop on the Exchequer nearly bankrupted Vyner and he only survived due to borrowing and crown protection. Vyner was also embroiled in a personal scandal, trying to marry his daughter to the Earl of Danby's son, even though Vyner's daughter was already said to be married. This was common knowledge

[56] TNA: C 8/296/106.

[57] TNA: C 7/581/73.

[58] CSP Venice. 364–382.

[59] De Krey. *London and the Restoration*. 140.

around London, and Marvell even reported it in his professional correspondence with the Corporation of Hull, describing the 'detestable and most ignominious story' about Vyner's daughter and adding that 'his late enterprising' in civic government was intended 'to subvert in all manners the Libertyes of the City'.[60] Thus, Vyner's professional and personal troubles provided an opportunity for the Common Council to manipulate and threaten the Mayor, 'compelling [him] ... to withdraw'. Secretary Alberti claimed that 'they will proceed against him to the extent of arrest and imprisonment from which his office does not exempt him', dishonouring the post of Mayor 'for the first time and forever'.[61] In a series of letters written to Secretary Coventry, Danby and Williamson, along with the Lord Keeper Sir Heneage Finch, described the recent disturbance. They claimed that the actions of Thompson, Player and the others were 'as if they were designed to give a trouble in the Parliament, as they have already done in the Citty'.[62] Secretary Alberti also expressed concerns, writing that although the 'quarrel' did not currently 'extend beyond the city of London', if 'people get exasperated there will be disturbances'.[63] Thus, their political activities were not only a danger within the Corporation of London, but within the national arena too.

Thompson and Nelthorpe's political situation became even more precarious as their efforts in the Common Council coincided with the parliamentary session of 1675, which according to De Krey 'transformed' national politics. The main point of dispute was Danby's Test Act, which required all 'office-holders to swear an oath against the alteration of government'—essentially attempting to purge the corporation of dissenters and nonconformists. This proposal caused uproar in both the House of Lords and the Commons and led to the king proroguing

---

[60] G. E. Aylmer. 2014. Vyner [Viner], Sir Robert. *ODNB*, https://doi.org/10.1093/ref:odnb/28318. Accessed 17 January 2020; Horsefield. The "Stop on the Exchequer" Revisited. 518–524; *The Poems and Letters of Andrew Marvell*, vol. 2. 150.

[61] CSP Venice. 364–382.

[62] The Lord Keeper, the Earl of Danby and Sir J. Williamson to Secretary Coventry. *SPO*, SP 44/43 f. 10, 13 March 1675; Whitehall. The Lord Keeper, the Earl of Danby and Sir J. Williamson to Secretary Coventry. *SPO*, SP 44/43 f. 12, 17 March 1675; Whitehall. The Lord Keeper, the Earl of Danby and Sir J. Williamson to Secretary Coventry. *SPO*, SP 44/43 f. 13, 20 March 1675.

[63] CSP Venice. 364–382.

parliament until 1677. Without parliament, Shaftesbury and other 'Country' party members instead 'turned to the city as a substitute arena for challenging the ministry', evident from the many meetings Williamson recorded in his intelligence notes between Shaftesbury and a 'knot' of civic politicians. The decision to prorogue parliament not only added to the determination of opposition forces, but also to those Anglican political leaders within the 'Court' faction.[64] As the City became the most important battleground for the ongoing political contest, Thompson and Nelthorpe's political positions, connecting the dissenting 'Country party' with the City opposition, took on greater importance and greater risk.

The difficulties encountered by Thompson and Company could be used to the advantage of certain courtly opponents, particularly Robinson who not only had links in parliament but also in the City's mercantile circles as a merchant and East India Company committee member from 1666 to 1677. Therefore, he was well placed to aid the circulation of rumour and gossip in London's commercial circles. That rumour and reputation could have such a significant effect is evident from the fortunes of the 'civic opposition' leaders in 1677. De Krey has argued that 'Edward Nelthorpe and Richard Thompson were forced to retire from civic affairs' following the failure of the bank. Whilst acknowledging that their collapse had an effect on their own political roles, De Krey does not link the collapse of the bank to the attempts just a few months later to remove their ally Player as Chamberlain 'and like-minded other colleagues' from the Corporation.[65] These are stated as two unrelated facts, and there is no recognition of the impact of the collapse of the bank within the higher politics of the 'Country' faction in parliament.

That such political manipulation took place on the back of the bank's failure is evident from state papers, which demonstrate the wider utility of the bank's collapse to leading Anglican figures. In January 1676, following the successful appointment of a judge to the Sherriff's court, Robinson wrote to Williamson that the conflict had been 'quietly ended' and 'Mr Richardson', 'an honest Lyall & quiett man', had been elected. He ended the letter with the sarcastic remark that 'the great Honeries Player & Thompson &co. find by demonstration they are not so powerful

---

[64] De Krey. *London and the Restoration*. 142–144; Lacey. *Dissent and Parliamentary Politics*. 77–79; Note by Williamson. *SPO*, SP 29/379 f. 73, 17 February 1676; Notes by Williamson. *SPO*, SP 29/379 f. 80, 18 February 1676.

[65] Seaward. Robinson, Sir John. *ODNB*; De Krey. *London and the Restoration*. 150.

as they made themselves', as they proved unable to overthrow the decision of the Corporation.[66] Just two months later Robinson informed Williamson that the banking partners had 'lost their reputations'. That this affected other 'opposition' leaders is evident from Robinson's closing statement in which he added, 'I heard the Chamberlain [Player] is diped with the above named' and finished by stating his desire for 'quiett' in the Corporation.[67] John Verney's newsletter to his father reveals that, shortly after this, Thompson and Nelthorpe were abruptly forced to abandon their places in the Common Council. John wrote that at a recent Common Council meeting 'the Recorder Sr John Howell asked where were the two Gentlemen that were wont to sett there (pointing out his finger to Tompsons seate)'.[68] Clearly, the political and commercial conflicts had a significant effect on the partners' credit and reputation.

To further ensure that Thompson and Nelthorpe would not return to politics, a caveat was added to the rules stipulating the 'Conditions to be observed when electing common councilmen'. This is evident in a draft and final version of a letter from December 1676 written by Lord Mayor Sir Thomas Davies, which was sent to the aldermen of London. The finished letter states that the king, in discussion with the Mayor and aldermen, required that the Corporation put into execution the 1673 'Act for the well Governing & regulating of Corporations' before the upcoming election to ensure that 'noe person doo sitt in Common Councell that is not qualifyed according to the said Act'. The Act was to be communicated to voters at the 'wardmote before the election' by the aldermen, who were to 'give publick notice & dirreccion' of the conditions so that voters may chose persons 'eminent in qualifications' for the 'honour & weale of their Citty'. In the draft, the mayor wrote out the conditions and noted down names next to them; the final letter only includes the conditions. In the draft letter, the condition that read 'noe person that hath summoned his creditors togeather not being able in due time to pay his debts but forc'd to compound' had 'Thompson' and 'Nelthorpe' written in the margin beside it. Underneath was the condition 'noe person That is an officer of the Citty that is bound to give his

---

[66] Sir John Robinson to Williamson. *SPO*, SP 29/378 f. 264, January 1676.

[67] Sir John Robinson to Williamson. *SPO*, SP 29/379 f. 265, 10 March 1676.

[68] BL: MS 636/29. *Verney Papers*. William Hall to Sir Ralph Verney, 16 March 1676, and 'John Verney to Sir Ralph Verney', 16 March 1676.

attendance on my Lord Mayor's person or the Court of Aldermen', with Sir Thomas Player's name noted next to it. Another condition, which did not make it into the final letter, has no names written next to it but could also refer to the bank partners. It excludes anyone 'that hath had a hand in setting upp an English manufacture in Ireland', which could refer to Nelthorpe's factory in Clonmel.[69]

Further evidence of a targeted attack on the opposition leaders, particularly Player, is evident from two newsletters. In a letter to Sir Edward Harley in June 1677, Marvell informed him that in a recent election at 'Common hall' there was 'an influenced designe ... to out Sir Thomas Playor'. A newsletter written by Thomas Barnes, an intelligence agent working for Secretary Williamson in the 1670s, professed to provide the reader with 'some of the present talk in town' and revealed a rumour that a letter had been 'sent from above to prevent Sir Thomas from being chosen'. This attempt to oust Player coincides with the date when Thompson and Nelthorpe fled their houses and went into hiding. However, unlike the bankers, Player was harder to remove from the Corporation. Marvell further informed Harley that the attack was unsuccessful due to an unexpectedly large turnout of 'fanatics' in support of Player. Indeed, Barnes reported that Player was re-elected with 'universal applause'.[70]

However, there is further evidence that this attack extended beyond the 'civic opposition' to the parliamentary 'country' faction, particularly one of its leading figures, the Earl of Shaftesbury. In 1676, due to the turbulent parliamentary session of 1675, Lord Treasurer Danby had a particular interest in ridding Parliament of his opponents and managed to obtain the support of the king. In February 1676, when the bank was still operating, Charles tried to persuade Shaftesbury to leave London. Later that month Danby convinced the king that Shaftesbury should be sent to the Tower, as Shaftesbury had been seen having regular meetings with City dissenters and 'parliamentary opposition' figures. However, Shaftesbury was not arrested due to Secretary Williamson's reluctance to sign the arrest warrant, Williamson also managed to convince the king to

---

[69] Notes of conditions to be observed in electing Common Council men. *SPO*, SP 29/387 f. 141, December 1676; The Lord Mayor of London to the Aldermen of the several wards. *SPO*, SP 29/387 f. 139, 12 December 1676.

[70] *The Poems and Letters of Andrew Marvell*, vol. 2. 352; T. B[arnes] to—. *SPO*, SP 29/394 f. 241, 3 July 1677; Marshall. *Intelligence and Espionage*. 201.

abandon this plan of action. Although unsuccessful, the actions of Danby and the king demonstrate the desire of powerful political leaders to eject Shaftesbury and reduce his influence.

Shaftesbury was connected to the bank through his business interests in London, which consisted of a range of landed investments, such as Exeter House in London, and in 'commerce and overseas plantations', holding stock in the Royal African and Hudson's Bay Companies as well as his proprietorship of the colony of Carolina. Shaftesbury biographer K. H. D. Haley noted Shaftesbury's business interests in the City and De Krey further speculated that Shaftesbury might have 'become directly involved' in the bank of Thompson and Company by 1675, although he provided no direct evidence to prove it. Williamson's intelligence notes, which De Krey cited, only record that Shaftesbury had '20,000*l*. in trade' which was 'diffused all over the town'. However, the newsletter written by John Verney to his father provides the missing evidence. After reporting the collapse of Thompson and Company, Verney wrote 'some say Shaftesbury is concerned 8000li in theire hands'. This demonstrates that the collapse of the bank was an even greater opportunity for Thompson and Nelthorpe's enemies to exploit than previously realised. It was an opportunity to spread rumours and bring 'quiet' not only to civic opposition groups but the 'country' faction in the houses of parliament as well. However, like Player, Shaftesbury would prove harder to remove. Indeed, it was not until February 1677, after challenging the legality of the new parliamentary session and failing, that Shaftesbury was arrested and sent to the Tower.[71] In light of Shaftesbury's potential involvement in the bank, Thompson and Nelthorpe's involvement in opposition politics becomes even more significant, with the collapse of their bank providing an access point to key figures in both the civic and parliamentary 'country' opposition.

---

[71] Haley. *The First Earl of Shaftesbury*. 404–405, 417–419; Tim Harris. 2008. Cooper, Anthony Ashley, first earl of Shaftesbury (1621–1683). *ODNB*, https://doi.org/10.1093/ref:odnb/6208. Accessed 20 May 2019; De Krey. *London and the Restoration*. 149; Notes by Williamson. *SPO*, SP 29/379 f. 80, 18 February 1676; BL: MS 636/29. *Verney Papers*. 'John Verney to Sir Ralph Verney', 16 March 1676.

IV

The collapse of the bank of Thompson and Company illuminates the close relationship between finance, commerce, and politics in Restoration London. It demonstrates how divisive 'court' and 'country' factions were in the 1670s and how all-enveloping those divisions could be in a person's life. Adopting leading roles in each field, the partners looked to enhance their individual and collective agency. In so doing, however, they adopted risky strategies that ultimately destroyed their political, commercial, and fiscal credit. Financially, the partners embarked on an innovative venture, which was heavily reliant on credit and public opinion. Commercially, they used their power, or capital, to secure lucrative deals that cut across traditional well-established practices. Politically, they took prominent positions in a nonconformist opposition group that tried to increase the power of the Common Council, alter established procedures, and influence higher politics. Whilst all these roles had the potential to enhance the partners' reputation, they also represented the multiplication of risk: the compromising of one role affecting the capacity to act in others. As such, the collapse of Thompson and Company highlights the socially and politically embedded nature of seventeenth-century finance and the importance of credit to institutions as well as individuals.

The kinds of risks faced by the partners of Thompson and Company were specific to their mercantile and civic identities. Thompson and Nelthorpe, through their roles as overseas merchants, bankers, and politicians, appear to have been constantly trying to gain power and influence within their economic, commercial, and political fields. They did so by adopting bold strategies and challenging existing hierarchies, which increased their power but also increased the risk attached to those roles. Therefore, the fate of Thompson and Company questions Bourdieu's model of fields and capital, which argues that an individual can attain a position of authority within a field by behaving according to the rules of the game and accruing capital or power. Instead, the fate of the partners shows that simply accruing power is not enough. The ways in which individuals use power and in what contexts are equally important. Whilst the partners of Thompson and Company did hold significant symbolic capital and credit in each field, their status was that of civic elites, not landed gentry, and their political positions were much lower ranking than their friends in the Commons and Lords. Unlike their political allies Shaftesbury and Player, an earl and a knight, respectively, the partners' capital was restricted and, arguably, easier to dismantle.

The bold and risky strategies of the partners also aided their collapse by increasing the level of risk inherent in each of their roles and the overlapping nature of their business activities, a mercantile partnership funded by their own bank, meant that once one role was compromised, they all were. The style of institution, type of trade they embarked on, and the networks the partners participated in and facilitated, all contributed to the collapse of Thompson and Company in 1678. But ultimately it was the partners' own strategies and the ways in which they used their power combined with the malice and impetus of their political opponents that sealed their fate.

Acknowledgement This chapter is derived in part from an article published in *Social History*. 2020. Copyright Taylor & Francis, available online: http://www.tandfonline.com/10.1080/03071022.2020.1732125.

CHAPTER 9

Aftermath

In her last will and testament, proved in 1696, Margaret Farrington, wife of the 'London merchant' John Farrington, stated that a legacy left to her by her mother, Anne Bearblock, was during Margaret's 'natural life' to be purely for her 'separate distinct and proper use' without the 'consent or intermeddling' of her husband. The legacy was held in trust for Margaret during her coverture and was hers to dispose of in her will. Margaret's share consisted of the profit and interest of 'fourscore pounds' and 'one full and equal third parte of the rest and residue of all and singular her goods chattels, debts and personall estate'. Her husband John was to have no part of this money. Whilst marriage settlements were usually taken out before marriage by the bride, a settlement could also be made for her once married, by someone else during the course of her life. In this case, Margaret's mother had taken out a settlement for her daughter known as 'separate estate', wherein property was 'held in trust for a wife's use during coverture, which was to be at her disposing', therefore also allowing her to make a will. Reasons why parents may take out such a settlement could be to protect their daughter financially, especially if they were 'concerned about a profligate son-in-law' or, in this case, a bankrupt son-in-law. This motivation is reflected in Margaret's will, which states that her legacy was not to be 'accountable or taken to bee any parte or partes of my said husbands estate nor bee subject or lyable in Lawe

---

© The Author(s), under exclusive license to Springer Nature
Switzerland AG 2022
M. Winter, *Banking, Projecting and Politicking in Early Modern England*, Palgrave Studies in Economic History,
https://doi.org/10.1007/978-3-030-90570-5_9

207

208   M. WINTER

or equity to the satisfaction of any of his debts or engagements whatsoever'. Instead, Margaret divided the remaining profits from the legacy into
thirds and distributed it among four of their five children. Their daughter
Anne Farrington, yet unmarried, was 'executrix' and received the lion's
share, which consisted of two-thirds of her mother's estate. Margaret and
John's 'second and third sons Francis and Ferdinando Farrington' were to
share the final third, whilst their daughter Rebecca, wife of John Philpott,
was to be paid £20 'and not more' out of her sister Anne's share.[1]
Her husband John and eldest son, John Farrington junior, witnessed
the will but her eldest son received no legacy from it. Presumably, John
Farrington junior would be the principal beneficiary of his father's will or
already had property and money settled on him.

The previous two chapters have outlined the collapse of the bank in
1678 and the reasons behind it, demonstrating how closely intertwined
politics, commerce, and finance were in the late seventeenth century and
how political factions could cause irreparable damage to a person's social
and economic credit as well as their ability to maintain a public office.
However, the narrative of Thompson and Company's decline does not
simply end in 1678. Whilst the partners stopped trading then, the collapse
of the bank stretched out into a series of Chancery court cases that
lasted until 1684 and caused a ripple effect through their wider kinship
and credit networks. The wider effects of the bank's collapse are well
evidenced in Margaret Farrington's will, which reveals the means she and
her mother went to in order to protect herself and her children from
the business failure of her husband. In their own pamphlet, the partners
emphasised the effect on their families, who had experienced the 'personal
Rigours' of bankruptcy.[2] Muldrew has argued that because the reputation of all household members was vital in obtaining credit, any damage
to an individual's reputation would affect the entire household through
'public knowledge' and association: the collapse of an individual's credit
would inevitably lead to the collapse of the household credit and wider
credit network.[3] The interconnected nature of individual and household
credit meant that their wives, children, and other household members

[1] TNA; PROB 11/421/381. Will of Margarett Farrington; Erickson. *Women and
Property*. 22, 26, 103, 105.

[2] *Case of Richard Thompson and Company*. 20.

[3] Muldrew. *Economy of Obligation*. 202, 274.

9 AFTERMATH   209

did suffer as a result—households were disbanded, families were relocated, and capital was lost. However, in contrast to Muldrew's argument, this did not lead to each household and every member within it losing their credit and therefore their ability to maintain themselves socially and economically. In the case of Thompson and Company the fate of the partners' households and their members was varied. As Margaret Farrington's will suggests, the partners' wives had different strategies and means by which to alleviate the social and economic impact of the bankruptcy, which meant that whilst they did experience setbacks, it did not necessarily destroy their credit outright. Additionally, the strategies and courses of action taken by these women had a knock-on effect on their children. This chapter examines the impact and aftermath of the collapse of the bank on the partners and their wider kinship and social networks. It works from the centre outwards, beginning with the fate of the four partners and steadily widening the scope to examine the effect on their wives, households, kin, and creditors and debtors. In doing so it demonstrates the connections and differentiations between personal, institutional, and household credit.

I

When the bank collapsed the partners fled and went their separate ways. However, only three of the partners went into hiding. A notice in the *Gazette* newspaper in 1677 only enquired after the whereabouts 'of the said Thompson, Page or Nelthorpe'.[4] Farrington had fallen victim to a different outcome of bankruptcy legislation, that of imprisonment in the King's Bench Prison. In his complaint to Chancery in 1684, Farrington recalled that he had returned to 'his house in London', where he 'was in a few days after arrested by many Creditors of the said Joynt Bank'.[5] Thompson and Nelthorpe managed to flee their homes and avoid detection by their petitioning creditors and the parliamentary commission. They achieved this through the help of their all-important kinship networks. Thompson fled to his brother-in-law Major Braman's house in Chichester, and Nelthorpe fled to a house on Great Russell Street in the London parish of St Giles in the Fields, which his kinsman and

[4] *The London Gazette*, 28 January 1677.

[5] TNA: C 7/581/73.

210   M. WINTER

close friend Andrew Marvell had taken for that purpose.[6] Thompson later joined Nelthorpe and Marvell in the Great Russell Street house with his wife, which was undoubtedly the safest location for them to be concealed as Marvell had taken significant caution in leasing the house. The lease of the house on Great Russell Street was under the name of Mary Palmer, Marvell's housekeeper who later claimed to be, and possibly was, Marvell's wife. According to Mary, Marvell instructed her to take the house and told her that she would be joined there by 'a ffriend or two who would come and Lodge' and they would take care of the rent and pay her housekeeping.[7] Through this arrangement, there was no way of tracing the house back to any acquaintance or kin of the partners. During their time in the Great Russell Street house Marvell was nominated to serve on the parliamentary committee to investigate the partners' bankruptcy, which included a search for the partners whereabouts.[8] Whether Marvell was actually active on this committee or just named is unknown. Either way, Marvell's duplicity is clear. Either he deceived the committee to protect his bankrupt friends, further demonstrating the practical utility of a strong kinship network, or he simply did not get involved with the committee at all.

Marvell, Nelthorpe, Mary Palmer (or Mary Marvell), and later Thompson and his family, cohabited together at the Great Russell Street house for about a year before circumstances changed. In August 1678, Marvell fell ill and died at the Great Russell Street house. Only a month later Edward Nelthorpe similarly succumbed to a quick illness and died. Mary Palmer, or Marvell, recalled that following Nelthorpe's death, and 'at the said Thompsons desire and Request', she continued to live in the Great Russell Street house with Thompson 'who himself dwelt there' and paid her to keep the house for him.[9] However, not long after

---

[6] Madam D. Thompson to Madam Braman. *SPO*, SP 29/402 f. 223, 30 March 1678; E. Braman to Madame Thompson. *SPO*, SP 29/402 f. 305, 6 April 1678; Dorothy Thompson to her brother-in-law, Major Braman. *SPO*, SP 29/401 f. 330, 7 January 1678; TNA: C 10/216/74.

[7] TNA: C 6/242/13.

[8] von Maltzhan. *An Andrew Marvell Chronology*. 116, 197; *The Poems and Letters of Andrew Marvell*, vol. 2. 208; Wall. Marvell's Friends in the City. 207; *Journal of the House of Commons*, vol. 9. 1667–1687. British History Online, http://www.british-history.ac.uk/commons-jrnl/vol9. 12 February 1678.

[9] TNA: C 7/589/82; C 6/242/13.

Thompson was himself arrested and taken to the King's Bench Prison where Farrington was also being held. The seventeenth-century records of the King's Bench do not survive in great number, but the information provided in the Chancery records and eighteenth-century records of the King's Bench can provide an insight into how Farrington and Thompson, the only surviving partners after 1678, lived after their bankruptcy.

Imprisonment for debt was rare, as creditors usually preferred other avenues of the law that were more likely to produce results. However, for creditors seeking more than just the return of their funds, and who wanted to destroy the debtor's reputation and chance of recovery, this could be a useful tool. Once imprisoned, a debtor had little motivation or ability to recoup their finances, and even less motivation to distribute what they had to disgruntled creditors. Whilst debtors' prison was generally unpleasant, especially for poor prisoners, wealthier prisoners could exploit the system. Prisons made 'provision for debtors to live and even conduct business in strictly defined areas outside the prisons known as the Rules'. The Rules consisted of 'Several square miles around the prison' in which prisoners could settle that offered more space and slightly more freedom but were still 'under the jurisdiction of the prison government'. Living within the Rules also meant that a prisoner could use, or abuse, the protections offered by imprisonment to avoid paying their debts. Whilst Farrington appears to have been a normal prisoner, confined by his creditors and renting a prison room, he did have some privileges. In 1684 Thompson complained to Chancery that despite Farrington's confinement, he was 'abuseing the rules of the Kings Bench and haveing his liberty to be in the Citty all most every day'. Whilst Thompson's statement infers that Farrington was breaking the rules, prisoners were actually permitted to leave the prison on 'day trips' to manage their affairs. In the same Chancery statement, Thompson claimed that the commission of bankruptcy had consumed his personal estate, arguing that he had 'made noo private settlement of any part of his reall estate' and that 'the comisioners of Bankrupt seized and sold the same for little more then one fourth part of the reall and true vallue thereof'. The sale of his estate was, Thompson argued, to his own 'great disadvantage and not in the least for the benefitt of the creditors'. However, Thompson still had some money to his name, as it turns out that he had moved into the prison Rules. In their 1684 statement to Chancery, Farrington and Mary Nelthorpe claimed Thompson had 'lately come into the Rules of the prison of the Kings bench and taken a house there' with 'his family'. This confirms that

212   M. WINTER

Thompson was one of the wealthier prisoners who could afford to live in relative comfort and possibly earn a living for his family.[10] This relative comfort was, however, still within the prison boundaries and both Thompson and Farrington's reputations would have been lost as a result of their imprisonment with little chance of returning to their previous careers or being trusted again.

Whilst the fate of Thompson, Farrington, and Nelthorpe is clearly outlined in the sources, what happened to Page is less frequently commented on. Despite being a partner, Page features rarely in the Chancery proceedings. When discussing the collapse of the bank, the other partners did not reference Page's actions, and Thompson claimed he had no knowledge of Page after he and Nelthorpe 'absconded' in 1677. The only mention of his condition are a few comments made by both Farrington and Thompson that Page was 'since dead', which would put his death at some time between 1677 and 1683, although no one appeared anxious to prove this fact. That Page had died is evident from the parish registers of St Mary Woolchurch, which record that an 'Edward Page' died 'suddenly in Woolchurch Market' on 7 June 1677. It is quite possible that the name 'Edmund' was mistaken for 'Edward' by the writer of the register and, indeed, in one of the court cases Page is mistakenly called 'Edward', John Greene claiming he 'did never heare that the said Nelthorpe was partner with Edward Page' but did know that the partnership included an 'Edmond Page'. The record of Edmund's death also matches Thompson's assertion in 1684 that he had been kept from Edmund's 'sight conversacion and knowledge of his Agende for seaven yeares last past or there abouts', dating his disappearance to 1677. Page appears to have died intestate. However, what happened to his share in the bank is mentioned in the Chancery records. Farrington claimed that 'before his death' Page had 'assigned all his Interest in the said moneys' to Farrington the 'better to enable [him] to satisfy an agreement ... with

---

[10] Muldrew. *Economy of Obligation.* 286; Earle. *Making of the English Middle Class.* 125; Joanna Innes. 1983. The King's Bench Prison in the Later Eighteenth Century. In *An Ungovernable People: The English and Their Law in the Seventeenth and Eighteenth Centuries,* eds John Brewer and John Styles, 250–298. London: Rutgers University Press. 256, 263; TNA: C 6/283/87; C 7/581/73; C 10/216/74; Thompson also refers to himself as being 'likewise a Prisoner in the Kings bench' in C 6/249/35.

9 AFTERMATH   213

their creditors to pay & discharge the debts so jointly contracted'.[11] How this arrangement affected Page's wife and family is unknown.

By 1678, then, only two partners remained living. How long Thompson and Farrington remained in the King's Bench prison is unknown, but both were certainly living there throughout the Chancery proceedings which went on until 1684. During those six years, Thompson and Farrington entered into and responded to legal action and managed to finalise payments with creditors once the commission of bankruptcy was superseded in the 1680s. Neither Thompson nor Farrington have left much trace in the records after 1684, save for what is known about them through their wives' wills. However, more is known about what happened to the wives of the partners after 1684. Margaret Farrington's situation has already been explored at the beginning of this chapter, and so the focus of the following discussion will be on the lives of Dorothy Thompson and Mary Nelthorpe, whose contrasting fates demonstrate the different ways in which women could employ their agency and formulate strategies at different stages of their lives to protect themselves from the law and from economic ruin.

II

When the partners fled into hiding in 1677, they did so without their wives. Whilst Edward Nelthorpe fled to the Great Russell Street house with Andrew Marvell, his wife Mary and the children, at Edward's instruction, were sent to stay with her mother in Finsbury. During this time, Mary claimed she was 'ignorant' of her husband's whereabouts, as it was 'not thought convenient' for her to know because the commission of bankruptcy had issued out a warrant against her for information and it was feared 'she might be compelled by the commissioners' to reveal his location.[12] Mary's claims of being kept in the dark further extended to much of her husband's business activities, displaying only limited knowledge of her husband's business in her answer to the Chancery court. Indeed, the statements made by Mary in Chancery suggest that she and her husband's social and economic life as a couple was divorced entirely

[11] TNA: C 6/249/35; C 7/581/73; C 6/283/87; C 6/275/120; Brooke. *Transcript of the Registers.* 243.

[12] TNA: C 10/216/74.

from Edward's business life. In contrast, Dorothy Thompson knew of her husband's whereabouts when the bank collapsed and even joined him in hiding when Richard moved to the Great Russell Street house. When Richard was in hiding at his brother-in-law Major Braman's house in Chichester, Dorothy wrote to her sister, Mrs. Braman, to thank her for their 'extraordinary favour'. By the date of this letter, 30 March 1678, Dorothy and Richard had moved to Great Russell Street and Dorothy apologised to her sister for being unable to 'recive' her in town as she is 'so unfortunate as to want a habitation to bid you welcome to'.[13]

Other than the housekeeper Mary Palmer, or Marvell, Dorothy was the only other female inhabitant of the Great Russell Street house and, according to the Chancery proceedings, she used this power and knowledge to help keep Mary Nelthorpe in the dark. In her answer to Chancery, Mary Nelthorpe claimed that when her husband fell sick in the Great Russell Street house, Richard and Dorothy took 'advantage of' the situation and 'did not acquaint' her of her 'husbands sicknesse till about twenty foure houres' before his death by letter on 17 September 1678. The following day Dorothy paid Mary a visit to inform her that Edward's 'disease had left him', but when Mary asked for her husband's whereabouts Dorothy refused on grounds that it 'might be dangerous', leaving Mary 'ignorant thereof'. Later that day, Mary received two letters: the first contained 'direccions' to her husband's 'aboade', and the second informed her that her 'husband was dead'. In this plan, Dorothy Thompson, rather than her husband, played the leading role in excluding Mary Nelthorpe and was complicit in all her husband's business decisions and economic actions. Dorothy's motivations are not recorded, but Mary Nelthorpe believed that the Thompsons made the decision to conceal her husband's whereabouts from her because they feared that 'Edward Nelthorpe would intrust' Mary rather than Richard with his 'personall estate', an estate that Mary believed amounted to £5000. On top of this, Mary claimed that the Thompsons were attempting to further 'extort money from' her and 'her three children'. It was for this reason, Mary argued, that she placed her trust in John Farrington to take out letters of administration for her husband's estate.[14]

---

[13] Madam D. Thompson to Madam Braman. *SPO*, SP 29/402 f. 223, 30 March 1678.
[14] TNA: C 10/216/74.

The Chancery proceedings therefore present Mary Nelthorpe as being deliberately excluded from the situation against her own and her husband's wishes. However, it is also possible that denial of knowledge and complicity in the affairs of the bank was a deliberate strategy on Mary Nelthorpe's part. The nature of equity law practised in Chancery meant that proceedings were based on arguments of morality and good conscience, so by stating that she had been poorly treated and was ignorant of a good deal of her husband's activities, Mary Nelthorpe might have been employing a strategy to protect herself in court. Emma Hawkes has argued it is unlikely that women 'were entirely without agency or ability' in the legal system, but that it was useful for women to be able to present themselves as such.[15] Dorothy was protected by her husband under the laws of coverture, which meant she could not be sued for her debts or economic insolvency, but as a widow Mary was not.[16] Mary's status as a widow could also explain why she did not administer her husband's estate but chose to elect John Farrington as administrator instead. Amy Erickson has argued that widows often renounced administration in such cases because they had their own assets and property which they needed to 'to protect from liability' of their 'husband's debts'.[17] In Mary Nelthorpe's case, she had lands settled on her during Edward's lifetime, and was aware that she had to maintain the estate for their children. The fragments of Nelthorpe's estate that remained in the bank were not worth the risk of losing her own separate estate. Therefore, it is possible that Mary employed a strategy that utilised her gender and status in court to protect herself and her children.

Similar to Mary Nelthorpe's Chancery statement, Farrington portrays Dorothy as a chief 'confederate' in the plotting and politicking that occurred after the collapse of the bank, particularly regarding the loss or concealment of the bank's books and papers. The location or fate of the books was an ongoing debate, with both Thompson and Farrington accusing one another of concealing or destroying them. Thompson claimed that Farrington had willingly surrendered himself to the Kings Bench in order to be under the rules and protection of the prison and

[15] Hawkes. "[S]he Will ... Protect and Defend Her Rights Boldly By Law and Reason...". 154.

[16] Muldrew. A Mutual Assent of Her Mind? 48.

[17] Erickson. *Women and Property.* 174.

216   M. WINTER

that his incarceration was a calculated move made to defraud Thompson, and the creditors, of the remaining money. Thompson further accused Farrington of burning the books, claiming that Farrington 'did publickly declare that he had burnt all his bookes of Accompt' and that Farrington had been observed by one of his servants who had attested it to be true. However, Thompson also believed that Farrington 'kept a true coppy or coppyes of them'.[18] Farrington's account places the blame not only on Richard Thompson, but on his wife Dorothy. Farrington accused Dorothy and Richard of conspiring to get him not only imprisoned but put 'to an Ignominious death for burning the said books & defrauding' the creditors of their money. They did this, Farrington argued, by spreading 'false informacion' and reporting so many 'untruths to some members of Parliament that they procured or occasioned a bill to be brought in the then house of commons in order to be passed into an Act of Parliament'. However, the creditors did not pursue this bill but 'stayed all prosecucion' against him.[19] There is no other record of this bill's existence and so the fate of the books and papers of the bank remains unknown. Farrington's statement situates Dorothy in the same socio-political networks as her husband and portrays her as equally capable of inflicting reputational damage.

As a result of their different marital status and actions taken, the fates of Dorothy Thompson and Mary Nelthorpe were starkly different. Both had agency and power but at different life stages. As Withington has argued, Dorothy Thompson's involvement in the affairs of the bank and politicking around its collapse demonstrates 'the kind of agency female citizens were capable of', particularly married women.[20] In contrast, Mary Nelthorpe's economic independence and social agency came in widowhood, when she was involved in multiple court cases, dealing both with cases of debt against her deceased husband and cases concerning her own management as *feme sole* of the businesses, real estate, and personal estate settled on her. This included leasing land in Beverley and taking over Edward's business ventures, most notably his mill at Caversham,

[18] TNA: C 6/283/87.

[19] TNA: C 7/581/73.

[20] Withington. *Politics of Commonwealth.* 229.

Oxford.[21] In April and May 1684, Mary was involved in a Chancery suit over the mill and letters patent granted to use Nelthorpe's 'engine or mill' invention to hull barley, which Nelthorpe had received a patent for in 1677 under the name of his associate Charles Milson.[22] The case reveals that letters patent had actually been granted to Mary Nelthorpe, John Green, John Hackshaw, and Charles Milson for the use of the mill for 14 years 'in trust and for the sole use and benefit of' Mary Nelthorpe. The patentees recruited Thomas Cartwright to hull the barley and finish it 'fitt for sale', signing articles of agreement in March 1682 that stated Cartwright was to have £12 for every ton of French barley and £32 for every ton of pearl barley, as well as 40 shillings per ton for his wages. Cartwright complained that Mary, Green, and Hackshaw were trying to defraud him of his rightful money, as he, being 'illiterate', could not do the accounts himself but claimed a bookkeeper, Thomas Speed, was appointed to do it for him. However, Mary denied this. According to her, Cartwright was to deliver the barley to Speed in London who would then sell it on Mary's behalf. Speed confirmed her account, stating that he was 'only accomptable to the said Mary Nelthorpe', not Cartwright. Mary also argued that Cartwright had not produced the agreed upon 30 tons of barley but was still paid for the same.[23] The case was most likely settled outside of court as no further proceedings can be found.

Mary Nelthorpe's control over her husband's real estate and business meant she was a wealthy widow with considerable agency. Mary was directly involved in managing the mill business, not just receiving the profits but entering into articles of agreement and defending her position in court. Clearly, the bankruptcy of her husband had not damaged her own credit beyond repair. Furthermore, she received a considerable legacy from her mother in 1686. Mary's mother, Elizabeth Sleigh, had remarried in 1658 but had organised a pre-marital settlement similar to that of Margaret Farrington, whereby Elizabeth retained control of her pre-marital estate 'during her life & at the time of her death', giving her new husband a lump sum only. Mary received a large legacy from her mother, consisting of £2000, all her 'greate jewells', and any remaining

[21] HHC: U DDBA/8/16. Copy of Lease for 11 years at £16 rent: Mary Nelthorpe of London, widow, to Roger Mason of Beverly. 1687.

[22] *Patents for Inventions*. 3.

[23] TNA: C 7/607/20. Cartwright v Nelthorpe. 19 April 1684; C 6/392/38. Cartwright v Speed. May 1684.

218   M. WINTER

estate after the other bequests.[24] It seems that Mary never remarried, as she was referred to in all documents throughout the 1680s as a widow. That she did not remarry is unsurprising, as Erickson has argued 'wealthy widows were the least likely of all widows to remarry' because they could afford not to.[25] Either Mary made no will or it has not survived.

In contrast, Dorothy Thompson's fate following the court cases is largely unknown. She wrote her will in 1708, by which time she too was a widow. Dorothy's will reveals that she lived in the parish of St Martin Ludgate in the house of her son, an unusual situation for a widow in this period who was normally left with her husband's house during her lifetime. However, she must have been relatively comfortable as she had a 'maid servant', Elizabeth Watson, to whom she left her 'weareing Apparrell' and £5. Other than this, Dorothy had a 'few household Goods and Implements of household standing', as well as 'the Rest and Residue of my Goods Chattells and personal Estate whatsoever', of which she unfortunately does not specify.[26] It appears that unlike Mary Nelthorpe, Dorothy Thompson was reliant on her children for support later in life and did not have independence or wealth in widowhood. Therefore, whilst Dorothy appears to have had power and agency during the bankruptcy and in the Great Russell Street house, she did not have the same power and agency later in life that Mary Nelthorpe did. The death of Edward Nelthorpe during the collapse of the bank may have been the crucial difference between the fates of Mary and Dorothy. After the collapse, Mary was forced to forge her own separate identity with the estate that Edward had transferred to her during his lifetime, and her decision to give Farrington the letters of administration to Edward's remaining estate, which was tied up in the bank, further demonstrates her efforts to remove herself from the negative credit networks that surrounded Thompson and Company and its collapse. Mary Nelthorpe therefore demonstrates that a spouse's loss of credit did not necessarily ruin both of their reputations or their potential for future business success.

Aside from the partners' wives, there is another 'wife' that needs consideration in this case whose precise identity is unclear. This is the

[24] TNA: C 5/94/96. Tryon v Nelthorpe. 15 July 1688; PROB 11/384/22. Will of Elizabeth Ireton, Wife. 5 July 1686.

[25] Erickson. *Women and Property*. 196.

[26] TNA: PROB 11/503/389. Will of Dorothy Thompson, Widow of Saint Martin Ludgate, City of London. 23 October 1708; Erickson. *Women and Property*. 187.

much-disputed Mary Marvell. In the Chancery court in 1681, Mary claimed 'she was lawfully married' to Andrew Marvell on 13 May 1667 'at the parish church of [blank] in the Little Minories London As by the Register book of the said church may appeare'. The church in Little Minories was the church of the Holy Trinity, the church register book of which, as Tupper pointed out, is unfortunately missing for the years 1662 to 1683. Therefore, the marriage cannot be proved. Further to this missing register, Mary claims that whilst she and Marvell lived together as man and wife 'in private', in public Marvell had asked her to 'conceal the said marriage and keep it as private as they could' and told Mary to go by her former name of 'Mary Palmer widdow'. The privacy surrounding the marriage came into great use later on when Mary took the lease of the Great Russell Street house in 'her owne name' to conceal the bankrupt Nelthorpe's whereabouts. However, the privacy of the marriage also cast doubts on Mary's claims to Marvell's estate after his death in August 1678. At this point, Mary took out letters of administration for Marvell's estate as his wife and became embroiled in the Chancery case over the £500 bond in Marvell's name. In response to Mary's claim in Chancery, Farrington stated that neither he nor Nelthorpe did 'know or believe that she was ever married to the said Andrew Marvell' and that during his lifetime Marvell did not at any time 'own or confese that he was married to the said Mary' and never lived with her 'as man & wife'. He claimed that Mary was 'the widow of a Tennis Court Keeper in or near the Citty of Westminster who died in a mean condicon' and that it was unlikely that Marvell would 'undervalue himselfe to intermarey with so mean a person as shee'. Instead, he argued Mary was Marvell's housekeeper who pretended to be his wife 'in hopes to gett money thereby from his friends & acquaintances'.[27]

Mary's status was debated in Chancery, but no conclusive answer was reached. If she was Mary Marvell, then her role was as Marvell's wife and a householder in the Great Russell Street residence who had a rightful claim to Marvell's remaining estate—if, that is, he had any. However, if she was

---

[27] Tupper. Mary Palmer. 367–392; Withington. *Politics of Commonwealth*. 224–227; Smith. *Andrew Marvell*. 197–198, 337–338; Kavanagh. Andrew Marvell "in Want of Money". 206, 208; Annabelle Patterson. 1990. Miscellaneous Marvell. In *The Political Identity of Andrew Marvell*, eds Conal Condren and A. D. Cousins, 189–208. Aldershot: Scolar Press. 191–192, 196–198; TNA: C 6/242/13; C 8/252/9.

220   M. WINTER

Mary Palmer her role changes to a widow who was employed as a servant or housekeeper by Marvell, Nelthorpe, and the Thompsons and either decided or was persuaded to pretend to be Marvell's wife. Mary Marvell or Palmer's situation was therefore entirely different to that of Dorothy Thompson or Mary Nelthorpe, as it was her marital status, and the social credit that accompanied it, which was under scrutiny in Chancery. Marvell left no will and, as proof of the marriage never appeared in court, Mary was entitled to nothing. She therefore had neither the economic and legal benefits of marriage nor the security it could bring in widowhood and, due to lack of evidence, had no recourse to the law.

III

The fate of the partners' and their wives also had a direct impact on their children, altering the composition and location of their households and the collective wealth of each family. The actions of the partners' wives had great significance for the wider household and further demonstrate that the breakdown of the householder's credit did not necessarily destroy the credit of the next generation.

At the time of Edward's death, his three children were still minors, and Mary requested 'maintenance' money for her children's 'educacion & placing out'.[28] The children's early lives, education, and careers are unknown. The only known record of Edward and Mary's children is from their eldest son Edward's will and an investigation into the correct title of the Nelthorpe family lands in Yorkshire in 1765.[29] These documents show that, despite their father's bankruptcy, their mother's successful estate management meant that the children inherited the lands and property in Yorkshire that Edward had inherited from his father. In 1765 Mr. Launders carried out an examination of the title to a vast estate in Yorkshire, which included the manor of Walkington, as well as other estates in Walkington, Redness, Whitefield, and Hatfield. He found that the estate had been transmitted through the Nelthorpe family, from Edward Nelthorpe's father to Edward and Mary, and after their

[28] TNA: C 10/216/74.

[29] TNA: E 134/7Geo3/East1. Interrogatories, Depositions taken at Beverley 13 April 7 Geo, 1767. Henry Liddell, Esq., Lenyns Boldero, Esq., v. Randle Hancock, Clerk. 25 October 1766–24 October 1767.

9 AFTERMATH **221**

deaths to their children via primogeniture, with the eldest son Edward receiving the estate either upon his majority or upon his mother's death.[30] However, Edward and his wife had no children. After Edward's death, the estate passed to his sister Mary Liddell, widow of Thomas Liddell, and then to their son Henry.[31] Edward and Mary's younger son, James Nelthorpe, appears not to have received any portion of the land, which could explain why in 1686 his grandmother, Elizabeth, left him a legacy of £500 but nothing for his elder brother and sister.[32] Their daughter Mary would most likely have received her own portion when she married. Mary Nelthorpe therefore managed to preserve an estate for her children that set them up well in later life.

Dorothy and Richard's children are harder to trace and did not inherit such a significant estate as that of the Nelthorpe children. When the bank collapsed Dorothy and Richard's surviving children, Edward and Samuel, were still young and must have moved with their parents to the Great Russell Street House. Edward's later career is untraceable, but his brother Samuel went on to become a 'mercer at Ongell on Ludgate Hill' and lived in the parish of St Martin Ludgate, as evident in his mother's will and his own will of 1741. The Thompson household in Woolchurch Market, however, may also have included Richard's children from his previous marriage, Anne and Robert, who were significantly older and appear to have already been provided for. Robert Thompson had already been engaged in an apprenticeship with his distant relation William Popple in Bordeaux. The apprenticeship is evident from a letter sent by Marvell to Popple which was addressed to 'Mr Robert Thomson' with the instruction that he pass it on to his 'Master'. Once Robert finished this apprenticeship, Richard gave his son 500 guineas to trade 'in the way of merchandize'. Whether Robert did embark on trade as a merchant is unknown, but both he and Anne were still alive in 1708 when

---

[30] HHC: U DDBA/8/49. Mr. Launder's remarks on the title to the Yorkshire Estate. 1765.

[31] TNA: PROB 11/574/150. Will of Edward Nelthorpe. 16 May 1720; PROB 11/564/136. Will of Thomas Liddell of Saint Andrew Holborn, Middlesex. 5 June 1718.

[32] TNA: PROB 11/384/22. Will of Elizabeth Ireton.

222 M. WINTER

Dorothy wrote her will as she left £10 a piece to her stepchildren.[33] The remainder of Dorothy's estate went to her sons, but as she owned no property herself this likely did not add up to a significant amount.

John Farrington's children are identifiable from his wife's will and further wills survive for their eldest son, John, and their daughter, Rebecca Philpott. John Farrington junior was 'of the Inner Temple London' and so must have received a good education in the 1670s prior to the bankruptcy of his father. In his 1715 will, John left the land he owned in 'the Parish of Newington Butts in the County of Surry', any land he might inherit from his sister Anne Thompson in 'Ship Yard', Southwark, and his land in Lincoln, to his wife Anne for her lifetime and then to his nephew John Philpott. It is unclear when and by whom this property was acquired, although it could have been settled on John Farrington junior whilst his father was still alive. If John's nephew died, then the estate was to be split between his two sisters, Anne Thompson and Rebecca Philpott.[34] Whether John junior inherited this land and property or acquired it through his own endeavours is unknown, but it does suggest that some wealth remained in the family after the bankruptcy of their father. Rebecca Philpott's will reveals that her son and the heir to her brother's estate died before her and so the sisters inherited John's land and property. Rebecca left her portion of the estate to her friend Sarah Lamb, thus ending the Farrington family ownership.[35]

In addition to children, the households of the four partners also included servants and apprentices. Of the apprentices, it can be assumed that their bonds were either transferred to a new master or ended entirely. Of the servants, it appears that only Thomas Speed retained his position with the Nelthorpe family under the management and employ of Mary Nelthorpe. Unlike the other bank employees, Gersham Proud and Edmond Portmans, who lost their positions when the bank collapsed, Speed was part of the household that managed to maintain some credit

---

[33] TNA: PROB 11/715/343. Will of Samuel Thompson, formerly Mercer of Saint Martin Ludgate, City of London. 26 January 1741; *The Poems and Letters of Andrew Marvell*, vol. 2. 348; TNA: C 7/581/73; PROB 11/503/389, Will of Dorothy Thompson.

[34] TNA: PROB 11/544/191. Will of John Farrington, Gentleman, Widower of the Inner Temple, Middlesex. 3 February 1715.

[35] TNA: PROB 11/685/128. Will of Rebecca Philpott, Widow of Saint Stephen Coleman Street London, City of London. 20 September 1737.

9 AFTERMATH 223

despite the ruin of the male householder. This demonstrates a separation between institutional or business credit and that of household credit, which is opposed to the model of credit outlined by Muldrew who argues that credit in the seventeenth century was centred around the household and that household and business accounts were 'mixed together'. The partners of Thompson and Company kept separate books for the bank and for their households, as evident from the witness depositions of their employees.[36] Therefore, upon their collapse, each household had an opportunity to regain or maintain their separate credit.

IV

Also implicated in Thompson and Company's collapse was the wider mercantile kinship network, comprised of the Thompson and Popple families. Sir Henry and Edward Thompson appear not to have suffered commercially or politically after the collapse of the bank and their main loss was personal: grief over the deaths of their friend Andrew Marvell and cousin Edward Nelthorpe. Indeed, Sir Henry was re-elected as an MP for York in 1679 and Edward Thompson's political career took off in the 1680s, serving as an alderman, Lord Mayor, and an MP for York. In addition to this, the Thompson brothers continued their involvement in opposition politics, becoming confirmed Whigs and demonstrating the banking partners' connections to later partisan conflicts. Sir Henry Thompson maintained connections with Sir Thomas Player and the London opposition group into the 1680s, connections which may have been first made through his banking cousins. In November 1682 it was reported that Sir Henry received letters and exclusionist propaganda works from Player, written in this instance by the playwright Elkanah Settle, who intended them to be acted out as 'playes ... in the Citty of Yorke'. Henry was also active in all Exclusion parliaments and was marked out by Shaftesbury as one of his 'worthy' parliamentary allies in 1679. Edward Thompson was also heavily involved in partisan conflicts in York and later national government. In 1683 Edward came into conflict with the Tory gentry faction in York over control of the civic militia and was brought in front of the King's council, in 1685 he was one of the five

---

[36] Muldrew. *Economy of Obligation*. 158; C 24/1069. 'Deposition of Gersham Proud' and 'Deposition of Edmond Portmans'.

224   M. WINTER

Whig aldermen purged from their positions and did not regain his position until 1688, and in 1685 he was taken into custody over his suspected role in the Monmouth Rebellion.[37] Despite his perceived involvement in plots and conspiracies Edward Thompson served as MP for York from 1689 until his death in 1701. Therefore, in the case of the Thompson brothers their earlier nonconformist politics did map onto their later Whiggism and suggest that had Thompson and Nelthorpe survived the collapse of the bank then they too would have taken up Whig politics.

Similarly, William Popple also experienced the personal loss of his uncle and cousin. However, unlike the York Thompson brothers, he and his business partner Robert Stewart were directly drawn into the collapse of the bank, accused in Chancery of withholding money from the partners that could have been used to pay off their petitioning creditors. Neither Popple nor Stewart ever appear to have given an answer to either Richard Thompson or John Farrington's bill of complaint, suggesting the claims made were either false or intended as leverage to encourage Popple and Stewart to pay or settle outside of court. Robbins has argued that whilst there is some evidence of Popple's indebtedness at the same time as Thompson and Company's insolvency, by 1684, the date of the Chancery proceedings against Popple and Stewart, Popple was described elsewhere as wealthy. Clearly, the failure of Thompson and Company did not compromise Popple's credit or business success. Indeed, Popple's business only suffered when he was forced to leave France in 1688, following the Revocation of the Edict of Nantes. However, he went on to have a successful career in English government as secretary to the Board of Trade from 1696 to 1707. In his religious and political outlook, Popple also links the banking partners to later partisan, particularly Whig, politics. Popple was a close friend of John Locke, evident in the frequent correspondence between Popple, his wife Mary, and Locke in the 1690s and early 1700s. Popple translated Locke's *Letter on Toleration* out of Latin, was secretary to him at the Board of Trade and at the Dry Club, which 'was founded by Locke to discuss religious liberty'. Popple also wrote

---

[37] Cruickshanks. Thompson, Sir Henry. *HoP*; Cruickshanks. Thompson, Edward. *HoP*; The deposition of Joshua Bowes of the parish of St Andrew's Holborn. *SPO*, SP 29/421/1 f. 147, 11 November 1682; Abigail Williams. 2008. Settle, Elkanah (1648–1724). *ODNB*, https://doi-org.sheffield.idm.oclc.org/10.1093/ref:odnb/25128. Accessed 4 June 2020; Phil Withington. 2008. Citizens, Soldiers and Urban Culture in Restoration England. *The English Historical Review* 123: 596–597, 607–608; Cruickshanks Thompson, Edward. *HoP*.

9 AFTERMATH   225

his own tract on religious toleration, *A Rational Catechism* published in 1687, and his manuscript commonplace book is further testimony to his political and religious views. The friendship between Popple and Locke also links him to the first earl of Shaftesbury, who was a close associate of Locke, and Popple was himself a close friend of the third earl.[38] Popple therefore provides another link between earlier nonconformist politics and later Whiggism, particularly linking the Restoration opposition politics of his banking cousins, his uncle Marvell, and his friend John Locke.

V

The collapse of Thompson and Company caused widespread disruption throughout their extensive credit and social networks. The use of a micro-historical approach, which does not just examine the bank as a business but also as a social and political entity, allows for an examination of the wider impact of the collapse of Thompson and Company. In doing so it becomes evident that the collapse of the bank disrupted and altered the composition of the partners' households and ended their business careers. However, as evident from family members' later careers and wealth, the collapse of Thompson and Company and ruin of its four partners did not completely destroy the household credit or the individual credit of each member of their respective kinship networks. Instead, it suggests that the household credit was somewhat separate from the institutional credit of the bank, which may have lessened the impact on the families of Thompson and Company's four partners. Additionally, there were ways and means through which household members, particularly wives, could further separate themselves from their spouse's financial activities and use the law in ways that would protect themselves and their children.

---

[38] TNA: C 6/526/178; Robins. Absolute Liberty. 199, 202, 192, 207–210, 208; E. S. de Beer. *The Correspondence of John Locke.* Oxford: Clarendon Press. vol. 4. 1978. Letters 1567, 1590, 1608, 1630, 1698; vol. 5. 1979. Letters 1704, 1906, 1986, 2002, 2036, 2041; vol. 6. 1980. Letters 2503, 2513, 2526, 2592, 2593, 2651; vol. 7. 1981. Letters 2708, 2714, 2740, 2821, 2868, 2877, 2967, 2971, 2985, 2999, 3011, 3085, 3088A, 3173, 3179; Seccombe. Popple, William (1638–1708). *ODNB*; William Popple. 1687. *A Rational Catechism, or, An Instructive Conference Between a Father and a Son.* London; BL: Add MS 8888. Tamberlane the Beneficient, a Tragedy; The Cid translated from Corneille; with several minor poems; all probably by Will. Popple sen. 1681–1701; J. R. Milton. 2008. Locke, John (1632–1704). *ODNB*, https://doi-org.sheffield.idm.oclc.org/10.1093/ref:odnb/16885. Accessed 4 June 2020; Robert Voitle. 1984. *The Third Earl of Shaftesbury, 1671–1713.* London: Louisiana State University Press. 67–68, 278.

226   M. WINTER

Although, as the case of Mary Palmer or Marvell shows, this was not an avenue that was open to all women.

Aside from family, other potential victims of the collapse of the bank were its debtors. In their pamphlet, the bank partners stated that in trying to 'comply' with their obligations to their creditors they were forced to call in loans made to debtors. As a result, 'Many of our Debtors broke, while we brought them under the same circumstances which obliged us to call upon them'. The danger this could place debtors in is evident from Edward Nelthorpe's cover up of Marvell's indebtedness to the bank. In his 1682 deposition in the £500 bond case, bank employee Gersham Proud recalled that when the bank collapsed Marvell was indebted by around £150. However, this was unknown to the creditors because Nelthorpe had asked for the debt to 'bee taken from the said Mr Marvell's account' and instead 'placed' and made out to be 'Mr Nelthorpe's debt' so that Marvell 'might not receive any trouble' from the commission of bankruptcy. Nelthorpe clearly did not want Marvell to be hassled by the commission for the money or for Marvell's reputation and credit to be sullied by the knowledge of his indebtedness. For many debtors though, the collapse of the bank may have offered relief as they could avoid repaying their debt. The partners' pamphlet suggests that many debtors did take full advantage of the situation, as they accused unnamed individuals of delaying payments and attempting to 'defraud' them.[39]

As previous chapters have shown, those most affected by the collapse of Thompson and Company were its creditors. However, as only limited evidence survives from a few of the wealthier creditors, the full extent of the damage is unknown. Fauconberg and Turner's surviving accounts show significant losses, but these are offset by their other successful investments and activities. The Corporation of Trinity House do show evidence of how Thompson and Company's collapse did impact upon wider credit networks. Trinity House had put £500 in the bank in the hope of making a profit from the interest accrued. However, the £500 was money originally entrusted to the corporation by 'Mr Merrick' who requested £30 a year interest on it from Trinity House. As the money was 'in Tompsone & Nelthorpes hands' there was nothing Trinity House could do, and they agreed that most of the £500 was 'likely to be lost'. The minutes

---

[39] *Case of Richard Thompson and Company.* 4, 15; TNA: C 24/1069. Interrogatory of Gersham Proud, 4 July 1682.

9 AFTERMATH 227

of Trinity House record the 'hardshipp put upon the Corporation' by Merrick's request for a return on his money and, as a result, 'Agreed to put out 600^{Li} into the East India Stock at 5 per Cent to pay Merricks Interest'.[40] The collapse of Thompson and Company did not cause the collapse of Trinity House, but it did compromise their credit networks and force them to take compensatory action. Thompson and Company's collapse therefore signalled the removal of yet another credit facilitator from seventeenth-century London's already struggling money market.

[40] LMA: CLC/526/MS30004/004. 223; LMA: CLC/526/MS30004/005. 49, 56.

CHAPTER 10

Conclusion

This book has undertaken a socio-economic microhistory of the bank of Thompson and Company, uncovering the origins, operation, and collapse of the bank, as well as the social, political, and commercial lives of the four founding partners. It is the first study that has taken Thompson and Company as its central focus, revealing much more about this institution and its four partners than was previously known or thought possible to discover with the available source material. The use of microhistorical methods has uncovered a much larger source base both within Chancery proceedings and in other institutional and personal records. One of the primary outcomes of this study is therefore methodological, demonstrating the utility of Chancery proceedings for historical reconstruction and particularly for uncovering lost businesses and business practices on a micro scale. Although Chancery proceedings were undertaken with an agenda and were often in pursuit of ulterior motives, by cross-referencing the legal proceedings with other sources it is possible to reconstruct the series of events and unearth significant amounts of detail. Indeed, the utility of Chancery records derives from the narrative nature of the proceedings, which focus as much on the context of a dispute as the dispute itself. When the two surviving partners, Thompson and Farrington, were trying to resolve their bankruptcy and draw in their debts in Chancery it was deemed necessary for them to explain the origin

© The Author(s), under exclusive license to Springer Nature Switzerland AG 2022
M. Winter, *Banking, Projecting and Politicking in Early Modern England*, Palgrave Studies in Economic History, https://doi.org/10.1007/978-3-030-90570-5_10

229

and operation of their venture in order to establish, in good equity and conscience, to whom the money or goods rightfully belonged. The institution was described by both Farrington and Thompson in enough detail to be able to analyse their practices and situate the institution within the commercial and financial culture of Restoration England without the use of their account books, ledgers, or papers. As such, it is a direct contradiction of Grassby's argument that 'original' books and papers are 'essential' for analysing the 'success and failure of private enterprise'.[1] In addition to uncovering the institution itself, and as the proceedings progressed, more and more people within the partners' social, commercial, and credit networks were drawn into the debates, providing further information as to the partners' identities, additional business schemes, and circles of influence that were previously unknown. Therefore, the reconstruction of Thompson and Company has successfully achieved one of the 'unifying principle[s] of all microhistorical research' in proving that 'microscopic observation will reveal factors previously unobserved'.[2]

The microhistorical case of Thompson and Company has revealed some significant information about the bank and its four partners. Chapters 2–4 examined the operation of the bank itself and identified Thompson and Company as a financial and commercial hybrid, acting as both an early deposit bank and mercantile partnership. The mixed identity of Thompson and Company further explains why the institution is absent from historiographies of banking in England and suggests that it can be better situated in the history of 'projecting', as a project that facilitated the financing of other projects as well as facilitating the circulation of credit in London and beyond. During its active years this project was highly successful, attracting over 200 customers who collectively deposited over £200,000 in the bank. Chapters 5 and 6 revealed more about the kinship networks that underpinned Thompson and Company and the credit networks it facilitated. Chapter 5 argued that uncovering the partners' identities and family relationships is important in order to understand how they came to set up such an experimental and risky venture. The wider kinship networks provided early career support in the form of skills acquisition and capital, as well as later support through the provision of commercial contacts and a network of like-minded political and religious

---

[1] Grassby. *Business Community*. 12.

[2] Levi. On Microhistory. 101.

10 CONCLUSION   231

associates. This is particularly true of the Thompson and Nelthorpe families who represent a commercial dynasty. Each branch of the family was involved in trade and politics in their respective locations, and used one another as sources of capital, experience, and support. Therefore, as well as being a partnership and facilitating various 'projects', Thompson and Company were also part of a wider network of mercantile businesses and political alliance. Chapter 6 further traced the creditors of Thompson and Company and used the limited surviving source material to reconstruct the networks of association and reputation through which the partners attracted customers. Knowledge of the creditors' identities led to uncovering some direct references to individuals' interaction with the bank and with other financial institutions, revealing the language used to describe financial transactions. Interestingly, this did not include the terms 'invest' and 'deposit' but revolved around an embodied language of 'hands' and 'putting' that reflects the physical exchange of specie and points to the interpersonal nature of credit relations in early modern England. Whilst only focussed on the surviving evidence from Thompson and Company's creditors, the language uncovered has significant implications for the ways in which individuals conceptualised money and their financial transactions. Further examination of this was not within the bounds of this book but is worthy of further study.

The final three chapters explored the economic, political, and social implications of the collapse of Thompson and Company. Despite the collapse of the bank being the most commented on aspect of Thompson and Company's history in previous scholarship, the wider impact of it has not previously been investigated. Chapter 7 demonstrated the significance of the collapse of Thompson and Company, its impact on bankruptcy legislation, and the extent to which it was publicly discussed and scandalised. Chapter 8 demonstrated how the networks discussed in Chapters 5 and 6 could not only have a positive impact on business success but could play an important negative role in business collapse. Indeed, networks played a significant part in the collapse of Thompson and Company in 1678, as enemies of the bank partners targeted not only them but also their friends and associates in a politically motivated attack. The political roles of partners Thompson and Nelthorpe have been recognised in previous scholarship but were not directly linked to the collapse of the bank. The collapse of Thompson and Company demonstrates the divisiveness of 'Court' and 'Country' opposition groups in 1670s London and gives greater significance to the role of Thompson and Nelthorpe

232   M. WINTER

within these circles. Chapter 9 returned to the family networks outlined in Chapter 5 and examined the impact of Thompson and Company's collapse on their families and associates. It argued that, in the case of Thompson and Company, there was a separation between household and institutional credit that meant not every household member lost their credit along with that of the male householder. This was primarily down to the actions of the partners' wives. Each wife interacted differently with both the business and the legal system, which was in part due to uncontrollable changes in their marital status but was also due to how they used their agency to manipulate their own situation. Their different strategies led to varying levels of success later in life and demonstrates that whilst women were legally restricted, there were many ways in which they could circumvent the law. Those who suffered most from the collapse were the creditors, whose efforts to regain their money led only to a small pay out.

The case of Thompson and Company highlights the intimate relationship between politics, commerce, and finance, demonstrating that whilst roles within each of those fields had the power to bolster reputation and success, they also increased the risk inherent within those roles. This book has, therefore, successfully uncovered a significant amount of detail about Thompson and Company that was previously unknown. However, as a traditional microhistory, the case of Thompson and Company has much broader, macro, ramifications for Restoration society, and its commercial, financial, and political culture.

In terms of commerce and finance, the case demonstrates the importance of understanding an institution, its origins, operation, and the implications of its success or failure. Historians and economists have stressed the importance of studying institutions due to their role in fuelling economic growth.[3] However, I argue that studying institutions is also important when examining economic instability and stagnation. Although Thompson and Company failed, the institution is still important for our understanding of individual and group responses to the changing economic and commercial fields and for understanding how new practices developed. In the basic narrative of financial development constructed by historians, the 1670s and 1680s feature very little. The narrative begins with the rise of goldsmith-bankers in the early-to-mid

---

[3] Ogilvie. *Institutions and European Trade*. 415; Carruthers. Rules, Institutions, and North's Institutionalism. 40; North and Weingast. Constitutions and Commitment. 803; Slack. *Invention of Improvement*. 257.

seventeenth century, their demise following the 1672 Stop on the Exchequer, and then the development of the market in stocks and shares and the establishment of the Bank of England in the 1690s, which is seen as the height of England's 'Financial Revolution'.[4] The 1670s and 1680s did not witness any significant economic growth or any particular triumphs in the public financing of the state. However, in those two decades there were a number of proposals for new financial institutions, such as offices of credit and changes to the assignability of credit instruments, as well as a 'a boom of pamphlets on economic improvement' and a rise in 'projecting' activities in England designed to combat 'distrust and political uncertainty'.[5] In this regard, Thompson and Company are important as a 'company' and 'project' established as a direct response to the financial and commercial environment of the 1670s—the 1672 Stop on the Exchequer, Anglo-Dutch wars, and coin shortage—and demonstrate the importance of experimentation and entrepreneurship at a time when traditional, or established, financial institutions and customs had broken down. Thompson and Company provides evidence of another type of institution to be included in the traditional narrative of financial development in England. Therefore, the case of Thompson and Company also has important implications for the chronology and nature of England's 'Financial Revolution'.

The 'Financial Revolution' is a contested area of historiographical debate, but most historians agree that it reached its height in the 1690s and early 1700s with a rapid increase in the type and number of financial outlets and the establishment of a system of long-term public debt.[6] Historians frequently refer to the development of England's 'Financial Revolution' in terms of governmental change and its impact upon the rights and abilities of financial institutions and individuals. Most prominent in this regard is the theory of North and Weingast, who argue that financial development in England was only possible after the constitutional change that followed in the wake of the 1688 Glorious

---

[4] Roseveare. *The Financial Revolution*; Richards. *Early History of Banking*; Muldrew. *Economy of Obligation*. 115–116.

[5] Wennerlind. *Casualties of Credit*. 97–98; Yamamoto. *Taming Capitalism*. 174, 183, 271.

[6] Dickson. *Financial Revolution*; Roseveare. *The Financial Revolution*; North and Weingast. Constitutions and Commitments. 803–832; Murphy. *The Origins of English Financial Markets*. 1–2, 15.

Revolution, in which 'the new institutions [of parliament and the crown] produced a marked increase in the security of private rights'.[7] Historians such as Murphy and C. D. Chandaman, amongst others disagree. They argue that the 'groundwork' for financial development had already been laid in the decades prior to 1688, and Murphy particularly emphasises that such 'groundwork' was not only implemented 'from above' but was 'demanded from below' by those who 'invested'.[8] However, these debates focus only on developments in public, not private, finance. The case of Thompson and Company, I argue, demonstrates the importance of private finance and individual entrepreneurship in the development of English finance in this period. The entrepreneurial venture of Thompson and Company was designed to facilitate private credit, offering interest-bearing deposits to a wide range of customers, whilst also creating profit-making opportunities for its partners. The demand, 'from below', for such a credit facilitator is evident from the number of creditors the bank attracted and the amount of money it dealt with. Clearly individuals were looking for opportunities and were willing to interact with 'projects' and experiments, which was an important development for the later expansion of financial outlets and opportunities. The importance of entrepreneurship 'for the outburst of experiment in the 1690s' has been recognised by Horsefield, and others, but only for 'enthusiastic projectors', most of whom never 'succeeded in putting their schemes' for institutions that facilitated public finance 'into practice'. Although the bank of Thompson and Company was not concerned with public finance, it represents a development in the provision of credit in England and can be seen as a part of 'two generations of propaganda' that 'helped to smooth the way for the outburst of experiment in the 1690s'.[9]

Another important way in which Thompson and Company contributed to financial development is through their institutional identity, showing how this developed in a society that had previously centred around interpersonal credit. Muldrew has argued that interpersonal credit in the

---

[7] North and Weingast. Constitutions and Commitments. 803–804; Wennerlind. *Casualties of Credit*. 108–109; Jongchul Kim. 2013. How Politics Shaped Modern Banking in Early Modern England: Rethinking the Nature of Representative Democracy, Public Debt, and Modern Banking. *Max-Planck-Institut für Gesellschaftsforschung. Discussion Papers*. 13.

[8] Murphy. Demanding "Credible Commitment". 180; Chandaman. *English Public Revenue*. 1; Desan. *Making Money*. 289.

[9] Horsefield. *British Monetary Experiments*. 102.

seventeenth century centred around the 'household' rather than the 'the individual or firm', with every member of the household responsible for upholding the reputation of the whole in order to build and maintain credit networks. According to Muldrew, the 'money market was transformed' in the 1690s with the growth of an 'institutional bank'—the Bank of England—and 'joint stock companies', which were a significant break from the 'individual' private banking system that collapsed in 1672 and the 'complex strings of interpersonal household credit'.[10] What is not explained here is how that leap from interpersonal to institutional and corporate was made. Stern has described 'Commercial corporations' as a 'critical step between household and informal regulation, on the one hand, and the "highly abstract and bureaucratized" forms of economic regulation embodied in the community of the nation-state on the other'.[11] Although Stern is discussing chartered companies, a similar blurring of the lines between informal and formal, interpersonal and institutional, household and company, is evident in the ways in which Thompson and Company were portrayed and described. Indeed, the bank appears to have been operating in a transition period from the interpersonal, household trust between individuals based on their knowledge of one another's reputations, towards institutional trust, whereby an established institution would take on a corporate identity beyond that of its founding partners.

In the case of Thompson and Company, this is true for their identity both as a bank and a commercial mercantile partnership. Gauci has argued that the increasing number of mercantile partnerships from the late seventeenth century onwards 'can be regarded as a major step towards a more corporate City, one in which the reputation of the individual still counted, but which saw a greater impersonality in the organization of overseas trade'.[12] Thompson and Company are a perfect example of this. They were both personal and corporate in the way they portrayed their own identity, using the surname of one partner but also the word 'company', which signified corporate association, and throughout their pamphlet and the Chancery proceedings they stressed that they had joined together in

---

[10] Muldrew. *Economy of Obligation*. 6, 115, 116, 123, 156, 158.

[11] Stern. *Companies*. 190.

[12] Gauci. *Emporium of the World*. 84.

236   M. WINTER

a 'society', 'partnership', and a 'company'.[13] Their creditors also blurred the lines between individual and institution, evident in the language they used to describe their financial transactions with Thompson and Company. When describing financial interaction with the bank, creditors used embodied language that signified a physical handing over or putting of money with the partners or into the company. Whilst this in some senses reflects the interpersonal nature of banking evident in the earlier seventeenth century, this language was often used alongside the concept of *company* or to refer to the *bankers* or *bank* as a group or institution, which points more to a corporate identity. Thompson and Company do not therefore belong to the historiography of earlier seventeenth-century interpersonal credit and individually based private banking, but also do not entirely fit with the corporate institutions that came to prominence in the 1690s. Combining the old with the new, Thompson and Company can be seen as a step towards the more corporate, national, institutions that characterise the 'Financial Revolution' in England.

In addition, the evidence of Thompson and Company's creditors questions the scope of the 'Financial Revolution' in terms of who was interacting with financial markets prior to the 1690s. Historians such as Wennerlind, Roseveare, and Temin and Voth, have argued that goldsmith-banks, and pre-1690s institutions more generally, only interacted with the 'moneyed community' or the 'landed gentry, merchants, and the government'.[14] Additionally, studies of gendered financial practices have suggested that women were also largely left out of financial markets prior to the 1690s.[15] However, the socio-economic composition of Thompson and Company's creditors demonstrates that the bank attracted a much broader range of clientele than other financial institutions, including amongst them the poorer sort as well as women and tradesmen. Historians studying only goldsmith-banks or state finance ventures have not come across the interaction of these sorts of people in the financial markets of seventeenth-century England, and therefore have seen it as a development that occurred only in the 1690s when more financial outlets, which accepted lower investments, appeared. Thompson and Company

---

[13] Withington. *Society.* 104, 105, 116; *Case of Richard Thompson and Company.* 3, 6, 12, 27; C 7/581/73; C 6/283/87; C 6/526/200; C 10/212/10.

[14] Roseveare. *The Financial Revolution.* 19; Wennerlind. *Casualties of Credit.* 94; Temin and Voth. Banking as an emerging technology. 150.

[15] Froide. *Silent Partners.* 11.

did also deal with merchants and some of the landed gentry, but large numbers of their clientele were tradesmen, women, and those of lesser means or at least not of extensive wealth. Their appeal to these sorts of people probably derived from their commercial identities as merchants and traders, as well as their civic, middling sort identities as citizens and officeholders, and the networks these engendered. Thompson and Company are just one example of such an institution and one that was previously neglected in the historiography of English finance. The reconstruction of the bank therefore brings into question how many more alternative, experimental institutions have been lost from the historical record. If, like the bank, other failed private institutions destroyed their books and papers then there could be a much broader story to tell of financial development in later seventeenth-century England.

Aside from the development of finance and commerce, the case of Thompson and Company also has important implications for financial collapse and prompts a rethinking of the role of reputation in the collapse of credit networks and institutions. Muldrew argues that 'access to goods, wealth and to the social status and power conferred by wealth – such as office holding or patronage – was dependent on access to the continual circulation of credit', and credit circulated successfully if everyone in the credit network upheld their 'financial obligations'.[16] However, the case of Thompson and Company suggests that sometimes the breakdown of credit was more complicated than simply failing financially. Accounts from both the partners and their creditors suggest that Thompson and Company were meeting their financial obligations—they survived two runs on the bank, paid out large sums of money, and offered numerous compositions to creditors—yet the bank still collapsed. Instead, it was manipulation of the partners' conferred 'social status and power' that was detrimental to their wealth and credibility, and ultimately caused their downfall. As Chapter 4 demonstrated, this was largely a result of the political roles and activism of Thompson and Nelthorpe and the enemies they had attracted in the Corporation of London. Therefore, a reverse of Muldrew's model is evident here. As the partners' social reputations failed, their finances came under scrutiny and, as a result of intense petitioning by their creditors, they became unable to meet their financial obligations.

[16] Muldrew. *Economy of Obligation.* 151, 153.

238   M. WINTER

Whilst the collapse of Thompson and Company did have a knock-on effect throughout their families and wider commercial and kinship networks, it did not cause a total loss of their credit. The wider Thompson family remained successful in both commerce and politics, as did their mercantile cousin William Popple. Even the bank's creditors, although no doubt out of pocket and some worse off than others, did receive a small percentage—3s per pound or 15 percent—of their original deposit. The most interesting implications of the collapse though are on the partners' wives and immediate families or households. The differing experience of the wives and families of Thompson and Company's partners after their bankruptcy suggests that household credit did not necessarily collapse along with that of one individual member's credit as Muldrew argues.[17] One explanation for this can be derived from the institutional identity and credit of the bank, which made the joint credit of the four partners distinct from that of their households, creating a buffer between them.

However, another explanation as to why household credit did not always collapse along with the householder's credit is explained by the different agency and strategies of each of the four partners' wives, best seen in the contrast between Dorothy Thompson and Mary Nelthorpe. Whilst Dorothy took a very active position in the events that occurred after the bankruptcy, Mary distanced herself entirely from the bank and denied any knowledge of it. Although Mary claimed her lack of knowledge was against her own wishes and was inflicted on her by her husband and the Thompsons, her actions could actually have been part of a more sophisticated strategy that used her situation to her own advantage in Chancery and in society. In this endeavour she was aided by the fact that her husband had settled lands on her before the bankruptcy and that she had no remaining ties to the bank after Edward's death in 1678. Mary and her children therefore managed to cultivate their own credit and reputation, distinct from the bank, and prosper with the family maintaining their estate into the eighteenth century and beyond. Dorothy, however, was not as independent in widowhood and relied on the support of her children in later years as her credit declined along with Richard's. Although this could be attributed to her continued marital status as a wife in the aftermath of the bankruptcy, the experience of Margaret Farrington shows that wives did not have to be dependent on their husband's wealth and

[17] Muldrew. *Economy of Obligation.* 148–149, 157–158.

credit. Margaret and her mother used a marriage settlement to avoid her and the children suffering from John Farrington's declining fortunes. The case of Thompson and Company therefore highlights the importance of agency and strategy as determinants of identity, status, gender, and power.

Similar arguments can be made regarding the four male partners of the bank. All four partners match the criteria for patriarchal masculinity, as married householders of middling rank with reasonable wealth as well as being citizens with respected professions.[18] Using Bourdieu's model of fields and capital, the partners all possessed social, economic, and symbolic capital in all three fields of commerce, finance, and politics. In terms of credit and economic identity, their respective householding status and 'considerable estates' meant that the partners were seen as credible and trustworthy.[19] In many ways their identities as middling sort, masculine married householders and citizens with significant wealth, allowed them to embark on such risky strategies. Their kinship networks provided them with the necessary skills and economic capital, and their commercial and political networks provided them with the contacts necessary to communicate their credit and obtain lucrative contracts and deals. However, despite matching all these different criteria of success, the partners and their joint venture were unsuccessful. This was largely because of the strategies they employed in each of their roles and their propensity to take risks.

The four partners were not just risk takers in one field but in all three of their roles in all three fields. Politically, those supportive kinship networks that provided vital skills and capital also situated the partners within a religious and politically dissenting milieu that attracted fierce opposition. Nelthorpe and Thompson became prominent opposition politicians in the Corporation of London, gaining status through those roles but also attracting powerful enemies. The collapse of the bank demonstrates the divisiveness of 'court' and 'country' factionalism in 1670s London, suggesting that, in this case, we can see distinctive party-like formations of opposition groups before the Exclusion Crisis and revelations of the Popish Plot that were 'systematic' in their approach

---

[18] Shepard. From Anxious Patriarchs to Refined Gentlemen? 291.

[19] Muldrew. *Economy of Obligation*. 153, 157–158; Alexandra Shepard. 2000. Manhood, Credit and Patriarchy in Early Modern England c. 1580–1640. *Past & Present* 167: 77, 89; *Case of Richard Thompson and Company*. 3.

240   M. WINTER

and increasingly hostile.[20] All four partners were prepared to embark on risky strategies in commerce and finance to make a profit, combining a 'bank' with a mercantile venture that was bank-financed. Nelthorpe and Thompson took this even further, funding not only mercantile trade but a variety of other commercial 'projects' of their own design. Whilst these ventures could have brought great profits, they also opened the partners up to rumour, gossip, and accusations of fraud, meaning that they were portrayed as crooks and swindlers after the collapse of the bank in 1678. That is not to say that the partners were simply diligent and honest traders who unfortunately ended up on the wrong side of the law. The partners' overall aim was to maximise profits for themselves, and they were prepared to use their creditors' money to fund their own schemes, with or without their creditors' knowledge. That money was then used to fund a wide variety of unstable and speculative ventures across the globe, particularly those carried out by Edward Nelthorpe. But unlike the deliberately fraudulent scheme of Thomas Pitkin in the 1690s, outlined by Kadens, Thompson and Company did not set out to defraud their creditors outright, a point proven by their eventual payment of a percentage of their creditors' deposits.[21] Rather the partners were 'projectors' and entrepreneurs whose risky 'projects' did not pay off. Despite having all the attributes necessary for success and power, the strategies the partners employed in all areas of their lives and careers led to their failure. What Thompson and Company ultimately reveals is the centrality of risk to everyday commercial life in Restoration London.

[20] Harris. *Politics under the Later Stuarts*. 62.
[21] Kadens. The Pitkin Affair. 48–570.

Appendix

© The Editor(s) (if applicable) and The Author(s), under exclusive
license to Springer Nature Switzerland AG 2022
M. Winter, *Banking, Projecting and Politicking in Early
Modern England*, Palgrave Studies in Economic History,
https://doi.org/10.1007/978-3-030-90570-5

The Creditors

Name	Residence	Occupation	Backwell account	Vyner account	East India Company	Royal African Company
Abbot, William	Greater London	Citizen, apothecary				
Allen, Anne	Gloucester	Widow	X			
Allen, William	Greater London	Merchant			Stock/bond holder	
Argill (Argall), Samuell	Greater London	Professional—Doctor in Physic				
Astey, Dorothy	Greater London	Widow				
Baker, John	City of London	Merchant			Personal Account	
Barnard, Daniell	Essex	Gent	X			
Beak, Samuell	City of London	Yeoman	X		Personal Account	
Beaman, John	City of London	Merchant				
Belasyse, Thomas, Viscount Fauconberg	London (also estate in Yorkshire)		X	X		
Berry, Anne	City of London	Gent				
Berry, Dan	City of London	Wife	X			
Billing, Thomas	City of London	Merchant				
Birkenhead, Theophilius	Greater London	Citizen—Blacksmith				
Blackwell, Isaak	Ireland?					
Bletzo, Francis	City of London	Citizen and cook	X			
Blunt, William	Greater London	Citizen				

(continued)

Name	Residence	Occupation	Backwell account	Vyner account	East India Company	Royal African Company
Bond, Elizabeth	City of London	Widow				
Boughte, Thomas						
Bowden, Moses						
Boyle, Robert	Greater London	Professional—Natural Philosopher		X		
Brigges, Thomas	Greater London					
Buller, Francis	Cornwall	Professional—Politician				
Buller, John	Cornwall	Professional—Lawyer				
Callis,						
Cannon, Richard	City of London	Citizen—Innholder	X			
Champion, Richard	London	Merchant				
Champneys, William	London	Merchant			Personal Account	
Charter, James	City of London	Citizen and cook				

(continued)

Name	Residence	Occupation	Backwell account	Vyner account	East India Company	Royal African Company
Cherret, Thomas	Greater London	Gent				
Chetwynd, Mary	City of London	Wife				
Chetwynd, Phillip	City of London	Merchant		X		
Churchman, Hester	Greater London	Wife				
Churchman, Sir John	Greater London	Gent	X	X		
Clare, Robert	City of London	Citizen	X			
Clarke, William	City of London	Professional—Physician				
Coleman, William	Plymouth, Devon	Captain				
Coles, Jane	Greater London	Widow/spinster				
Conyers, Mary		Widow/spinster				
Cornwallis,						
Cotton, Sir Robert	Cheshire	Professional—Politician				
Crispe, John	City of London	Merchant	X		Stock/bond holder	
Crispe, Stephen	Colchester, Essex	Citizen—Quaker activist and writer				

(continued)

Name	Residence	Occupation	Backwell account	Vyner account	East India Company	Royal African Company
Crosley, Leonard	London					
Dayle, Susan	London	Widow				
Dayn (Dunn), Thomas	Greater London	Citizen—Goldsmith				
De Tente, James						
Dickson, Abraham	Somerset					
Dixon, Elizabeth	London	Wife				
Dixon, John	London	Citizen and Feltmaker				
Draper, Robert	Berkshire	Gent				
Dubois, John	City of London	Merchant	X		Personal Account	Stockholder
Durham, William	London	Professional—Clergyman				

(continued)

Name	Residence	Occupation	Backwell account	Vyner account	East India Company	Royal African Company
Elis, Edward						
Irby, Elizabeth	London	Spinster				
Irby, Sir Anthony	Greater London	Professional—Politician				
Farrer, Elizabeth	Greater London	Widow				
Fenn, Robert	City of London	Merchant	X			Stockholder
Fitch, Thomas	Greater London	Merchant			Personal Account	
Fleetwood, Anne	London	Widow	X			
Fox, William	Greater London	Citizen				
Frampton, Tregonwell	Newmarket, Suffolk	Professional—Racehorse trainer	X			
Frampton, William	Dorset	Gent				
Fryer, George	Greater London	Mariner				
Gardiner, Thomas	London	Merchant				
Gauden, Phillip						
Gerard, Sir Gilbert	Greater London	Professional—politician	X			
Gilbert, Thomas	Oxford	Professional—Minister	X			
Gladman, John	Greater London	Citizen				
Glandvill, William	Kent	Professional—lawyer				Stockholder

(continued)

(continued)

Name	Residence	Occupation	Backwell account	Vyner account	East India Company	Royal African Company
Godolphin, John	Greater London	Captain			Correspondence	
Goodwyn, Sarah	London	Widow/spinster				
Gore, Gerrard	Sussex	Gent	X			
Gorges, Ferdinando	City of London	Merchant	X			
Gower, Thomas	City of London	Professional—Minister				
Grahme, Randalph	Yorkshire, with house in London	Citizen—Woollen draper	X			
Grant, Anne	Greater London	Widow				
Green, Thomas	City of London	Citizen—Goldsmith	X			
Gregory, Francis	Hambledon, Buckinghamshire	Professional—Church of England Clergyman and writer	X			
Griffith, Edward	Greater London	Merchant			Personal Account	
Grigges, James	Greater London	Mariner				
Grist, William		Mariner				
Grove, Benjamin	Greater London	Citizen				
Grove, John	Greater London	Merchant	X		Personal Account	
Grove, Ruth		Widow/spinster				
Guyn, Ryc	City of London	Citizen—Fishmonger				
Hall, Thomas	City of London					

(continued)

248 APPENDIX

(continued)

Name	Residence	Occupation	Backwell account	Vyner account	East India Company	Royal African Company
Harris, Thomas						
Harris, Jane	City of London	Mariner				
Harsent, Jane	City of London	Widow/spinster				
Harvey, John	City of London	Merchant	X		Personal Account	
Haward, John	Snowfields, Surrey	Citizen—Book seller				
Hickes, James	City of London	Citizen—senior clerk in the inland letter office				
Horwood, John	Greater London/Algiers	Mariner				
Hoskins, Sir John	Herefordshire	Professional—Lawyer and Natural Philosopher	X			
Hudson, John	City of London	Citizen—Goldsmith				
Humphreys, Stephen	Sussex	Gent				Stockholder
Hunt, Thomas	City of London	Merchant	X		Personal Account	
Impey, Thomas	Greater London	Gent				
Ingram, Frances	Yorkshire—Thirsk	Widow				
Jackson, Isaak	Greater London	Citizen—silkthrower				
Jackson, Richard						
Jennes (Jeenes), John	City of London	Citizen—Upholder				
Jekyll, John	City of London	Citizen—haberdasher				
Keate, Sir Jonathan	City of London	Merchant	X		Stock/bond holder	

(continued)

(continued)

Name	Residence	Occupation	Backwell account	Vyner account	East India Company	Royal African Company
Kemble, John	Greater London	Citizen—Clerk				
Kempthorne, Sir John	Portsmouth	Naval officer/Captain	X			
King, George	London	Citizen—Goldsmith				
Kirk, Thomas	London	Citizen				
Laughton, John	Lincolnshire	Gent				
Lawrence, Edward	Greater London	Professional—Minister				
Lawson, Godfrey	Yorkshire—Leeds	Merchant Adventurer				
Lawson, Ralph	Greater London	Gent				
Legrand, Mick						
Lewis, Henry	City of London	Citizen—Scrivener	X			
Lyle, John	Greater London	Master & mariner				
Lyster, Bernard	London					
Maddison, Ralph	Greater London	Gent				
Mainwaring, Charles	London	Citizen—haberdasher				
Mandesley, Thomas	Greater London	Citizen—grocer	X			
Manshell, George						
Marcer, Elizabeth		Widow/spinster				

(continued)

(continued)

Name	Residence	Occupation	Backwell account	Vyner account	East India Company	Royal African Company
Marsh, Miles	London	Gent				
Mason, Charles	City of London	Professional—Doctor				
Matson, Ellen		Widow/spinster				
Mayo, Israell	Hertford	Gent				
Medlicott, Thomas	Abingdon, Berkshire (also a house in London)	Professional—Lawyer	X	X		
Morgan, Jane	City of London	Widow/spinster				
Morrise, John	City of London	Merchant	X			Stockholder
Muddle, Abraham	Mayfield, Sussex	Gent				
Neast, Thomas	Gloucester	Gent				
Nevill, Elizabeth	Greater London	Widow				
Newman, Thomas	London/Zant	Merchant	X			
Nicolls, Alice	Hertford	Widow/spinster				
Norborne, William	Greater London	Citizen				
Norman, Mary	Greater London	Spinster				
Oubell, James						
Palmer, Edward	City of London	Merchant	X		Stock/bond holder	
Palmer, William	Greater London	Merchant			Personal Account	Stockholder
Parkman, Thomas	Devon?	Citizen—Taylor				

(continued)

(continued)

Name	Residence	Occupation	Backwell account	Vyner account	East India Company	Royal African Company
Partridge, Anne	London	Widow				
Peck, Henry	Greater London	Mariner				
Perkyns, Benjamin						
Pert, Rich						
Peter, Lord William	London	Gent	X			
Petre, John	Essex	Gent				
Petty, Tho		Mariner				
Piggot, William	City of London	Citizen	X			
Pockins, William	City of London	Merchant				
Poore, Nathaniel	City of London	Citizen—Goldsmith				
Powell, Rebecca	London	Widow				
Powell, Robert	City of London	Citizen—Draper				
Prowse, Richard	Devon	Gent	X			
Pym, Christopher	Surrey	Gent				
Radford, Anne	Greater London	Widow/spinster				
Ramsden, William	Hull	Merchant			Correspondence	
Rawlins, Giles	City of London	Citizen	X			

(continued)

(continued)

Name	Residence	Occupation	Backwell account	Vyner account	East India Company	Royal African Company
Reeve, Anne	London	Widow				
Richardson, Joshua	City of London	Professional—Rector				
Rigden, Mr.	Yorkshire					
Robbins, Mary	Buckinghamshire or Surrey	Widow	X			
Robbinson, Alexander	London	Mariner				
Robinson, Humphrey	Greater London	Citizen	X			
Robinson, Mary	City of London	Widow				
Russell, Mary	London	Widow/spinster				
Salisbury, Susan	London	Widow				
Sankey, Ann	Greater London	Widow				
Saverton alias Sabbarton, Joseph	Greater London	Gent				
Savile, Dan	London	Citizen—painter stainer				
Savile, Francis	London	Citizen				
Seamour, Richard	London	Citizen				
Sherwyne, Richard	Greater London	Professional—Deputy Receiver				
Smith, Anne		Widow/spinster				
Smith, John						

(continued)

(continued)

Name	Residence	Occupation	Backwell account	Vyner account	East India Company	Royal African Company
Smithson, Anthony	London	Gent				
Smythe, John	London	Merchant				
Southerby, James	Greater London	Merchant	X		Stock/bond holder	
Starr, Elizabeth		Widow/spinster				
Stephenson, Robert	City of London	Merchant	X		Personal Account	Stockholder
Streete, Beth	City of London	Widow				
Symson, John	London	Mariner				
Temple, Sir John	Ireland	Gent				
Temple, John	City of London	Citizen—Goldsmith-banker				
Thompson, Henry		Mariner				
Thompson, John	Greater London	Mariner				
Thorner, Mary	London	Widow				
Thornhills, Johan						
Thorold, Grissilla	London	Widow				
Thorowgood, John		Merchant				
Tilden, Richard	Greater London	Merchant	X		Other business	Stockholder
Todd, William	Yorkshire	gent				

(continued)

(continued)

Name	Residence	Occupation	Backwell account	Vyner account	East India Company	Royal African Company
Travers, James	Liverpool	Merchant				
Tredcroft, Edward	London/Fort St. George India	Merchant			Correspondence	
Trinity House	City of London	INSTITUTION				
Tunny, Richard						
Turner, Sir William	Greater London	Merchant—Woollen Draper and silk merchant	X			
Turner, Symon	Greater London	Citizen				
Vanbrugge, Giles	City of London	Gent				
Vear, Jo:	City of London	Citizen, painter and stainer				
Villiers, George, Viscount Grandison	Hertfordshire	Gent		X		
Wallop, John	Hampshire	Gent				
Warburton, Mr.	Ireland					
Watson, Anne	City of London	Widow				
Watts, Edward	City of London	Merchant	X	X	Personal Account and Stock/bond holder	
Welding, Anne	Greater London	Widow				
Weston, John	Greater London					
Whitehead, George	London	Citizen				

(continued)

(continued)

Name	Residence	Occupation	Backwell account	Vyner account	East India Company	Royal African Company
Whitley, George	Greater London	Gent				
Wilkins, Maudlin		Widow				
Wilkinson, William	City of London	Citizen—Skinner				
Williams, Nathaniel	Greater London	Citizen—Joiner				
Williamson, Henry	City of London	Citizen—Upholder				Stockholder
Wiseman, Sir Robert	Essex	Professional—Judge and Jurist	X			
Woodward, Robert	Greater London	Citizen—grocer				
Young, William	Greater London	Citizen—Carpenter	X			

Sources TNA: C 8/328/50; *Boyd's Inhabitants of London*; *The Little London Directory of 1677*; The National Archives wills PROB; London Metropolitan Archives wills and probate documents; History of Parliament http://www.historyofparliamentonline.org/; Brook. *Transcript of the Registers*; London Hearth Tax: City of London and Middlesex, 1666. British History Online. http://www.british-history.ac.uk/london-hearth-tax/london-mddx/1666. Accessed 19 May 2020; Woodhead. *Rulers of London*; Customer Account Ledgers of Edward Backwell. 6, 14, 16, 20, 22, 25, 29, 44, 52, 64, 79, 89, 91, 94, 100, 101, 103, 105, 106, 107, 108, 115, 125, 129, 137, 148, 156, 162, 169, 175, 184, 190, 191, 197, 201, 205, 205, 223, 228, 238, 243, 253, 262, 267
TNA: Exchequer, E 406/16. Goldsmiths' assignment book, Second series. 1676–1680, ff.106, 113, 163, 410, 239; TNA: Exchequer E 406/17. Goldsmiths' assignment book, Second series. 1680–1696, ff.335–337; TNA: Exchequer E 406/18. Goldsmiths' assignment book, Second series. 1698–1703, f.114; Personal Accounts, BL: IOR/L/AG/1/1/2. Ledger B. ff.102, 153; IOR/L/AG/1/1/3. Ledger B. ff.283, 404, 355; IOR/L/AG/1/1/4. Ledger C. ff.184, 230, 302, 386, 108, 311; IOR/L/AG/1/1/5. Ledger D. ff.35, 141, 90, 152, 222, 318, 436, 518; IOR/L/AG/1/1/6. Ledger E. ff.19, 88, 127, 115, 149, 291, 323, 366, 315, 534; IOR/L/AG/1/1/7. Ledger F. ff.342, 250, 277, 58, 298; IOR/L/AG/1/1/8. Ledger G. ff.360,

415, 393, 422, 88, 432; IOR/L/AG/1/1/9. Ledger H. ff.285, 420, 516, 518, 282, 370, 186, 285, 374; IOR/L/AG/1/1/10. Ledger J. ff.202,353, 422

Stock or bond holder: BL: IOR/L/AG/1/1/4/f.170; IOR/L/AG/1/1/5/f.209, 222, 305, 18; IOR/L/AG/1/1/6/ff.344, 439, 366, 359, 367; Correspondence: BL: IOR/E/3/34. East India Company Original Correspondence. 1673–1674, ff.150–53, 137–38, 246–55; IOR/E/3/87. Letter Book 4. 1666–1672, f.97, 103, 105, 121; IOR/E/3/93. Letter Book 10 (Old Company). 1698–1709, ff.1–6; IOR/L/L/2/364. Lease. 29 July 1682; IOR/L/L/2/365. Mortgage. 27 April 1683; IOR/L/L/2/366. Assignment of lease. 25 January 1690; TNA: T 70/600. Company of Royal Adventurers Trading with Africa. (No. 3) Home Ledger. 1664–1674, ff.237, 222, 39, 212, 156–7; T 70/601. Company of Royal Adventurers Trading with Africa. Home Ledger 3. 1678–1680, ff.193, 122, 235.

Bibliography

Manuscript Primary Sources

Borthwick Institute for Archives

Will of Edward Nelthorpe of Walkington. July 1640.
Will of Matthew Alured of Harthill. September 1694.

The British Library

Add MS 8888. Tamberlane the Beneficient, a Tragedy; The Cid translated from Corneille; with several minor poems; all probably by Will. Popple sen. 1681–1701.

Add MS 28051. Original correspondence of the family of Osborne, Dukes of Leeds, on matters of private business; 1669–1788.

Add MS 28089. *Papers relating to the English Colonies in America.* The proposalls of Ferdinando Gorges, Esq., for the sale of the province of Maine in New England to his Maiestye. 24 February 1676.

Add MS 34195. Collection of original letters, warrants, and papers, many of which refer to the expenses of the Tower Establishment and other offices, the repayment of Crown Loans, the transfer of South Sea Stock, etc.

Add MS 34515. Mackintosh Collections. Vol. XXIX. Notes and extracts from the papers at Welbeck Abbey.

Add MS 38849. Hodgkin Papers. Vol. IV. Pepys and Danby papers.

© The Editor(s) (if applicable) and The Author(s), under exclusive license to Springer Nature Switzerland AG 2022
M. Winter, *Banking, Projecting and Politicking in Early Modern England*, Palgrave Studies in Economic History,
https://doi.org/10.1007/978-3-030-90570-5

258 BIBLIOGRAPHY

Add MS 41255. Note-Book of Thomas Belasyse, 2nd Viscount Fauconberg of Henknowle. 1671–1710.
Add MS 65141. Clifford Papers. Vol IV. 1662–1713.
Egerton MS 3351. Vol. XXVIII.
IOR/B/32. Court Minutes. 22 April 1672–10 April 1674.
IOR/E/3/34. East India Company Original Correspondence. 1673–1674.
IOR/E/3/87. Letter Book 4. 1666–1672.
IOR/E/3/93. Letter Book 10 (Old Company). 1698–1709.
IOR/H/42. Miscellaneous papers.
IOR/L/AG/1/1/2 and 3. Ledger B. August 1664–March 1669.
IOR/L/AG/1/1/4. Ledger C. April 1669–April 1671.
IOR/L/AG/1/1/5. Ledger D. May 1671–July 1673.
IOR/L/AG/1/1/6. Ledger E. August 1673–December 1675.
IOR/L/AG/1/1/7. Ledger F. January 1676–May 1678.
IOR/L/AG/1/1/8. Ledger G. June 1678–June 1682.
IOR/L/AG/1/1/9. Ledger H. July 1682–June 1694.
IOR/L/L/2/364. Lease for 61 Years. 29 July 1682.
IOR/L/L/2/365. Mortgage. 27 April 1683.
IOR/L/L/2/366. Assignment of lease. 25 January 1690.
Microfilm 636/29. *Verney Papers from Claydon House.* November 1675–September 1676.
Ogilby, John, and William Morgan. 1677. *LARGE AND ACCURATE MAP OF THE CITY OF LONDON. Ichnographically describing all the Streets, Lanes, Alleys, Courts, Yards, Churches, Halls and Houses, &c,* http://www.bl.uk/onl inegallery/onlineex/crace/l/largeimage87902.html.
Stowe MS 191. Historical Papers, consisting chiefly of Instructions to Ambassadors; 1651–1680.
Stowe MS 201. Essex Papers vol. II. f. 410.
Stowe MS 204. Essex Papers vol. V. f. 341.
Stowe MS 205. Essex Papers vol. VI. f. 461.
Stowe MS 207. Essex Papers vol. VIII. f. 448.
Stowe MS 210. Essex Papers vol. XI. f. 442.

EAST SUSSEX RECORD OFFICE

SAS/DD 510. Release by way of Mortgage (following lease for a year). 2 May 1682

GUILDHALL ARCHIVES

CLC/L/HA/C/011. Register of apprentice bindings for the Haberdashers Company.

BIBLIOGRAPHY 259

MS 15858/1 or CLC/L/HA/C/008. Index to registers of freemen of Haberdashers Company.

HAMBURG STATE ARCHIVE (STAATSARCHIV HAMBURG)

MS 521-1. Register book of the Church of the English Court.

HERTFORDSHIRE ARCHIVES AND LOCAL STUDIES

DE/P/F81/77. *Letters from William Cowper to Judith, also letters from other correspondents.* Letter from Mary Popple to Edward Nelthorpe. 26 June 1677.

HOARE'S BANK ARCHIVE

HB/1/1. Goldsmith's Workbook 1684–87.
HB/5/F/1. Customer Ledger A 1673–1683.
HB/8/A1-22. Releases and Discharges 1675–1712.
HB/8/B/1. Bond by Lord Conyers D'Arcy to Richard Hoare for £145. 2 March 1685/6.
HB/8/M/1. Miscellaneous receipt notes for money credited—1671, 1676–1822.
HB/8/M/2/2. Handwritten cheques from Ann Clobery to Richard Hoare. 1677–1681. Cash Book.

HULL HISTORY CENTRE

C DMX/168/1. Andrew Marvell Manuscripts. 17 January 1660–31 May 1660.
U DDBA/8/8. Articles of Agreement between Roger Heath of the Inner Temple, London, esq. and Edward Nelthorpe of Redness, esq. 4 July 1639.
U DDBA/8/15. Account of monies due to Mary Sleigh, a daughter of Edmund Sleigh, esq. citizen and alderman and mercer, under will of her father. 1657–1662.
U DDBA/8/16. Copy of Lease for 11 years at £16 rent: Mary Nelthorpe of London, widow, to Roger Mason of Beverly. 1687.
U DDBA/8/35. Lease at peppercorn rent: Edward Nelthorpe, citizen merchant of London and his wife Mary to Matthew Alured of Beverly, esq. 6 March 1665.
U DDBA/8/49. Mr. Launder's remarks on the title to the Yorkshire Estate. 1765.
U DDFA/37/1. Cash Book of Henry Thompson, merchant at Bordeaux. 1647–1648.

260 BIBLIOGRAPHY

U DDFA/37/2. Memorial book of Henry Thompson. 1647–1648.
U DDFA/37/3. Journal of Henry Thompson. 1647–1648.
U DDFA/37/4. Journal of Henry Thompson at York and Amsterdam. 1655–1657.
U DDFA/37/5. Journal of Henry Thompson at Bordeaux. 1655–1667.
U DDFA/37/6. Wine merchant's account book (Edward Thompson?). 1662–1665.
U DDFA/39/6. Letter: Duke of Buckingham to Sir Henry Thompson, York, 24 August 1666.
U DDFA/39/8. Letter: Henry Thompson, Escrick to Thomas, Viscount Osborne, Lord High Treasurer of England, 5 July 1673.

The Library of Congress

MSS97733. *London Newsletters Collection.* Reel 2.

London Metropolitan Archives

ACC/0413/A/04/001. Will of Theophilus Birkenhead. 15 September 1693.
CLA/024/06/001/004. 1641 Bond for £80 11s. 6d., Richard CHAMPION merchant of London to John LINCH citizen and clothier.
CLC/509/MS05107/002, Miscellaneous accounts, chiefly clients', but also some private accounts, 1673–1692.
CLC/509/MS05105. Book of sales, 1664–1671, followed by accounts relating to his personal estate, 1671–1691.
CLC/521/MS18242. Agreement whereby Dame Mary Sternell, alias Starling (nee Garford), widow of Samuel Sternell, gives George, Viscount Grandison, her intended husband, £2000 on condition that her remaining real and personal estate will not be under his control. 18 November 1674.
CLC/526/MS30307. List of masters, deputy masters, elder brethren and secretaries. 1660–1950.
CLC/526/MS30004/004. *Corporation of Trinity House.* Court Minutes 1670–1676.
CLC/526/MS30004/005. *Corporation of Trinity House.* Court Minutes 1676–1681.
COL/AD/01/49. Letter Book YY. 1673–1676.
COL/CA/09/03/001. List of Names of Aldermen.
COL/CC/01/01/045 (Microfilm X109/082). Common Council Journal. 10 November 1669–22 September 1673.
COL/CC/01/01/046 (Microfilm X109/083). Common Council Journal. 20 December 1673–22 October 1678.
DL/AM/PW/1685/067. Will of Richard Seymour. 1685.

MS1174/001. Court Minute Book of the Eastland Company 1666–1682.
MS 6428 (2). Clayton & Morris Ledger 1672–1675.
P69/MRY15/B/013/MS01009. Churchwardens' vouchers and papers and miscellaneous overseers' vouchers for the united parishes of St Mary Woolnoth with St Mary Woolchurch Haw.
P69/MRY15/B/018/MS07661. Collection of miscellaneous papers relating to the united parishes of St Mary Woolnoth with St Mary Woolchurch Haw containing, inter alia, churchwardens' appointments, apprenticeship indentures and bonds of indemnity.

THE NATIONAL ARCHIVES

Admiralty:
ADM 106/289/7. Jonas Shish, A. Beare, J. Uthwat and Phineas Pett. 27 October 1673.
ADM 106/236/86. 31 October 1677.
ADM 106/323/139. 10 December 1677.
ADM 106/323/415. 12 December 1677.
ADM 106/323/143. 28 December 1677.

Chancery:
C 6/148/7. Archdale v Lownes. 1661.
C 7/455/40. Dixon v Farrington. 1662.
C 10/153/9. Bletso v Baines. 1668.
C 10/157/10. Bletso v Baines. 1669.
C 10/119/112. Smithson v Smithson 1670.
C 5/59/43, Page v Jago, 23 January 1671.
C 5/488/20. Godfrey v Mayoe. 1671.
C 8/178/138. Thompson v Bickley. 1673.
C 7/510/27. Poyntz v Nelthorpe. December 1673.
C 8/268/47. Squibb v Nelthorpe. 1674.
C 10/189/39. Hamerton v Nelthorpe. 1675.
C 8/296/106. Terrezy v Nelthorpe. 12 May 1676.
C 8/327/60. Cordary v Savile. 1676.
C 10/402/10. Cordary v Savile. 1676.
C 5/551/85. Scadding v Corbee. January 1676–May 1677.
C 7/522/35. Farrington v Holland. January 1677.
C 8/328/50. Lord Grandison v Thompson. 12 February 1679.
C 6/275/120. Wallis v Marvell. 16 November 1681.
C 6/247/21. Marsh v Towers. 1681.
C 7/589/82. Wallis v Farrington. 11 January 1682.
C 7/587/95. Marvell v Farrington. 23 January 1682.

262 BIBLIOGRAPHY

C 8/252/9. Farrington v Palmer. February 1682.
C 6/242/13. Farrington v Palmer. 18 February 1682.
C 6/276/48. Farrington v Marvell. 1 July 1682.
C 24/1069. Interrogatories relating to Farrington v Marvell. 1–24 July 1682.
C 10/484/71. Farrington v Nelthorpe. 12 April 1683.
C 10/212/10. Cowper and Thompson v Foach, Farrington and Nelthorpe. 14 July 1683.
C 6/526/200. Farrington v unknown. 20 July 1683.
C 6/392/39. Cooper v Foach. 21 November 1683.
C 22/811/30. Nuthall v Cowper and others. 1683.
C 10/211/16. Cowper v Nuthall. 1683.
Final Decree C 78/1058 no. 4. accessed via *The Anglo-American Legal Tradition* http://www.uh.edu/waalt/index.php/C78_1683. John Nuthall and Elizabeth his wife v. John Cooper, executor of Nicholas Cooper; John Hall; and Richard Thompson. 17 November 1683.
C 6/526/178. Farrington v Unknown (Popple and Stewart). 31 March 1684.
C 7/607/20. Cartwright v Nelthorpe. 19 April 1684.
C 6/249/35. Farrington v Foach. 22 April 1684.
Final Decree C 78 1133 no. 3. Accessed via *The Anglo-American Legal Tradition* http://www.uh.edu/waalt/index.php/C78_1684. Robert Cowper, gent; and John Cowper, gent, only sons of Nicholas Cowper, gent, deceased; Richard Thompson; and John Hall v. John Foach; John Farrington; and Mary Nelthorp. 9 May 1684.
C 6/283/87. Thompson v Farrington. 30 May 1684.
C 6/392/38. Cartwright v Speed. May 1684.
Final Decree C 78 1133 no. 2. Accessed via *The Anglo-American Legal Tradition* http://www.uh.edu/waalt/index.php/C78_1684. John Farrington, administrator of Edward Nelthorpe v. Mary Marvell; and John Greene, administrators of Andrew Marvell, esq. 13 June 1684.
C 7/581/73. Farrington v Thompson. 7 July 1684.
C 6/411/29. Farrington v Hall. 18 July 1684.
C 10/216/74. Thompson v Nelthorpe. 8 November 1684.
C 5/94/96. Tryon v Nelthorpe. 15 July 1688.
C 10/275/13. Cooper v Nelthorpe. 1688.
C 8/349/43. Nelthorpe v Cowper. December 1692.
C 109/24. Attwood v Ware: Letters and accounts of William Attwood, merchant: London, Exeter, York; Hamburg, Genoa etc. 1660–1689.

Exchequer:
E 406/16. Goldsmiths' assignment book, Second series. 1676–1680.
E 406/17. Goldsmiths' assignment book, Second series. 1680–1696.
E 406/18. Goldsmiths' assignment book, Second series. 1698–1703.

BIBLIOGRAPHY 263

E 134/7Geo3/East1. Interrogatories, Depositions taken at Beverley 13 April 7 Geo, 1767. Henry Liddell, Esq., Lenyns Boldero, Esq., v. Randle Hancock, Clerk. 25 October 1766–24 October 1767.
Records of the Colonial Office, Commonwealth and Foreign and Commonwealth Offices, Empire Marketing Board, and related bodies:
CO 389/11. Entry Books of Commissions, instructions, petitions, warrants, correspondence, etc. 1673–1684.

Royal African Company:
T 70/600. Company of Royal Adventurers Trading with Africa. (No. 3) Home Ledger. 1664–1674.
T 70/601. Company of Royal Adventurers Trading with Africa. Home Ledger 3. 1678–1680.

Wills:
PROB 11/262/31. Will of Edmund Sleigh, Alderman of London. 3 February 1657.
PROB 11/331/295. Will of Isaac Blackwell of Hamburg. 5 November 1669.
PROB 11/347/293. Will of Nicholas Cowper, Gentleman of Bobbingworth, Essex. 10 March 1675.
PROB 11/362/434. Will of Dame Frances Ingram, Widow. 1 April 1680.
PROB 11/364/64, 'Will of Robert Clare, Chirurgion of London', 2 October 1680.
PROB 11/365/74. Will of Elizabeth Bond, Widow of the City of London. 17 January 1681.
PROB 11/366/377. Will of Robert Draper, Gentleman of Windsor, Berkshire. 31 May 1681.
PROB 11/367/180. Will of Ralph Lawson. 14 July 1681.
PROB 11/369/326. Will of William Coleman, Captain of Plymouth, Devon. 4 March 1682.
PROB 11/372/258. Will of Phillip Chetwind, Clothworker of London. 19 February 1683.
PROB 11/373/82. Will of William Grist, Mariner of Rotherhithe, Surrey. 14 May 1683.
PROB 11/373/120. Will of Gerrard Gore of Shillinglee Park, Sussex. 21 May 1683.
PROB 11/375/341. Will of Elizabeth Irby of Saint Margaret Westminster, Middlesex. 8 March 1684.
PROB 11/375/426. Will of Anne Allen, Widow of Gloucester, Gloucestershire. 3 April 1684.
PROB 11/377/28. Will of William Durham, Clerk Rector of saint Mildred Bread Street, City of London. 1 August 1684.

264 BIBLIOGRAPHY

PROB 11/377/468. Will of Doctor Samuel Argall, Doctor in Physic of Saint Martin in the Fields, Middlesex. 7 November 1684.

PROB 11/380/51. Will of Thomas Impey of Uxbridge, Middlesex. 7 May 1685.

PROB 11/380/471. Will of Grissilla Thorold. 23 July 1685.

PROB 11/381/82. Will of John Simson, Mariner of Saint Mary Magdalene Bermondsey, Surrey. 8 August 1685.

PROB 11/381/180. Will of James Nelthorpe, Merchant of London. 2 October 1685.

PROB 11/381/495. Will of Ranald Grahme of Nunnington, Yorkshire. 2 December 1685.

PROB 11/384/22. Will of Elizabeth Ireton, Wife. 5 July 1686.

PROB 4/8496. Barnard, Daniel, of Walthamstow, Essex, yeoman. 13 September 1686.

PROB 11/385/116. Will of William Durham, Clerk Rector of Letcombe Bassett, Berkshire. 2 November 1686.

PROB 11/389/107. Will of Anne Grant, Widow of Saint Mary Newington, Surrey. 8 November 1687.

PROB 11/391/166. Will of Thomas Neast, Gentleman of Twyning, Gloucestershire. 10 May 1688.

PROB 11/392/405. Will of Richard Cannon, Innholder of The Red Heart Fetter Lane, City of London. 22 September 1688.

PROB 11/394/81. Will of James Hicks, Gentleman of London. 17 January 1689.

PROB 11/395/360. Will of Sir John Churchman of Inner Temple, Middlesex. 13 June 1689.

PROB 11/396/143. Will of John Thorowgood, Merchant of Lyme Regis, Norfolk. 22 July 1689.

PROB 11/399/141. Will of William Frampton of Moreton, Dorset. 10 April 1690.

PROB 11/420/234. Will of Daniel Savile, Painter Stainer of London. 31 May 1694.

PROB 11/421/381. Will of Margarett Farrington, Wife of London. 1 October 1694.

PROB 11/423/142. Will of Alexander Robinson, now belonging to their Majesty's Ship Neptune, Mariner. 13 November 1694.

PROB 4/7721. Beaman alias Ballmon, John, of St Mary Woolchurch, London. 20 February 1695.

PROB 11/430/429. Will of James Grigg or Griegg, Mariner of Stepney, Middlesex. 26 March 1696.

PROB 11/447/76. Will of Mary Norman, Spinster of Saint Martin in the Fields, Middlesex. 4 August 1698.

BIBLIOGRAPHY   265

PROB 11/448/194. Will of John Simson, Mariner of Saint John Wapping, Middlesex. 17 November 1698.

PROB 11/452/159. Will of William Grist, Mariner of Ratcliffe, Middlesex. 1 September 1699.

PROB 11/454/384. Will of Simon Turner, Skinner of London. 8 March 1700.

PROB 11/459/28. Will of James Nelthorpe of Charterhouse Yard, Middlesex. 8 January 1701.

PROB 11/464/461. Will of Robert Woodward, Founder and Pewterer of Saint Botolph Without Aldgate, London. 23 May 1702.

PROB 11/471/311. Will of Alexander Robinson, now belonging to her Majesty's Ship Dunkirk. 26 August 1703.

PROB 11/484/164. Will of John Hudson, Goldsmith of London. 13 September 1705.

PROB 11/492/208. Will of Richard Prowse, Gentleman of Tiverton, Devon. 22 January 1707.

PROB 11/497/90. Will of Thomas Kirk, Skinner of Saint Giles Cripplegate, City of London. 21 October 1707.

PROB 11/499/343. Will of John Laughton, Gentleman of Boston, Lincolnshire. 31 January 1708.

PROB 11/503/389. Will of Dorothy Thompson, Widow of Saint Martin Ludgate, City of London. 23 October 1708.

PROB 11/516/373. Will of Anne Reeve, Spinster of London. 27 July 1710.

PROB 11/523/320. Will of George Fryer, Mariner being outward bound to Sea for the now intended Voyage to Smyrna of Saint John Wapping, Middlesex. 16 October 1711.

PROB 11/531/97. Will of Isaac Jackson, Silkthrower of London. 13 January 1713.

PROB 11/544/191. Will of John Farrington, Gentleman, Widower of the Inner Temple, Middlesex. 3 February 1715.

PROB 11/549/235. Will of Anne Reeve, Widow of Kensington, Middlesex. 3 December 1715.

PROB 11/558/91. Will of Thomas Cherret or Cheret, Gentleman of Saint Martin in the Fields, Middlesex. 17 May 1717.

PROB 11/561/145. Will of Gerrard Gore, Merchant of London. 2 December 1717.

PROB 11/564/136. Will of Thomas Liddell of Saint Andrew Holborn, Middlesex. 5 June 1718.

PROB 11/565351. Will of Nathaniel Williams, Joiner of Saint Andrew Holborn, Middlesex. 10 October 1718.

PROB 11/574/150. Will of Edward Nelthorpe. 16 May 1720.

PROB 11/590/153. Will of George Whitehead of Saint Botolph without Bishopgate, City of London. 20 March 1723.

266 BIBLIOGRAPHY

PROB 11/685/128. Will of Rebecca Philpott, Widow of Saint Stephen Coleman Street London, City of London. 20 September 1737.
PROB 11/715/343. Will of Samuel Thompson, formerly Mercer of Saint Martin Ludgate, City of London. 26 January 1741.

Post Office Record Office

POST 94/15. *Letter book, postmaster and packet agents, England.* September 1673–February 1675.
POST 94/17. *Letter book, postmaster and packet agents, England.* February 1675–October 1677.
POST 94/19. *Letter book, postmaster and packet agents, Ireland.* August 1672–October 1677.

The Samuel Pepys Library

MS 2875. Journal of the Green Ribband Club at the King's Head Tavern over against the Temple in Fleet Street, 14 November 1678 to 29 June 1681. *The Samuel Pepys Library, Magdalene College Cambridge.* 465–491.

Sheffield City Archive

BFM/129. Matthew Ashton's (later Frank's) account book.

State Papers Online

Note of a bond of Edward Thompson of York, Richard Thompson of Stepney, and Edward Nelthorpe in 3000l to Edward Smith and Edward Lee, merchants of London. *State Papers Online*, SP 29/193 f.8, 1 March 1667.
Case of Edward Thompson, merchant, presented to Council. *State Papers Online*, SP/29/193 f.6, March 1667.
The Lord Lieutenant to Lord Arlington. *State Papers Online*, SP 63/334 f.83, 18 August 1673.
The Lord Lieutenant to Lord Arlington. *State Papers Online*, SP 63/334 f.97, 23 August 1673.
James Hickes to Williamson. *State Papers Online*, SP 29/337 f.26, 5 September 1673.
Sir Thomas Player to Sir Joseph Williamson. *State Papers Online*, SP 29/337 f.38, 9 September 1673.
Sir Robert Southwell to Williamson. *State Papers Online*, SP 29/337 f.68, 19 September 1673.

BIBLIOGRAPHY 267

John Paige to Williamson. *State Papers Online*, SP 29/337 f.150, 13 October 1673.

Warrant to the Commissioners of Prizes to pay to Sir Robert Southwell. *State Papers Online*, SP 44/26 f.169, 20 December 1673.

Warrant to the Commissioners of Prizes to pay 100l. to Thomas Hawkes, merchant, for his services about the East India prizes, and particularly in advancing their sale. *State Papers Online*, SP 44/26 f.170, 28 January 1674.

The Lord Keeper, the Earl of Danby and Sir J. Williamson to Secretary Coventry. *State Papers Online*, SP 44/43 f.10, 13 March 1675.

Whitehall. The Lord Keeper, the Earl of Danby and Sir J. Williamson to Secretary Coventry. *State Papers Online*, SP 44/43 f.12, 17 March 1675.

Whitehall. The Lord Keeper, the Earl of Danby and Sir J. Williamson to Secretary Coventry. *State Papers Online*, SP 44/43 f.13, 20 March 1675.

Order in Council on the petition of William Strangh, citizen and merchant of London. *State Papers Online*, SP 29/370 f.284, 19 May 1675.

Francisco Terrezy &a. against Mr. Nelthorp touching their share in the 10000[L] for relinquishing their Contract for the East India Prizes to be heard 28th. *State Papers Online*, Privy Council: Registers, PC 2/64 f. 465, 14 July 1675.

Summons for Witness in the cause above. *State Papers Online*, Privy Council: Registers, PC 2/64 f. 465, 14 July 1675.

Original Warrants for making free the following ships. *SPO*, SP 29/364 f.19, 18 November 1675.

Sir John Robinson to Williamson. *State Papers Online*, SP 29/378 f.264, January 1676.

Note by Williamson. *State Papers Online*, SP 29/379 f.73, 17 February 1676.

Notes by Williamson. *State Papers Online*, SP 29/379 f.80, 18 February 1676.

Sir John Robinson to Williamson. *State Papers Online*, SP 29/379 f.265, 10 March 1676.

Order in Council. *State Papers Online*, SP 29/381 f.97, 5 May 1676.

Warrant to send Nathaniel Ponder to the Gate House. *State Papers Online*, Privy Council: Registers, PC 2/65 f.217, 10 May 1676.

Report of Sir Leoline Jenkins in the case of Sir John Shorter and the Hamburgher. *State Papers Online*, SP 82/16 ff.38–39, 31 May 1676.

Similar affidavits by the following persons concerning the following ships, the only difference being that the ship is sometimes a foreign built ship made free. *SPO*, SP 29/389, ff.100, 101, 30 June 1676.

Passes granted for the following ships during the period included in this volume. *SPO*, SP 30/D, 1 July 1676.

Notes of conditions to be observed in electing Common Council men. *State Papers Online*, SP 29/387 f.141, December 1676.

The Lord Mayor of London to the Aldermen of the several wards. *State Papers Online*, SP 29/387 f.139, 12 December 1676.

268 BIBLIOGRAPHY

Dorothy Thompson to her brother-in-law Major Braman. *State Papers Online*, SP 29 401 f.330, 7 January 1678.

T. B[arnes] to —. *State Papers Online*, SP 29/394 f.241, 3 July 1677.

Edward Nelthorp to Williamson. *SPO*, SP 29/400 f.181, 25 January 1678.

Madam D. Thompson to Madam Braman. *State Papers Online*, SP 29/402 f.223, 30 March 1678.

E. Braman to Madame Thompson. *State Papers Online*, SP 29/402 f.305, 6 April 1678.

James Hickes, senior clerk in the inland Letter Office, to the Duke of York. *SPO*, SP 29/442 f.178, 1678.

Richard Thompson to his brother-in-law Major Braman. *State Papers Online*, 29/417 f.499, 5 February 1681.

Richard Thompson to his brother-in-law, Major Braman. *State Papers Online*, SP 29/416 f.52, 24 June 1681.

The deposition of Joshua Bowes of the parish of St Andrew's Holborn. *SPO*, SP 29/421/1 f.147, 11 November 1682.

The examination and further deposition on oath of Stephen Thompson. *State Papers Online*, SP 29/428 f.298, 13 July 1683.

Edward Thompson to Secretary Jenkins. *SPO*, SP 29/428 f.282, 13 July 1683.

Elizabeth Farringdon to the King. *State Papers Online*, SP 29/429 f.400, July 1683.

Elizabeth Farringdon to the King. *State Papers Online*, SP 29/429 f.401, 1683.

The King to the Deputy Lieutenants of the East Riding of Yorkshire. *State Papers Online*, SP 31/2 f.21, 26 June 1685.

PRINTED PRIMARY SOURCES

1676. *An Answer to Two Letters Concerning the East-India Company*. London [EEBO].

1678. *An Excellent New Ballad Between Tom the Tory, and Toney the Whigg. To the Tune of Shittle-Come-Shite*. London [EEBO].

Barbon, Nicholas. 1690. *A Discourse of Trade*. London [EEBO].

Birch, Thomas. 1757. *The History of the Royal Society of London for Improving of Natural Knowledge, from Its First Rise. In Which the Most Considerable of Those Papers Communicated to the Society, Which Have Hitherto Not Been Published, Are Inserted in Their Proper Order, as a Supplement to the Philosophical Transactions*. London.

Brooke, J. M. S. 1886. *Transcript of the Registers of the United Parishes of St Mary Woolnoth and St Mary Woolchurch Law*. London. Bowles and Sons.

1677. *The Case of Richard Thompson and Company: With Relation to Their Creditors*. London [EEBO].

BIBLIOGRAPHY 269

1685. *The Case of John Hinde Goldsmith with His Creditors Justly Stated*. London [EEBO].

Christie, W. D. 1874. *Letters Addressed from London to Sir Joseph Williamson While Plenipotentiary at the Congress of Cologne in the Years 1673 and 1674*. 2 vols. London. Camden New Series 8–9.

E. S. de Beer. 1978. *The Correspondence of John Locke*, vol. 4: Letters Nos. 1242–1701. Oxford. Clarendon Press.

E. S. de Beer. 1979. *The Correspondence of John Locke*, vol. 5: Letters Nos. 1702–2198. Oxford. Clarendon Press.

E. S. de Beer. 1980. *The Correspondence of John Locke*, vol. 6: Letters Nos. 2199–2664. Oxford. Clarendon Press.

E. S. de Beer. 1981. *The Correspondence of John Locke*, vol. 7: Letters Nos. 2665–3286. Oxford. Clarendon Press.

Covert, Nicholas. 1700. *The Scrivener's Guide Being Choice and Approved Forms of Presidents of All Sorts of Business Now in Use and Practice, in a Much Better Method Than Any Yet Printed, Being Useful for All Gentlemen, but Chiefly for Those Who Practice the Law, viz. Assignments, Articles of Agreement, Acquittances, Bargains and Sale, Bills, Conditions, Copartnerships, Covenants, Deeds, Defeazances, Grants, Joyntures, Indentures, Letters of Attorny, Licenses, Obligations, Provisos, Presidents for Parish Business, Releases, Revocations, Wills, Warrants of Attorny, &c*. London [EEBO].

Defoe, Daniel. 1697. *An Essay Upon Projects*. London.

1758. *The Grants, Concessions, and Original Constitutions of the Province of New-Jersey. The Acts Passed During the Proprietary Governments, and Other Material Transactions Before the Surrender Thereof to Queen Anne*. Philadelphia [ECCO].

Journal of the House of Commons, vol. 9, 1667–1687. British History Online. https://www.british-history.ac.uk/commons-jrnl/vol9.

Knight, R. M. 1640. *Englands Looking In and Out. Presented to the High Court of Parliament Now Assembled*. London [EEBO].

Lambe, Samuel. 1657. *Seasonable Observations Humbly offered to His Highness the Lord Protector*. London [EEBO].

Latham, Robert, and William Matthews. 1971. *The Diary of Samuel Peyps*. Vol. 7. London: Harper Collins.

1878. *The Little London Directory of 1677*. London [ECCO].

London Gazette Database. 24 January 1677. https://www.thegazette.co.uk.

London Gazette Database. 28 January 1677. https://www.thegazette.co.uk.

Malynes, Gerard. 1622. *Consuetudo, vel lex mercatoria, or the ancient law-merchant*. London [EEBO].

Marvell, Andrew. 1677. *An Account of the Growth of Popery and Arbitrary Government in England*. Amsterdam [EEBO].

270 BIBLIOGRAPHY

Marvell, Andrew. 1681. *Miscellaneous Poems by Andrew Marvell Esq.* London [EEBO].

Mun, Thomas. 1664. *England's Treasure by Forraigne Trade. Or The Ballance of Our Forraign Trade Is the Rule of our Treasure.* London [EEBO].

1676. *The Mystery of the New Fashioned Goldsmiths or Bankers. Their Rise, Growth, State, and Decay, Discovered in a Merchant's Letter to a Country Gent, Who Desired to Bind His Son Apprentice to a Goldsmith.* London [EEBO].

1691. *Plain Dealing: In a Dialogue Between Mr. Johnson and Mr. Wary His Friend, a Stock-Jobber, and a Petitioner Against the E-- I-- Company, About Stock-Jobbing, and the Said Company.* London [EEBO].

1876. *Patents for Inventions. Abridgments of Specifications Relating to Grinding Grain and Dressing Flour and Meal, A.D. 1623–1886.* London.

Margoliouth, H. M. 1967. *The Poems and Letters of Andrew Marvell*, vol. 2, 2nd edn. London.

Margoliouth, H. M., Pierre Legouis, and E. E. Duncan-Jones. 1971. *The Poems and Letters of Andrew Marvell*, vol. 2, 3rd edn. Oxford: Clarendon Press.

Petty, William. 1662. *A Treatise of Taxes & Contributions.* London [EEBO].

Popple, William. 1687. *A Rational Catechism, or, An Instructive Conference Between a Father and a Son.* London.

1677/8. *Reasons Most Humbly Offered to the Consideration of Parliament, Why a Bill Now Depending Before Them, Against Richard Thompson and Partners Should Not Be Passed.* London [EEBO].

1677/8. *Reasons Offered by Several of the Creditors of Richard Thompson and Partners, for Stopping All Proceedings Upon the Statute, and for the Speedy Acceptance of Their Proposal of 6s. 8d. per Pound.* London [EEBO].

Robinson, C. J. 1882. *A Register of the Scholars Admitted into Merchant Taylor's School, from A.D. 1562 to 1874*, vol. 1. London.

Royal Commission on Historical Manuscripts. 1912. *Calendar of the Manuscripts of the Marquess of Ormond, K. P. Preserved at Kilkenny Castle*, vol. 3. London.

Royal Commission on Historical Manuscripts. 1912. *Calendar of the Manuscripts of the Marquess of Ormond, K. P. Preserved at Kilkenny Castle*, vol. 4. London.

Sellers, Maud. 1917. *The Acts and Ordinances of the Eastland Company.* York.

Sellers, Maud. 1918. *The York Mercers and Merchant Adventurers, 1356–1917.* London: Surtees Society.

Shaw, William A. 1909. *Calendar of Treasury Books Preserved in the Public Record Office*, vol. 4, *1672–1675.* London: His Majesty's Stationery Office.

Yarranton, Andrew. 1677. *England's Improvement by Sea and Land to Out-Do the Dutch Without Fighting, to Pay Debts Without Moneys, To set at Work all the Poor of England with the Growth of Our Own Lands. To Prevent Unnecessary Suits in Law; With the Benefit of a Voluntary Register. Directions Where Vast Quantities of Timber Are to Be Had for the Building of Ships: With the Advantage of Making the Great Rivers of England Navigable. Rules to Prevent Fires*

in London, and Other Great Cities; With Directions How the Several Compa-
nies of Handicraftsmen in London May Always Have Cheap Bread and Drink.
London [EEBO].

SECONDARY SOURCES

Allen, David. 1976a. Political Clubs in Restoration London. *The Historical Journal* 19: 561–580.
Allen, David. 1976b. The Political Function of Charles II's Chiffinch. *Huntington Library Quarterly* 39: 277–290.
Allison, K. J. 1969. *A History of the County of York East Riding*, vol. 1, *The City of Kingston Upon* Hull. London: Victoria County History.
Allison, K. J. 1974. *A History of the County of York East Riding*, vol. 2, *Dickering Wapentake*. London: Victoria County History.
Allison, K. J. 1976. *A History of the County of York East Riding*, vol. 3, *Ouse, Derwent and Wapentake and Part of Harthill Wapentake*. London: Victoria County History.
Allison, K. J. 1989a. *A History of the County of York East Riding*, vol. 6, *The Borough and Liberties of Beverley*. London: Victoria County History.
Allison, K. J. 1989b. Lists of Officers. In *A History of the County of York East Riding*, vol. 6, *The Borough and Liberties of Beverley*, ed. K. J. Allison, 198–206. London: Victoria County History.
Amussen, Susan D. 2012. Political Economy and Imperial Practice. *The William and Mary Quarterly* 69: 47–50.
Appleby, Joyce. 2011. *The Relentless Revolution: A History of Capitalism*. New York: W. W. Norton & Company.
Ashton, Robert. 1960. *The Crown and the Money Market 1603–1640*. Oxford: Clarendon Press.
Aylmer, G. E. 2002. *The Crown's Servants: Government and Civil Service Under Charles II, 1660–1685*. Oxford: Oxford University Press.
Baker, John H. 1979. The Law Merchant and the Common Law Before 1700. *The Cambridge Law Journal* 38: 295–322.
Baker, John. 2019. *Introduction to English Legal History*, 5th edn. Oxford: Oxford University Press.
Barry, Jonathan, and Christopher Brooks. 1994. *The Middling Sort of People: Culture, Society and Politics in England, 1550–1800*. Basingstoke: The MacMillan Press.
Beaven, A. P. 1908. *The Aldermen of the City of London, Temp. Henry III.-1908: With Notes on the Parliamentary Representation of the City, the Aldermen and the Livery Companies, the Aldermanic Veto, Aldermanic Baronets and Knights, etc*, vol. 2. London: Corporation of the City of London.

272 BIBLIOGRAPHY

Beckert, Sven, and Christine Desan. 2019. *American Capitalism: New Histories*. New York: Columbia University Press.

Bisset, Anna B. 1996. *The Eastland Company York Residence: Register of Admissions to the Freedom 1649–1696*. York: Borthwick Institute Publications.

Blomefield, Francis. 1739. *An Essay Towards a Topographical History of the County of Norfolk*, vol. 1. London: W. Miller.

Bottomley, Sean. 2014. Patent Cases in the Court of Chancery, 1714–58. *The Journal of Legal History* 35: 27–43.

Bourdieu, Pierre. 1985. The Social Space and the Genesis of Groups. *Social Science Information* 24: 195–220.

Bourdieu, Pierre. 1992a. *The Logic of Practice*, trans. Richard Nice. Cambridge: Cambridge University Press.

Bourdieu, Pierre. 1992b. *Language and Symbolic Power*, ed. John B. Thompson, trans. Gino Raymond and Matthew Adamson. Cambridge: Polity Press.

Braddick, Michael J. 2000. *State Formation in Early Modern England c.1550–1700*. Cambridge: Cambridge University Press.

Braddick, Michael J., and John Walter. 2010. Introduction. Grids of Power: Order, Hierarchy and Subordination in Early Modern Society. In *Negotiating Power in Early Modern Society: Order, Hierarchy and Subordination in Britain and Ireland*, eds Michael J. Braddick and John Walter, 1–42. Cambridge: Cambridge University Press.

Brenner, Robert. 1993. *Merchants and Revolution: Commercial Change, Political Conflict, and London's Overseas Traders, 1550–1653*. Cambridge: Cambridge University Press.

Brewer, John. 2010. Microhistory and the Histories of Everyday Life. *Social and Cultural History* 7: 87–109.

Brooks, Christopher W. 1998. *Lawyers, Litigation and English Society Since 1450*. London: Hambledon Press.

Brooks, Christopher W. 2008. *Law, Politics and Society in Early Modern England*. Cambridge: Cambridge University Press.

Brown, Frank E. 1986. Continuity and Change in the Urban House: Developments in Domestic Space Organisation in Seventeenth-Century London. *Comparative Studies in Society and History* 28: 558–590.

Burdon, Pauline. 1982. The Second Mrs Marvell. *Notes and Queries* 227: 33–44.

Burdon, Pauline. 1984. Marvell and His Kindred: The Family Network in the Later Years—I The Alureds. *Notes and Queries* 31: 379–385.

Burdon, Pauline. 1985. Marvell and His Kindred: The Family Network in the Later Years—II Nelthorpes, Thompsons, and Popples. *Notes and Queries* 32: 172–180.

Burke, Peter. 2001a. *New Perspectives on Historical Writing*, 2nd edn. Cambridge: Polity Press.

BIBLIOGRAPHY   273

Burke, Peter. 2001b. History of Events and the Revival of Narrative. In *New Perspectives on Historical Writing*, ed. Peter Burke, 283–300. Cambridge: Polity Press.

Burnard, Trevor, and Giogrio Riello. 2020. Slavery and the New History of Capitalism. *Journal of Global History* 15: 225–244.

Butler, Sara M. 2004. The Law as a Weapon in Marital Disputes: Evidence from the Late Medieval Court of Chancery, 1424–1529. *Journal of British Studies* 43: 291–316.

Carlos, Ann M., and Larry Neal. 2004. Women Investors in Early Capital Markets, 1720–1725. *Financial History Review* 11: 197–224.

Carlos, Ann M., and Stephen Nicholas. 1996. Theory and History: Seventeenth-Century Joint-Stock Chartered Trading Companies. *The Journal of Economic History* 56: 916–924.

Carlos, A. M., E. Fletcher, and L. Neal. 2015. Share Portfolios in the Early Years of Financial Capitalism: London, 1690–1730. *Economic History Review* 68: 574–599.

Carlton, Charles. 1974. *The Court of Orphans*. Leicester: Leicester University Press.

Carruthers, Bruce G. 1996. *City of Capital: Politics and Markets in the English Financial Revolution*. Chichester: Princeton University Press.

Carruthers, Bruce G. 2007. Rules, Institutions, and North's Institutionalism: State and Market in Early Modern England. *European Management Review* 4: 40–53.

Chandaman, C. D. 1975. *The English Public Revenue, 1660–1688*. Oxford: Oxford University Press.

Chapman, Alison A. 2018. The Lay Reader's Guide to *Milton v. Cope*: Trust, Debt, and Loss in Chancery. *Milton Quarterly* 52: 113–127.

Chernaik, Warren L. 1983. *The Poet's Time: Politics and Religion in the Work of Andrew Marvell*. Cambridge: Cambridge University Press.

Christie, W. D. 2005. *A Life of Anthony Ashley Cooper First Earl of Shaftesbury 1667–1683*, vol. 2. Massachusetts: Forgotten Books.

Churches, Christine. 2000. Business at Law: Retrieving Commercial Disputes from Eighteenth-Century Chancery. *The Historical Journal* 43: 937–954.

Cioni, Maria L. 1982. The Elizabethan Chancery and Women's Rights. In *Tudor Rule and Revolution: Essays for G. R. Elton from His American Friends*, eds Delloyd J. Guth and John W. McKenna, 159–182. Cambridge: Cambridge University Press.

Clark, Dorothy. 1938. Edward Backwell as a Royal Agent. *The Economic History Review* 9: 45–55.

Clark, Dorothy. 1971. A Restoration Goldsmith-Banking House: The Vine on Lombard Street. In *Essays in Modern English History: In Honour of Wilbur Cortez Abbott*, 3–47. London: Harvard University Press.

274 BIBLIOGRAPHY

Clay, C. G. A. 1984a. *Economic Expansion and Social Change: England 1500–1700*, vol. 1, *People, Land and Towns*. Cambridge: Cambridge University Press.

Clay, C. G. A. 1984b. *Economic Expansion and Social Change: England 1500–1700*, vol. 2, *Industry, Trade and Government*. Cambridge: Cambridge University Press.

Coates, Ben. 2004. *The Impact of the English Civil War on the Economy of London, 1642–50*. Ashgate: Routledge.

Cockerell, H. A. L., and Edwin Green. 1976. *The British Insurance Business 1547–1970: An Introduction and Guide to Historical Records in the United Kingdom*. London: Heinemann Educational.

Condren, Conal, and A. D. Cousins. 1990. *The Political Identity of Andrew Marvell*. Worcester: Scholar Press.

Dari-Mattiacci, Giuseppe, Oscar Gelderblom, Joost Jonker, and Enrico C. Perotti. 2017. The Emergence of the Corporate Form. *The Journal of Law, Economics, and Organization* 33: 193–236.

Davies, K. G. 1952. Joint-Stock Investment in the Later Seventeenth Century. *The Economic History Review* 3: 283–301.

De Krey, Gary S. 1985. *A Fractured Society: The Politics of London in the First Age of Party 1688–1715*. Oxford: Clarendon Press.

De Krey, Gary S. 1990. London Radicals and Revolutionary Politics, 1675-1683. In *The Politics of Religion in Restoration England*, eds Tim Harris, Paul Seaward, and Mark Goldie, 133–162. Oxford: Oxford University Press.

De Krey, Gary S. 2005. *London and the Restoration 1659–1683*. Cambridge: Cambridge University Press.

de Roover, Raymond. 1948. *The Medici Bank: Its Organization, Management, Operations, and Decline*. New York: New York University Press.

de Roover, Raymond. 1949. *Gresham on Foreign Exchange: An Essay on Early English Mercantilism with the Text of Sir Thomas Gresham's Memorandum for the Understanding of the Exchange*. London: Harvard University Press.

de Roover, Raymond. 1974. *Business, Banking, and Economic Thought in Late Medieval and Early Modern Europe: Selected Studies of Raymond de Roover*. Chicago: The University of Chicago Press.

Desan, Christine. 2008. From Blood to Profit: Making Money in the Practice and Imagery of Early America. *The Journal of Policy History* 20: 26–46.

Desan, Christine. 2015. *Making Money: Coin, Currency, and the Coming of Capitalism*. Oxford: Oxford University Press.

de Vries, Jan. 2008. *The Industrious Revolution: Consumer Behaviour and the Household Economy, 1650 to the Present*. Cambridge: Cambridge University Press.

Dickson, P. G. M. 1967. *The Financial Revolution in England: A Study in the Development of Public Credit 1688–1756*. London: Routledge.

BIBLIOGRAPHY 275

Diprose, John. 1868. *Some Account of the Parish of Saint Clement Danes.* London: Diprose and Bateman.

Dzelzainis, Martin. 2013. Andrew Marvell, Edward Nelthorpe, and the Province of West New Jersey. *Andrew Marvell Newsletter* 5: 20–25.

Dzelzainis, Martin, and Edward Holberton. 2019. *The Oxford Handbook of Andrew Marvell.* Oxford: Oxford University Press.

Earle, Peter. 1991. *The Making of the English Middle Class: Business, Society and Family Life in London, 1660–1730.* London: University of California Press.

Earle, Peter. 1994. The Middling Sort in London. In *The Middling Sort of People: Culture, Society and Politics in England, 1550–1800,* eds Jonathan Barry and Christopher Brooks, 141–158. Basingstoke: The MacMillan Press.

English, Barbara. 1990. *The Great Landowners of East Yorkshire 1530–1910.* Hertfordshire: Harvester Wheatsheaf.

Erickson, Amy Louise. 1990. Common Law Versus Common Practice: The Use of Marriage Settlements in Early Modern England. *Economic History Review* 43: 21–39.

Erickson, Amy Louise. 1993. *Women and Property in Early Modern England.* London: Routledge.

Erikson, Emily. 2008. The Real Network Society. *Historical Methods* 41: 163–166.

Erikson, Emily. 2013. Formalist and Relationalist Theory in Social Network Analysis. *Sociological Theory* 31: 219–242.

Erikson, Emily. 2014. *Between Monopoly and Free Trade: The English East India Company, 1600–1757.* Princeton: Princeton University Press.

Erikson, Emily, and Sampsa Samila. 2015. Social Networks and Port Traffic in Early Modern Overseas Trade. *Social Science History* 39: 151–173.

Everitt, Alan. 1985. *Landscape and Community in England.* London: A&C Black

Ewen, Misha. 2019. Women Investors and the Virginia Company in the Early Seventeenth Century. *The Historical Journal* 62: 853–874.

Farr, David. 1994. Notes and Documents: Oliver Cromwell and a 1647 Case in Chancery. *Historical Research* 71: 341–346.

Feingold, Mordechai. 2017. Projectors and Learned Projects in Early Modern England. *The Seventeenth Century* 32: 63–79.

Field, Jacob F. 2018. *London, Londoners and the Great Fire of 1666: Disaster and Recovery.* Oxford: Routledge.

Fischel, W. J. 1960. The Jewish Merchant-Colony in Madras (Fort St. George) During the 17th and 18th Centuries: A Contribution to the Economic and Social History of the Jews in India. *Journal of the Economic and Social History of the Orient* 3: 78–107.

Flather, Amanda. 2011. Gender, Space, and Place. *Home Cultures* 8: 171–188.

Fontaine, Laurence. 2014. *The Moral Economy: Poverty, Credit, and Trust in Early Modern Europe.* Cambridge: Cambridge University Press.

276 BIBLIOGRAPHY

Forster, G. C. F. 1961. York in the 17th Century. In *A History of Yorkshire: The City of York*, ed. P. M. Tillott, 160–206. London. Victoria County History.

Forster, G. C. F. 1969. Hull in the 16th and 17th Centuries. In *A History of the County of York East Riding*, vol. 1, *The City of Kingston Upon Hull*, ed. K. J. Allison, 90–173. London. Victoria County History.

Forster, G. C. F. 1989. Beverley in the 17th Century. In *A History of the County of York East Riding*, vol. 6, *The Borough and Liberties of Beverley*, ed. K. J. Allison, 89–111. London: Victoria County History.

Foster, Joseph. 1874. *Pedigrees of the County Families of Yorkshire*, vol. 3, *North and East Riding*. London: W. Wilfred Head.

Froide, Amy M. 2017. *Silent Partners: Women as Public Investors During Britain's Financial Revolution, 1690–1750*. Oxford: Oxford University Press.

Gadd, Ian Anders, and Patrick Wallis. 2002. Introduction. In *Guilds, Society and Economy in London 1450–1800*, eds Ian Anders Gadd and Patrick Wallis, 1–14. London: Institute of Historical Research.

Gauci, Perry. 2001. *The Politics of Trade: The Overseas Merchant in State and Society, 1660–1720*. Oxford: Oxford University Press.

Gauci, Perry. 2002. Informality and Influence: The Overseas Merchant and the Livery Companies, 1660–1720. In *Guilds, Society and Economy in London 1450–1800*, eds Ian Anders Gadd and Patrick Wallis, 127–139. London: Institute of Historical Research.

Gauci, Perry. 2007. *Emporium of the World: The Merchants of London 1660–1800*. London: Hambledon Continuum.

Gervais, Pierre. 2017. In Union There Was Strength: The Legal Protection of Eighteenth-Century Merchant Partnerships in England and France. In *Market Ethics and Practices, c. 1300–1850*, eds Simon Middleton and James E. Shaw, 166–183. Oxford: Routledge.

Giffard, Hardinge Goulburn, and Viscount Tiverton. 1914. *The Principles and Practice of Prize Law*. London: Gale.

Ginzburg, Carlo. 1980. *The Cheese and the Worms: The Cosmos of a Sixteenth-Century Miller*, trans. John and Anne Tedeschi. Maryland: The John Hopkins University Press.

Ginzburg, Carlo, and Carlo Poni. 1991. The Name and the Game: Unequal Exchange and the Historiographic Marketplace. In *Microhistory and the Lost Peoples of Europe*, eds Edward Muir and Guido Ruggiero, 1–10. London: The Johns Hopkins University Press.

Glaisyer, Natasha. 2005. "A Due Circulation in the Veins of the Publick": Imagining Credit in Late Seventeenth- and Early Eighteenth-Century England. *The Eighteenth Century* 46: 277–297.

Glaisyer, Natasha. 2006. *The Culture of Commerce in England, 1660–1720*. London: Boydell & Brewer.

BIBLIOGRAPHY 277

Goldie, Mark. 1990. Danby, the Bishops and the Whigs. In *The Politics of Religion in Restoration England*, eds Tim Harris, Paul Seaward, and Mark Goldie, 75–105. Oxford: Oxford University Press.

Goldie, Mark. 2001. The Unacknowledged Republic: Officeholding in Early Modern England. In *The Politics of the Excluded, c.1500–1850*, ed. Tim Harris, 153–194. Basingstoke: The MacMillan Press.

Grafe, Regina, and Oscar Gelderblom. 2010. The Rise and Fall of the Merchant Guilds: Re-Thinking the Comparative Study of Commercial Institutions in Premodern Europe. *The Journal of Interdisciplinary History* 40: 477–511.

Graham, Aaron. 2016. Military Contractors and the Money Markets, 1700–15. In *The British Fiscal-Military States 1660-c.1783*, eds Aaron Graham and Patrick Walsh, 83–112. London: Routledge.

Graham, Aaron. 2019. Credit, Confidence, and the Circulation of Exchequer Bills in the Early Financial Revolution. *Financial History Review* 26: 63–80.

Grassby, Richard. 1995. *The Business Community of Seventeenth-Century England*. Cambridge: Cambridge University Press.

Grassby, Richard. 2001. *Kinship and Capitalism: Marriage, Family, and Business in the English-Speaking World, 1580–1740*. Cambridge: Cambridge University Press.

Greaves, Robert L. 1990. *Enemies Under His Feet: Radicals and Nonconformists in Britain, 1664–1677*. Stanford: Stanford University Press.

Greif, Avner. 1998. Historical and Comparative Institutional Analysis. *The American Economic Review* 88: 80–84.

Grenfell, Michael James. 2014. *Pierre Bourdieu: Key Concepts*, 2nd edn. Oxford: Routledge.

Griffiths, Paul, Adam Fox, and Steve Hindle. 1996. *The Experience of Authority in Early Modern England*. Basingstoke: The MacMillan Press.

Häberlein, Mark. 2012. *The Fuggers of Augsburg: Pursuing Wealth and Honour in Renaissance Germany*. Virginia: University of Virginia Press.

Hadfield, Andrew, and Simon Healy. 2012. Edmund Spenser and Chancery in 1597. *Law and Humanities* 6: 57–64.

Halasz, Alexandra. 1997. *The Marketplace of Print: Pamphlets and the Public Sphere in Early Modern England*. Cambridge: Cambridge University Press.

Haley, K. H. D. 1968. *The First Earl of Shaftesbury*. Oxford: Oxford University Press.

Hancock, David. 1995. *Citizens of the World: London Merchants and the Integration of the British Atlantic Community, 1735–1785*. Cambridge: Cambridge University Press.

Hancock, David. 2005. The Trouble with Networks: Managing the Scots' Early-Modern Madeira Trade. *The Business History Review* 79: 467–491.

278 BIBLIOGRAPHY

Harris, Tim. 1990a. Introduction: Revising the Restoration. In *The Politics of Religion in Restoration England*, eds Tim Harris, Paul Seaward, and Mark Goldie, 1–28. Oxford: Oxford University Press.

Harris, Tim. 1990b. "Lives, Liberties and Estates": Rhetorics of Liberty in the Reign of Charles II. In *The Politics of Religion in Restoration England*, eds Tim Harris, Paul Seaward, and Mark Goldie, 217–241. Oxford: Oxford University Press.

Harris, Tim. 1993. *Politics Under the Later Stuarts: Party Conflict in a Divided Society 1660–1715*. London: Routledge.

Harris, Tim, Paul Seaward, and Mark Goldie. 1990. *The Politics of Religion in Restoration England*. Oxford: Oxford University Press.

Hawkes, Emma. 2000. "[S]he Will … Protect and Defend Her Rights Boldly by Law and Reason …": Women's Knowledge of Common Law and Equity Courts in Late-Medieval England. In *Medieval Women and the Law*, ed. Noel James Menuge, 145–161. Woodbridge: Boydell Press.

Hirst, Derek, and Stephen N. Zwicker. 2011. *The Cambridge Companion to Andrew Marvell*. Cambridge: Cambridge University Press.

1932. *Hoare's Bank: A Record 1673–1932*. London: Private.

Hofri-Winogradow, Adam. 2012. Parents, Children and Property in Late 18th-Century Chancery. *Oxford Journal of Legal Studies* 32: 741–769.

Holderness, B. A. 1984. Widows in Pre-Industrial Society: An Essay Upon Their Economic Functions. In *Land, Kinship and Life-Cycle*, ed. R. M. Smith, 423–442. Cambridge: Cambridge University Press.

Hoppit, Julian. 1987. *Risk and Failure in English Business 1700–1800*. Cambridge: Cambridge University Press.

Horsefield, J. Keith. 1960. *British Monetary Experiments 1650–1710*. Cambridge: Harvard University Press.

Horsefield, J. Keith. 1982. The "Stop of the Exchequer" Revisited. *The Economic History Review* 35: 511–528.

Horwitz, Henry. 1995. *Chancery Equity Records and Proceedings 1600–1800: A Guide to Documents in the Public Record Office*. London: Stationery Office Books.

Horwitz, Henry. 1997. Record-Keepers in the Court of Chancery and Their "Record" of Accomplishment in the Seventeenth and Eighteenth Centuries. *Historical Research* 70: 34–51.

Horwitz, Henry, and Patrick Polden. 1996. Continuity or Change in the Court of in the Seventeenth and Eighteenth Centuries? *Journal of British Studies* 35: 24–57.

Hubbard, Eleanor. 2012. *City Women: Money, Sex, and the Social Order in Early Modern London*. Oxford: Oxford University Press.

Hudson, Pat. 2014. Slavery, the Slave Trade and Economic Growth: A Contribution to the Debate. In *Emancipation and the Making of the British Imperial*

BIBLIOGRAPHY 279

World, eds Catherine Hall, Nicholas Draper, and Keith McClelland, 36–59. Manchester: Manchester University Press.

Hunt, Edward S. 1994. *The Medieval Super Companies: A Study of the Peruzzi Company of Florence*. Cambridge: Cambridge University Press.

Hunter, Pamela. 2012. *Through the Years: Tales from the Hoare's Bank Archive*. London: Constable and Robinson.

Innes, Joanna. 1983. The King's Bench Prison in the Later Eighteenth Century. In *An Ungovernable People: The English and Their Law in the Seventeenth and Eighteenth Centuries*, eds John Brewer and John Styles, 250–298. London: Rutgers University Press.

Jones, J. R. 1956. The Green Ribbon Club. *Durham University Journal* 49: 17–20.

Jones, J. R. 1961. *The First Whigs: The Politics of the Exclusion Crisis 1678–1683*. London: Oxford University Press.

Jones, W. J. 1979. The Foundations of English Bankruptcy: Statutes and Commissions in the Early Modern Period. *Transactions of the American Philosophical Society* 69: 1–63.

Jones, J. R. 1996. *The Anglo-Dutch Wars of the Seventeenth Century*. Essex: Routledge.

Kadens, Emily. 2010. The Pitkin Affair: A Study of Fraud in Early English Bankruptcy. *American Bankruptcy Law Journal* 84: 483–570.

Kadens, Emily. 2015. Pre-Modern Credit Networks and the Limits of Reputation. *Iowa Law Review* 100: 1–21.

Kamerick, Kathleen. 2013. Tanglost of Wales: Magic and Adultery in the Court of Chancery circa 1500. *The Sixteenth Century Journal* 44: 25–45.

Kavanagh, Art. 2013. Andrew Marvell "In Want of Money": The Evidence in John Farrington v. Mary Marvell. *The Seventeenth Century* 17: 206–212.

Kerridge, Eric. 1988. *Trade and Banking in Early Modern England*. Manchester: Manchester University Press.

Kim, Jongchul. 2011. How Modern Banking Originated: The London Goldsmith-Bankers' Institutionalisation of Trust. *Business History* 53: 939–959.

Kim, Jongchul. 2013. How Politics Shaped Modern Banking in Early Modern England: Rethinking the Nature of Representative Democracy, Public Debt, and Modern Banking. *Max-Planck-Institut für Gesellschaftsforschung. Discussion Papers*. 1–23

Klinck, Dennis R. 2010. *Conscience, Equity and the Court of Chancery in Early Modern England*. Ashgate: Routledge.

Knights, Mark. 2005. *Representation and Misrepresentation in Later Stuart Britain: Partisanship and Political Culture*. Oxford: Oxford University Press.

280 BIBLIOGRAPHY

Lacey, Douglas R. 1969. *Dissent and Parliamentary Politics in England, 1661–1689: A Study in the Perpetuation and Tempering of Parliamentarianism.* New Brunswick: Rutgers University Press.

Lane, Frederic C. 1937. Venetian Bankers, 1496–1533: A Study in the Early Stages of Deposit Banking. *Journal of Political Economy* 45: 187–206.

Laurence, Anne. 2008. The Emergence of a Private Clientele for Banks in the Early Eighteenth Century: Hoare's Bank and Some Women Customers. *The Economic History Review* 61: 565–586.

Leng, Thomas. 2016. Interlopers and Disorderly Brethren at the Stade Mart: Commercial Regulations and Practices Amongst the Merchant Adventurers of England in the Late Elizabethan Period. *The Economic History Review* 69: 823–843.

Leng, Thomas. 2020. *Fellowship and Freedom: The Merchant Adventurers and the Restructuring of English Commerce, 1582–1700.* Oxford: Oxford University Press.

Leunig, Tim, Chris Minns, and Patrick Wallis. 2011. Networks in the Premodern Economy: The Market for London Apprenticeships, 1600–1749. *The Journal of Economic History* 71: 413–443.

Levi, Giovanni. 2001. On Microhistory. In *New Perspectives on Historical Writing*, 2nd edn, ed. Peter Burke, 97–119. Cambridge: Polity Press.

Lyon Turner, G. 1911. *Original Records of Early Non-Conformity Under Persecution and Indulgence*, vol. 2. London: T. Fisher Unwin.

Magnússon, Sigurdur Gylfi, and István M. Szijártó. 2013. *What Is Microhistory? Theory and Practice.* Oxford: Routledge.

Marshall, Alan. 1994. *Intelligence and Espionage in the Reign of Charles II, 1660–1685.* Cambridge: Cambridge University Press.

Marshall, Alan. 1996. Sir Joseph Williamson and the Conduct of Administration in Restoration England. *Historical Research* 69: 18–41.

Mathias, Peter. 2000. Risk, Credit and Kinship in Early Modern Enterprise. In *The Early Modern Atlantic Economy*, eds John J. McCusker and Kenneth Morgan, 15–35. Cambridge: Cambridge University Press.

McGowen, Randall. 1998. Knowing the Hand: Forgery and the Proof of Writing in Eighteenth-Century England. *Historical Reflections* 24: 385–414.

Melton, Frank T. 1986. *Sir Robert Clayton and the Origins of English Deposit Banking, 1658–1685.* Cambridge: Cambridge University Press.

Mitchell, David. 1995. Innovation and the Transfer of Skill in the Goldsmiths' Trade in Restoration London. In *Goldsmiths, Silversmiths and Bankers: Innovation and the Transfer of Skill, 1550 to 1750*, ed. David Mitchell, 5–22. London: Sutton Publishing.

Mitson, Anne. 1993. The Significance of Kinship Networks in the Seventeenth Century: South-West Nottinghamshire. In *Societies, Cultures and Kinship 1580–1850*, ed. C. Phythian-Adams. Leicester: Leicester University Press.

BIBLIOGRAPHY 281

Muir, Edward. 1991. Introduction: Observing Trifles. In *Microhistory and the Lost Peoples of Europe*, eds Edward Muir and Guido Ruggiero, vii–xxviii. London: The Johns Hopkins University Press.

Muir, Edward, and Guido Ruggiero. 1991. *Microhistory and the Lost Peoples of Europe*. London: The Johns Hopkins University Press.

Muldrew, Craig. 1998. *The Economy of Obligation: The Culture of Credit and Social Relations in Early Modern England*. Basingstoke: Palgrave Macmillan.

Muldrew, Craig. 2001. "Hard Food for Midas": Cash and Its Social Value in Early Modern England. *Past & Present* 170: 78–120.

Muldrew, Craig. 2003. "A Mutual Assent of Her Mind"? Women, Debt, Litigation and Contract in Early Modern England. *History Workshop Journal* 55: 47–71.

Murphy, Anne L. 2005. Lotteries in the 1690s: Investment or Gamble? *Financial History Review* 12: 227–246.

Murphy, Anne L. 2006. Dealing with Uncertainty: Managing Personal Investment in the Early English National Debt. *History* 91: 200–217.

Murphy, Anne L. 2009a. *The Origins of English Financial Markets: Investment and Speculation Before the South Sea Bubble*. Cambridge: Cambridge University Press.

Murphy, Anne L. 2009b. Trading Options Before Black-Scholes: A Study of the Market in Late Seventeenth-Century London. *The Economic History Review* 62: 8–30.

Murphy, Anne L. 2013. Demanding "Credible Commitment": Public Reactions to the Failures of the Early Financial Revolution. *The Economic History Review* 66: 178–197.

Murphy, Anne L. 2019. Performing Public Credit at the Eighteenth-Century Bank of England. *Journal of British Studies* 58: 58–78.

Musa, Shavana. 2015. Tides and Tribulations: English Prize Law and the Law of Nations in the Seventeenth Century. *Journal of the History of International Law* 17: 47–82.

Namier, Sir Lewis. 1960. *The Structure of Politics at the Accession of George III*, 2nd edn. London: MacMillan.

Neal, Larry, and Stephen Quinn. 2001. Networks of Information, Markets, and Institutions in the Rise of London as a Financial Centre, 1660–1720. *Financial History Review* 8: 7–26.

North, Douglass C., and Barry R. Weingast. 1989. Constitutions and Commitments: The Evolution of Institutions Governing Public Choice in Seventeenth-Century England. *The Journal of Economic History* 49: 803–832.

Ogborn, Miles. 2007. *Indian Ink: Script and Print in the Making of the English East India Company*. London: University of Chicago Press.

Ogilvie, Sheilagh. 2011. *Institutions and European Trade: Merchant Guilds, 1000–1800*. Cambridge: Cambridge University Press.

282 BIBLIOGRAPHY

Ormrod, David. 2003. *The Rise of Commercial Empires: England and the Netherlands in the Age of Mercantilism, 1650–1770*. Cambridge: Cambridge University Press.

Patterson, Annabelle. 1990. Miscellaneous Marvell. In *The Political Identity of Andrew Marvell*, eds Conal Condren and A. D. Cousins, 189–208. Aldershot: Scolar Press.

Peltonen, Marku. 2005. Politeness and Whiggism, 1688–1732. *The Historical Journal* 48: 391–414.

Peltonen, Matti. 2001. Clues, Margins, and Monads: The Micro-Macro Link in Historical Research. *History and Theory* 40: 347–359.

Pettigrew, William. 2013. *Freedom's Debt: The Royal African Company and the Politics of the Atlantic Slave Trade, 1672–1752*. Chapel Hill: University of North Carolina Press.

Pincus, Steven C. A. 1995. From Butterboxes to Wooden Shoes: The Shift in English Popular Sentiment from Anti-Dutch to Anti-French in the 1670s. *The Historical Journal* 38: 333–361.

Pincus, Steven C. A. 1996. *Protestantism and Patriotism: Ideologies and the Making of English Foreign Policy, 1650–1668*. Cambridge: Cambridge University Press.

Priestley, Margaret. 1956. London Merchants and Opposition Politics in Charles II's Reign. *The Bulletin of the Institute of Historical Research* 29: 205–219.

Purdy, J. D. 1974. Kilham. In *A History of the County of York East Riding*, vol. 2, *Dickering Wapentake*, ed. K. J. Allison, 247–263. London: Victoria County History.

Quilter, Matthew. 2004. Daniel Defoe: Bankrupt and Bankruptcy Reformer. *The Journal of Legal History* 25: 53–73.

Quinn, Stephen. 1997. Goldsmith-Banking: Mutual Acceptance and Interbanker Clearing in Restoration London. *Explorations in Economic History* 34: 411–432.

Quinn, Stephen, and William Roberds. 2007. The Bank of Amsterdam and the Leap to Central Bank Money. *American Economic Review* 97: 1–48.

Rabb, Theodore K. 1966. Investment in English Overseas Enterprise, 1575–1630. *The Economic History Review* 19: 70–81.

Raymond, Joad. 2003. *Pamphlets and Pamphleteering in Early Modern Britain*. Cambridge: Cambridge University Press.

Raynes, Harold E. 1948. *A History of British Insurance*. London: Sir Isaac Pitman & Sons.

Razzell, Peter, and Christine Spence. 2007. The History of Infant, Child and Adult Mortality in London, 1550–1850. *The London Journal* 32: 271–292.

Richards, R. D. 1927. The Evolution of Paper Money in England. *The Quarterly Journal of Economics* 41: 361–404.

BIBLIOGRAPHY   283

Richards, R. D. 1928. A Pre-Bank of England English Banker—Edward Backwell. Reprinted from *The Economic Journal* 38, Supplement No. 3: 335–355.

Richards, R. D. 1929. *The Early History of Banking in England*. London: Routledge.

Robbins, Caroline. 1967. Absolute Liberty: The Life and Thought of William Popple, 1638–1708. *The William and Mary Quarterly* 24: 190–223.

Rommelse, G. 2010. The Role of Mercantilism in Anglo-Dutch Political Relations, 1650–74. *Economic History Review* 63: 591–611.

Roseveare, Henry. 1987. *Markets and Merchants of the Late Seventeenth Century: The Marescoe-David Letters, 1668–1680*. Oxford: Oxford University Press.

Roseveare, Henry. 1991. *The Financial Revolution 1660–1760*. London: Longman.

Ruggiero, Guido. 2001. The Strange Death of Margarita Marcellini: *Male*, Signs, and the Everyday World of Pre-Modern Medicine. *The American Historical Review* 106: 1141–1158.

Safley, Thomas Max. 2013. *The History of Bankruptcy: Economic, Social and Cultural Implications in Early Modern Europe*. New York: Routledge.

Samuel, Edgar. 2002. Diamonds and Pieces of Eight: How Stuart England Won the Rough-Diamond Trade. *Jewish Historical Studies* 38: 23–40.

Scala, Gail Ewald. 1974. An Index of Proper Names in Thomas Birch, "The History of the Royal Society" (London, 1756–1757). *Notes and Records of the Royal Society of London* 28: 263–392.

Scammell, G. V. 1972. Shipowning in the Economy and Politics of Early Modern England. *The Historical Journal* 15: 385–407.

Scott, Jonathan. 1990. England's Trouble: Exhuming the Popish Plot. In *The Politics of Religion in Restoration England*, eds Tim Harris, Paul Seaward, and Mark Goldie, 107–131. Oxford: Oxford University press.

Scott, W. R. 1968. *The Constitution and Finance of English, Scottish and Irish Joint-Stock Companies to 1720*, vol. 1. Cambridge: Cambridge University Press.

Sgard, J. 2013. Bankruptcy, Fresh Start and Debt Renegotiation in England and France (17th to 18th Century). In *The History of Bankruptcy: Economic, Social and Cultural Implications in Early Modern Europe*, ed. Thomas Max Safley, 223–235. New York: Routledge.

Shepard, Alexandra. 2000. Manhood, Credit and Patriarchy in Early Modern England c. 1580–1640. *Past & Present* 167: 75–106.

Shepard, Alexandra. 2003. *Meanings of Manhood in Early Modern England*. Oxford: Oxford University Press.

Shepard, Alexandra. 2005. From Anxious Patriarchs to Refined Gentlemen? Manhood in Britain, circa 1500–1700. *Journal of British Studies* 44: 281–295.

Shepard, Alexandra. 2015a. *Accounting for Oneself: Worth, Status, and the Social Order in Early Modern England*. Oxford: Oxford University Press.

284 BIBLIOGRAPHY

Shepard, Alexandra. 2015b. Minding Their Own Business: Married Women and Credit in Early Eighteenth-Century London. *Transactions of the Royal Historical Society* 25: 53–74.

Slack, Paul. 2015. *The Invention of Improvement: Information and Material Progress in Seventeenth-Century England*. Oxford: Oxford University Press.

Smith, Edmond. 2018. The Global Interests of London's Commercial Community, 1599–1625: Investment in the East India Company. *The Economic History* Review 71: 1118–1146.

Smith, Nigel. 2011. How to Make a Biography of Andrew Marvell. In *The Cambridge Companion to Andrew Marvell*, eds Derek Hirst and Steven N. Zwicker, 194–219. Cambridge: Cambridge University Press.

Smith, Nigel. 2012. *Andrew Marvell: The Chameleon*. Hampshire: Yale University Press.

Snarr, Hal W. 2014. *Learning Macroeconomic Principles Using MAPLE*. New York: Business Expert Press.

Spicksley, Judith. 2007. "Fly with a Duck in thy Mouth": Single Women as Sources of Credit in Seventeenth-Century England. *Social History* 32: 187–207.

Spicksley, Judith. 2008. Usury Legislation, Cash, and Credit: The Development of the Female Investor in the Late Tudor and Stuart Periods. *The Economic History Review* 61: 277–301.

Spurr, John. 2008. Later Stuart Puritanism. In *The Cambridge Companion to Puritanism*, eds John Coffey and Paul C. H. Lim, 89–106. Cambridge: Cambridge University Press.

Spurr, John. 2011a. *Anthony Ashley Cooper, First Earl of Shaftesbury 1621–1683*. Surrey: Routledge.

Spurr, John. 2011b. Shaftesbury and the Politics of Religion. In *Anthony Ashley Cooper, First Earl of Shaftesbury 1621–1683*, ed. John Spurr, 127–151. Surrey: Routledge.

Stern, Phillip J. 2007. Politics and Ideology in the Early East India Company-State: The Case of St Helena, 1673–1709. *The Journal of Imperial and Commonwealth History* 35: 1–23.

Stern, Phillip J. 2011. *The Company State: Corporate Sovereignty and the Early Modern Foundations of the British Empire in India*. Oxford: Oxford University Press.

Stern, Phillip J., and Carl Wennerlind. 2014a. *Mercantilism Reimagined: Political Economy in Early Modern Britain and Its Empire*. Oxford: Oxford University Press.

Stern, Phillip J., and Carl Wennerlind. 2014b. Introduction. In *Mercantilism Reimagined: Political Economy in Early Modern Britain and Its Empire*, eds Phillip J. Stern and Carl Wennerlind, 3–22. Oxford: Oxford University Press.

BIBLIOGRAPHY 285

Stern, Phillip J. 2014. Companies: Monopoly, Sovereignty, and the East Indies. In *Mercantilism Reimagined: Political Economy in Early Modern Britain and Its Empire*, eds Phillip J. Stern and Carl Wennerlind, 177–195. Oxford: Oxford University Press.

Stobart, Jon, Andrew Haan, and Victoria Morgan. 2007. *Spaces of Consumption: Leisure and Shopping in the English Town, c. 1680–1830*. Oxford: Routledge.

Szijártó, István M. 2017. Probing the Limits of Microhistory. *Journal of Medieval and Early Modern Studies* 47: 193–198.

Tadmor, Naomi. 1996. The Concept of the Household-Family in Eighteenth-Century England. *Past & Present* 151: 111–140.

Tadmor, Naomi. 2001. *Family and Friends in Eighteenth-Century England: Household, Kinship, and Patronage*. Cambridge: Cambridge University Press.

Temin, Peter, and Hans Joachim Voth. 2005. Credit Rationing and Crowding Out During the Industrial Revolution: Evidence from Hoare's Bank, 1702–1862. *Explorations in Economic History* 42: 325–348.

Temin, Peter, and Hans Joachim Voth. 2006. Banking as an Emerging Technology: Hoare's Bank, 1702–1742. *Financial History Review* 13: 149–178.

Temin, Peter, and Hans Joachim Voth. 2008. Private Borrowing During the Financial Revolution: Hoare's Bank and Its Customers 1702–24. *Economic History Review* 61: 541–564.

Temin, Peter, and Hans Joachim Voth. 2013. *Prometheus Shackled: Goldsmith Banks and England's Financial Revolution After 1700*. Oxford: Oxford University Press.

Thirsk, Joan. 1978. *Economic Policy and Projects: The Development of a Consumer Society in Early Modern England*. Oxford: Oxford University Press.

Thompson, John B. 1992. Editor's Introduction. In Pierre Bourdieu, *Language and Symbolic Power*, ed. John B. Thompson, trans. Gino Raymond and Matthew Adamson, 1–31. Cambridge: Cambridge University Press.

Thomson, Patricia. 2014. Field. In *Pierre Bourdieu: Key Concepts*, ed. Michael James Grenfell, 65–80. Oxford: Routledge.

Tillott, P. M. 1961. *A History of Yorkshire: The City of York*. London: Victoria County History.

Todd, Barbara J. 2014. Fiscal Citizens: Female Investors in Public Finance Before the South Sea Bubble. In *Challenging Orthodoxies: The Social and Cultural Worlds of Early Modern Women*, eds Melinda S. Zook and Sigrun Haude, 53–74. Ashgate: Routledge.

Trivellato, Francesca. 2020. Renaissance Florence and the Origins of Capitalism: A Business History of Perspective. *Business History Review* 94: 229–251.

Tucker, P. 2000. The Early History of the Court of Chancery: A Comparative Study. *The English Historical Review* 115: 791–811.

Tupper, Fred S. 1938. Mary Palmer, Alias Mrs. Andrew Marvell. *Modern Language Association* 53: 367–392.

286 BIBLIOGRAPHY

Turner, Henry S. 2014. Corporations: Humanism and Elizabethan Political Economy. In *Mercantilism Reimagined: Political Economy in Early Modern Britain and its Empire*, eds Phillip J. Stern and Carl Wennerlind, 153–176. Oxford: Oxford University Press.

Van Hoftstraeten, Bram. 2016. The Organization of Mercantile Capitalism in the Low Countries: Private Partnerships in Early Modern Antwerp (1480–1620). *TSEG* 13: 1–24.

Voitle, R. 1984. *The Third Earl of Shaftesbury, 1671–1713*. London: Louisiana State University Press.

von Maltzahn, Nicholas. 2003. Andrew Marvell and the Lord Wharton. *The Seventeenth Century* 18: 252–265.

von Maltzhan, Nicholas. 2005. *An Andrew Marvell Chronology*. Basingstoke: Palgrave Macmillan.

von Maltzahn, Nicholas. 2019. Marvell, Writer and Politician, 1621–1678. In *The Oxford Handbook of Andrew Marvell*, eds Martin Dzelzainis and Edward Holberton, 3–25. Oxford: Oxford University Press.

von Maltzahn, Nicholas, and Rory Tanner. 2012. Marvell's "Maniban" in Manuscript. *The Review of English Studies* 63: 764–778.

Wall, L. N. 1959. Marvell's Friends in the City. *Notes and Queries* 6: 204–207.

Wallis, Patrick. 2008. Consumption, Retailing, and Medicine in Early-Modern London. *The Economic History Review* 61: 26–53.

Walsh, Claire. 1995. Shop Design and the Display of Goods in Eighteenth-Century London. *Journal of Design History* 8: 157–176.

Weiser, Brian. 2003. *Charles II and the Politics of Access*. Suffolk: Boydell Press.

Wennerlind, Carl. 2011. *Casualties of Credit: The English Financial Revolution, 1620–1720*. Cambridge: Cambridge University Press.

Whyman, Susan E. 1997. Land and Trade Revisited: The Case of John Verney, London Merchant and Baronet, 1660–1720. *The London Journal* 22: 16–32.

Whyman, Susan E. 1999. *Sociability and Power in Late-Stuart England: The Cultural Worlds of the Verneys 1660–1720*. Oxford: Oxford University Press.

Winter, Mabel. 2020. The Collapse of Thompson and Company: Credit, Reputation, and Risk in Early Modern England. *Social History* 45: 145–166.

Withington, Phil. 2001. Views from the Bridge: Revolution and Restoration in Seventeenth-Century York. *Past & Present* 170: 121–151.

Withington, Phil. 2005. *The Politics of Commonwealth: Citizens and Freemen in Early Modern England*. Cambridge: Cambridge University Press.

Withington, Phil. 2007. Company and Sociability in Early Modern England. *Social History* 32: 291–307.

Withington, Phil. 2008. Citizens, Soldiers and Urban Culture in Restoration England. *The English Historical Review* 123: 587–610.

Withington, Phil. 2010. *Society in Early Modern England: The Vernacular Origins of Some Powerful Ideas*. Cambridge: Polity Press.

BIBLIOGRAPHY 287

Withington, Phil. 2011. Andrew Marvell's Citizenship. In *The Cambridge Companion to Andrew Marvell*, eds Derek Hirst and Steven N. Zwicker, 102–121. Cambridge: Cambridge University Press.

Wood, Alfred C. 1935. *A History of the Levant Company*. Oxford: Oxford University Press.

Woodhead, J. R. 1965. *The Rulers of London 1660–1689*. London: London & Middlesex Archaeological Society.

Woolfe, Maurice. 1970–1973. Foreign Trade of London Jews in the Seventeenth Century. *Transactions & Miscellanies (Jewish Historical Society of England)* 24: 38–58.

Wrightson, Keith. 2000. *Earthly Necessities: Economic Lives in Early Modern Britain*. London: Yale University Press.

Wrightson, Keith. 2004. *English Society 1580–1680*. London: Routledge.

Wrightson, Keith. 2005. Mutualities and Obligations: Changing Social Relationships in Early Modern England. *Proceedings of the British Academy* 139: 157–194.

Wrightson, Keith. 2011. *Ralph Tailor's Summer: A Scrivener, His City and the Plague*. New Haven: Yale University Press.

Yamamoto, Koji. 2018. *Taming Capitalism Before Its Triumph: Public Service, Distrust, and 'Projecting' in Early Modern England*. Oxford: Oxford University Press.

Yamamoto, Koji. 2011. Piety, Profit and Public Service in the Financial Revolution. *English Historical Review* 126: 806–834.

Zahedieh, Nuala. 2010. *The Capital and the Colonies: London and the Atlantic Economy, 1660–1700*. Cambridge: Cambridge University Press.

Zahedieh, Nuala. 2013. Colonies, Copper, and the Market for Inventive Activity in England and Wales, 1680–1730. *Economic History Review* 66: 805–825.

Internet Sources

History of Parliament

Bolton, P. A., and Basil Duke Henning. RAMSDEN, William (c.1618–80), of Hull, Yorks. *The History of Parliament: British Political, Social & Local History*, http://www.historyofparliamentonline.org/volume/1660-1690/member/ramsden-william-1618-80 [accessed 12 February 2018].

Bolton, P. A., and Paula Watson. INGRAM, Sir Thomas (1614–72), of Sheriff Hutton, Yorks and Isleworth, Mdx. *The History of Parliament: British Political, Social & Local History*, http://www.historyofparliamentonline.org/volume/1660-1690/member/ingram-sir-thomas-1614-72 [accessed 20 July 2018].

288 BIBLIOGRAPHY

Bolton, P. A., and Paula Watson. THOMPSON, Francis (c.1655–93), of Humbleton, Yorks. *The History of Parliament: British Political, Social & Local History*, http://www.historyofparliamentonline.org/volume/1660-1690/member/thompson-francis-1655-93 [accessed 13 May 2020].

Bolton, P. A., and Paula Watson. THOMPSON, William (1629–92), of Scarborough, Yorks. *The History of Parliament: British Political, Social & Local History*, http://www.historyofparliamentonline.org/volume/1660-1690/member/thompson-william-1629-92 [accessed 13 May 2020].

Crook, B. M. FARRINGTON (FARINGTON), Richard (c.1644–1719), of South Street, Chichester, Suss. *The History of Parliament: British Political, Social & Local History*, http://www.historyofparliamentonline.org/volume/1660-1690/member/farrington-%28farington%29-richard-1644-1719 [accessed 16 July 2019].

Cruickshanks, Eveline. THOMPSON, Edward (c.1639–1701), of York. *The History of Parliament: British Political, Social & Local History*, http://www.historyofparliamentonline.org/volume/1660-1690/member/thompson-edward-1639-1701 [accessed 31 May 2019].

Cruickshanks, Eveline. THOMPSON, Sir Henry (c.1625–83), of York and Marston, Yorks. *The History of Parliament: British Political, Social & Local History*, http://www.historyofparliamentonline.org/volume/1660-1690/member/thompson-sir-henry-1625-83 [accessed 13 June 2019].

Cruickshanks, Eveline, and Richard Harrison. COTTON, Sir Robert (1644–1717), of Hatley St. George, Cambs. *The History of Parliament: British Political, Social & Local History*, http://www.historyofparliamentonline.org/volume/1690-1715/member/cotton-sir-robert-1644-1717 [accessed 18 May 2020].

Cruickshanks, Eveline, and Richard Harrison. COTTON, Sir Robert, 1st Bt. (c.1635–1712), of Combermere, Cheshire. *The History of Parliament: British Political, Social & Local History*, http://www.historyofparliamentonline.org/volume/1690-1715/member/cotton-sir-robert-1635-1712 [accessed 18 May 2020].

Edwards, E. R. COWPER, Sir William, 2nd Bt. (1639–1706), of The Castle, Hertford. *The History of Parliament: British Political, Social & Local History*, http://www.historyofparliamentonline.org/volume/1660-1690/member/cowper-sir-william-1639-1706 [accessed 31 May 2019].

Edwards, E. R., and Geoffrey Jaggar. KEATE, Sir Jonathan, 1st Bt. (1633–1700), of The Hoo, Kimpton, Herts. *The History of Parliament: British Political, Social & Local History*, http://www.historyofparliamentonline.org/volume/1660-1690/member/keate-sir-jonathan-1633-1700 [accessed 12 February 2018].

BIBLIOGRAPHY 289

Ferris, John P. GORE, Sir John (1621–97), of Sacombe, Herts. *The History of Parliament: British Political, Social & Local History*, http://www.historyof parliamentonline.org/volume/1660-1690/member/gore-sir-john-1621-97 [accessed 27 June 2018].

Gauci, Perry. TURNER, Sir William (1615–93), of St. Paul's Churchyard, London. *The History of Parliament: British Political, Social & Local History*, http://www.historyofparliamentonline.org/volume/1690-1715/member/ turner-sir-william-1615-93 [accessed 12 February 2018].

Helms, M. W., and B. M. Crook. FARRINGTON, John (c.1609–80), of Chichester, Suss. *The History of Parliament: British Political, Social & Local History*, http://www.historyofparliamentonline.org/volume/ 1660-1690/member/farrington-john-1609-80 [accessed 26 June 2019].

Helms, M. W., and Eveline Cruickshanks. BULLER, Francis (1630–82), of Shillingham, nr. Saltash, Cornw.; the Middle Temple and Isleham, Cambs. *The History of Parliament: British Political, Social & Local History*, http:// www.historyofparliamentonline.org/volume/1660-1690/member/buller-fra ncis-1630-82 [accessed 18 May 2020].

Helms, M. W., and John P. Ferris. MARVELL, Andrew (1621–78), of Highgate Hill, Mdx. and Maiden Lane, Covent Garden, Westminster. *The History of Parliament: British Political, Social & Local History*, http://www.histor yofparliamentonline.org/volume/1660-1690/member/marvell-andrew-162 1-78 [accessed 13 June 2019].

Helms, M. W., and Paula Watson. BULLER, John (c.1632–1716), of the Middle Temple and Morval, nr. East Looe, Cornw. *The History of Parliament: British Political, Social & Local History*, http://www.historyofparliamentonline.org/ volume/1660-1690/member/buller-john-1632-1716 [accessed 12 February 2018].

Helms, M. W., and Paula Watson. IRBY, Sir Anthony (1605–82), of Whaplode, Lincs and Westminster. *The History of Parliament: British Political, Social & Local History*, http://www.historyofparliamentonline.org/volume/ 1660-1690/member/irby-sir-anthony-1605-82 [accessed 12 February 2018].

Henning, Basil Duke. Braman, John (1627–1703), of Chichester, Suss. *The History of Parliament: British Political, Social & Local History*, http://www. historyofparliamentonline.org/volume/1660-1690/member/braman-john-1627-1703 [accessed 14 June 2019].

Rowlands, Edward. GRAHME, Ranald (c.1605–85), of Petty France, Westminster and Nunnington, Wath, Yorks. *The History of Parliament: British Political, Social & Local History*, http://www.historyofparliamentonline.org/volume/ 1660-1690/member/grahme-ranald-1605-85 [accessed 26 July 2018].

290 BIBLIOGRAPHY

OXFORD DICTIONARY OF NATIONAL BIOGRAPHY

Ashton, Robert. 2017. Crisp, Sir Nicholas, first baronet (c.1599–1666). *Oxford Dictionary of National Biography*, https://doi-org.sheffield.idm.oclc.org/10.1093/ref:odnb/6705 [accessed 27 June 2018].

Aylmer, G. E. 2008. Backwell, Edward (c.1619–1683). *Oxford Dictionary of National Biography*, https://doi.org/10.1093/ref:odnb/986 [accessed 13 May 2020].

Aylmer, G. E. 2014. Vyner, Sir Robert, baronet (1631–1688). *Oxford Dictionary of National Biography* (Oxford, 2004–2020), https://doi.org/10.1093/ref:odnb/28318 [accessed 17 January 2020].

Barnard, Toby. 2008. Butler, James, first duke of Ormond (1610–1688). *Oxford Dictionary of National Biography*, https://doi-org.sheffield.idm.oclc.org/10.1093/ref:odnb/4191 [accessed 10 January 2020].

Clark, Charles E. 2004. Gorges, Sir Ferdinando (1568–1647). *Oxford Dictionary of National Biography*, https://doi-org.sheffield.idm.oclc.org/10.1093/ref:odnb/11098 [accessed 11 August 2018].

Clarke, Elizabeth R. 2008. Jekyll, John (1611–1690). *Oxford Dictionary of National Biography*, https://doi.org/10.1093/ref:odnb/67136 [accessed 16 February 2018].

De Krey, Gary S. 2008a. Dubois, John (*bap.* 1622, *d.* 1684). *Oxford Dictionary of National Biography*, https://doi.org/10.1093/ref:odnb/67399 [accessed 12 February 2018].

De Krey, Gary S. 2008b. Ireton, John [created Sir John Ireton under the protectorate]. *Oxford Dictionary of National Biography*, https://doi.org/10.1093/ref:odnb/14453 [accessed 31 May 2019].

De Krey, Gary S. 2008c. Player, Sir Thomas (*d.* 1686). *Oxford Dictionary of National Biography*, http://www.oxforddnb.com/view/article/22364 [accessed 2 July 2018].

Gentles, Ian J. 2004. Ireton, Henry (*bap.* 1611, *d.* 1651). *Oxford Dictionary of National Biography*, https://doi-org.sheffield.idm.oclc.org/10.1093/ref:odnb/14452 [accessed 14 June 2019].

Greaves, Robert L. 2009. Nelthorpe, Richard (*d.* 1685). *Oxford Dictionary of National Biography*, https://doi.org/10.1093/ref:odnb/19891 [accessed 31 May 2019].

Harris, Tim. 2008a. Cooper, Anthony Ashley, first earl of Shaftesbury (1621–1683). *Oxford Dictionary of National Biography*, https://doi.org/10.1093/ref:odnb/6208 [accessed 20 May 2019].

Harris, Tim. 2008b. Green Ribbon Club (*act.* C.1674–c.1683). *Oxford Dictionary of National Biography*, https://doi.org/10.1093/ref:odnb/92786 [accessed 31 May 2019].

BIBLIOGRAPHY 291

Henry, John. 2009. Wilkins, John (1614–1672). *Oxford Dictionary of National Biography*, https://doi-org.sheffield.idm.oclc.org/10.1093/ref:odnb/29421 [accessed 13 February 2018].

Hunter, Michael. 2015. Boyle, Robert (1627–1691). *Oxford Dictionary of National Biography*, https://doi-org.sheffield.idm.oclc.org/10.1093/ref:odnb/3137 [accessed 13 February 2018].

Hutchings, Victoria. 2004. Hoare, Sir Richard (1648–1719). *Oxford Dictionary of National Biography*, http://www.oxforddnb.com/view/article/13385 [accessed 23 May 2017].

Kelliher, W. H. 2004. Marvell, Andrew (c.1584–1641). *Oxford Dictionary of National Biography*, https://doi-org.sheffield.idm.oclc.org/10.1093/ref:odnb/18241 [accessed 13 May 2020].

Kelliher, W. H. 2008. Marvell, Andrew (1621–1678). *Oxford Dictionary of National Biography*, https://doi-org.sheffield.idm.oclc.org/10.1093/ref:odnb/18242 [accessed 13 May 2020].

Knights, Mark. 2008. Osborne, Thomas, first duke of Leeds (1632–1712). *Oxford Dictionary of National Biography*, https://doi.org/10.1093/ref:odnb/20884 [accessed 13 May 2020].

Lynch, Beth. 2004. Ponder, Nathaniel [*called* Bunyan Ponder] (1640–1699). *Oxford Dictionary of National Biography*, https://doi.org/10.1093/ref:odnb/67702 [accessed 12 February 2018].

Marshall, Alan. 2008. Williamson, Sir Joseph (1633–1701). *Oxford Dictionary of National Biography*, https://doi.org/10.1093/ref:odnb/29571 [accessed 16 February 2018].

McIntyre, G. S. 2004. Hoskins [Hoskyns], Sir John, second baronet (1634–1705). *Oxford Dictionary of National Biography*, https://doi-org.sheffield.idm.oclc.org/10.1093/ref:odnb/13840 [accessed 15 August 2018].

Melton, Frank. 2007. Clayton, Sir Robert (1629–1707). *Oxford Dictionary of National Biography*, https://doi-org.sheffield.idm.oclc.org/10.1093/ref:odnb/5579 [accessed 13 May 2020].

Miller, John. 2004. Howard, Henry, sixth duke of Norfolk (1628–1684). *Oxford Dictionary of National Biography*, https://doi.org/10.1093/ref:odnb/13907 [accessed 6 February 2018].

Milton, J. R. 2008. Locke, John (1632–1704). *Oxford Dictionary of National Biography*, https://doi-org.sheffield.idm.oclc.org/10.1093/ref:odnb/16885 [accessed 4 June 2020].

Morgan, Basil. 2004. Osborne, Peregrine, second duke of Leeds (*bap.* 1659, *d.* 1729). *Oxford Dictionary of National Biography*, https://doi-org.sheffield.idm.oclc.org/10.1093/ref:odnb/20879 [accessed 1 June 2020].

Pinfold, John. 2007. Frampton, Tregonwell [*called* the Father of the Turf] (*bap.* 1641, *d.* 1728). *Oxford Dictionary of National Biography*, https://doi.org/10.1093/ref:odnb/10062 [accessed 18 July 2018].

292 BIBLIOGRAPHY

Scott, David. 2015. Alured, Matthew (*bap.* 1615, *d.* 1694). *Oxford Dictionary of National Biography*, https://doi-org.sheffield.idm.oclc.org/10.1093/ref:odnb/66498 [accessed 13 June 2019].

Seaward, Paul. 2008. Robinson, Sir John, first baronet (*bap.* 1615, *d.* 1680). *Oxford Dictionary of National Biography*, https://doi.org/10.1093/ref:odnb/37904 [accessed 10 December 2018].

Seccombe, Thomas, revised by C. S. Rogers. 2013. Popple, William (1638–1708). *Oxford Dictionary of National Biography*, https://doi-org.sheffield.idm.oclc.org/10.1093/ref:odnb/22545 [accessed 11 July 2019].

Slater, Victor. 2004. Belasyse, Thomas, first Earl Fauconberg (1627/8–1700). *Oxford Dictionary of National Biography*, https://doi.org/10.1093/ref:odnb/1978 [accessed 28 March 2019].

Williams, Abigail. 2008. Settle, Elkanah (1648–1724). *Oxford Dictionary of National Biography*, https://doi-org.sheffield.idm.oclc.org/10.1093/ref:odnb/25128 [accessed 4 June 2020].

Wynne, S. M. 2008. Palmer [née Villiers], Barbara, countess of Castlemaine and suo jure duchess of Cleveland (*bap.* 1640, *d.* 1709), royal mistress. *Oxford Dictionary of National Biography*, https://doi.org/10.1093/ref:odnb/28285 [accessed 15 February 2018].

Yale, D. E. C. 2004. Finch, Heneage, first earl of Nottingham (1621–1682). *Oxford Dictionary of National Biography*, https://doi.org/10.1093/ref:odnb/9433 [accessed 5 February 2019].

Zaller, Robert. 2006. Breman [Braman], John (*bap.* 1627, *d.* 1703). *Oxford Dictionary of National Biography*, https://doi-org.sheffield.idm.oclc.org/10.1093/ref:odnb/67420 [accessed 13 May 2020].

OTHER

Boyd's Inhabitants of London and Family Units 1200–1946—Unpublished Index accessed via *Findmypast*, https://search.findmypast.co.uk/search-world-records/boyds-inhabitants-of-london-and-family-units-1200-1946.

C. Hoare and Co. *Hoare's Bank*, https://www.hoaresbank.co.uk/about-us [accessed 25 May 2017].

Calendar of State Papers Relating to English Affairs in the Archives of Venice, Volume 38, 1673–1675, *British History Online*, https://www.british-history.ac.uk/cal-state-papers/venice/vol38 [accessed 20 May 2020].

City of London, Haberdashers, Apprentices and Freemen 1526–1933, accessed via *Findmypast*, https://www.findmypast.co.uk/articles/world-records/full-list-of-united-kingdom-records/education-and-work-records/city-of-london-haberdashers-apprentices-and-freemen-1526-1933.

Customer Account Ledgers of Edward Backwell, 1663–72. *Royal Bank of Scotland Heritage Hub*, https://www.rbs.com/heritage/people/edward-backwell.html [accessed 28 March 2019].

Inflation Calculator. *Bank of England*, https://www.bankofengland.co.uk/monetary-policy/inflation/inflation-calculator?number.Sections%5B0%5D.Fields%5B0%5D.Value=60&start-year=5.10459405001771&end-year=1110.8 [accessed 6 March 2019].

London Hearth Tax: City of London and Middlesex, 1666, *British History Online*, http://www.british-history.ac.uk/london-hearth-tax/london-mddx/1666 [accessed 19 May 2020].

Records of London's Livery Companies Online: Apprentices and Freemen 1400–1900, *Institute of Historical Research*, https://londonroll.org/.

Sheriff Hutton Park. *Historic England*, https://historicengland.org.uk/listing/the-list/list-entry/1001462 [accessed 13 June 2019].

INDEX

A
Aboab, Jacob, 196
Alured, Matthew, 126
Anglicans, 19, 20, 35, 141, 187, 188, 190, 200
Apprenticeship, 29, 30, 32, 33, 48, 105, 122, 149, 221
Articles of agreement, 28, 37, 44, 82, 83, 87, 89, 95, 157, 158, 217
Attachments, 162, 163

B
Backwell, Sir Edward, 7, 41, 63, 65–67, 77, 78, 81, 82, 87, 169, 255
Banking
European, 82
Fuggers, 58, 82
Goldsmith, 6, 7, 28, 41, 61, 63, 64, 73
Medici, 58, 82
Peruzzi, 58, 82

scrivener, 8, 41, 61, 63, 64, 82, 143
Bank of England, 7, 12, 38, 41, 42, 54, 61, 133, 155, 233, 235
Bankruptcy
acts, 97, 160, 162, 169
commission of, 67, 96, 98–100, 128, 136, 159, 161, 163, 166, 168, 170, 171, 178, 211, 213, 226
legislation, 159, 160, 165, 169, 178, 209, 231
statute, 1, 46, 50, 163, 164, 167, 171
Belasyse, Thomas, viscount and later earl Fauconberg, 51, 76, 77, 242
Beverley, 32, 123, 125, 126, 216, 220
Bookkeeper, 43, 139, 162, 165, 217
Bourdieu, Pierre, 17, 18, 182, 204, 239
Braman, Major John, 119, 120, 139, 209, 210, 214

© The Editor(s) (if applicable) and The Author(s), under exclusive license to Springer Nature Switzerland AG 2022
M. Winter, *Banking, Projecting and Politicking in Early Modern England*, Palgrave Studies in Economic History,
https://doi.org/10.1007/978-3-030-90570-5

295

296 INDEX

Butler, James, duke of Ormond, 96, 97, 154

C

Chancery court, 1, 21, 25, 51, 80, 83, 116, 139, 153, 154, 160, 198, 208, 213, 219
Citizens, 19, 28–30, 32, 35, 36, 43, 48, 58, 67, 68, 80, 89, 95, 114, 115, 120, 126, 140, 149, 151, 152, 195, 216, 224, 237, 239, 242–252, 254, 255
Civic opposition, 35, 36, 144, 189–192, 200, 202, 203
    Thompson and Nelthorpe's roles within, 187
Clayton and Morris, 63–65, 87
Coffeehouse, 174, 175
Common Council (of London), 1, 19, 140, 141, 143, 144, 198
Company
    joint stock, 88, 89, 235
    regulated, 33, 88, 89
    and society, 11
Composition, 13, 67, 78, 82, 97, 99, 102, 143, 159, 161, 163–165, 169–171, 175, 178, 179, 186, 220, 225, 236, 237
Conformism, 187
Cooper, Anthony Ashley, First Earl of Shaftesbury, 189
Corporation of London, 5, 24, 35, 144, 145, 181, 187, 192, 198, 199, 237, 239
'Country party', 20, 192, 200
'Court Party', 20
Credit, 6, 8–15, 21, 23, 28, 29, 35, 41, 42, 49, 51, 52, 59, 60, 62, 64, 68–70, 73, 75–77, 81, 82, 86, 95, 101, 103, 105, 106, 114, 117, 122, 131, 132, 135, 137–139, 147, 150, 155, 156,

169, 172, 173, 177, 182, 183, 201, 204, 208, 209, 217, 218, 220, 222–227, 230–239
Creditors, 2, 12, 14, 15, 23–25, 27, 28, 30, 37, 42, 44–51, 53, 61, 62, 64, 66–71, 74, 76, 77, 79–82, 87, 90, 93, 94, 96–100, 114, 115, 131–133, 135, 136, 138–142, 145–155, 158–179, 181, 184–187, 198, 201, 209, 211, 213, 216, 224, 226, 231, 232, 234, 236–238, 240, 242
    of other institutions, 151
    of Thompson and Company, 30, 66–71, 73, 76, 77, 79, 82, 97, 98, 100, 132–134, 136, 140, 145, 147, 150, 170, 236

D

Debtors, 45, 50, 51, 53, 61, 74, 87, 88, 98, 131, 139, 154, 159–162, 165, 168, 169, 175, 178, 209, 211, 226
De Krey, Gary S., 8, 19, 20, 27, 28, 35, 36, 79, 121–123, 143, 144, 148, 182, 188–191, 198–200, 203
Deposit, 7, 9, 27, 28, 42, 44, 45, 49, 50, 58, 59, 61, 65, 68, 73, 75, 76, 78, 82, 85, 87, 88, 94, 96, 99, 131–135, 137, 138, 140, 143, 144, 146, 150, 151, 153, 158, 163, 175, 230, 231, 234, 238, 240
Dissenters, 1, 35, 36, 123, 141, 143, 189, 199, 202. *See also* Nonconformists
Dubois, John, 79, 141, 143, 144, 198, 245

INDEX   297

E
East India Company, 5, 54, 63,
    75–77, 79, 135, 144, 152, 181,
    184, 192–198, 200, 242–255
Employees
    clerks, 43
    servants, 43, 117, 118, 222
Exchange bank, 10, 59, 60, 133

F
Factors, 15, 17, 28, 31, 58, 74, 80,
    90–92, 103, 161, 230
Farrington, John
    early career, 30
    family of, 115
    fate after collapse, 208
Farrington, Margaret, 118, 207–209,
    213, 217, 238
Financial instruments
    bill obligatory, 51
    bill of Exchange, 31, 51–53
    bond, 51, 52, 137
    inland Bill, 51, 61
    mortgage, 53, 63
    promissory note, 61, 62
    statute staple, 53, 54
Financial Revolution, 6, 14, 66, 67,
    71, 72, 75, 84, 155, 233, 236
Fractional reserve, 44, 61, 64, 82, 85,
    99, 101, 133

G
Great Russell Street, 4, 209, 210,
    213, 214, 218, 219, 221

H
Hamburg, 33, 34, 153
Hickes, James, 146
Hind, John, 173
    Hind and partners, 173

Hoare's bank, 6, 8, 65, 70, 78, 79,
    132, 134
Household
    as an economic unit, 11, 117
    of the partners, 209, 220, 225
Hull, 47, 104, 106, 109, 112, 123,
    125, 126, 142, 145, 146, 168,
    199, 217, 251

I
Institutions, history of, 11
interest, 9, 15, 27, 37, 41–45, 51, 53,
    57, 59, 61, 62, 65, 68, 69,
    74–76, 81, 82, 85, 87, 88, 99,
    100, 105, 109, 119, 123, 131,
    133–137, 147, 154, 172,
    175–177, 202, 203, 207, 212,
    226, 227, 234
Invest, 75, 76, 78, 134, 136, 137,
    231
    investment, 131, 134
Ireland, 5, 47, 91, 96, 97, 154, 172,
    177, 186, 202, 242, 253, 254

K
Keate, Sir Jonathan, 79, 116, 146,
    248
King's Bench Prison, 209, 211–213

L
Lambe, Samuel, 60
Lombard Street, 7, 38, 41, 63, 114
The London Gazette, 209

M
Marriage
    Marvell's marriage, 112
    the partners' marriages, 116, 117
    settlement, 15, 117, 207, 239

298 INDEX

Marvell, Andrew, 2, 4–6, 20, 28, 29, 36, 51, 84, 105, 107, 112, 114, 123, 125, 126, 139, 144, 145, 150, 189, 210, 213, 219, 223
Marvell, Mary (Palmer), 4, 5, 28, 57, 139, 210, 214, 219, 220, 226
Matthews, George, 96, 97
Merchant Adventurers Company, 33
Microhistory, 2, 3, 8, 54, 229, 230, 232
Monmouth Rebellion, 144
Muldrew, Craig, 11–14, 60, 65, 66, 68, 74, 75, 102, 117, 138, 155, 159, 161, 162, 164, 165, 208, 209, 212, 215, 223, 234, 235, 237–239
Mun, Thomas, 59, 60, 81, 137

N
Nelthorpe, Edward
early career, 230
family of, 5, 105, 111, 121–123, 125, 128, 129, 220, 222, 231
fate after collapse, 181, 185, 212
politics of, 5, 35, 123, 126, 129, 189, 199–201, 203, 224
Nelthorpe, James, 31, 91, 92, 109, 111, 114–116, 121, 125–127, 136, 137, 139, 221
Nelthorpe, John, 125, 126
Nelthorpe, Mary, 54, 57, 128, 211, 213–218, 220–222, 238
Nelthorpe, Richard, 127
Networks
credit, 131
kinship, 21, 25, 104–107, 109, 114, 122, 123, 126, 128, 129, 131, 141, 209, 210, 223, 225, 230, 238, 239
political, 15, 16, 122, 156, 216, 239
social, 1, 11, 15, 25, 155, 209, 225

Nonconformists, 1, 20, 35, 36, 119, 121, 122, 126, 189, 191, 199, 204, 224, 225. *See also* Dissenters

O
Office holding, 35, 237
Osborne, Thomas, earl of Danby, 35, 189

P
Page, Edmund
early career, 30
family of, 129
fate after collapse, 212
Partnership, 15, 28–30, 32–35, 37, 38, 43, 44, 58, 80, 82, 84, 85, 88–91, 93–95, 97, 99–101, 104, 107, 115–118, 131, 138, 157, 173, 186, 196, 197, 205, 212, 230, 231, 235, 236
Pitkin affair, 23, 161, 165, 168, 169, 240
Player, Sir Thomas, 43, 147, 148, 187, 188, 191, 195, 198, 199, 202, 223
Popple, William, 5, 53, 91, 112, 126, 152, 221, 224, 225, 238
Portmans, Edmond, 43, 44, 139, 222, 223
Post Office, 46, 146, 147, 176, 177
Privy Council, 24, 184, 185, 189, 193, 194, 196, 198
Prizes, 34, 192–198
prize goods, 94, 157, 192, 195
prize taking, 192, 193, 195
Project, projecting, 9, 10, 25, 82, 83, 85, 86, 95–98, 100–102, 230, 233
Proud, Gersham, 43, 44, 118, 222, 226

R

Richards, R.D., 7, 8, 22, 28, 60, 61, 63–65, 72–75, 87–89, 134, 233
Risk, 17, 59, 60, 75, 76, 78, 81, 89, 95–97, 103, 129, 132–134, 172, 183, 185, 192, 193, 200, 204, 205, 215, 232, 239, 240
Robinson, Sir John, 57, 181, 188, 189, 201
Rodrigues, Alphonso, 196, 197
Royal African Company, 77–79, 94, 131, 143, 144, 242–255
Run on the bank, 44
Rye House Plot, 144

S

Serra, Anthony Gomes, 196, 197
Ships
  Alphon, 193
  Arms of Camphire, 193
  Constant Friendship, 185–187
  Europe, 193
  Papenburg, 193
  shares in, 75–77
Shop (bank office), 38, 41, 42, 111, 140
Speede, Thomas, 43, 44, 139
Spinsters, 48, 67, 68, 70, 148, 244, 246–253
Stop on the Exchequer, 6, 7, 62, 65, 73, 80, 133, 143, 155, 169, 172, 198, 199, 233

T

Terrezy, Francisco, 196, 197
Third Anglo-Dutch War, 63, 94, 157, 191, 192, 195
Thompson, Dorothy, 114, 119, 120, 210, 213, 214, 216, 218, 220, 222, 238

Thompson, Edward, 34, 106, 107, 109, 111, 112, 123, 127, 128, 139, 146, 223, 224
Thompson, Richard
  early career, 212
  family of, 105, 107, 111, 123
  fate after collapse, 13, 204, 212
  politics of, 122
Thompson, Robert, 109
Thompson, Sir Henry, 109, 114, 116, 125, 189, 190, 223
Thompson, Stephen, 127, 146
Tory, 20, 141, 142, 223
Treasury Orders. *See* Stop on the Exchequer
Trinity House, Corporation of, 42, 57, 135, 150, 151, 168, 226
Turner, Sir William, 30, 51–53, 77–79, 86, 135, 149, 150, 162, 178, 226, 254

V

Verney, John, 48, 50, 57, 135, 162, 173–176, 201, 203
Vyner, Sir Robert, 41, 63, 65–67, 81, 82, 87, 137, 143, 169, 198, 199
  bank of, 66, 81
  political involvement, 143

W

Whig, 19–21, 122, 141–145, 190, 223, 224
Whitley, Roger, 135, 172, 176, 177, 255
Widows, 48, 67, 69, 70, 137, 140, 147, 148, 150, 154, 215, 217–222, 242–255
Williamson, Sir Joseph, 43, 46, 146, 147, 174, 181, 188–191, 193, 195, 199–203

intelligence, 43, 147, 188, 191, 200, 202, 203

and the post office, 146

Woolchurch market, 38, 42, 212, 221

Y

Yamamoto, Koji, 10, 84–86, 94, 95, 100, 233

Yarranton, Andrew, 60, 74, 137

York, 31, 33, 34, 103, 104, 106, 107, 109, 123, 125, 126, 146, 147, 149, 150, 176, 189, 190, 223, 224

Printed in the United States
by Baker & Taylor Publisher Services